Exploring the urban

PROFESSOR H. J. DYOS

Exploring the urban past

Essays in urban history by
H. J. DYOS

Edited by
DAVID CANNADINE
and
DAVID REEDER

CAMBRIDGE UNIVERSITY PRESS

Cambridge
London   New York   New Rochelle
Sydney   Melbourne

Published by the Press Syndicate of the University of Cambridge
The Pitt Building, Trumpington Street, Cambridge CB2 1RP
32 East 57th Street, New York, NY 10022, USA
296 Beaconsfield Parade, Middle Park, Melbourne 3206, Australia

First published 1982

Printed in Great Britain at the
University Press, Cambridge

Library of Congress catalogue card number: 82-1209

British Library Cataloguing in Publication Data
Dyos, H. J.
Exploring the urban past.
1. Cities and trams—History
I. Title   II. Cannadine, David   III. Reeder, David
909'.09732   HT111
ISBN 0 521 24624 5

ISBN 0 521 24624 5 hard covers
ISBN 0 521 28848 7 paperback

For
OLIVE DYOS

Contents

Acknowledgements

We would like to acknowledge the following periodicals and publishers for permission to reprint these articles and essays: Chapter 1 is reprinted from *The Victorian City: Images and Realities*, ed. H. J. Dyos and M. Wolff (1973), by permission of Routledge & Kegan Paul; Chapter 2 from *Urbanity and Suburbanity: an inaugural lecture delivered in the University of Leicester, 1st May 1973*, by permission of Leicester University Press; Chapter 3 from *Britain and the Netherlands*, ed. J. S. Bromley and E. H. Kossman (1971), by permission of Martinus Nijhoff BV; Chapter 4 from *The Quality of Urban Life*, ed. H. J. Schmandt and W. Bloomberg (1969), by permission of Sage Publications, Inc.; Chapter 5 from the *International Review of Social History*, II (1957), by permission; Chapters 6, 7 and 8 from the *Journal of Transport History* I (1953), II (1955) and III (1957), respectively, by permission of Leicester University Press; Chapters 9 and 10 from *Victorian Studies* XI (1968) by permission; and Chapter 12 from *Collins' Illustrated Atlas of London* (1973), by permission of Leicester University Press.

We are also grateful to the staff of Cambridge University Press, and in particular to Patricia Williams and Stephen Barr, for their exemplary kindness, help and consideration.

D. N. C.

D. A. R.

Introduction
H. J. Dyos and the urban process

by DAVID REEDER

Jim Dyos became a leading figure in the new and burgeoning field of urban history during the 1960s. By the time of his sudden death in 1978 he had succeeded in acquiring an almost legendary reputation as the doyen of British urban historians. Professional colleagues have frequently expressed admiration for his single-minded commitment to the historical study of the city, and the manner and style of the several pioneering contributions he made to it. Yet Dyos published only one book-length study in urban history, an account of the *Victorian Suburb* (1961), although he had also collaborated with D. H. Aldcroft in writing a volume of transport history. With these exceptions, the principal part of his creative endeavour was embodied in occasional essays written over a period of nearly thirty years as contributions to journals and books, and as distillations of public talks and lectures.

The purpose of this volume is to provide a tangible memorial to Dyos's scholarship. It collects together and reproduces a selection from his essays in the hope of making them more readily available for study and discussion. Whilst the main concern of the editors in making this selection is to provide a coherent volume of readings which will be useful to students and teachers of urban history, they have also endeavoured to illustrate the range of Dyos's scholarly interests and the obligations which he had felt to publicise materials, review developments and point to future directions for research. The editors have chosen to include, therefore, some of his general and speculative writings on the study of urbanisation, as well as examples from the more specific, research-based articles on nineteenth-century urban topics. The latter cover such matters as transport development and street improvements, the house-building industry, suburban development, housing conditions and the literature of the slums.

All these subjects were relatively new and somewhat unfashionable when Dyos first wrote about them, but they now form basic components in the study of the nineteenth-century city, and they are of importance also, as Dyos was at pains to insist, to all students of modern British economic and social history. As individual pieces of writing, some of his contributions to these subjects quickly became recognised as 'classics' in their own right, capable of being read more than once with great profit and enjoyment. As a collection of pieces, they have still much to teach about the rise of the modern city. In effect, the essays in this volume furnish a guide to the history of the urban process, offering both precepts and examples on the basis of investigations into and reflections on Victorian London as the representative type of 'big city' environment and a foretaste, therefore, of the kind of environment in which many of us live now.

1

The Part One essays, to start by highlighting the general writings first, offer a commentary on the significance of urbanisation as an increasingly global experience in the nineteenth and twentieth centuries. Urbanisation can be defined in all sorts of ways, of course, and the literature of urban sociology is like a paper-chase of such definitions. It seemed altogether preferable, Dyos would tell his students, to think of it initially as simply a process of population concentration that results in an increase in the number and size of towns and cities, and alters the balance of population distribution as between country and town, the latter defined in terms of size or density. From this point of view the period from the early 1800s to about the mid-twentieth century formed a distinct phase. Before 1800 the rate of urbanisation – the speed at which the ratio of the urban to the non-urban population changed – was low and inconspicuous; whilst after the mid-twentieth century, when the growth of the world's population accelerated to something like twice what it had been, there may have been – as in some parts of the Third World – a greater growth of population outside cities than in them, so that the rate of urbanisation slows down even though the growth of cities remains phenomenal.

In the Part One essays, Dyos is concerned with arguing, directly or indirectly, that any general explanation of economic and social change in the modern period should take fully into account the circumstances that gave rise to and flowed from the urbanising process, especially during the classic phase of the nineteenth century when British society first became urbanised. It is easy to appreciate that urbanisation was related most closely then to the development of new industrial technology, and more generally of economic development, and that the mechanism of the process was primarily that of immigration from the countryside, with towns and cities absorbing more than any simple tabulation of the rural–urban flow might suggest because death-rates in cities remained higher by and large than those prevailing in rural districts and small towns. But when we ask what shaped the kind of urban society brought into being, as Dyos was doing in the general essays, we have to take account not only of population change, and the impact of technology, but of the kind of environment formed in the city and the values

which it embodied. Dyos regarded technology as having the most fundamental influence, without giving it an overall deterministic role, not merely,
however, from the impact of innovations such as transport developments
but also because of the way that the city came to function as in itself a kind of
machine for living in.

The city was an independent variable as well as a dependent variable in
relation to broader processes of change. These are not mutually exclusive
possibilities or sequential changes, but they represent a set of repercussions
which can and do normally occur together. The great challenge to the urban
historian, nevertheless, is to assess the impact of the city as an independent
variable. How can we identify the ways cities have influenced economic
development or the structures of society? What methods are there for
showing how urbanisation entailed new modes of conduct, social disciplines,
values, attitudes? Or to put the matter as Dyos represents it in his essay on
the quality of urban life, how can we show that changes in quantity, in the
scale of human settlement, affected the quality of life which is lived in them?
Dyos draws attention to linguistic and methodological difficulties in moving
from a discussion of the structural indicators of urbanisation to one
concerned with psychological perceptions of the quality of urban life, and he
suggests that much of what the city has come to mean for its citizens may
well be inaccessible to historians. Yet he believed profoundly in the need for
historians to make a greater effort 'to interpret more subtly and richly the
impact of urbanisation on the mind and spirit of city dwellers'.

The theme of the meaning of the city, and of the interdisciplinary methods
necessary to acquiring the art of reading the city, was raised most explicitly
in the concluding reflections (with Michael Wolff) to the two-volume
symposium on the Victorian city. It was necessary, this huge enterprise had
implied, to examine the total phenomenon of the nineteenth-century city,
not only how it had come into being, and what it actually comprised, but also
how the vast changes taking place there were perceived and experienced at
the time. In other words, the Victorian city had to be studied subjectively as
well as objectively, in terms of its symbolic meanings and associations, and
through the literary imagination, with its special task of making acceptable
fears of the terrifying and unknown. The reflective essay on the Victorian
city follows this up by laying emphasis on the sensational impact of
urbanisation: how new concentrations of people on an entirely new scale did
indeed begin to generate new energies, new attitudes and all sorts of new
calculative possibilities that were bound to disturb older assumptions and
methods of social regulation. At the same time, however, as the essay notes,
older political and social structures, and older modes of procedure survived
in the Victorian city, and older perceptions and values were filtered through
an intellectual and literary commentary on the city in ways that helped to
mediate the culture shock of urban change.

Dyos was intrigued by the ambiguity of the response to the growth of the city in the nineteenth century, from which came some of the more persistent confusions about the meaning of city life. This was, in a sense, what his inaugural lecture was about. One point it makes is that the city has so often been represented as a place with a kind of split personality, embodying a duality of human possibilities – the apex of human endeavour, yet the pit of human suffering and degradation. Such images were imaginative representations of more subtle truths. They were a function, Dyos thought, of one of the more compelling ironies of urban existence that tug at so many students of urban life. He was referring here to the contrast between the promise which the city held out for a richer life – its role as the great equaliser – and the actual conditions of living to be found there. The modern city had been taken over by a pathological state of urbanism, which he described as a kind of suburbanity.

Dyos was evidently not afraid to insist on the relevance, the social urgency even, of his chosen field. This is not to imply that he put history at the service of some contemporary ideology of urban reform. On the contrary, the overriding concern in the study of the urban past was to afford a *perspective* on the predicaments of the urban present. That might be done partly from interpreting the images which city life had evinced and showing how they were formed – a procedure for which Dyos had a special talent as he demonstrated in giving illustrated lectures on the Victorian city – and more basically from systematic investigations of the realities out of which the images were composed. For Dyos Victorian London was the most relevant choice among English cities for such pursuits; it also had the advantage of providing much fascinating theatre in the variety of the human condition which it contained.

In focussing so much of his attention on London as *the* Victorian city, and of central importance to understanding the nature and implications of the urban process, Dyos was resisting the tendency in British post-war history to look for the springs of economic and social change in the provincial towns and cities. He was ready to agree that in some respects the latter was indeed a proper emphasis. Victorian London did seem to have missed the main thrust of the industrial revolution, and was not much affected by the social movements and radical politics that flowed round but not through the metropolitan city. What must be kept firmly in mind, nevertheless, Dyos argued, was an interlocking economic connection between metropolis and provinces, and the 'true influence of each upon the other in political and cultural terms'. Whether Dyos correctly assesses that influence may be arguable, but his general essay on the metropolitan process in this volume certainly highlights aspects of London's changing role in a system of cities. Whilst Victorian London was an accumulator of people and wealth (and to that extent parasitic on other cities), it was also 'the generator, the great influencer of tastes and values, images and opinions'. Several of Dyos's essays, not just the essay in Part One, draw attention to the cultural and psychological impact of the metropolis.

2

Dyos had strong emotional as well as academic links with London. It was truly for him that 'dear, damned, distracting town'; and he continued to render in his writings a lasting impression of Victorian London as a place. But he also thought that the major task of the urban historian was to inject the sense of place into general explanations of change, getting it logically tied in by relating the larger processes at work to the places in which they occurred. The urban historian had to demonstrate the dynamic influence of urbanism in and through the history of place and by giving the processes at work a name and a habitat. His own approach to these matters was through an exploration of the manner and significance of Victorian London's coming into being. Thus he concentrated mostly on the self-evident products of the urban process, the massing of physical structures and the social massing of the people. The Part Two essays in this volume can be regarded as contributing to that overall theme by discussing how external agencies (including the railway) were factors in the transformation of Victorian London. The Part Three essays more directly confront the city as a physical and social mass, explaining how the fabric of Victorian London was made to become the effigy of its social structure. Looking back on this work now one can detect an underlying consistency of purpose. The topics may reflect changing interests and obligations, but they were being presented as case-studies in urban change and the process of accretive growth; and they were concerned not only with what happened to the city, but what this meant for the lives of ordinary Londoners.

Take, for example, the earliest, modest writings on the railway and the city. These were intended ostensibly to fill out a bit of the story of the social repercussions of transport development in the nineteenth century. The railway had evidently a great potential for change, but the question was how that potential could be studied in carefully defined ways. Dyos had already investigated the impact of railways on the timing and pace of suburban development in the nineteenth century in his Ph.D. thesis on the development of Greater London, south of the Thames. He chose now to examine how the construction of railway lines and terminals affected the lives of those people who were displaced by them. Thus he endeavoured to spell out the human terms in the simultaneous equation connecting transport and urban development.

Dyos was the first to count the social costs of railway development in Victorian London, quantitatively in terms of how many were displaced from a study of the demolition statements themselves, and also, if somewhat more tentatively, by trying to assess change qualitatively, finding out what happened to the displaced, and how far the workmens' tickets provided after the Cheap Trains Act benefited the London poor and relieved pressure at the centre. This was undoubtedly a kind of urban history, albeit approached from the outside, with the city as the dependent variable, and it served to bring Dyos in touch with the way that Victorian London worked as a place in which to live, and with some of the processes going on there. He was beginning to make the point in these early essays that the commercial zeal for building railway terminals in Victorian London, in itself a symptom and a means of strengthening the concentrative power of the capital, and of accelerating thereby the centripetal tendencies in London's growth, served to intensify the pressure of numbers on city space. These essays constituted, therefore, a kind of rehearsal for what Dyos eventually presented as the real drama of city life as expressed in the movement of people about the city, and in a continuous contest for social space.

This last theme was heralded also in the essay on metropolitan 'improvements', even if the stated purpose of the article was to explain why London had contrived to plan its new streets in quite a different way from that of Paris. Dyos makes something of a paradox out of how these schemes, with the potential to help make of the capital an object of pride and a symbol of national greatness, were governed in the event more by financial expediency, and justified on essentially practical grounds. Yet traffic congestion, if temporarily alleviated, was never materially lessened, and schemes intended to improve the physical and moral condition of the lowest class initiated processes that deteriorated their condition even more. This was the greater paradox. The street improvements, like the building of railway lines and terminals later, and the reconstruction and extension of London's commercial centre, afforded any number of new opportunities for exercising a kind of ruthless opportunism in the destruction of the ugly and unhealthy bits of the old city, without much understanding until later in the century of the consequences of such random slum clearances in adding immeasurably to the congestion of living conditions in the neighbourhoods that were spared.

3

The central area of Victorian London, where population growth was concentrated until the 1860s, felt the impact of change most directly and it was there or thereabouts that the social residues of the urban process were piled up and took shape as slums. Dyos was the first modern historian to consider how such malformations in the urban fabric occurred and were perceived at the time. When he wrote the essay included here the slum scarcely had a history as such; yet it was one of the analogues of the new urban civilisation that was coming into existence in the Victorian commonwealth. There was a need, Dyos believed, to study other perceptions of it than those of the social commentators, and to work through a whole declension of types if the slums of Victorian Britain were to be assigned a proper place in the urban history of these times. Despite new work on the origins of housing policies in Victorian London, this challenge has not yet been taken up.

When Dyos comes to survey the literature of slum life he makes some interesting general points, the first of them about how London excited the curiosity of so many writers in the nineteenth century. The theme of the city as an object of curiosity and a point of discovery comes back into his introduction to *Collins' Illustrated Atlas of London*. This new type of atlas imposed a rational order on the city as well as providing a guide to the streets, but it told us little about what went on behind the surface appearances. In contrast, many of the writings on London catered to a taste and an appetite for safely conducted journeys into *unknown* lands. They also served, Dyos points out, to reinforce the sense of the poor as inhabiting a nether world, an image that was symptomatic of how the poor were being distanced by the very investigations made of them. In this kind of literature the term slum crept into existence with the same kind of stealthy insistence with which the urban poor had been forming their ranks; and the more the slum was observed the more the realisation grew of the dangers it presented to society.

Thus we can trace in the writings which Dyos reviews a distinctly modern and conscious experience of the extremity of the human condition, an apprehension not only of the plight of individuals but of the social distance that had opened up between different communities. We can also trace a growing sense of the explosive energies penned up within the city waiting to be released. The crisis of the late-Victorian city Dyos saw as a crisis of perceptions, and of all the writers of the time he believed that C. F. G. Masterman had conveyed the sense of crisis most effectively in an image of the ghetto as a kind of human pinfold. Masterman's pessimistic vision of the rising up of the urban masses 'out of the abyss', was a prophetic epitaph on the Victorian city.

Dyos was moved himself by a kind of compassion for the predicaments of urban man. The sense of indignation in his writing about the housing conditions of the urban poor did not mean, however, that he saw himself drawing up an indictment of the past for its misdeeds. On the contrary, he went to some lengths in maintaining that the builders of the Victorian city, not least the anonymous army of the speculative house-builders of the suburbs, were more sinned against than sinning, whatever the contemporary image or the attempt to fasten the blame for poor housing on them. The problem of the housing of Londoners was at root economic, and a function of

Introduction

how Victorian London worked as a private city whose allocations of living space were made according to the logic of a capitalistic organisation. An aspect of this logic was the connection between inferior environmental conditions in the centre and a house-processing operation that was concentrated mainly on the suburbs.

The interconnections between slums and suburbs were spelt out in a joint essay with myself contributed to the symposium on the Victorian City, but not reproduced here to avoid duplicating material already contained in earlier essays. But it did serve to emphasise that the suburb-building operation formed part of a dynamic of urban growth whose larger structures and mechanisms – especially the financial mechanisms – had always to be kept in mind. The key to this dynamic was London's commercial success: the wealth generated in the commercial metropolis was used first by the middle class to shape a new environment in the suburbs, and it was the source too of the resources for a self-generating investment to keep the machinery of suburban housing production going. Hence the pace and timing of suburban development in Victorian London, and the capital investment needed to sustain it, had implications for the housing and living space of the entire urban community.

It is interesting to notice how this argument about the dynamic of urban growth was already implicit in his earliest writings on the speculative builders and developers of Victorian London, where he relates studies of the Victorian housing industry in London to a larger analysis of the logistics of suburban development. Dyos makes his work on the size-structure of the London housing industry, based on the District Surveyor's Returns of house-building, contribute towards exposing the mechanisms of an accretive process of urban growth – and the same is true of his studies of the business operations of speculative house-builders, including the detailed study of the operations of a south London builder that Dyos had come across initially in researching the history of Camberwell for his book on the Victorian suburb. At the same time his account of what lay behind the making of the urban fabric helps us to a better understanding of the Victorian city as an artifact by demonstrating the nature of its housing products. Dyos taught us in fact to recognise the congruence between the fabric of the Victorian suburb and the social needs it was meeting. The lecture he gave to the Victorian Society, published here for the first time, followed up as it was by a personally conducted tour of the landscape which his south London builder had formed, serves to heighten our perceptions of the new urban milieu of the nineteenth century. It added to the explanation he had already given of suburbia as an urban society of less marked extremes which represented, his inaugural lecture had claimed, a new kind of urban existence, 'a kind of suburbanity'.

xviii

4

Whatever the subject Dyos kept coming back to the central question of the meaning of urban change, challenging thereby some of our stereotype images, especially of the suburb. But what mattered to him above all was the opportunity which his studies gave to work towards a dispassionate reading of the social contest that was written into the fabric of the city; and he had wanted to take this much further by looking more closely into the life and institutions of suburbia to see how the suburb worked as a social strategy. This notion of the battle for space in the Victorian city was important to him methodologically, for here surely was a process going on that was not confined to *a* place, and therefore a means not only of reinforcing the idea of place, however necessary that may be, but was also a link between the micro- and the macro-aspects of the urban process, between the making of the individual town or suburb and the urbanisation of society.

In his studies Dyos was attempting to make sense of the big city environment through examining the processes involved in its making. He offers us a perspective that can help to make the city more meaningful and accessible. Dyos knew that for many people the modern city was, in truth, a frightening and bewildering prospect, made up, as it was, of a landscape of surfaces and a special language of signs at once so familiar and yet so incomprehensible as to form almost the 'structure of chaos'. The point of his work on the urban past was to show that there was a pattern and organising principles at work, as the changing environment of the city was shaped and adapted to new uses.

The editors of this volume believe there is much to be gained from putting these essays together. They convey a real sense of continuity. They show how particular studies of Victorian London formed the basis for general views about the urban process, and that over the years Dyos was fashioning a distinctive approach to urban history. In reading through them we are able to have a glimpse of the urban historian in the making. This is the more important because of the influence which Dyos has had on the nature and course of urban history in Britain. It seems only fitting, therefore, and a tribute to Dyos's reputation as a creative force in British urban history, to conclude this volume with a critical appreciation of his overall place in the historiography of the subject.

PART ONE

The Urbanising World

1

The Victorian city in historical perspective

To all appearances the Victorian city is now virtually a thing of the past. The actual city, the physical monument, that pile of solemn but exuberant shapes that has been for so long and for so many people the very emblem of urbanity is at last melting away. Those massive realities that once commanded the ground in such numbers are being furiously singled out as trophies by conservationists or reduced to rubble by property developers. The urban past has never had a very secure future. The ponderous and ever-accumulating mass that no Victorian generation could perceive as complete has remained intact, it now seems, for only the first two post-Victorian generations. Only now therefore can we be conscious of the whole cycle. We can even sense the shape of some of the things to come. The technologies that underpinned these first cities of the industrial era are being superseded by others with quite different implications, and the processes that built up such high densities in those cities may even be going into reverse. For the urban mass no longer generates forces of attraction directly proportionate to its density. Density, though susceptible to almost limitless engineering possibilities, is no longer a necessary condition of urban intercourse. No human settlement in Britain lies beyond the city's range. The perspective we get of the Victorian city from the ground is therefore a finite, tentative, historical one. In such respects it seems no longer contemporary.

Yet, if we look harder, what we see is something rather different. Our evolving cities are still governed by the ways in which earlier occupants of the ground divided their fields or settled their estates, and the centres of commercial gravity if not their circumferences are commonly still fixed where earlier convenience required. Inertia is part of the dynamic of urban change: the structures outlast the people who put them there, and impose constraints on those who have to adapt them later to their own use. The fact is that the framework of growth, however hastily devised, tends to become the permanent structure, and to be held fast by property titles and convenient routines that can seldom be undone at a stroke. Even urban clearways are making surprisingly clean-cut slices through the elaborate

3

residues of nineteenth-century growth. Within that arena the relative standing of neighbourhoods changes less than that of their salient as a whole, largely because housing produced in the mass must conform to standard specifications and be occupied by correspondingly uniform social groups. Then, as now, the social framework devised by developers, whether with eyes open or shut, becomes embodied in the structures themselves and is a bequest no less lightly given away than a more strictly entailed inheritance. Even when neighbourhoods decay such covenants remain, for houses built for the servant-keeping classes decline inexorably into whole districts of one-roomed dwellings. The configuration of the ground, the prevailing wind, the means of locomotion, the location of the gas-works, the precise whereabouts of cemeteries, golf-courses, schools, hospitals, parks, sewage works, factories, railway sidings, and shopping centres – all amenities whose distribution tended to be settled at an early stage of urban growth – are ineradicable influences on subsequent patterns of urban life. To that extent what happened in the nineteenth century plainly matters still.

There is nevertheless a more fundamental reason for regarding the Victorian city as belonging to the present. The growth of cities in the nineteenth century not only marked the beginning of a period in which so many of the aches and aspirations of modernity were first felt but the beginnings of processes which have had since to be seen in unified global terms. It was then that the urbanisation of the world first gathered momentum and a framework for the contemporary history of man became perceptible. It was then that the inherent characteristics of our present social condition became actual in comprehensive terms: the city as the environment of the social mass could be seen taking shape and its ultimate possibilities visualised. Britain was the first to complete this modern transformation, just as she had been the first to undergo the industrialisation of her economy, and represents therefore the prototype of all industrialising, urbanising, modern-ising societies. Here, indeed, was a foretaste of the way we live now.

1

What unifies these Victorian and latterday phases of urbanisation as a universal experience is, above all, the sharp awareness of multiplying numbers, of man by the million, of whole systems of growth points, of a prospect of cities without end, and of a political arithmetic that must embrace them all. The obsession with numbers which characterised the social investigations of the Victorians themselves was almost congenitally determined and the inevitable prefix to so many of their judgments, as to ours. For the unprecedented acceleration in the growth of the population gave to cities for the first time in six thousand years a totally new role. No longer dominated by the numbers and capacities of those living off the land, these new aggregates could generate their own energies, impose their own demands on the countryside, and develop a new culture. Though they first grew more by taking people off the land than by breeding them, British cities were, by the end of the nineteenth century, coming within reach of maintaining their numbers for themselves. That transition, presently followed by other European countries and their overseas settlements, was within a century being made throughout the world, under constraints not basically different from those prevailing in Victorian Britain. Once again the control of death preceded the control of birth, though with much more dramatic effect in our own time. Urbanisation among the emerging countries in the third quarter of the twentieth century has become in consequence a simple function of population growth and the cities the decanters for agrarian poverty. Perhaps one-third of the world's population already live in urban places of some description and even the most halting extrapolations would bring this urban concentration to something like that of Britain in mid-nineteenth century before the end of the twentieth. Britain alone could be described as predominantly urbanised by the end of the nineteenth century; already the most advanced countries are comparably so; the rest are following behind.

The Victorian city is part of our culture in a still more general sense. The promise of modernity, however distant, is abundance and equality, the material and ideological products of the dual revolution in England and France in the late-eighteenth century, and the city is its exponent, if not its redeemer. Here, new opportunities for communication intersected, new patterns of human relationships began to form, new institutions sprang up, new values, sensations, conventions and problems were expressed; while older perceptions, behaviour and limitations changed their pitch or dis-appeared altogether: everywhere a flickering failure of absolutes in ideas and attitudes, a stumbling advance towards free association between people, a more democratised urbanity. The humanisation of mankind became for the first time a momentarily imaginable possibility, even if the petty realities of individual lives too often remained stubbornly gross and seemingly hopeless. In the modern world, the path of progress has been an urban one. The very existence of the city has been a demonstration of the capacity, however uneven, to lift human effort beyond subsistence and a preoccupation with the brute facts of mere existence; and the urbanisation of the whole population is an index, however crude, of rising standards of material welfare. Here is a measure of our civilisation.

What is so conspicuous in the city is the gathering of vast crowds of ordinary people for everyday purposes, something hitherto impossible. It has by the last quarter of the twentieth century become such a routine of urban life that deserted streets betoken something wrong. Perhaps nothing illustrates better than our joint numerosity the affinities we have with the first modern city-dwellers of Victorian Britain and the differences that exist between us both and the generations that went before. Modern man is essentially thick on the ground. On the lower and darker side of pre-Victorian respectability what we see is a vast ignorable pit of shadows from which few ever emerged to make any distinguishable mark of personal achievement. The traditional urban mob was personified only by its ringleaders and remained essentially anonymous and undifferentiated. The modern aspect of the crowd militant as we see it developing early in the nineteenth century included implicit disciplining, the dawning of a new sense which the urban working classes began to have of themselves, and the heightened sensitivity felt by the ruling classes towards popular unrest. What also began to happen at the same time, though barely perceptibly, was something that can only be described as a process of faces appearing in the crowd.

In conditions of urbanisation, a dominant culture is always faced by new groups of people previously thought of as beneath consideration. The close juxtaposition of rich and poor, of the mercantile and servile elements in urban society, which had persisted since ancient times, only began to break down in England during the eighteenth century and it was not until the nineteenth that this disintegration became at all marked. Before this time the allocation of social space was determined more than anything by the divisions between crafts and between townsmen and aliens, though the accumulation of private property, the award of public honours and the expanding scope for conspicuous consumption had also helped to draw such groups apart. The analogue to this process was the suburb, at one time a no-man's-land for all that was disreputable – dungheaps, gallows, stinking trades, bloodsports, low taverns, prostitutes, thieves and the mob – and at another the means for keeping such things at a safe distance. It represented at once a glint of mutual perception between the middle and working classes and a blindfolding of their social relations wherever it happened at least during the nineteenth century. To that extent they are symptoms of the Victorian city as a phenomenon of modernity, of the capacity for sustained awareness of other societies or cultures. What the Victorian city began to do by way of opening up the possibilities of the dual revolution was to permit this sustained awareness of differences in social conditions to take place. Here, almost for the first time, was some visible prospect of the advancement of whole classes but, more than that, a stirring consciousness among the lower ranks of society of the removable differences in the quality of human life. It was the city which enabled such things to be seen.

It was not an ennobling experience through and through. For the working classes had been thought of as sub-human for so long that it was almost natural for them to display, or for their superiors to see them as displaying their reputation for animality – brute strength, brute instincts, brute deserts. The faces in the crowd were as often as not seen to be marked by strong drink, violent passions, degraded character. The great unwashed were socially unclean, too, and the typical attitudes first expressed to this emergent group by those above them were also stereotyped – a blend of contempt, fear, hate and physical revulsion. Threaded into such attitudes was a mixture of awe and envy derived from general knowledge of the profligacy of the working classes, itself partly dependent on the common, if not first-hand, observation that prostitutes, like prize-fighters, ordinarily came from the lower orders. The pornography of the period assumed that all servants, shop girls and labourers were inexhaustibly libidinous. To the respectable classes such things spoke of an almost totally unregenerative condition redeemable in very few instances and then only by acts of grace and forgiveness. They remained deeply gloomy about the lower reaches of the Victorian city and conceived the notion of a residuum to cover the unknowable poor. Slum missionaries brought back their tales of horror and pathos from this nether world as if they had been journeying in darkest Africa. They were for the most part, as it seems now, both deaf and dumb, incapable of hearing the authentic tongue of the voiceless or of telling the prisoners how to escape. The poor man was in truth a long way from paradise and the rich man from longing for his touch, but the gulf between them was no longer fixed and the city itself was capable of closing it in other ways.

The Victorian city was essentially a great leveller, even though it began, like the railway, by hardening the categories of those using it and directing them into socially segregated compartments. To be sure, its population was distributed more explicitly in this regard by night than it was by day, and there were always incongruous pockets of privilege and understood affiliations. Urban society developed diversity, too, so that the range of its modes of behaviour and particular attributes became almost a function of size. Yet the city was above all the province of anonymity and the nondescript. In it the individual's identity tended to be smudged and made less distinguishable; he could lose himself in the crowd, become part of the common multiple, disappear. This is precisely what he could never do in village society. There, understood roles, systems of deference and clear lines of demarcation designating ground to be covered or avoided, still expressed the animus of feudalism. The difference between the city and the village was not so well established everywhere, especially in the nascent industrial cities, where the lords of the loom and the mine were creating conditions in which individuals could be marked men and their lives could be moulded to new forms of serfdom. The general tendency was altogether less idiosyncratic and more organisational. The urban masses were in truth composed, not of social atoms, but of individual human beings. Yet for purposes of social action, as for mutual perception, it was the extra-familial grouping, the collective label, more generalised identification of ordinary needs, more abstract reference to people as such, that now began to pass into common parlance about the city. Inhospitable to the stranger, unyielding even to its own, the city was nevertheless a great force towards equalising its inhabitants.

2

There we are bound to pause. The characteristics of urban life are still in far too great a flux to be quite sure what we are seeing. That the Victorian city leapt beyond the accepted human scale and imposed on its citizens new patterns of association does not mean that it was utterly inhumane. The inhumanities of the Victorian city derived largely from the crisis of numbers and of personal identity which it provoked, though the problems of coming to terms with the new environment itself were not all solved with human regard. Far from it, but it does seem clear that the curse of privatism, the headlong and egocentric pursuit of private wealth and power irrespective of the hurt done to others, was sufficiently inhibited in Britain to avoid complete havoc. Municipal responsibilities were shouldered sometimes with a casualness that was almost venal but in ways that headed off the worst aspects of what Tawney called the tyranny of functionless property. It is also not difficult to see that the loosening tissue of personal ties that bound up each pre-urban community implied release as well as insecurity. The blank wall that faced the newcomer to the city cannot obscure the fact that the whole civilising process, of which the city is the most powerful agent, has involved a lengthening of the lines of human communication, not a constriction of them. Larger networks of social intercourse had already breached the city walls in feudal times; the city of the industrial era merely extends these possibilities to all and sundry.

The passage to urbanity which the Victorian city offered was not contrived exclusively within itself but evolved to a degree that is seldom acknowledged from rustic beginnings of various kinds. Modern industry began to a large extent outside the existing towns and moved into them only when water-power gave way to steam or the entrepreneurial advantages of an urban location outweighed those of an industrial colony. As it did so the whole economic matrix began to shift from country-dominated town to town-dominated country. In the context of a larger transition still, the city as a type was shifting in power and influence from the condition it had known under the Renaissance as a state literally of its own to that of an organ of the nation-state – the administrative, economic and cultural hub of a much larger whole. Beyond this focus again lies the control mechanism of the metropolis and a system of world cities. The self-evident physical and social mass that we see in any one of them does little of itself, however, to distinguish its generic urbanity. The mere possession by a place of a given number of digits to denote size, density or employment is not enough to clinch the matter, and the sociological hypothesis that urban life is characterised by impersonal, secondary and contractual relationships has been submitted to surprisingly few historical tests. We know next to nothing even of kinship patterns in the Victorian city, let alone its more elaborate community structures and the sense of belonging or separation that permeated its various social layers. What we can perhaps perceive is that the Victorian city was a hybrid growth, drawing one strain from its commercial past, another from its rustic environment, a third from its own necessities. Its interpenetration by a rural culture, planted there by its country-bred citizens and kept alive by force of family upbringing and an apparently unquenchable longing for some semblance of pastoral bliss, is one of its fundamental, if elusive, aspects. The functional affinities of the city with villages and market towns remains a persistent, if sometimes surprising, one, even though we see in the seasonal movements of the wayfaring classes and their less nomadic counterparts, the landed squirearchy of London's West End, some evidence of how the life of the city and the village was periodically mediated.

In the nineteenth century no English city had severed itself from its rural connections. The largest of them still conducted extensive back-yard agriculture, not merely half-a-dozen hens in a coop of soap-boxes, but cow-stalls, sheep-folds, pig-sties above and below ground, in and out of dwellings, on and off the streets, wherever this rudimentary factory-farming could be made to work. The larger the city the more liable was it to contain these things in relative abundance, not simply because there was some kind of living to be made out of it but because the gobbling up of the countryside had meant swallowing villages whole. Their old way of life slowly eroded but its associations were often deliberately reinforced to generate a new kind of village atmosphere. Moreover, in back-streets of a certain formation or social composition, lived little communities that knew themselves so well, that shared their common identity with such jealous pride, that for all ordinary purposes of life they comprised a village of a sort that was not basically distinguishable from those surrounded by fields. The old face-to-face relationships more readily associated with the traditional village were implanted in the heart of the Victorian city in its slums. That kind of situation is palpable still, just as the transient and impersonal characteristics commonly attached to the city itself are to be seen nowadays transfixing so many suburbanised and urban-tenanted villages far from its doors. The recognised territorial and sociological distinctions between the city and village which held good, with certain exceptions, in the nineteenth century are in some sense now being turned inside out, and clear dividing lines between them are becoming even more difficult to draw.

The sense of community – at once enlivening and stifling – that was once carried in the very marrow of village society has never quite deserted the cities, even though it occurs only in small pockets, for poverty and injustice

9

tend to bind those that share them, and the city tolerates both. It even succeeds in perpetuating uncharacteristically urban events, like the August bank holiday walk by thousands together out of Leeds onto the moor, which goes on under its own momentum and a desire by those taking part to declare a common identity. There are, too, latent capacities which are brought into the open only in an emergency, like that secret understanding between complete strangers that de Tocqueville recalled in his *Souvenir* when he wrote of a kind of morality peculiar to times of disorder, and a special code for days of rebellion. A city like Liverpool has its own language of the walls, not merely through its babble of posters or the forlorn *graffiti* of telephone kiosks and public lavatories, but in the rank subtleties inscribed with chalk or aerosol spray on its most public surfaces. This is city talk, not country: urban walls were endless, disowned almost, open invitations to fly-posting and sloganising alike. In the village street virtually every brick was a personal belonging, every act public knowledge, all information by word of mouth.

So much of this sub-literary world of the city's streets must remain inscrutable. Of the millions of yards of street ballads hawked for sale before the last quarter of the nineteenth century only scraps survive, but they probe for us other ephemeralities, and give us a glimpse of the imaginative content of a million brief lives, a view from the gutter, and in terms of popular appeal an anticipation of the tabloids of our own time. The true verbal and graphic equivalent of urbanism is journalism proper, the best lens we have for a close-up of the Victorian city, of its disconnections, intimacies, conflicts, aberrations, incidents – of its whole symbiotic continuum and style. The concentration of people in such numbers created for the first time the readership on the required scale to launch newspapers and magazines in their thousands and to give vent to opinion and interest of almost every kind. Here is the earliest running commentary we have on what it felt like to have the city burgeoning out at such speed and throwing up issues of such novelty and discord. What is omitted from those pages and by whom is as important to the reading of them as it is to the reading of history itself, and what is pictured and how is as revealing of their readers' receptivity as the magazine advertisement of today. The hard social substance of the city was at first filtered by convention and only gradually was the distance interposed between readers and reality by such means foreshortened, chiefly by humour, and finally disposed of altogether. The city street and the city poor ultimately came into some kind of focus – the faces in the crowd even began to wear recognisable expressions – and the actual distance between them and the well-to-do was paced out, if only vicariously. It was an object-lesson patiently conducted though perhaps barely half-learned. Even a man as humane and concerned with the predicament of the poor as Mayhew could not, despite his own best feelings and judgments and the insuppressible empathy of his interviewing, prevent himself from setting the poor at a distance. This he did partly by confusing the poor in general with the most depressed and degraded of their number, and partly by stressing the discontinuities in the hierarchy of the urban working class. What the illustrated magazines and the products of the slum presses teach us is that there are attitudes toward the city and its mechanisms of amelioration that we have hardly begun to clarify, and that the contents of a whole uncatalogued archive of material are as yet unread.

3

Much of the urban historian's task is concerned with the art of reading the city. That art is architectonic and archaeological as well as literary. If we want simply to evoke the urban landscape that we have lost we must not only lift off the encrustations of the motor age but reinvest with their own coarse original grain the places which we have veneered over. There are severe limits to this, for so many of the incidental noises, smells, colours, sense of place have gone beyond recall: who, for instance, even now remembers the vivid litter of bus tickets on London pavements, the sulphurous flavour of a pea-souper, the horsy din and strain of Ludgate Hill? If we want to be more than mere resurrectionists and breathe some life and meaning into the language of the city we must expect to study it with all the senses. Engels is in this respect a surer guide than Augustus Hare simply because he had the imagination to search for an organising principle behind the masquerade of the principal streets and to look for it, not among the historical relics that were dotted about, but in the conditions of contemporary life and work that bore testimony everywhere he looked. Behind the assertive commercial façade of Manchester he detected a deeper meaning than the simple proposition that it pays to set up shop where customers collect. The fuller message of these streets to him was that, without conscious design, the city had revealed its inherent structure in the organisation of its own space. It was as if Mill's civilising process, whereby pain and suffering are kept from the sight of rulers, had preserved Manchester's merchant princes from the spectacle of the means of their own enrichment. The workers' quarters were concentrated always round the back, and their presence expressed by mere allusion.

That is no longer such a startling discovery. The relationships between the slums and suburbs of other cities are now seen to have been equally expressive of their respective production functions, and the capacity of the upper classes to spin a web of communications that enabled them to commute to the centre without being encumbered by needless distractions no less developed. The precise topography of the paths along which they moved and the extent to which the separation of the classes was adjusted behind them as they pushed further afield can be read with little difficulty from any residue still left on the ground – the symbolic language of domestic architecture and the more explicit references in the layout, naming and furnishing of the streets. In every place there is some such little tale to tell, of what it was that once meant so much to people living there, of how such things could never last, and why it all had to be repeated, more or less, just along the road. And if we could work down the social heap to its very bottom the stones would have much more to say, of how much had to be done just to keep going, of how the numbers grew and the room shrank, of how the ground eventually opened and swallowed everything up. Thankfully, we cannot read many of these hieroglyphs any longer for ourselves, for the sight of them eventually brought about their destruction, but we can see the urban decay organically following the urban growth, the wretchedness mirroring the contentment, the poverty subtending the riches, and recognise in it all a structure, not of chaos, but of logically related parts.

Behind these landmarks and structures lie private worlds of thought and feeling that we are conscious though not cognisant of, things that matter in any understanding of the Victorian city but which are buried too secretly to be explored by ordinary historical means. The quality of urban life which we seek cannot, except in a very limited sense, be quantified. It says something for the affective conditioning of large areas of Victorian life that the Victorians' chief sense of fact was numerical, that they should have felt compelled to quantify their qualitative statements about urban society above all. The city has always had an inexorable calculus. But numbers have no feelings and are at best mere explanatory agents. What satisfactions and hurts, what sense of community or deprivation, what consciousness of beauty or ugliness or merely of environment and actuality, stirred those very countable people we long to know. Our best informants are those imaginatively concerned with the contemporary scene, above all the novelists, who penetrate sometimes the very structure of feeling and prevailing values, and persuade us of the truths they utter, though without a shred of proof. What they have to tell us about the impact of urbanism as an all-enveloping experience is perhaps less direct and sure-handed. What they offer over all is simply evidence about the city in a new form.

In evaluating what the Victorian novel has to say about the city we have to keep reminding ourselves of its underlying predisposition to treat its subject as a hostile environment, and to recognise that this is an aspect of the tendency of the high culture of Victorian Britain to express a pre-urban system of values. There was, Jerome Schneewind pointed out some years ago, a fundamental Victorian debate that straddled formal philosophy, styles of consciousness and imaginative expression – a debate that surfaced, for example, in the arguments between Intuitionists and Utilitarians about ethics. For the former, good behaviour was the result of sympathy and emotional understanding; for the latter, of wise calculation and the observation of agreed rules. Each had its appropriate setting. Intuitionism suited small groups, typically friendly and personal; Utilitarianism, large groups, typically strangers. We might say that the one was the ethic of the family and the village, and the other of the crowd and the city. The tradition that had been brought into life by the family and the village had in turn suffused Victorian literature and helped thereby to sharpen the concept of the city as its destroyer, the enemy of culture and moral values, the ally of anarchy, materialism and the deadly sins. What the Victorian novel tried to do in fact was to redeem the city, to domesticate the unruly scene, to personalise the dreadful anonymity, to make a family of the crowd. The popular bardic literature of the great Victorian writers was committed to the task of drawing the whole literate nation into a kind of cousinship that embraced especially its newly awakening and wayward members. The great authors – a type of uncles and aunts reinforcing the parental roles of Queen, Church and Ministerial Government – ventured dutifully into city streets where the squire and the justices no longer could and policemen seldom dared to go, to exhort and reassure, to embrace and admonish its unfamiliar types, and to offer the souls that might be saved an avenue of escape.

What we see in this whole literary enterprise – as in drawing and painting, too, though their social outlines are far less clear and much slower to form – is a gigantic effort by creative artists to adapt to the highly original scenes and experiences of the city without abandoning the categories set for them by the pre-urban generations that had gone before. They approached it from the outside, on the basis of intuitionist values, quintessentially humane, paternally structured and pastoral – the counterpart to the painters' preoccupation meanwhile with landscape and portraiture and of the dramatists with melodrama and urban stereotypes. The idea of an urban nature, so exultantly proclaimed by Lamb at the very beginning of the century in a famous letter to Wordsworth, was unthinkable among creative artists for a very long time. The standard of comparison implicitly invoked instead was the tamed nature of rural England. Some of the most revealing passages come at points where the transition from this supposedly earthly paradise to the city occurred – as, for example, in the initiation of the country-born into the shock city of Manchester in *Mary Barton*, or, in reverse, in the intrusion of the city-bred villainy of Mr Slope into the pastoral peace of Barchester. Sometimes such gaps were too wide to be bridged, even in the imagination. The emotional difficulty offered to sensitive newcomers to the city comes out with unexpected force in the tendency shown by the working-class poets of the shock city itself to increase their use of their beloved country dialects to echo their rural past rather than to portray the social realities on their own doorsteps.

By the end of the nineteenth century this choice of attitudes towards the

13

city had become less invidious, and the city as an object for the expression of continuous art, unflawed by rustic associations, much more readily accepted. Dickens was the necessary pioneer. He had always been the great exception, not so much in his preference for any city-derived values (for he thought he was as anti-Utilitarian as anyone), but in his inability to forgo the city as a locale or to disguise his excitement at its vitality and diversity. He was as incapable of deserting it as Hardy was of developing any empathy with it. No one has been able to match his subtle and unerring command of the curious social topography of London, and the intensity of his love affair with his mass readership has about it a preview of modern encounters between popular artist and mass audience.

But there was no general readiness on the part of novelists, poets and painters to make such materials as Dickens's so unaffectedly urban until the 1890s. Perhaps the city at that time occupied a place in the English imagination similar to that of sex and was similarly repressed. It was not something to celebrate with open joy but remained within the Puritan tradition a source of guilt and alarm. The fact of the city, as of manufacturing industry, was never accepted with any real trust, and both have been contested suspiciously ever since. The world's first nation of city-dwellers remains its most reluctant. The release of imaginative energies to interpret the city in the 1890s was part of a general, albeit partial, adjustment to the facts of life – an adjustment which also included a somewhat more realistic attitude towards the mysteries of sex, a correlation which no English Baudelaire quite portrayed. Yet for the first time a whole generation of artists was growing up that was not afraid of the city, and could make it appear something less than a monster.

The very note of terror and obscurity that had been struck so insistently by some of the massed structures of the earlier part of the century was being subdued, their awful rhetoric stilled. Once the demands of commerce and industry could no longer be met by designs drawn exclusively from the ancient or the rural world the city became the theatre of opposing aesthetic forces, and the looming shapes of railway termini, viaducts, factories and penitentiaries were deposited relentlessly among them. These vast structures owed rather more to eighteenth-century inspiration than to the modular possibilities of cast iron and reinforced concrete, but during the latter part of the nineteenth century the beginnings of a great rebuilding of business quarters, in London at least, helped to open the way for a more cosmopolitan explosion of architectural style than the city had ever known. Meanwhile, a more domestic theme wound persistently on – the declension of the villa of the country gentry into the suburban semi-detached. Here many things met. Among the railway suburbs of the largest cities the dominant influence by the end of the century was unquestionably the picturesque, a fitting architecture perhaps for an urban middle class still dreaming dreams of landed possessions and of a haven for the family. The suburb was a supremely ambivalent invention and therefore a key element in the history of the Victorian city. It was fitting that the architectural forms of the suburb should have diverged from the purely urban, for the suburb was, after all, a gesture of non-commitment to the city in everything but function. Even the functions might be abstracted in garden cities or model villages or communitarian colonies, and the cities abandoned to their shame. The final phase of the Victorian city was in several respects a fugitive one, not only for the middle classes retreating to their laburnum groves but for the masses following behind in workmen's trains or making for emigrant ships instead.

4

The whole of this long Victorian episode in the process of urbanisation might well be thought of as a kind of training that society had to undergo. It was not a simple programme of adaptation to changed circumstances or a new environment, but a fundamental restructuring of attitudes, the acquiring of new social techniques, the acceptance of new codes of discipline, the pursuit of new opportunities. The sequence was neither settled in advance nor even known and it could never be considered complete. The adjustment proceeded at a different rate for different groups, and it involved the absorption of new knowledge not merely by the young but by whole classes. The process was literally that of acculturation to an urban way of life. We see symptoms of it on every level, not merely in the daily flows along commuter corridors or in the scrupulous calculations of site values, but in the cell-like accretion of municipal powers, the sectarian shepherding of the poor, the organisation of charity, the rise of spectator sports, the widening scope for enjoyment and freer association. In this larger education the pub occupied a peculiar and versatile position, a place in which many roles were played and adaptations made, both in the institution itself and in those frequenting it. We do not even now recognise all the subtleties of this socialisation. More generally, however, the most fundamental lesson that urban society had to learn was that it could no longer neglect to take account of the implications of its own actions, to remain ignorant of itself. It had on the contrary to undertake a continuous series of acts of self-knowledge, to adopt an empirical stance and to develop, implicitly or explicitly, some kind of social policy.

Natural laws, which under divine authority had acquired benevolent force in the eighteenth century, no longer served. That God made the country and man the town did not immediately annul the proposition that Nature should flourish everywhere: that, for example, even the city slum was a natural phenomenon, the proper habitat of the ever-present poor, and that the nomads whom Mayhew found filtering through them could be seen as belonging to a lower natural order, ordained to their underworld. Yet the

15

inclination to refuse to tamper with so-called natural forces was not in tune with technology and the encouragement it gave to rising expectations of life. The rash assault of the railways (to take Wordsworth's phrase) and the vastly more blatant interference with the natural landscape by industrialisation itself developed the overriding notion that permanence was giving way to change and helped to place cultural emphasis on functional achievement and human responsibility. The conscience of the new rich became an index of the relative deprivation of the urban poor. The sense of crisis that began to pervade the whole social condition was entirely man-made.

The concept of Nature as a cultural force was therefore inclined to become by the middle of the century tremendously confused and its moral and spiritual sanctions neutralised – though not, as we now know, extinguished. We see Victorian urban society wrestling with its lessons, to be or not to be natural, especially when it came to the drains. 'It might be worthwhile, sometimes, to inquire what Nature is,' remarks Dickens in a familiar passage in *Dombey and Son*, 'how men work to change her, and whether in the enforced distortions so produced, it is not natural to be unnatural.' He then takes the reader into a slum and reflects on outraged Nature, ending thus: 'When we shall gather grapes from thorns, and figs from thistles; when fields of grain shall spring up from the offal in the bye-ways of our wicked cities, and roses bloom in the fat churchyards that they cherish; then we may look for natural humanity and find it growing from such seed.' The authority of a traditional concept is plainly giving way to a recognition of the primacy of human needs. The old idea that there was something natural about suffering, something to be tolerated, begins to yield to the new idea that men should use whatever political and technical skills they can command to raise the level, demeanour and satisfactions of human life in the city – use it to lift the potential of its whole culture. The city, which was being spoken of in mid-Victorian England as the burial pit of the human species, was a promise that these things could be done – a promise that partly explains the Liberals' positive enthusiasm for the city, as it does the reformation of urban government they sought so zealously.

For the time being the city was a laboratory of public medicine. Discovering the pathological and psychological consequences of human density, and learning the fearful capacity of some of the most mortal diseases to bridge the widest social gaps, took a dreadful time – the etiology of typhus even was not fully known until the twentieth century. No emergent society ever proceeded so far in urbanising itself with such little established fact about its implications, nor ever will: the rate of urbanisation among the emergent countries of today rests substantially on the control of crude death-rates first demonstrated when the major advances in public health were being pioneered in the nineteenth century. At first sight, such progress was matched by what now seems to have been a shocking perversity in

16

actually taking the first steps – taking due pains to collect drinking water where sewers did not discharge, to build sound homes and to eat enough good food. Such lessons were in fact part of a much larger syllabus that included the training of a multiplying band of experts of every kind to make and run a machine fit for living in, and to adapt the human being to the machine – to make of him, conceivably, a sentient machine himself. In fact a more systematic and fundamental interference with the behaviour of the individual was required than any earlier society had known. Small wonder therefore that the political counterpart to the psychological challenge of delivering up full personal freedom of action which urban society required, namely centralisation, should have been so bitterly fought over in mid-century. However, within another generation sanitary reform had been so completely accepted within the canon of municipal improvement that the only real issue was, not how much public money could be spent, nor what men should do to stay alive, but who should pay. Ridding the cities of their slums eventually meant rehousing their occupants below cost and taxing the country for most of the difference. The ultimate lesson of urbanisation is that no one is left out.

That was also the ultimate message of the Church, framed as it still was by rural conventions, dispensing a pastoral role. For Nonconformists, who had never encountered in the towns the resistance to their teachings that they had found in the country, the cities were a larger opportunity, which they seized, and from which they proselytised with varying success the industrial valleys of Wales and the North of England. The Established Church was an older institution, bereft in the cities of its natural setting and of its single-handed job of saving the souls of people who had so little hope of bodily ministrations. It now found the emphasis given by urbanisation to the relief of bodily suffering a chalice difficult to refuse. The settlement movement must have seemed to many at the time the noblest gesture engendered by the late-Victorian city, but its Christian purpose tended to be enlisted in practice more in the cause of bestowing middle-class attitudes on the poor than in enrolling them in the company of heaven. Whatever adamant of religious feeling of their own the urban working classes had, they did not seek their salvation in Protestantism. The forces that activated any such allegiances were inclined rather to be derived from deep cultural or ethnic roots which, in the circumstances of the city, meant in turn forming enclaves of streets and, in circumstances recognised widely in the cities of the twentieth century, providing bases for ghettos or for urban guerrilla warfare.

5

Two final observations may serve as both warning and exhortation. One is the ready familiarity one feels with the Victorian city – its people, its problems, the basic patterns of its life – almost as if it belonged to a long-remembered experience of one's own. In several senses, this is almost literally true. The camera, through which we perceive so much of our own world, has transmitted to us a whole gallery of likenesses and recognisable shapes that draws us and them involuntarily closer. At one end of the gallery these celluloid images actually spring into action or their living representatives tell us face to face how it all was, and the sense of identification and unbroken continuity becomes irresistible, sometimes movingly so. These impressions are not in themselves out of place, for the distinction our language draws between past and present is not so tidily sustained in our perception of the world about us, and standard intervals of chronological time are not the only way of structuring human experience. Yet we must beware of becoming involuntary ventriloquists and of mixing up the scenery, of failing to distinguish between the things that once were and no longer are, of creating fantasy. We have tried to clarify the sources of the images of contemporary life that were current in the Victorian city and to set them against the prevailing realities of the time. It is as well to remember that although their world is part of our own, ours was never part of theirs.

The second observation is that there is a great deal yet to be said about the Victorian city itself, especially in regard to the definition and mutations of an urban culture in all parts of Britain and among British possessions overseas, not to mention those larger inter-cultural studies that are needed before we can take proper stock of the way the twentieth century has shaped, and been shaped by, the rise of the city. The vast intercontinental transfers of population and power and the formation of large nation-states in the nineteenth century have made that period one of the hinges of history, and the enormous strides taken by industrialisation and technology have made its cities the template for the whole structure of modern life. The city has set us the task of examining everything that has claimed to be permanent and essentially human in our heritage and systems of values. What we see therefore as urgent in the serious study of these things is some means of connecting the humanistic and the scientific traditions that are available. We shall then be able to interpret more subtly and richly the impact of urbanisation on the minds and spirits of city-dwellers and learn more intimately the secrets both of the way we live now and of the way we might live.

2

Urbanity and suburbanity

You were good enough to say, Mr Vice-Chancellor, when you invited me to give this inaugural lecture, that it wasn't strictly necessary – or words to that effect. Since you did so the most recently installed professor of economic history in this country, Donald Coleman at Cambridge, has taken stock of what he describes as 'this dying ritual': of the 32 persons who have become professors in his subject since 1945 no fewer than 15 have crept into their chairs without a word.[1] I confess I also thought of taking that vow of silence. My own academic life has been immured in Leicester so long – I came here, as you delicately forbore to point out, before most of my present students were born – that I have never been aware of taking any step that might properly be accompanied by any ceremonial. What has happened, quite simply, is that the University has given me the opportunity to indulge my historical curiosity in the way I chose, and I have been lucky enough to catch one of the biggest breakers to have risen in Modern History since the war. This is an opportunity, therefore, for me to reflect on the course of urban history in the light of the urban tendencies of our times, to consider the proper limits of the subject and to suggest some of the directions in which it might now most happily go. It is an opportunity, too, for me to thank the University of Leicester for being the first in this country to mark the emergence of urban history as a recognisable corpus of knowledge in this way and, on a purely personal level, to offer this lecture as a small gesture of my gratitude to the University for its own distinctive urbanities over the last two decades and more.

1

The civilities of university life are in themselves no guide to what I have to say, though they do embody some of the assumptions still commonly attached to certain types of urban institution. They are assumed to be – and sometimes actually are – places in which the frictions of human contact and aspiration have produced in time a kind of polish, a series of mannerly procedures, a certain good humour and gentle regard, even between the direst opponents – the kind of thing that Macaulay, writing in 1849, saw in Charles II, who apologised on his death-bed for having been 'a most unconscionable time dying' – the last glimpse, Macaulay wrote, 'of that exquisite urbanity, so often found potent to charm away the resentment of a justly incensed nation'.[2] I think that's a bit old-fashioned, even in universities, and the sense of urbanity as pertaining to the relatively refined characteristics of townsmen has been out of date much longer still. Urbanity in that sense had gradually been accepted in the course of the seventeenth and eighteenth centuries, when urban was still a derivative of urbane and a mark of some respect, as in the pseudonym of the editor of the *Gentleman's Magazine*, Sylvanus Urban, Gent. The term urbanity itself was in frequent use for most of the nineteenth century, though, one suspects, with rapidly diminishing significance for the palpable differences between urban and rural life, except among those at the top. There was in this sense nothing urbane, for instance, about life in 'the Ghetto' – C. F. G. Masterman's term for that 'enclosure into which is penned our labouring population' in London around the turn of the nineteenth century.

Outside, some incredible distance beyond its borders, [he explained] is the world that counts; those that look before and after, meditate, design and aspire. Within are those to whom the twentieth century belongs . . . Here are lives not even kindled by the resourcefulness, subtlety, and individual enterprise of the avowed criminal, but in incredible multitude, shabby, ineffective, battered into futility by the ceaseless struggle of life

– the self-same 'suffocating vulgarities and tyrannies' of huge cities for which Chesterton also felt disgust as they crushed the 'overlooked, overcharged, sweated' people in them 'into a sort of jam'.[3] Whether we have the same gut reactions or not, here is a type of urban existence we can still recognise, a type of urbanity – a type of sub-urbanity, if you like – in which the city is not the deliverer of mankind but the destroyer, literally as well as figuratively. I do not have the time to explore at all searchingly the imagery of the city which would project both this feeling for the city and a contrary one. Without both *caritas* and *cupiditas* – the city four-square and the city of destruction – the perspective is distorted. All I can do in this respect this evening is to try and open the aperture of urbanity a little and to change the visual focus from time to time.

The more general meaning that the word was tending to adopt at the time – around the beginning of this century – when Masterman and Chesterton were writing the words I quoted just now was, of course, what we should characteristically refer to today as urbanism, meaning by it the general state or condition of urban life. Yet H. G. Wells could still include among his *Anticipations* in 1901 a prospect of a diffused 'urbanity', as he put it, beyond the 'urban regions'.[4] F. W. Maitland, the great historian of medieval municipal institutions, when referring to a long-standing practice of corporate boroughs which had become a scandal by common consent rather than by misdemeanour (namely, the sale of corporation property for the corporators' gain), indicated in his Ford Lectures to the University of Oxford in 1897 an inherent difference in this respect between modernity and antiquity, and he said, if he could so use the words, between urbanity and rusticity.[5] The term therefore fits my period well for I must talk somewhat about the nineteenth century, but I also choose to speak of urbanity in this lecture, rather than urbanism, in order to point to something in particular and in order to resist a little a tendency in the writing of urban history which I shall later explain. The difference in form and stress between the words urban and urbane is similar to that between human and humane. And if that stress is nowadays hard to apply the difficulty itself will suggest to you one of the compelling ironies of urban existence that tug at so many students of urban life – that great gap between the promise of modernity, the vision of abundance and equality, and its fulfilment by the cities which are its agents.

The civilising possibilities of cities can seldom have seemed as remote as they do at the present day among the pavement people of Calcutta and Hong Kong, or to anyone caught in the crossfire of urban guerrillas from Mexico City to Belfast, or among the barely perceived pathological poor of our large cities. The history of urban man cannot, of course, be seen in an unflickering focus, any more than the city can be disconnected in our minds from its counterpart, the country, as though the urbanisation of human society were a unilinear process bestowing benefits all round. It has clearly not done that. Indeed, as Raymond Williams points out in his most recent book, what London, for example,

had to show, more fundamentally, even to modern experience, than the uniform cities of the early Industrial Revolution, was a contradiction, a paradox: the coexistence of variation and apparent randomness with what had in the end to be seen as a determining system: the visible individual facts but beyond them, often hidden, the common condition and destiny.[6]

The accent I lay on urbanity is meant, despite the inherent and historical contradictions of the term, to help us to hold on to the individual facts, to keep us alert to human idiosyncrasies quite as much as to the more anonymous forces of history which fix the larger boundaries to ordinary lives, and to require in us the effort to find the connections between them.

The problem is not so much the problem, long familiar to economic historians above all, of finding the typical, representative facts on which to rest an analysis of the systematically repeated operations of economic activity, as it is that of finding a way of representing the disjunctive, individuated occurrences that are strung together in everyday experience with even less systematic organisation than news items in an evening paper. The problem, I am saying, is of finding the individual in the crowd, the community in the mass, personal identity among the statistics – a problem of values as well as of material fact, a problem that straddles many fields and makes demands on many disciplines. From his point of view Mr Williams sees this primarily as a problem of language; from mine I see it also as a problem of historical method; but our sympathies converge at some points completely, as in that passage in *The Mill on the Floss* where, having portrayed the urbanities of good society, with its claret and velvet carpets and its dinner engagements six weeks deep, George Eliot makes us look at the history of unfashionable families: 'good society', she writes,

floated on gossamer wings of light irony, is of very expensive production; requiring nothing less than a wide and arduous national life condensed in unfragrant, deafening factories, cramping itself in mines, sweating at furnaces, grinding, hammering, weaving under more or less oppression of carbonic acid – or else, spread over sheepwalks, and scattered in lonely houses and huts on the clayey or chalky corn-lands, where the rainy days look dreary. This wide national life is based entirely on emphasis – the emphasis of want, which urges it into all the activities necessary for the maintenance of good society and light irony.[7]

We cannot fail to notice in passing that this kind of connection is one that can be made even more easily in contemporary society, where the demands of the cities as a whole on the suppliers of their foodstuffs and raw materials of every kind are spread far and near, throughout the non-urban Third World, with obvious economic and political consequencies. We are daily made aware of such social discrepancies, and of their alarming tendency to increase almost as fast as the economic growth of the most rapidly expanding economies. We are also made aware of the effects of the 'filthy and polluting cities' upon the whole ecological balance of the inhabited globe. But I am far from wanting to press on you a view of the pathological condition of latterday urbanity as its normative condition. I only mention these dysfunctional aspects of urban economies at this point to suggest, however tentatively, the lengths to which even a relatively narrowly conceived cost-benefit analysis of the city as a generalised phenomenon in contemporary life would have to go if it is to have any real meaning. In the last resort, the issue of whether any kind of urbanity can prevail in human society seems likely to depend on the capacity of the world's largest cities to resist the course of development prophesied for them by so many writers at the turn of the nineteenth century. And the test of whether they have done so will predictably be their capacity to maintain and improve the quality of all their hundreds of millions of human lives, nothing less. That is a good reason, I think, for approaching the study of the processes at work within a framework that includes the humanities as well as the social sciences.

2

The urban transformation I have been alluding to is an astonishingly recent experience in the history of human society. If we set aside the question of how cities began, six or seven or eight thousand years ago, it is very clear that in terms simply of the relative extent to which populations have been concentrated in this way the threshold of modern urban existence can be fixed around the year 1800. I am not, of course, suggesting that civilisations other than our own were not dominated by their urban institutions – too much of the cultural legacy that we draw from classical antiquity is an urban one for that. All I am saying is that by any measurable index of the urbanisation of whole populations the process which has brought us to our present urban condition proceeded at markedly different rates before and after the nineteenth century.

The figures are scarcely in dispute. By 1800, when the world's population is generally reckoned as having been less than 1,000 million, not more than 3 per cent could be described as being urbanised: there were perhaps not more than 750 concentrations of 5,000 or more people throughout the world, and more than half of its entire urban population was contained in some 45 cities of 100,000 or more; no country could be described as having been completely urbanised and, indeed, only two – the United Kingdom and the Netherlands – contained much more than a tenth of their populations in urban concentrations of some kind. In the course of the next 150 years, while the world's population was increasing about 2½ times, the number of places containing 5,000 or more inhabitants multiplied so fast that by 1950 they contained, not 3 per cent, but 30 per cent of the total; by then, too, the 45 cities of 100,000 inhabitants or more had swollen to 875, of which about 50 contained a million apiece. Looked at in this global way, the urbanisation of the human population as a whole is clearly a contemporary phenomenon which is still developing very fast.

The leading American demographer in this field, Kingsley Davis, has calculated that the rate of change we were seeing in the 1950s was twice that of the preceding 50 years: by 1960, in his view, not less than a third of the population of the world was living in urban places of some size, and it is even possible to extrapolate current trends with enough confidence to predict that, by the end of the century, the average distribution as between the city and the country will roughly correspond with the situation existing in Britain alone around the middle of the nineteenth century, when half the population could be described as urban. The period within which our present urban condition became actual is, as I say, remarkably short, all the more so when we keep in mind that Britain alone could have been described as fully urbanised as recently as 1900. By now all the most advanced countries are in a comparable state; the rest, albeit painfully, are already falling into line.

In any explanation of this remarkable transformation of modern times, what happened in the nineteenth century and, above all, what happened in Britain, matters still. To anyone now living in or within the domain of a

Victorian city, as we all do, the link is as close and strong as the grip still held, by a kind of mortmain, over this part of the university site by Lutyens' Memorial Arch in Victoria Park. The elevation of these buildings could not be allowed to challenge the city's own memorial to the missing, itself a distant echo of that other arch in Flanders. In any city the divisions of the land, the structures that were first built, the whole paraphernalia that were first needed to make a place work or give it a sense of purpose, all add in some degree to the inertia of its mass. Even Victoria Park is itself a congress of many pre-Victorian influences. A quite different measure of how the legacy of the urban past continues to shape not only the urban present but our urban future in Great Britain is suggested by the downward trend in existing housing densities: 28 dwellings per acre for pre-1881 housing, 20 per acre for areas developed between 1881 and 1920, 13 per acre for the period 1921–41 – a profile of suburban trends in the past and an inkling of renewal problems for the future. In spite of itself, in spite of its aspirations to modernity and progress, in the face (if you like) of its most characteristic image as the place of the future, the city, any city, embodies its own past with infinite tenacity. Even so restless a place as Leicester cannot entirely abandon its past.

More fundamentally perhaps, the urban transformation of Britain in the nineteenth century matters to what came after as a prototypical experience. Concentrating the population, not just into a few large cities that might in 1843 justify an historian's judgment of it as *The Age of Great Cities*, but into towns of every size, was a process that was taking place twice as fast in England and Wales in the first half of the nineteenth century as it was anywhere else, and still markedly faster in the half-century that followed, when only the United States, Prussia, Saxony and Australasia had come up to her earlier rate. Not only so, but the capacity of the towns to generate their own natural increase, and even to begin to yield a surplus for migration, both between themselves and for export overseas – that is, to stop devouring people from the country on the scale practised by London in the eighteenth century (when it arguably took half the natural increase of the whole country to keep her supplied with a growing population) – also occurred sooner here than anywhere else.

The terrifying toll of life taken by the cities right down to the 1870s, as well as the compensatingly high birth-rates, both changed with almost dramatic suddenness in the last decade or so of the nineteenth century and the first decade of the twentieth. The extraordinary holding operation that had been mounted in the name of sanitary improvement in one urban burial pit after another during the three decades around mid-century had merely kept crude death-rates at near-crisis levels. Mortality still varied with the size and density of urban populations, so that even in 1893 a man born and brought up in Manchester could not expect to live much more than half as long as a countryman born at the same time – a tendency that was evident in varying degrees in all the other urbanising countries of the time – but, within another two decades, urban death-rates were no longer pushing up the national average. How far urban birth-rates had been leading since the 1870s in the opposite direction is still not clear, but in terms both of fertility and mortality there can be little doubt the cities were now the critical factor in determining the national wellbeing.

By the 1921 census the proportion of the population designated 'urban' had reached a level it could scarcely ever exceed, some 80 per cent. Though the cities, the smaller towns, and the suburbs which clung to them both in ever-growing numbers, continued to require more land as the total population grew and households divided with greater alacrity as prosperity increased, the process of urbanisation (if by it we mean a shift in the proportion of the population contained in towns) had in this country come to an end. That it was virtually completed in the Victorian period is one reason why so much of the research now going on in urban history should be concentrated on the nineteenth century.

That episode in our urban history is a prelude to our own times in so many respects. So much that was new in it sprang directly from its sheer numerosity, concentrated as it so plainly was into such a fascinating and at times horrifying series of growth points; and the Victorians' awareness of their own multiplying numbers – one might almost say obsession with them – rapidly took hold of their sense of fact, of what had to be done to cope with them, of how their successes might be measured. The relatively thin stream of statistics that had till now been supplied almost entirely to measure movements of trade, tax yields, and so on, now began to foam with figures on the incidence of disease, the condition of the urban environment, the statement of employment, poverty, crime, urban institutions of every kind, with the new statistical societies of the 1830s and 1840s busying themselves from the start with statistics of the highest social relevance. For all their patchiness and uncertain bearing, these statistical accumulations – I am not speaking merely of official sources – probably represent the most accessible and unheard-of materials that are available anywhere to illustrate and explain the inexorable calculus of the city.

Such progressions, as those watching them came to recognise, amounted (or at least seemed to amount) to fundamental changes in the quality of life:

We had thought that a city of four millions of people were merely a collection of one hundred cities of forty thousand [Masterman wrote]. We find it differing not only in degree, but in kind, producing a mammoth of gigantic and unknown possibility.... This, then, is the first thing to note of us, not our virtue or vices, beauty, apathy, or knowledge; but our overwhelming, inconceivable number – number continually increasing, multiplying without a pause, coming not with observation, choking up the streets of the great city, and silently flowing over the dismal wastes beyond.[8]

Numbers on this scale, and the apparently incoherent, almost unintelligible, tangle of incidental shapes that went with them, had already begun to produce – and not only in London – those instinctive reactions to these human aggregates for which the sociologists have since provided a suitably misunderstood term, *anomie*. But one thinks immediately of the fate of Mrs Bulstrode in *Middlemarch*, for whom the anonymity of a numbered house in an obscure row was terrifyingly like life without hope, a threat of becoming a mere cypher herself. Yet the numbers had a contagion of their own and the aggregates produced required a different organisation of their social space from that prevailing in pre-industrial towns, a different kind of social discipline, a new sense of time, and of the division between work and leisure.

But even if Jane Jacobs's historical hypothesis of cities-first-rural-development-later cannot yet be accepted, the cities of the industrial era did not inaugurate something entirely new. The idea that the city, having served its time as commercial centre or even commercial principality, should at this time have emerged from its chrysalis as a separate component within the nation-state and become instead not merely the control mechanism but the entire social framework, that the city should at this point have become, in one sociologist's phrase, society itself, constitutes one of the problems of definition that still plague urban historians. The city would not release rusticity that readily – May Day and Jack-in-the-Green became and remained the province of chimney sweeps in London till the twentieth century. But there can be little argument that with the coming of the dual revolution in England and France in the eighteenth and nineteenth centuries, it was the cities that first saw that faltering failure of absolutes in ideas, conventions, institutions and behaviour, and which permitted instead a more democratised kind of urbanity. Maitland's long view told him that

Mere numbers are important. I am persuaded [he said] that we hurry the history both of our villages and of our towns because we fill them too full. There are some thoughts which will not come to men who are not tightly packed.[9]

As I have argued elsewhere, it was here that the humanisation of mankind became for the first time a momentarily imaginable possibility, even if the petty realities of individual lives remained stubbornly gross and seemingly hopeless. In the most general terms, it was these new industrial towns which first enabled such things to be seen, where those who might otherwise have remained almost totally lost to view on the underside of pre-Victorian respectability perceived, though not always in advance of the respectable classes themselves, the potentiality of the removable differences in the quality of human life. I wouldn't want to do more than hint at the part played by the cities in the political education of the middle and working classes (and, incidentally, in the advance of the Liberal party and of Nonconformity) without allowing for all kinds of variation in time and place and group and class, for which there is scarcely time this evening.

26

What I think can be recognised, even on this level of analysis, is the role of the Victorian city as both theatre and laboratory, a place literally for demonstration, as it has remained. In regard to the latter, it is clear enough now that no urbanising nation ever proceeded so far with so little knowledge as to the pathological and psychological implications of such high human densities, though these were not in fact as high, in terms of persons per acre, as those reached in a number of Continental cities. What we see happening, especially when account is taken of the unremitting inquiries being undertaken by public and private agencies into so many aspects of the urban condition of the nation, is a gigantic act of self-knowledge, a readiness demanded by the conditions themselves to adopt an empirical stance, and to work out, bit by bit, and with lessening reluctance, either implicitly or explicitly, some kind of social policy. This, indeed, was when the bedrock of the collectivist coral island we now inhabit was laid down.

One can almost see urban society wrestling with its lessons, lessons that included not only the training of a multiplying band of experts of every kind to make and run a machine fit for living in but to adapt the human being to the machine – to make of him, conceivably, some kind of sentient machine himself. 'I see cities peopled with machines', declared Disraeli's hero in *Coningsby*; even Henry James could write of London in the 1880s as a 'tremendous human mill'.[10] These are not such novelties to us because we are never called upon to face such challenges unprepared: the political counterpart to the psychological challenge of surrendering so much personal freedom of action to the urban machine was in the mid-nineteenth century centralisation of administrative controls, a campaign beside which the battles over comprehensive schooling or the London ringways are a sideshow. As to the Victorian city as theatre, why you have only to watch the turns as they come onto the stage in Asa Briggs's *Victorian Cities* – the Manchester 'shocker' of the 1840s, the *pas de seul* of Leeds around its own town hall in the 1850s, the pantomime season in Birmingham in the 1870s with Chamberlain as the magic fairy, and so on. There was a national audience for each of them.

For all this celebration of municipal achievement it has to be admitted, I think, that the fact of the city has been accepted in this country only with a certain reluctance. Certainly the idea of it, in the nineteenth century, the touchstone (if you like) of its urbanity, was itself a curious alloy. The prevailing culture of mid-Victorian England tended to express a pre-urban system of values, and to imply a countryman's view of the city – of Cowper's 'gain-devoted cities' whither flowed 'The dregs and faeculence of every land' – a subverted environment devoid of Nature, calculating threatening, vicious, in some sense inhuman.[11] For the most part, not only novelists, poets and other men of letters, but painters, architects, dramatists, Churchmen – all were inclined to approach the city, so to speak, from the outside, on the basis rather of intuitionist values, quintessentially humane, pastoral. It is not suprising that it was now, largely I suppose through Matthew Arnold, that the agrarian term 'culture' tended to oust the urban term 'civilisation'. Its exponents tended to be out of sympathy with what might be regarded as the natural basis of acceptable behaviour for getting onto terms with the more open, volatile society of the city, namely Utilitarianism. Experience led in one direction; emotion lingered behind or led in quite a different direction. There was, we should now say, a tension – that tension, indeed, which Raymond Williams explores with such sensibility in his unsentimental elegy of rural life. In political debate, of course, attitudes were different, and the city was not entirely friendless even within the charmed circle at the centre of high Victorian culture. Towards the close of the nineteenth century, too, a new generation of artists had appeared that could look the city in the face and write about it or portray it without a shudder – unless, characteristically enough, it was done through the new urban art of the detective story. There was, unquestionably, throughout this critical phase of urbanisation a deep-seated ambivalence towards the city among those who set English society its norms, as in some sense I think there still is.

The most eloquent demonstration of that, of course, is the suburb – that unanswerable argument in favour of the romanticism of the Englishman. If, once upon a time, you brought him up on a diet of the Bible, *Pilgrim's Progress*, Shakespeare, and the pastoral poets, what (as David Eversley once asked) do you expect? Such habits of mind die hard. Before the period I have been speaking of the suburb was nothing of the kind: far from being this most favoured locality on the Surrey–Sussex borders, with pixies on the lawn and John Betjeman at the garden gate, it had been the haunt, in the Middle Ages, of all that was most disreputable in urban, above all in London, society – a nether world of dungheaps, stinking trades, bloodsports, gallows, low taverns, prostitutes, foreigners, thieves, the poor and the mob. The transition to what, in our ethnocentric way, we would regard as authentic suburbanity came relatively late and, in this country at least, constituted from the start a welcome retreat from the city. The story of that diffident courtship of the country by the urban middle classes and of how and why they accepted the suburban embrace is surely too well known to be repeated now: a pattern of movements perhaps more like a series of children's games than the gestures of a love affair – first leapfrogging the suburban slums of the medieval city, then follow-my-leader as the mansions of the landed aristocracy and their minions set off up-wind in the seventeenth and eighteenth centuries, and finally 'he' or touch-last as the working classes set out in hot pursuit in the late-nineteenth and twentieth centuries. The merits of Epsom to the City stockbrokers whom Defoe found there at the beginning of the eighteenth century differ little from those living now in Camberley –

that 'mingling of density and rurality', which Henry James described in the 1870s, 'where the charm of seclusion seems to merge itself in that of proximity to the city market'.[12] All that has changed since is our sense of proximity, and perhaps of seclusion: the romantic idyll of pastoral bliss remains, the castles are still being placed on the ground. During the nineteenth century, however, suburbanity looked especially golden, a state of existence that offered what we should now speak of as a complete range of environmental and social controls: access to the cheapest land for those with most security of employment and the time and money to spend in getting to and from it; opportunity for the manipulation of social distinctions for those most adept at it; isolation from rapid social change for those most vulnerable to it.

There were hidden mechanisms, as well as new transport technologies, at work here. Understandably enough, the respectable classes used part of their earnings from the urban economy to put a safe distance between themselves and their social inferiors, not merely by the purchase of a season ticket from a railway station in the suburbs but by investment in a variety of suburban enterprises from speculation in land or commuter systems to housing, provisioning, entertaining and the supplying of professional and financial services of many kinds, the earnings of one suburb sometimes literally providing the investment for the next. These things all required their own support operations and the personnel to run them, and the structure they supported therefore had to be underpinned by a social order capable of transmitting the habits and tastes of the middle classes through intervening social layers to the upper strata of the working classes; or, conceivably, providing opportunities which the working classes could develop in their own distinctive ways. Once working, this suburban apparatus could obviously be used more intensively, as by a government made weary by thinking how to house the urban masses at densities which medical opinion would tolerate and at rents that would not be asking too much either of family budgets or of middle-class philanthropy. It saw in the suburbs a gleam of hope, a way out for itself, and it too became a fugitive from the city, until very recently. The workmen's ticket was not, as things turned out, a passport to the suburbs for everyone; much more effective in the general deployment of the urban working classes were precisely the means that had given the middle classes their opportunity – more secure employment, higher pay, shorter working hours – though these depended on the operation of less easily governed mechanisms.

What is, of course, so striking is the sheer fact of suburban accretion itself: the little houses all in a row, the gently diminishing densities and latterly of front elevations, the palpable mutations of Palladian villas and Dutch interiors into various states of semi-detachment – of the Beautiful into the Picturesque – and the development of special accents and what Nicholas

Taylor calls in his new book being published this week 'the intricate iconography of their personal landscapes' – so many sign languages for houses and gardens and occupants alike, more diverse and sophisticated than they are often supposed to be – but amounting in the end to a more striking fact still, a gesture of non-commitment, of defiance almost, to the city itself.[13]

This is a gesture we can still recognise, even though we do not completely understand it, especially if we glance at other parts of the English-speaking world. The great merit of the United States to an historian, of course, is that it gives him the opportunity of looking into the future without being accused of deserting the past. And the great merit of Los Angeles in this context is, as Robert Fogelson has demonstrated so meticulously in his history of the place, that it had already emerged by 1930 as 'the archtype, for better or worse, of the contemporary American metropolis' – a metropolis rejected entirely in favour of its suburbs. It provides a disturbing prospect of a still more pervasive suburbanity. But the book begins in retrospect with an innocent question posed by a man walking its streets in the early 1930s.

As I wandered about Los Angeles, [he wrote] looking for the basic meaning of the place, the fundamental source of its wealth and its economic identity, I found myself quite at sea. The Chamber of Commerce people told me about the concentration of fruit, the shipping, the Western branch factories put up by concerns in the East. But none of these things seemed the cause of a city. They seemed rather the effect, rising from an inexplicable accumulation of people – just as the immense dealings in second-hand automobiles and the great turnover of real estate were an effect. It struck me as an odd thing that here, alone of all the cities in America, there was no plausible answer to the question, 'Why did a town spring up here and why has it grown so big?'[14]

Here the natural spring of urban history bubbles out. What is it, deep below, that forces these things out, just here, in these shapes, with these consequences? One thinks immediately of the same nagging curiosity in the mind of Friedrich Engels, sent from Germany to learn the family business in Manchester in 1842, but who must for his own sake also know the organising principle behind the masquerade of the streets. For him the city's organisation of its social space was a replication of Mill's civilising process, whereby all repugnant necessities are kept from the sight of rulers – sometimes it seems too much so – which in Manchester's case meant screening from her merchant princes the spectacle of the slums which allowed labour costs in the mills to be held down; the suburban shuttling to and fro by public transport between their counting houses and the suburbs along the city's commercial façades was simply one of the refinements of an urban civilisation. On the only occasion known to me when A. J. P. Taylor assumed the mantle of urban historian some years ago, he had at once simpler and more poetic reasons to offer for Manchester: its merchant princes were certainly like the men of the Renaissance, he thought, in exalting the individual to a quite ruthless degree, but they lacked one

Renaissance characteristic, aesthetic taste. There was no spot in Manchester to which you could confidently lead a blindfold stranger and then say to him, 'Now open your eyes!' He recalled that Norman Douglas had a theory that English people walked with their eyes on the ground to avoid the excrement of dogs on the pavement. 'The explanation in Manchester is simpler,' he explained: 'they avert their eyes from the ugliness of their surroundings.'[15]

3

In presenting what will certainly have struck my students, if not others, as all too Olympian a view of our urban world, I have left a good deal unsaid and smoothed out a good many historical irregularities, but I wanted particularly to stress the importance of the interconnections between four explanatory factors: population, technology, values, environment. This I have done partly because the socio-economic problems of the city are inherently those of human interaction within and against such a mass – to insist on its physical as well as social framework – and partly in order to approach less arbitrarily than I otherwise should a task I can no longer avoid. An inaugural lecture is perhaps above all an occasion for academic propaganda, for the enunciation of doctrine, and for the encouragement of the faithful. My task, I ask you to recognise, does not square up so easily to these demands: there is no received doctrine and there are already so many faithful that it would be rash to encourage any more.

I should explain that at this time there are over 700 individual pieces of serious research going on in this country into a great many aspects of the urban past, from the archaeology of urban development in the Dark Ages to commuting patterns in the modern metropolis, from York in the age of reform to Blackpool in the age of affluence; and in one country after another – in the United States, Canada, Australia, Italy, Germany, Austria, Sweden, Japan – groups of urban historians are forming, in the way we have seen happen here in the course of the last ten years. The printed material now appearing on the urban past, even of this country, is well beyond one man's capacity to grasp completely. Urban history tends, to quote the words of Eric Hobsbawm, to be 'a large container with ill-defined, heterogeneous and sometimes indiscriminate contents. It includes anything about cities.'[16] It begins to look, indeed, rather like modern cities themselves. So I propose concentrating in the time that's left simply on two or three cardinal issues – the nature of urban history, its limits, and some of its methodological possibilities.

Urban history, it must by now be clear, is a field of knowledge, not a single discipline in the accepted sense but a field in which many disciplines converge, or are at any rate drawn upon. It is a focus for a variety of forms of knowledge, not a form of knowledge in itself. It can have, therefore, no absolute tests of admissibility, unless and until we can be quite clear what we mean by 'urban' and are confident that we can define it in exclusive terms. There's the rub. The very nature of the case, the varying conventions established by usage, and the materials by reference to which such a category could be upheld, all work against such a neat solution. I was indicating earlier that the all-embracing historical process that we have to understand is that of urbanisation itself, a process involving not only the concentration of populations at certain densities, and shifts in their occupational and social structures, but a number of cultural adaptations, too. This is obviously a process affecting different parts of a community at any one time in different degrees and involving therefore the study not merely of those parts defined as having become urban but those in process of becoming so. What is and what is not urban is moreover incapable of being determined with any great statistical accuracy at any one time – not by size, nor by density, nor by degree of nucleation – owing to the wide variety in census conventions and local conditions, which also makes the application of standard criteria, even within the same community, over a long period of time somewhat suspect. There have, as I have been saying, always been more subtle cognitive processes at work. In his great speech on the Reform Bill, Macaulay thought it proper to refer to the engulfed village of Marylebone as

that great city which lies to the north of . . . Oxford-street, – a city superior in size and in population to the capitals of many mighty kingdoms; and probably superior in opulence, intelligence, and general respectability, to any city in the world,

and a woman standing for the first time on top of the Empire State Building had to exclaim, 'The sun and the stars are the suburbs of New York.'[17]

We certainly lack a suitable lexicographer's definition of what is urban, nor perhaps do we yet want one: our best definitions are likely to remain operational ones. We still know too little about the distinctive attributes of urban communities to be able to identify them accurately in comprehensive historical terms, and indeed that is, in one sense, what urban history is all about, or should be – clarifying and defining by whatever theoretical or empirical means seem most promising the differences between the forms and behaviour of urban communities, both in themselves and over and against rural communities. That done, if ever it is, the specialism of urban history must dissolve, with that even more inchoate entity, social history, into the kind of history of society which Hobsbawm dreams of.

What we cannot afford to forget in our more or less abstract formulations of these things is that the abstractions are not ends in themselves, that they have in the end to be reified, to be brought together in recognisable places, to provide a visible focus for our efforts to understand this kind of human predicament in the past. It is all too easy in academic life to lose sight of the obvious. The two most obvious facts about the city, now or to contemporary eyes in the past, are its physical and social mass – as Macaulay and the woman on the skyscraper were saying – and the two things are clearly related. It is, of course, true that we are now seeing our cities turned inside out, with the physical mass at the centre coinciding with the social mass less often, which is in turn being dispersed like dust. Our sense of place is changing. It is indeed becoming more difficult to get a sense of place at all.

Yet the inherent connections between form and function, scale and structure, remain, and in the history of every large city that comes to mind it has invariably been so. But in its present state of development the social totality implicit in the study of urban history is tending to be carved up entirely among a hungry family of social scientists, who are becoming doubtful whether the city can be studied as a separate entity at all. It has been said:

the decisive features of urban life in modern times are not spatially distributed in a way that justifies urban history, or for that matter urban sociology, as a special field . . . for the student of modern society it is indeed nearly coterminous with social history.[18]

That is the view of Stephan Thernstrom, the arch-apostle of the so-called 'new urban history', which has in the course of the last five years been daring any old urban historian on the other side of the Atlantic to show his face, and largely getting away with it. Like the 'new economic history', this approach has already developed the aura if not the apparatus of a minor discipline in its own right. It commonly depends to a substantial extent on quantitative evidence, is concerned primarily with the less visible, inarticulate mass of ordinary people, and looks for its concepts chiefly to sociological theory, though (unlike the kind of general economic theory available to the 'new economic historians') it does not have on hand a general social theory at all adequate for its purposes, nor does it offer the same scope for counter-factual types of analysis.

The study of the urban past has been influenced far more by sociologists in the United States than it has been in this country, though there has also been a strong tradition of local history against which the 'new urban history' has to a great extent been a reaction. The explanation of such differences is complex. There is no time at this point to trace in any detail, as I have done elsewhere, the phases through which urban history may be said to have passed since it was practised so effortlessly by those English local antiquarians-cum-town-boosters in the late eighteenth century, except perhaps to remark that there does appear, both here and in the United States, to have been a rough relativity between phases of economic and social development and the preoccupations of historians which would help to explain both the relatively late start of urban history in this country and the closer coupling of it with sociology in the States.

Be that as it may, what we are now seeing there, in the emergence of the 'new urban history', is one aspect of the attempt to find a solution to what Norman Birnbaum regards as a problem which is as troubling to sociology as it is fundamental to it – what he describes as 'the insertion of the dimension of time in systematic analysis'.[19] I cannot presume to challenge that judgment of sociology but as I sample the first fruits of this new growth I do grow somewhat apprehensive of its outcome for the study of urban history at large. There is no question that this infusion of new ideas and the application of new techniques has been remarkably invigorating, especially to anyone suffering unduly from orthodoxy (as we all do from time to time) – though I have been inclined to wonder sometimes whether the exercises are often not more important as a regimen than as a cure. Historians are always being asked to jump through new hoops. That is their occupational hazard. But what concerns me about these particular hoops is their diameter. They are so narrow. That is, of course, precisely what gives them their rigour. The central issues of the 'new urban history' form a paradigm of the development of American society in the nineteenth and twentieth centuries: population movement, ethnicity, social class and the power structure, as revealed, largely by computer methods, in the manuscript census data, voting lists, street directories, savings bank records and the like, for the years 1850 to 1880.

Apart from raising a cheer for finding a means of making the customary objects of so much history its subjects, there seem two things worth saying. First, that if we can judge by what has been produced so far (and limiting ourselves to the work of scholars who have identified themselves with this group), this is a field which seems, paradoxically enough, only incidentally concerned with the city and perhaps only incidentally with history itself. The focus is on social change at large, on processes involving relations between social groups whose locations are in a state of general flux; and though the scenario typically includes the city it appears more as an arena than as part of the drama. The city as such, the whole interlocking apparatus without which urban life could not function, the relations between generations of buildings and generations of men that my simple model of the Victorian city earlier on illustrated in part, the history of how and why it took the shape it did, here and not there, does not come in. Apart, too, from the various intra-urban aspects of the matter which have been snapped up by geographers as fast as sociologists have dropped them, there is the whole question of the development of systems of cities and the task, say, of applying empirically central place theory.

As I say, the reason why the 'new urban history' eschews these things is that it sees itself in effect as a branch of empirical sociology. The second thing that might be said about it is that, like a good deal of work depending primarily on demographic analysis, it appears to be somewhat indifferent to the human content of the city, to have no place for the individual's experience of it, and to offer little scope for the elucidation of its culture, whether conceived in the conventional or anthropological sense. There is, too, an obvious predilection for themes especially susceptible to quantification, which is, however, much less of a danger than it may seem, if only because it requires all methodological assumptions to be made explicit – something which must be regarded as a distinct gain in itself.

The ways of urban historians are many and it is not yet clear which of them will lead out of the maze they find themselves in. I do not say crisis, which is the term most often used to describe the current challenge to urban history. The challenge that comes with the vast outpouring of writings having some general semblance of urban history, mainly in the form of facile biographies of individual towns or cities, or countless, minuscule, urban-centred happenings, is simply a challenge to the digestion, not to the head. Even now the number of absolutely first-class studies of individual cities is pitifully small and scarcely a major city in this country has yet been given definitive treatment. That should trouble us much more.

But urban historians also express embarrassment on account of the considerable variety of approaches that are being made in their subject. I do not think they need do so. On the contrary, the lack of agreement as to whether to pursue the ecological approach that stems from Robert Park and Louis Wirth, as developed by Otis Duncan and Leo Schnore, and more elaborately adapted by Eric Lampard; or the more generally environmental approach anticipated by Christopher Tunnard and altogether more explicitly handled by Sam Bass Warner Jr and Roy Lubove (an approach with which my own work may be most readily associated); or the approach through the comparative study of characteristic institutions as demonstrated by Asa Briggs, Julius Rubin, John Kellett and Brian Harrison; or the approach through imagery in the manner of Anselm Strauss or Kevin Lynch or Raymond Williams; or the approaches through locational or small area analysis of Alan Pred, David Ward and Richard Lawton; or even the approach through first and last things, as understood by Patrick Geddes, Lewis Mumford, Jane Jacobs – or, for that matter, Spengler or Toynbee: the lack of agreement, I say, as to which of these, or other approaches, to follow gets neither rebuke nor dogmatic guidance from me. I find their catholicity positively healthy.

4

Two things only need now be said. One is that the growth of cities and the phenomenon of an urbanising world together represent one of the largest historical dimensions of modern times, and that the urban content of that history, whether expressed implicitly or explicitly, is bound to increase and add to the challenge confronting urban history still more. The other is that as this happens the identity and the role of urban history will be more closely defined through the work of urban historians themselves, especially in the degree to which they seek out the differences within and between urban societies. What is, I think, already clear is that the authentic measure of urban history is the degree to which it is concerned directly and generically with cities themselves and not with the historical events and tendencies that have been purely incidental to them; and that, whether concerned with cities as more or less isolated or systematic or universal phenomena, it is the study of the characteristically symbiotic relationships of their different characteristics, of the ways in which their components fitted together or impinged on other things, that distinguishes urban historians from those who may be said merely to be passing through their territory.

Their subject differs from local history to the extent that it is concerned with a more pervasive historical process, and from municipal history in being occupied with vastly more than certain types of local government; it differs, on the other hand, from social history in its quite specific commitment to explaining the development of both the urban milieu and its uses, and from sociology in its dominant concern with explaining the urban past; it differs, too, from its first cousins in this country, economic history and geography, in being more interested than they can afford to be, in their different ways, in the humanistic and functional elements composing the urban scene; and it differs, incidentally, from a variety of other historical specialisms, such as agricultural, industrial, business, transport, military or town-planning history in not being concerned with specific forms of activity.

The city, I have been saying, is too large and complex a phenomenon to be left to a single academic discipline, and it has rightly become a matter for geographers, economists, economic historians, sociologists, demographers, social psychologists, political scientists, literary historians, archaeologists, civic designers and engineers. Their commitment to the city is bound to be partial; that of the urban historian has to be total. And if we are ever to understand so completely the secret of how to live so close together in such numbers that we can plan to enjoy it more and more and not less and less, it will be due in some small degree to the understanding which urban history has brought to the achievement of a common urbanity.

3

Greater and greater London: metropolis and provinces in the nineteenth and twentieth centuries

I think I should begin this essay on the Celtic fringes of Britain. I should then move rapidly on to London, which is a well-trodden route, and having planted my flag there survey the country behind me. My first Celtic reference must be to a man born in Edinburgh to Catholic Irish parents; who was raised and educated in that city, qualified as MD there in 1885, and then went to practice for a time in Southsea. Two years later he published his first novel, *A Study in Scarlet*, and a year later wrote for *The Nineteenth Century* a farcically statistical article 'On the Geographical Distribution of the British Intellect'. What Dr A. Conan Doyle had done by way of research was to trace some 1,150 men of *DNB* standing who belonged to what he described as 'the intellectual walks of life', and out of the 824 'English roll of honour' he located 235 of London birth – a ratio of 1 : 16,000 as against 1 : 34,000 in the provinces (though Edinburgh he demonstrated as having a ratio of 1 : 5,500). He also remarked, a little incredulously, on the fact that such a large number of clever people had been born abroad. The pre-Cambrian level of intellectuality, so to speak, was located in the distant hills to which the ancient Britons had been driven – Cornwall and Wales – but for its utter depths one had to turn to the bottomless bogs of western Ireland. This seems to have caused Conan Doyle no surprise. What his lists of provincial and metropolitan alumni actually meant is anybody's guess. What he himself suggested was that they showed the way in which the centralisation of wealth for centuries back had drawn the brightest intellects in every walk of life towards the metropolis. What was suggested to the readers of *The Nineteenth Century*, perhaps, was that London was at last capable, with all this talent, of proving itself under the same constraints that municipal boroughs in the provinces had been doing for two or three generations already. That year, 1888, was the year of the foundation of the London County Council.

My second Celtic reference is to a man who was born in Belfast and died in Dublin six years after Conan Doyle was born, another medico who turned to letters, John Fisher Murray. He contributed to *Blackwood's* in the 1830s a series of sketches of London life gathered at first hand, and these were republished in that capital of the Anglo-Scottish community, Edinburgh, under the title *The World of London*. Among them was this passage:

London is not merely a *place*, it is an abstraction, a connecting and necessary link in our chain of thought; it is the workshop of artificers in mind, their storehouse, their market, their solace, and their reward; the centre of great and important changes in the political and social history of man; the forms to which rays of intelligence from the furthest horizon of earth converge, concentrate, and are reflected back again upon the public mind; not merely our fashions, luxuries, tastes, are thence imported, but our opinions come 'cut and dry' from London; we are dictated to from London, in London we are governed, they make our laws in London; in short, London is the head, the brain, the heart, the noble viscus of our body politic, and we in the provinces are but outlying extremities, subsidiary, secondary; we are hardly allowed to know whether our toes are cold until we are so instructed by leading articles from London![1]

Here already, in Murray's view, was the cosmopolitan centre of almost everything, not only a lens for a wider world but a focus for provincial life – a threat, perhaps, not only to what Bagehot a generation later called its 'motley picturesqueness' but to the cultural independence of communities large and small, in town and country, across the whole face of England and those Celtic territories beyond.

1

The image we get is of some gigantic Roman candle erupting with ideas every morning and illuminating every 'cranny of the kingdom' by its uniform metropolitan light.[2] Can that already have been true? I rather doubt it. One of the easiest historical perspectives to lose is a sense of distance. We should remember not only the rusticities of London life a century ago but how accessible the country was and how much of it had to be crossed to reach some place even remotely like it. Richard Jefferies found as much wild life twelve miles from St Paul's in the 1880s as he did in the seclusion of Worcestershire;[3] H. G. Wells tells us in *Kipps* how the inhabitants of Folkestone even in Edwardian times regarded London as a distant country; and in Hardy's *The Mayor of Casterbridge* the descent of royalty from the metropolis comes to Dorchester like a progress from the Middle Ages. Victorian England was indeed 'an island like a little book, full of a thousand tales,'[4] and each tale told of innumerable elements in provincial society that separated them from each other and even from themselves. But somewhere, in each of them, a kind of metropolitan leaven became active in the period I am considering, and it is this that intrigues me. A Portuguese, travelling by train from Southampton to London in the early 1890s, wrote of his sense of money irrigating the whole scene:

The train, still journeying, seemed to me to go along drawn by the focus of attraction of the capital, London, of which all this part of England is a suburb. The devouring inspiration exercised by the capital was the phenomenon that pre-occupied me.[5]

That is the theme which occupies me too.

What this essay suggests, in fact, is that far from there having been too much emphasis by historians on the metropolitan centre of national life there may have been in some respects too little. The pursuit comparatively recently of provincial themes by local and economic historians has been refreshing enough, but there is some inclination to overstate the rise of the provinces in both political and economic terms. I am inclined myself to share the reaction expressed in a broadcast talk by T. C. Barker a year or two ago to the provincial approach to explanations of economic growth in the eighteenth century,[6] and to call for another, more explicitly metropolitan, approach to the nineteenth century as well. My basic hypothesis is that the centripetal tendencies in the organisation of economic and social life which had been inaugurated by the establishment of an unusually highly centralised state at the end of the Middle Ages have persisted ever since. The shift of resources into the exploitation of the northern provinces, and others, in the eighteenth and nineteenth centuries might be represented simply as an interlude in a much longer historical trend. And it occurred, not as an abatement of the centripetal forces which were concentrating the population and economic power on London, but primarily as a redeployment of provincial resources, some of them having been, as it were, processed in London *en route*. The industrialisation of the North was achieved more than anything by an alteration in the balance of productive forces engaged in agriculture, manufacturing production and exchange in the country at large, but not by imposing a halt on the growth and influence – nor perhaps even on the general economic stimulus – of London. Indeed, London's dominance in the economy, and its sway in social and political affairs, had already advanced well before the time when a new technology released industry from the coalfields and shifted the whole centre of gravity of the economy back in a southerly, London direction in the twentieth century.

By this time, the whole process was about to enter a second phase, in which the centripetal tendencies helped to release powerful centrifugal ones. Building up a metropolitan focus produced a strong metropolitan echo. The process of 'metropolitanisation' that I think we can see building up in the nineteenth and twentieth centuries has involved, in fact, two processes that have overtaken each other as echoing ripples do on a pond. One process caused London to subsume a growing share of the national life, including economic activities, and meant packing London with people from the country, with country ways, with provincial attitudes perhaps, foreign customs certainly, which produced in the capital a concentration of wealth or control over it, and therefore a disproportionate share per head of the benefits (and, conceivably, the penalties) of a relatively rich society. The second process has involved a centrifugal deployment of the metropolitan population, its investment capital and something of a metropolitan culture, if that is the right word, which is now beginning to bite into – homogenise might be a better term – provincial ways and attitudes.

39

The tensions produced by this ebb and flow are as much psychological as political, as much social as economic, and I am bound to overlook much in the space I have, and be obliged, too, to cover a lot of ground familiar to British historians. I also run the danger of stereotyping what was actually diverse. As Henry James once pointed out, 'One has not the alternative of speaking of London as a whole, for the simple reason that there is no whole of it. . . . Rather it is a collection of many wholes, and of which of them is one to speak?'[7] The journalist, George R. Sims, got round this when writing his encyclopaedia, *Living London* (1901), by identifying a whole spectrum of Londons: apart from Scottish, Irish and Welsh London, there were Jewish, French, German, Money, Musical, Hooligan, Kerbstone, Waterside, Sweated and Afflicted Londons – and many more. Nor were these purely literary devices. I am encouraged by the fact that the place was so vast that almost anything one can say about it is bound to be true.

One small point of definition that might be noted at this point is that neither 'provinces' nor 'metropolis' had assumed their modern meaning until the beginning of the period that concerns me.[8] Late-Georgian London was so obviously on an urban scale of its own that it could be referred to still, quite unambiguously, as Town; and places out of town belonged simply to 'the Country'. It was not until provincial political leaders began using the term, with the kind of off-hand deliberation whereby Negro leaders in our own day have made their demands uncompromisingly 'black', that the provinces found their radical identity and their voice. This had happened by the 1840s. But the term still kept its pejorative overtones. It was still possible to refer, as Horace Smith did, in 1836, to 'a provincialism of mind as well as of accent'; and the notion that to be provincial was to be vulgar, unpolished, less than civilised, was already too deeply embedded to be cast away so easily. Macaulay alone, and then only in an election address, could hold forth on what his first biographer was compelled to caption the 'Loveliness and Intelligence of Leeds'.[9] 'Metropolis' was not stretched to cover the whole of London until Pierce Egan and his imitators pursued their respective rakes round Regency London in its geographical and social entirety.[10] The first book known to me to include Westminster and Southwark as well as the City under this name is James Grant's *The Great Metropolis*, published in 1836. Even towards the end of the century the *Oxford English Dictionary* insisted that this was a term 'somewhat pompously used for London. Also, in recent use, occasionally applied to London as a whole, in contradistinction to *the City.*'

2

London was in fact already an amorphous lump, with no clear geographical orientation beyond the swerving river, no tangible centre, no one point of assembly, yet so big that it was most natural to describe it in terms of strange, unexplored continents.

Behold, within the Arctic circle, as I may call it, [wrote John Fisher Murray] the migratory Esquimaux of Camden Town . . . behold the Antarctic regions of Wandsworth, Kensington Common, and Peckham Rye; cast your astonished eye over the vast continent of Southwark . . . its adjacent islands of Lambeth and Rotherhithe, and the archipelagic neighbourhoods of Kent Road, St George's in the Fields, Bethlem Hospital, and the Marsh Gate.[11]

Exotic figures of speech were a commonplace in descriptions of Victorian London[12] and are a minor echo of its world-wide commercial expansion, but they also give a hint how insular and remote from each other in terms of geographical and social distance the communities that composed London were felt to be.

Its social geography, though intricate and mercurial, developed very clearly along lines of social class, and London submitted earlier than other cities to the fracturing of its sense of community into too many fragments to permit it to give clear expression to its local needs. 'The bond of companionship that held the "*outsides*" together', wrote Murray, 'is broken; every man is absorbed in his own business or reflections.'[13] By the 1880s, if not before, it was possible to identify whole districts that were not only distinguishable from each other in the broadest middle-and-working-class terms, but in degrees of fashionableness, in terms of skilled and unskilled, in the division between clerical and manual occupations. By then, when the geographical expression called London contained over four million people, the prospect of creating a coherent community of it had vanished. Its parts had never been securely joined together and the pressure of population under which it expanded tended to force them further apart. The original ingredients of commerce and government – the Cities of London and Westminster – had not mixed, and now the built-up area had swallowed numerous surrounding villages and half-digested them, visible still as a boa-constrictor's meal but squashed out of shape, socially and physically. It is not difficult to see how the structure altered nor easy to miss its meaning. The huge scale of this suburban deployment, the reflection in its social geography of the division of labour in London's economy, and not least the imitative tendencies of the age and the place, made the capital by the last quarter of the nineteenth century not only an exceptional place, requiring an exceptional form of government, but something of a prototype for the provincial conurbations of the future. It was a place – or rapidly coming to be one – without a clear civic identity or even the desire for one, a vast congeries of socially homogeneous neighbourhoods rather than balanced communities.

Its municipal government, when it developed, therefore drew little inspiration or direction from the provinces. There is perhaps some irony in the fact that the aggrandisement of London which occurred in the nineteenth century took place without its appearing to share either immediately or directly or positively in any of the current movements which led to the rise of the provinces. In a limited sense it might be said that London missed the mainstream of the industrial revolution, the direct thrust of the movement for municipal reform, and the advance of radical politics – the things which account most readily for the provincial emphasis of so much nineteenth-century British history. The reform of municipal government in the provinces on a uniform basis of reasonably democratically elected councils dated, of course, from the reforms of the early 1830s, though it is possible to trace earlier beginnings, and to find the magistrates still enthroned in various ways later on. But the attempt to form some kind of fellow feeling between townsmen and town councillors, whether it was successful or not, had no answering echo in London. The real beginning of representative government there did not come before the establishment of the London County Council in 1888, and then only on a rising tide of national reform and in an interval allowed by the tide of Irish affairs. That year provided the date on which every town of more than 50,000 inhabitants and some smaller ones (61 all told in England and Wales) became county boroughs, independent of the counties themselves, which were also being put on an elective basis at the same time. London was indeed a county itself.

It is true that London had had for twenty years or so before 1888 lively enough debates on the general question of municipal reform, and some important reformers: James Beal and the Metropolitan Municipal Association were active enough, but they roused no general sympathies.[14] Curiously enough, it was the move of a middle-aged Welshman, John Lloyd, a man who had spent twenty years managing country estates in Breconshire, and who had gone up to London to read for the Bar, which led to the formation of the most effective organisation yet established, the Municipal Reform League. The ancient Corporation of the City of London had declined the opportunity of forming a single government of London in the 1830s, and the commissioners who looked at the matter again nearly twenty-five years later had succumbed to the argument from scale – that an aggregate of two millions could not enjoy self-government because it did not have real self-knowledge nor a focus of self-interests. The thing was fit only for administration. How prophetic that decision was I dare not think, now that we are under the shadow of the Royal Commission on Local Government in England. London, though fit for a province in itself, was therefore saddled for more than a generation with a kind of vastly inflated vestry, in the shape of the Metropolitan Board of Works.

The radical spirit that had once been capable of infusing the whole of London seems to have been smothered under the sheer weight of numbers. The collapse of Chartism, which was marked if not secured in London, was simply the most conspicuous demonstration of the failure of the collective will of the London working man in this period. For a generation or more it is difficult to see any convincing sign of a change of heart. Indeed, it was not until the 1880s that London was again capable of producing its own discontents in sufficient numbers to command any degree of national attention. It remained till then completely overshadowed by the provinces. 'London is always the last to stir,' complained the Chartist *Northern Star* in 1841, 'or when it takes the initiative, such is its overwhelming bulk, and the consequent segregation of its parts, that no powerful and well compacted concentration of popular energy is produced.'[15] There can be little question that the factory movement, the co-operative movement, the real driving force in Chartism and the anti-corn law movement, were all decidedly provincial; and there is force in the contention that in other directions too – in the anti-slavery and the tariff reform movements, for example – the real strength of reform was located in the industrial towns of the Midlands and the North, even though their headquarters, and a modicum of support, were found in London. Of course, Bright's Law, as it might be called, that the cotton districts of Lancashire and the West Riding of Yorkshire ought to govern England, at least to the extent that its laws accorded with the prevailing sentiments in those two counties, lost a good deal of its force at Westminster. Yet it was a natural expectation. Forty years on, however, it was the massive concentration of wealth, population and business enterprise of London that was being looked to for a radical lead. The programme in this case was socialism, its prophet the complex personality of H. M. Hyndman, its instrument the Social Democratic Federation.

Metropolitan socialism, revolutionary or non-revolutionary, was however a damp squib. The Fabians and the SDF were alike uncongenial to provincial working men, but London working men themselves could not yet get off their knees. All that carried easily to the provinces was the noise of sporadic disturbance like the Hyde Park or the Trafalgar Square riots or the great dock strike of 1889. The theory of revolution, tempered more by foreign than by provincial experience, or the subtleties of political permeation, remained muffled. The Independent Labour Party, which was formed at Bradford in 1893, was in so many respects nearer the natural centre of gravity of moderate working-class opinion, while London remained hostile to it. Justifiably enough, Ben Tillett could caricature it still in 1914 as the Sphinx of Labour.[16] Trade-unionism remained persistently weak in London despite the surges of support for the new unionism after 1889, and there were marked limitations in the ranks of London labour generally right through to 1914. The basic reason was, of course, that unlike so many of the industrial towns, London was not based on a single manufacturing industry of importance but on a wide variety of service trades, mostly conducted on a small scale and except for two or three of them – furniture and clothing particularly – fairly widely dispersed. They were vulnerable, too, to seasonal

43

and cyclical fluctuations in trade. The workforce was drawn mainly from overlapping markets for casual labour, of which important sections were highly disorganised and liable to sweating and other abuses. It was also scattered and divided, a situation which, as Dr Pelling has pointed out, gave to the Liberal party the chance of speaking with one voice in one constituency and another in the next.[17] Not that this had much effect, for it was the Liberals' failure to hold the capital after 1885, quite as much as their shortcomings elsewhere (especially in Birmingham), which accounts for their ultimate decline. Labour could occupy the vacuum in London once the blockage of London socialism had been overcome. This it had barely done by 1914. The post-war advances showed how important the potential of London had been to Labour all along, and in this sense it might be said that the influence of London on national politics had been felt only negatively.

But what London was doing, not so much in response to provincially inspired political movements but with *itself*, was an altogether more positive influence – news, as Asa Briggs remarks, for the first time in Manchester and Birmingham.[18] The job to be done after the establishment of the LCC, and the completion of a properly structured two-tier system of local government with the forming of the metropolitan boroughs eleven years later, was something new in scale and possibilities. Fulfilling the kind of large-scale municipal programme set forth in J. F. B. Firth's *Municipal London* (1876) meant doing battle with narrow interests of all kinds, vested as well as vestrified, business as well as civic. It also raised important questions of municipal identity and democratic participation, of a kind which rapidly growing boroughs elsewhere recognised in some degree as their own – questions, indeed, that are a long way from being answered yet. When one reflects how little is yet known in detail about the structure and operation of urban politics in the nineteenth century, it would be rash to grant London any very special priorities in municipal progress. Some of the first object-lessons the new LCC members studied were, after all, provincial in origin: municipal housing was one, municipal hospitals another. But there was now talk of giving London a soul and a meaning, of municipalisation galore and 'strong' government. The expence entailed soon contributed to the division of the Council on clear party lines. It was really this, and the curious anaesthetising of Londoners' larger loyalties – divided as they seemed to be between an expression of increasing vagueness known as London and their own more recognisable municipal bit of it, embodied in the local town hall – which seem now to have been such a foretaste of a universal experience.

There was, of course, another reason altogether for curiosity in provincial places about London's corridors of power, namely the concentration of the administrative control of the state there. To London municipal politicans, who fought in the front rank against the stealthy advance of the central government into local affairs, and whose own local government had been impeded to some extent by the jealousy of the Lord God of Westminster, it was ironic that London itself should have become identified in the provinces with the aggressions of Whitehall. The two images blurred. I cannot give much attention to the point here, but we can see clearly enough from the researches of the administrative historians that the effect of piecemeal, unpremeditated, badly administered legislation on localities up and down the country in the half-century before 1880 had been to build up in the hands of the central administrators an almost continuously augmented power. It had not been ruptured at the close of Edwin Chadwick's reign, for the Local Government Act Office kept all the major and effective controls of the old Central Board of Health and on top of these obtained new discretionary powers, while the sheer force of circumstances prevailing alike in industrial city or residential suburb – as local authorities tried, more or less ineptly, to draft by-laws, settle boundaries, prepare plans and estimates for water and drainage schemes, compose differences with other Boards, and so on – made them turn in voluntary denial of the 'voluntary principle' to Whitehall for help. This tendency was most marked, naturally, in smaller places, but the bewildering barrage of legislation – for example, in public health before 1875 – was bound to mean the exercise of more or less arbitrary central power in regard to places of every size. The great leveller, of course, was sewage. How to get rid of it, where and how to sweeten it, or simply how to forget about it, this was the problem that made so many proud places turn like tired children to Whitehall. London became a kind of advice bureau for these provincial administrators, who were in any case inclined to use what technical services were going to save local expense, a persistent but debilitating tendency in the annals of local government.[19] The subsequent history of this process belongs so much to our own day that I may be excused for going no further, except perhaps to remark that local councils nowadays accept more money on the whole in grants from central government than they raise in revenue from their own ratepayers. This creates at the same time doubts in parliament about their competence to spend it and disillusion in their own communities about their capacity to apply their rateable income to the things local people want. The metropolis has always been the seat of this power, the exercise of which has tended to polarise relations between London itself and the people at the other end. The combined image of it hardened.

The political importance, if not the political leadership, of the capital at the turn of the nineteenth and twentieth centuries was, of course, in tune with changes in the whole distribution of the population between London and the rest of the country. I do not need to give any elaborate statistics to demonstrate the national fixation of our time that London and its region have been draining the rest of the country of people and wealth almost incontinently. Although the proportion of the population of England and Wales living in south-east England has scarcely changed since censuses were

first taken[20] – 38.6 per cent in 1801 and 38.8 per cent in 1961 – the growth of
Greater London itself has been undeniably persistent. The term itself did
not come into regular statistical use before 1875, though the idea of a
London greater than its formal boundaries goes back to Wren. The largest
administrative area for London that had yet been invented, the metropolitan
police district, remained largely a statistical abstraction, and its easy
circumference of London and its suburbs has long disappeared. But if we
consider the population of the area covered by Greater London since the
beginning of the nineteenth century, we see that it accounted for about 12
per cent of the population of England and Wales in 1801 and grew steadily
throughout the nineteenth century to reach 20 per cent by 1901, where it
remained until 1951. The main industrial areas of the country in the
Midlands and the North, which had been growing substantially more
rapidly as a group than Greater London in the first half of the nineteenth
century, were then overtaken. In terms of the proportion of the total
population contained in them, they had probably reached their peak by
1901: certainly, from 1921 their proportion of the gainfully occupied
population – the Midlands apart – was actually declining. The powers of
absorption of Greater London were by now prodigious. In the last decade of
the nineteenth century it gathered in or retained about a quarter of the net
increase of the whole country. This intake slackened off over the next couple
of decades but picked up dramatically in the 1920s and 1930s, by absorbing
more than a third of the national increase. The Barlow Report of 1940
understandably referred with alarm to the related phenomena of the
continued drift from the land and the suburban conquest of it in London and
the south-east, which it saw as taking place largely at the expense of the rest
of the country. The distribution within this area later changed a bit as
London began adding to its labour force disproportionately in office and
service employment; and there is some evidence that over the last decade or
two London has begun to reiterate a long-established tendency to spawn
industries further afield and, of course, to distribute some of its population in
what we must call overspill. The summary picture we now have in
consequence is of London and the south-east as the leading export region in
the country, with the Port of London itself handling about 35 per cent of
exports, as measured in value terms.[21]

3

None of this is really new. The situation is, in fact, not unlike that of the early
eighteenth century, when the commercial vortex of London, which sucked
in the overwhelming part of the import, export and re-export trade of the
country, was based on a great infrastructure of provincial roads and
waterways, and on key markets of its own for industrial raw materials,
capital and labour. Then, too, the migration into the provinces of a certain

amount of metropolitan industry contributed directly to the progress of industrialisation, while the expansion of a number of finishing trades in London itself, along with the ordinary demands of London to be provisioned, undoubtedly added to the impetus of it still more. The detailed ramifications of this internal trade, the extent to which market towns became major collecting centres for primary products, the way in which metropolitan influences encouraged commercial farming and improvements in inland transport – these matters are all known too imperfectly for the role of London as an engine of economic growth in the rest of the eighteenth century to be stated with any great precision.[22]

Can it really be that the rise of the industrial North was some kind of clandestine extra-mural activity of London? Is Georgian London to be thought of as an independent variable in the growth of the national economy and, by implication, of its provincial towns? And, if it was, how far into the nineteenth century did this relationship last? How extensive in fact was the London city region in this period? The questions are easier to ask than to answer, for we badly need a full-scale economic history of Victorian London. What is clear enough is that London did not lose its position as the chief manufacturing centre of the country in the Victorian period, though this has rather been obscured by the complexity of its industrial structure and the undramatic character of its development. Far from there being, through the growth of the railway system, a vast transfer of trading outlets to other ports, London, mismanaged though it was, held on to its share. And the net effect of increasing rail communication between the provinces themselves was to tie them in still more firmly to the hub of the system: as early as the 1860s the economist Cliffe Leslie was talking of a complete revolution in the scale of local prices in the United Kingdom 'which the railways are lifting towards the metropolitan level'.[23]

Nor did London's influence on money markets slacken, despite the growth by 1914 of a dozen or more provincial stock exchanges (some of which offered specialised dealings), largely because much of their business was actually executed in London. The importance of the London market was, of course, cosmopolitan, but its overwhelming emphasis on foreign issues presumably had some bearing, however indirect, on the habits of both provincial investors and the pattern of home investment. I mean, the connections between the export of capital on the scale involved and the under-investment in human capital in the industrial back-streets, though traced quite unconsciously at the time, were not only fundamental to the operational success of those same mill-towns but a powerful ingredient in the whole response of the working people in them to the political choices open to them. It was also, it might be added, a basic assumption in their judgments on London itself. One such popular image, for example, was that portrayed by Augustus Mayhew in his confessedly unfashionable novel,

Paved with Gold; or the romance and reality of the London streets (1858):

the metropolis has been transformed, [he wrote] into a huge spider's web, with railway fibres radiating from its centre [and] the citizen, like the round-bellied insect itself... is seen to dart along the lines when there is anything... that promises a 'good catch' for him.

(This is Cobbet's image of the parasitic metropolis, with stockjobbers skipping up from Brighton, or living like drones in Islington.)

Did provincial savings have the same kind of mobility, I wonder? London increased in importance as a source of capital for railways and public authorities in the second half of the nineteenth century – a result of company amalgamation in the one case and the growth of insurance business in the other – but, except for some idea about the contribution of the landed interests, we know next to nothing about the geographical distribution of the investors themselves. How far the finance of house-building, for example, was confined to its locality, in any part of the country in the nineteenth century, we do not know. One small clue to the matter may lie in the origins of mortgage funds collected together by one large London builder of the last quarter of the century: almost a third of the £280,000 he raised, mainly through London solicitors, between 1867 and 1895, came from outside London, including substantial sums from the West Country, Yorkshire and the Midlands – the biggest individual sum of all, £20,000, coming from a clergyman in Northampton.[24] What this kind of evidence suggests is the uninterrupted growth of a region exercising a critical influence on the economic performance of neighbouring ones. The question whether London's was the dominant influence in the metropolis/provinces partnership, whether it amounted to a major stimulus to the economic growth of particular regions of the country, or whether it constituted some kind of drag on progress in the larger sense, no one has yet troubled to find out.

One important thing that will have to be done if we are to get the dynamics of this relationship right is a comprehensive study of the patterns of internal migration and the structure of labour markets. What Ravenstein's calculations in the 1880s seem to suggest, for example, is that there were certain functional relationship between different parts of the country and the metropolis.[25] Warwickshire, he demonstrated, had for some time been dispersing more of its population to northern industrial districts and to Greater London than it drew from them both in return. That is, it 'fed' London and the North, and made up this net loss by drawing in from the rest of England and Wales many more people than it dispatched to those areas. Nothing can be deduced positively about the direction and volume of exchanges between London and the provinces from Cairncross's well-known study, partly because he was concerned with net gains and losses and not with flows.[26] What one discovers from the census enumerators' books themselves is a much more complex pattern, a flux and reflux considerably in excess of the net movement, and possibly having an orientation different from it. London's catchment area changed little in the course of the nineteenth century. It included the whole country, though the great bulk came from southern England, and there is little evidence that greater ease of movement encouraged people to travel further. The composition of these movements from different parts of the country sometimes varied interestingly – more West Country women and more Lancashire men and women in 1911 than 1851, for example – but the migratory connections between London and the provinces told most in the proportions of native Londoners to be found in different districts.

Half the people of London in 1851 were not, strictly speaking, Londoners at all, but had been born elsewhere. The proportion soon declined, and by 1881 stood at a third. In Mayfair, the affluent centre, however, about 60 per cent of the population in 1881 had been born outside London; in Bethnal Green, virtually all slum and semi-slum in the East End, the figure was only 12 per cent. Charles Booth suggested that there was in fact an inverse ratio between the proportion of provincial immigrants and the poverty of the district. I have already argued this point in another essay and concluded that the slums of Victorian London are indeed more properly thought of as settlement tanks for submerged Londoners than as settlement areas for provincial immigrants.[27] My point now is that there must have been a much more subtle process of acculturation to the city going on than historians have yet worked out. Some rather promising work on the widespread introduction of the Irish into London and of alien Jews into the East End is now in hand, but the general question of the extent to which other less specific immigrants, particularly from the country, were conditioning urban life by keeping their country attitudes and connections – a question that lies very near the root of the difference between urban and rural life – will be more difficult to answer.

The images of London, not only in the minds of migrants from the provinces but of those left behind, especially before the era of mass communications, are bound up very closely with the forces of attraction and tension between London and the rest of the country. Durkheim propounded, in his *De la division du travail social* (1893), a law of social attraction which depended very much on the size and what he called the moral density of towns. He saw the social mass exercising an attraction in proportion to its density and scale. Llewellyn-Smith, who wrote on immigration into London in Booth's massive work, explained that what brought people up from the country, apart from 'the gigantic lottery of prizes' was 'the contagion of numbers', a sense of excitement about things going on under bright lights that was so different from dull, rural routine.[28] It did not matter perhaps that this appetite had to give way for so many to a diet of nettles – that, in terms of C. F. G. Masterman's bitter cry *From the Abyss* (1902),

We pack ourselves into small cottages . . . choke up the public houses . . . overflow into canal barges, and railway arches, and disused drains . . . are pushed into the gutters where we ply unwelcomed articles, and children's toys, and publications obscene to the limit, beside the heedless stream that ever hurries past.

The same dark thoughts of Harriet Carker in *Dombey and Son* did not impede the daily one-way traffic of foot-passengers bound for London whom she watched on the outskirts,

who went shrinking on . . . swallowed up in one place or other of its immensity . . . food for the hospitals, the churchyards, the prisons, the river, fever madness, vice, and death . . .: they passed on to the monster, roaring in the distance, and were lost.

What compelled them all on in some degree was that sensation known even to a sensitive countryman like Richard Jefferies, who, delighted though he was to find kestrels hovering over Surbiton, had to admit to

the immense City inducing a nerve-restlessness . . . there is a magnetism stronger than that of the rock which drew the nails from Sinbad's ship . . .. It is not business . . . it is not 'society', it is not pleasure. It is the presence of man in his myriads. I often go to London, [he confessed] without any object whatever but just because I must, and, arriving there, wander whithersoever the hurrying throng carries me.[29]

This metropolitan magnetism impregnated the work of so many Victorian novelists, in fact. Even when writing about the country they did so time and again under the brooding presence of the town. These were places not so much of the country itself, like Hardy's Casterbridge – little more than 'a street ruled by a mayor and corporation yet echoing with the thump of the flail, the flutter of the winnowing fan, and the purr of milk into the pail'. They were places, to quote Hardy still, 'which are as foreign bodies set down, like boulders on a plain, in a green world with which they have nothing in common'. Above them all, whether manufacturing or market town, new dynasties of mill-owners or old neighbourhoods of landed gentry, loomed London, the unseen if not the visible presence. Throughout Hardy's life-long development of the tragedy of the urban invasion of the countryside, in particular, London exercised a distant but dominant influence, the supreme goal of what he described in an article in *Longman's Magazine* in 1883 as 'the tendency of rural populations towards large towns . . . to flow uphill when forced by machinery'. He might have said much the same of authors when impelled by royalties. 'The work which we collective children of God do', sneered Matthew Arnold in 1869, 'our grand centre of life, our *city* for us to dwell in, is London!'[30] The purely literary and dramatic attractions of London were unequalled anywhere at this time. The mass journalism that Arnold was attacking began in the last quarter of the century, in the wake of *The Daily Telegraph* and *The Daily Mail*, and it reinforced these tendencies still more. It did so, for instance, not only by recruiting writers from the country like Richard Jefferies and working their genius to death, but by the subsequent build-up of circulations and increasingly powerful means of opinion-forming. The climacteric came, I suppose, between the wars, and the later transsubstantiation of *The Manchester Guardian*. The scuffles for unassailable control still going on are part of the mopping-up operations. It is hard to resist the conclusion that we seem to be approaching very fast the calamity so feared by T. S. Eliot of 'the disappearance of the peripheral cultures of England'.[31] Gwyn Thomas, an acidulous Welsh writer, when asked quite innocently why he resisted the pull of London, put the danger more pungently in a broadcast talk the other evening. The London writers, he explained, are susceptible to a kind of dandruff of the brain, a flaking away of their cerebral capacities.

4

London was literally the Babylon of the Victorians. Robert Mudie, a Scot who edited *The Sunday Times* long before the seductions of the colour supplements, seems to have invented the phrase in his *Babylon the Great: or, men and things in the British capital*, which was published five years after he had reached it, in 1825. George R. Sims, a Londoner by birth – and perhaps the first Victorian to have had one of his works published in full by both colour supplements on the same day ('Christmas Day in the Workhouse') – was still echoing Mudie's theme in his *Ballads of Babylon* in 1880. London, if the contemporary pamphlets and melodramas which circulated widely in the provinces are to be believed, was the great weight depressing the scales of Victorian manners and morals. The stories, if not novel, were impressive, and say a good deal about anti-London feeling. Thus, London was reliably reported to be experiencing infanticide at the rate of 300 per annum, with not less than 10,000 women living there who had murdered their children. Such terrifying catalogues of London's sins were, after all, being sold openly on the streets. What they told was of the decline in churchgoing, the increase in Sunday-drinking, Sunday-trading, Sunday-travelling, a surge in crimes of violence, floods of pornography, low amusements, 80,000 prostitutes, 60 miles of shops open on a Sunday, 2 million dying speeches of felons pouring from slum presses each week, penny theatres, casinos, singing and dancing saloons, gambling, racing, 10,000 places for getting strong drink – the pit was unfathomable! 'All this is in London!' proclaimed a pamphlet published in 1857, under the title *The Masses Without! A Pamphlet for the Times on the Sanatory, Social, Moral and Heathen Condition of the Masses*. The author, a certain John Knox, then set off for Birmingham, Manchester, Liverpool, Edinburgh, Glasgow, but with much reduced expectations.

George Wilson M'Cree, who went from Newcastle-upon-Tyne to become a slum missionary in London in 1848 and became popularly known as the bishop of St Giles in the course of the next twenty-five years, found a certain amount of hope in the situation, and having quantified the work of the devil called the role of the opposing army: 361 London City Missionaries, who visited between them nearly 2 million houses a year, ministered to a quarter of a million sick, handed out 6,000 Bibles, 2½ million tracts, held 36,000 Bible classes and 3,700 out-of-doors services, confirmed 1,300 persons and saved 863 drunkards – what labours! What mountains to be moved! It was all a chilling confirmation that London must be a doomed city. The daily prayer which Mr M'Cree suggested might be said in support cannot have lifted spirits very far:

O Lord, our God, [it ran] save London from the fate of Sodom, Nineveh, and Babylon! and may it become, even in our time, the light of the world, the salt of the earth, the habitation of holiness, the perfection of beauty, the joy of the whole universe – yea, may London become they holy city, O King of Heaven![32]

Clearly, London was much more often inclined to be regarded as the city of destruction than as the city foursquare. 'This London, Agrah! Is the Devil's Own Shop' ran the title of one anonymous Irish ballad.[33] So far as my own reading of such literature has gone, it is also clear that London invited more sharply divided opinions, more deep-seated ambivalence than any other city or town in Victorian England. It is an interesting speculation whether London did not perform some necessary Freudian function for provincial minds. How hungrily were George W. M. Reynolds's entrancing *Mysteries of London* (1846–50) – or Mayhew, Greenwood, Hollingshead, Sala, Sims or Stead, for that matter – devoured in provincial places, and how securely lodged in provincial prejudices were their metropolitan melodramas and side-shows and stereotypes? One cannot tell. But what I do want to suggest is that London occupied a unique and identifiable place in the national psyche which someone has got to probe very thoroughly before we can understand properly its relations with the provinces, either then or now. What is the real meaning of Richard Jefferies's apocalyptic vision, *After London* (popular edition 1908), when the metropolis sinks back into primeval swamp and English cities are 'kept in awe by troops of Welshmen, Irish, and even the western Scots . . . opening the doors of the houses, helping themselves to what they will'?

There is one set of images of London for Londoners and another of London for provincials or foreigners. To get at them we would have to compile what Eric Hobsbawm has called in a marvellously apt phrase 'the dictionary for the language of the voiceless'.[34] Benjamin Brierley, the little-known Lancashire dialect writer, a handloom weaver and silk warper who helped found the Manchester Literary Club and wrote over forty books between the 1860s and 1890s, is the kind of chap to supply some of the entries. In the book he called *Ab-o th'yate in London; or, southern life from a northern point of view* (1868), in which he describes his first visit to London, he begins by saying as he leaves Manchester by train, 'Farewell, owd England . . . Th'owd woman said – "Farewell, owd England!" too; an' then we sit as quiet as moice.' And when he got into a street brawl the distinction comes out again: 'I thowt I'd let 'em see ut they'd getten howd of an Englishman, an' not a Lunnoner.'

One of the things Ben Brierley did was to visit the Crystal Palace. When it had housed the Great Exhibition, it had had the same kind of introductory function in bringing provincial people to London, though on a more democratic basis, as the annual meetings in different towns of the British Association for the Advancement of Science and of the National Association for the Promotion of Social Science also performed. It was visited by over six million people; vast numbers came by excursion from provincial towns. The Exhibition provided, however, another kind of link, for its success depended on rousing support for it as an idea in the provinces, both to help in raising public money, in obtaining exhibits, and in promoting savings clubs to pay for visits. Every mayor in the kingdom was asked to form a committee, a great banquet was given by the Lord Mayor of London to obtain their support, and a suitable sprinkling of provincial representatives, like John Gott of Leeds, stepped on to the Royal Commission itself.[35] Without the support of the principal provincial towns, some of which had already held exhibitions of their own, it is doubtful whether it would have been a success.

It only confirmed, however, the national ascendancy of London in such matters. The concentration of national treasures and institutions, public spectacles, public buildings, public persons, most of the panoply of kingship, all conferred a kind of bonus on Londoners, which was not *totally* spurned, and the obverse of which has been a kind of provincial deprivation. It is only recently, in 1967, that the Arts Council (which dispensed nearly £6 million in the year ending March 1968) felt compelled to appoint a Regional Adviser and, in the words of its chairman, 'in simple justice call a relative halt to expansion in many London plans... until at least something comparable to the London density of culture is available in other parts of the country'.[36]

It would, I believe, be possible to widen this point if one could get a satisfactory breakdown of the distribution of public revenue in other ways, because what parliamentary returns relating to local taxation and expenditure suggest is the possibility that there was some subsidisation of London, even in the Victorian period, through the practice of making government loans at very low rates of interest for inordinately long periods in order to finance public improvements of various kinds. London borrowed much of what it needed on the open market, but it was still the case that of the £150 million or so of public debt of local authorities in 1881 about half represented the debts of London and some half-a-dozen other large towns.[37] It is impossible to substantiate this point here, but one cannot help wondering whether there were places below a certain size which contributed through the tax system to the general welfare of those above it. It would not somehow be surprising to find a kind of undistributed middle of places that helped to keep the rest going.

Be that as it may, there were transfers of another kind going on with the ebb and flow of the London season. The quite precise chronology – May-June-July, Epsom to Goodwood – and the unvarying convention of retreating to the country the moment it was over gave a rhythm not only to metropolitan life but to countless communities in the country. According to G. C. Brodrick, writing in 1881, the West End of London – which had its own gentry – was half-emptied of inhabitants during eight or nine months of the year.[38] The convention in London clubs (which occupied a position in the upper ranks of English society repeated nowhere else) was to have both 'town' and 'out of town' membership – something again virtually unknown, for example, on the Continent, but quite common in institutions of many kinds in London. Part of the explanation of this is, of course, that England contains no former capitals, no provinces in the sense in which that word applies to most countries of the rest of Europe, no regions – despite geographers' inventions of heptarchies and the like – which are distinctive and separable from the rest. The big towns of England, the French writer Cohen-Portheim once suggested in a revealing little book, *England, the Unknown Isle* (1930), are really no more than colonial towns. 'The word "province" in its continental sense is unknown in England,' he wrote, 'nor is there any reality to which it would correspond.' As to London, it remained unique, 'a formation for which no name exists'.[39] The capital has remained where it was planted when the exchequer was settled there under Henry II and the common bench added soon after. Had the campaigns against Scotland under the early Edwards come off, as Tout suggested,[40] the capital might have settled at York, but given that failure and the wealth of London it was natural that it should have remained in the south, and become the national accumulator.

5

For a whole variety of reasons, of which I have been able to examine all too few, London got a reputation for smartness in fashion as well as in business which no provincial town that was not itself a kind of annexe of London – like Cheltenham perhaps or Brighton – could rival in the nineteenth century, nor even since. Perhaps someone will confirm or deny whether those 'waves of fashion' which J. B. Priestly identified in his *English Journey* of the 1930s, 'rising in Berkeley Square and then slowly travelling out' do indeed at last 'ebb and dwindle into semi-detached villas outside Newcastle'? The social indices are different now.[41] I have, as I said I would, taken up a metropolitan standpoint. Historically speaking, I am sure this is the best perspective. But let me return now to John Fisher Murray, whom I quoted near the beginning of these remarks. He told the story of a master tailor from a provincial town, a provincial snip, who, finding his genius unappreciated in this vast metropolis, where, probably, he never rose higher in his profession than the manufacture of military inexpressibles at fourpence a pair, returned in disgust to his native village. There his presence was sufficiently indicated by a capacious signboard over his door bearing the inscription, in flaming yellow – 'SNAGGS, tailor, from LONDON'.[42]

That sign says practically everything that I have taken this essay to say.

4

Some historical reflections on the quality of urban life

I write this essay in the English Midlands, in a temporary building circa 1915 which was erected as quarters for nurses alongside the former lunatic asylum then doing duty as a military hospital. Around me stretch the nobler architectural edifices of the latest tenant of this site, the University of Leicester, and beyond it the ancient city of that name, now containing nearly 300,000 people set in a conurbation half as numerous again. The making of this complex of buildings and of this fourteenth city of the kingdom is not difficult to explain, even to the narrow point at which the towering memorial arch in the park, originally dedicated to the dead of World War I, came to exercise its peculiar hold over the height and character of the university buildings which have crept towards it base. But how far can one go in discerning the quality, not simply of these artifacts, but of the life of the community that created and used them?

A diverse economy of small and moderate-sized firms, unruffled industrial relations, a high level of female employment, an escape from serious damage from bombing, have meant for the city and its inhabitants little acquaintance with poverty, no overgrown fortunes, a hundred years of prosperity, and a hard cover of Victorian buildings. Local people still refer unconsciously to a League of Nations report of the 1930s that put Leicester second in riches in Europe after Lille. Be that as it may, the local community has both the satisfaction of thinking it is so and some of the attributes that come from really believing it. The city's weekly bank clearings are indeed about double those of its larger neighbour, Nottingham, and building societies flock here to scoop up the savings.

The city itself embodies the qualities of bourgeois success. It has a rather puffy pride without a real sense of community, a desire to lead without any real taste for adventure, some suspicions of the intellectual life without any declared antagonism towards it, a complete spectrum of religious sects without much feeling of piety. The city has demolished all three of its theatres since the war and given their sites to shops and a building society. It now gives its tentative support to a tiny repertory company, temporarily housed on the edge of a bus terminus but with imaginative energies unconfined, and substantially more to bingo halls and working men's clubs, which flower here supremely well. It has destroyed practically every one of its pre-Victorian buildings and, the town hall excepted, put virtually nothing of architectural merit in their place. It barely manages to stay in the First Division of the Football League. Yet there is a core of thrift, a tenacious spirit of independence, a feeling for natural beauty, some compassion for the handicapped, an earnest of pleasantness in most things, a kind of urbanity. To some it is clean; to others dull. Its motto pledges allegiance to both. *Semper eadem.*

There is much more to be said about Leicester than this, but significantly less could be said with confidence by anyone who had not lived in the place long enough to use it well, make friends and come to belong to it. Londoners like myself need longer because they are usually full of metropolitan conceits, especially a disbelief in provincial variety and excellence – the notion that to be provincial is to be deprived. They have also to combat local chauvinism, which in Leicester is levelled against Nottingham and London in that order. These things are an illustration of something important in the discussion of the quality of urban life in its historical perspectives. They point to the fact that there is a limit to the range of places that can be known sufficiently for the purpose, and they contain a warning that, like index numbers, their interpretation cannot be taken very far at second hand.

For these reasons, the horizons of this essay are not very distant ones in time or space. They do not stretch much beyond 150 years from the present. The examples given come mostly from Britain and a very few from the United States. Little even of this can be traversed descriptively for reasons that we are about to discuss. Almost the nearest approach for the historian must be through a consideration of some of the more important factors conditioning the quality of urban life – not so much those elusive qualities themselves. However, an incidental advantage of this is that the analysis is capable of being extended, *mutatis mutandis*, to include a wider area and conceivably a longer period. In what follows the discussion will centre on three main themes that are interwoven with each other: size and distribution of urban populations; technological influences bearing on the urban household and the community; and public administration and amenities.

1

There are things about urban life that historians can never tell. It is one thing to discover and explain why people have collected together in one place rather than another, why they have manufactured these things rather than those, how they have added to their numbers with unnatural speed or watched them slowly ebb away, how such communities have organised their social space and how they have occupied it. These matters left their marks, as often as not, either in documents or on the ground – not always very legibly perhaps but in some discernible palimpsest which told of what once went on. They assumed, that is, a verifiable public aspect of urban life. Such materials have sometimes permitted historians to write vivid, dispassionate urban biographies which come near to activating the urban past with the same flickering locomotion and new-found excitement of the early films. We see the likeness to ourselves and are satisfied with its authenticity. Sometimes the images speak and we hear what they have to say. They tell us how the various urban containers were made and a little of what went into them, and we get in consequence a more solid sense of form, if not of substance.

Seldom can the historians tell us all the things that mattered to the objects of our curiosity, especially how good or bad it *felt* to be alive in the conditions of the time. What did these urban contents think of their urban containers, without our hindsight and within their own preoccupations and scales of values? Who can tell? Rarely, if ever, has the historian been able to light up those private worlds of individual thought and feeling in a way which enables us to tell what consciousness of beauty or ugliness or sheer actuality was there, what sense of justice or oppression, what sense of community or deprivation, what satisfaction or hurts. These things have remained in historical darkness since cities began and they probably always will. The evidence for them is hardly ever tangible enough to be looked at in true perspective. Indeed, it is rarely possible to look directly at them at all, and the circumstantial evidence for the simplest bread-and-butter questions bearing on them is invariably so partial that they remain in the limbo of controversy.

It has to be recognised that the quality of life can probably be interpreted in all its pregnant meaning only by the creative artist, especially by the novelist, who is above all imaginatively concerned with the contemporary scene. The best of them penetrate the very structure of feeling and make everyday situations bear a kind of responsibility for conveying those qualitative things that no ordinary historical document can record. In Mrs Gaskell's first novel, *Mary Barton* (1848), for example, there are points where we no longer feel observers – as we do in her second novel, *North and South* (1855) – but real participants in working-class family life at the full onset of the new industrialism. The quality of that experience, the real meaning of community among industrial workers lately sucked in from rural villages, and something of the start of a tradition of working-class solidarity have an undeniable objectivity. Even among the other industrial novels of that period this objectivity seems comparatively rare, and for the most part we discover instead fictionalised commentaries on social values or imaginative propaganda for social reform. The original possibilities of going beyond rhetoric and giving sober meaning to that actual quality of life that belongs to what Carlyle had named industrialism are realised more vividly still in the early D. H. Lawrence:

The real tragedy of England, as I see it, is the tragedy of ugliness. The country is so lovely: the man-made England is so vile.... It was ugliness which betrayed the spirit of man, in the nineteenth century. The great crime which the moneyed classes and promoters of industry committed in the palmy Victorian days was the condemning of the workers to ugliness, ugliness, ugliness: meanness and formless and ugly surroundings, ugly ideals, ugly religion, ugly hope, ugly love, ugly clothes, ugly furniture, ugly houses, ugly relationship between workers and employers.

Here, from the brain of one imaginative son of a Midlands mining area, is an analysis of social values and the quality of the life they framed in terms that are honest but unlikely to have been true for the mass of the people who were subject to these things. It is only human to find ways of fending off harsh experience from which there is no real escape, and familiarity with squalor must have bred indifference or blindness or self-rewarding deceits at least as often as contempt or protest. However, such avenues do not remain open forever, and we must hope to see one day that the revulsion from ugliness had some kind of positive historical dimension too.

There are some clues to this already in the way in which urban life invites ambivalence. The city appears in ancient and modern writing as the genius of degradation as well as civilisation, the place of destruction as well as salvation, the object of aspiration and the source of despair. Almost any reflections on city life bear this out. Take a quite inconspicuous example – the unsigned comments on the Post Office London Directory which appeared in 1849 in an improving little magazine named *Hoggs's Weekly Instructor:*

London! word of wonderful import – symbol of a mighty apparent unity – of one mass of human beings, vast and world-like, gravitating together by a system of mutual dependency – yet word, motive with ideas, diverse as the poles and opposite as positive and negative in thought – 'of life's extremes, the grandeur and the gloom,' the boldest and most striking phenomena are seen in thee. London! the word describes, as with the graver of a Prometheus, palpable and distinct, a circle replete with unequals and antagonisms. . . . Here wealth, groaning with satiety, sighs for some new world of pleasure, and poverty, maddened with hunger, seeks from day to day any world, it cares not which, save this.

Rusticity was never, so runs the underlying theme, like this. It was therefore easy for the city to assume more often the literary role of symbolising the downward rather than the upward tendencies in human nature. That bias, accentuated by the horrors – both real and imaginary – of the industrial cities of modern times, has provided one of the persistent themes of recent literary history. The city has had few friends among modern novelists, fewer still among poets. It has had, to use the modern jargon, a poor image, and it is difficult to make due compensation for this in assessing its qualities. Our own imaginations trip us up. Did Victorian towns really stink as unfailingly of sulphur and open sewers as Port Sunlight did of soap? Was there never any innocent fun in the slums nor dark crime in the suburbs? Can the cultural slope always have run, like the trains, *up* to London? There is a strong spirit of anti-urbanism in both British and American thinking which is rooted, no doubt, in more fundamental parts of the national psyche, just as its outcome leads in all kinds of unexpected directions.

In Britain this bias helps to explain, for example, why the English (and still more markedly the Welsh) should have been such reluctant city-dwellers, accepting their lot with a devious determination to bring as many rustic features as possible onto the urban scene. The English social historian David Eversley, has put it this way:

The example of the Eisteddfod is to me a very mild example of our pretentious rurality; we bring up our children on a diet of the Bible, Shakespeare and the pastoral poets; we never have conceded that we have industrialized. What is the semi-detached house except the desperate nineteenth-century attempt to try and maintain an outlook on your own plot of ground?

It is the kind of romantic yearning that can move whole generations and never be expressed in words. The English hardly knew they had such a preference until drawing-board architects tried to stand streets on end and lift public housing toward twenty stories in the last few years. The tenants then noticed that no birds sang so high in the sky and neighbours dropped in less. Feet on the ground, a bit of green, curves and slopes, chance encounters, the children in sight, a place of one's own – these might almost have been written into the genetic code of the ordinary people whose great-grandparents had in so many cases left the country to join the town. It is no accident that the English seem to prefer to speak of town and country planning. The garden city movement, whose antecedents go much earlier than Ebenezer Howard, very properly became the chief contribution which the English had to make to the art of living close together. Perhaps this fact helps to account for the relatively graceless failure of British town planners, both professional and amateur, in using pure urban forms. The long debate over rebuilding the bombed environs of St Paul's in London in recent years has unconsciously plumbed depths like these.

One more comment in this connection will help to broaden the historical perspective a little. When he was painting his brilliant miniature of Manchester in *Encounter* some years ago (March 1957), the English historian A. J. P. Taylor could not help turning for its true epitome to a stretch of green:

The most revealing spot in Manchester is not the historic centre, not even the Royal Exchange, but Victoria Park. This is still a private estate, with toll-gates and keepers in uniform. Gothic palaces jostle each other; gardeners dust the soot from the leaves of the trees; and the ghosts of merchant princes walk in the twilight. These were the men who gave Manchester its historical character. We think of them in retrospect as Radicals; and so they were in lack of respect for traditional authority or in their ruthless destruction of whatever stood in their way. But they were far from a belief in economic quality or even in democracy, if we mean by that putting the needs of the majority first. They had succeeded by their own energy; and they supposed that the duty of society was discharged if it gave others the chance to do the same. It did not worry them that, while the rich man was in his mansion, the poor man at the gates of Victoria Park lived in a slum. The road to success lay open for those who wished to take it. Like the men of the Renaissance they exalted the individual. They lacked one Renaissance characteristic. Of all dominant classes, they were the least equipped with aesthetic taste. Perhaps Money is less beautiful than Intrigue or Wickedness – the Renaissance routes to power; or perhaps it is so beautiful in itself as to destroy the need for beauty elsewhere. At any rate, the result is the same: Manchester is irredeemably ugly. There is no spot to which you could lead a blindfold stranger and say happily: 'Now open your eyes.' Norman Douglas had a theory that English people walked with their eyes on the ground so as to avoid the excrement of dogs on the pavement. The explanation in Manchester is simpler: they avert their eyes from the ugliness of their surroundings.

The municipal park, however regimented its borders and quaint its taboos, has been the saving grace of a good many of the ugly bits of England. It was a Victorian transmutation of the English landscaped park of the eighteenth century and of the botanic garden which developed with such force in the late-Georgian and Regency period. Before long, it also formed a focus for ideas on gardens from all over Europe and collected its flora from all over the world – perhaps the most beautiful residue of the English Empire. It provided a blend of the exotic and the indigenous in a way which no other English art could excel and contributed more subtly than we tend to think to the quality of urban life both then and since. The park open to the public was an unexceptionable way of making public gestures. Sometimes parks were produced simply by public demand, sometimes by a patron's deed of gift, sometimes simply by opening the gates of a private or royal estate. The Victoria parks of England were above all expressions of good manners. Commons were different. They were survivals in the suburbs of an agrarian culture which had been overrun, like ancient fairs reduced to roundabouts and palmistry. Their scrubby acres tended to be less inviolate than parks barricaded with ornamental railings, at least until preservation societies rose late in the nineteenth century to defend what was left of them against railways, brick-makers and allotment holders. Recreation grounds came later still and were, like public baths, municipal all through. Collectively, the parks, commons, walks, burial grounds, made a decent difference to the places that had them. They gave a place style. What happened when the railings were removed for scrap metal during World War II was another matter. They no longer closed at dusk.

These few reflections throw into sharper relief the historian's ordinary qualifications for making judgments of value about the quality of urban life. Rarely does the evidence which he normally handles help very much. His main struggle to discover what really happened, or how attitudes actually changed and why, may require him now and then to navigate as best he can the little unfathomed inlets of intangible things that impinge on his theme; but he cannot cast himself adrift on such a sea, however benign. The truth is that there can be no reliable *historical* chart to the quality of urban life without a new discipline for connecting the historical and literary traditions of scholarship, and it would be idle in the course of these few remarks to try and create one. An essence like the quality of urban life, secreted in every joint and carried on by every nerve of the urban organism, is bound to be more fugitive than its own minutiae. The state of the streets, the programme of concerts in the civic hall, the efficiency of the postal service, the proximity of friends, all help to make life more or less agreeable and add to or subtract from its quality, but they cannot be aggregated or synthesised into a neat overall result. The historian cannot do what Joyce has done in *Dubliners* or *Ulysses* or what T. S. Eliot did with such economy in 'The Waste Land' – however much he admires their grasp on what eludes him in the self-same London or Dublin. For the historian it is one thing to recognise the factors germane to a sense of the quality of life; it is another to take readings of the satisfactions they gave.

2

Quality is, after all, a slippery concept. In one sense it can mean degrees of excellence in almost anything; in another simply the sum of its attributes; but in ordinary usage it has gathered vague overtones that have given it an historical perspective of its own. The only way of describing this is to say that the whole notion has been democratised. Trollope described in one place in *Barchester Towers* (1857) how 'the quality, as the upper classes in rural districts are designated by the lower with so much true discrimination, were to eat a breakfast, and the non-quality were to eat a dinner'. As a substantive, used without sarcasm, to indicate those in the higher ranks of society, the term had become a colloquialism and was now beginning to go out. It had not, apparently, become an urban term, perhaps because 'the quality' remained essentially a landed aristocracy. The pursuit of quality as the hallmark of approval, the only true sign of breeding, as distinct from its natural, unconscious expression, arose with the middle classes and when it was duly pinned down became bourgeois. In the Victorian period 'high class' 'select', 'family', 'quality' became interchangeable tradesmen's terms for their middle-class clientele and the stuff they bought. It is difficult to find writers of that time who were free of such constraints and who were ready to describe the things the working classes – or more accurately the poor – bought or the way they lived in terms of the quality of the goods or of their lives. To have spoken of quality when writing about their *condition* would have been a serious misuse of terms. This is no longer true. Outward appearances matter less, except to the undistributed middle, and the quality of life, be it urban or rural, is now the way it is lived at large.

There is also a sociological difficulty. What meaning are we to attribute to urban life itself? Clearly, it is impossible to go into the whole ambience of urbanism, though it does have an obvious bearing on the quality of life that occurred. The question is directed rather at the generic differences between urban and rural life. In what important respects has the experience of living in towns differed, if at all, from life in the country, and are such differences those of quality rather than degree? Is there some urban continuum along which villages, market towns, small industrial towns, industrial cities, metropolises, are strung out, and in which some discernible differences in the quality of life may be found? Any such budding idiosyncracies tended to be blurred in the beginning, of course, by the interpenetration of rural and urban economies: urban life could not begin at any level before cultivators produced more food and raw materials than they themselves consumed; it could not go on unless urban products or services found outlets beyond the communities that provided them. Moreover, the beginnings of modern industry occurred for the most part outside the towns and penetrated them only when advancing technology and entrepreneurial demands made the towns themselves gigantic machines for both living and working in. The historical patterns are in fact quite complex. Wherever it occurred, the transition from country-dominated town to town-dominated country was neither smooth nor sudden, and rural and urban features have persistently occurred out of context. Nor has this been confined to economic life.

Although a large literature has already grown up on the subject, the distinctive attributes of urban and rural life, the resemblances and differences between life in the village and in the city as well as between towns of different sizes and functions cannot be discerned with real clarity even for those places still under our own gaze. And as for towns used by generations now dead, generic distinctions have simply not yet been identified by sustained historical research. We do not know enough by way of observation how to isolate distinctively *urban* behaviour from rural behaviour, or know how far to go in rejecting such distinctions altogether. There are several hypotheses. We may tentatively accept the proposition that urban life is essentially impersonal, secondary, contractual, but we can easily find a whole range of mixed examples in which it is not so. Though common sense tells us that we cannot fail to recognise a city when we see one, the inhabitants of certain city neighbourhoods – locations often better known by reference to individual streets than by more general place-names like Highgate or Greenwich Village – know that they form a community which for all the ordinary purposes of social life is indistinguishable from that of the authentic village enclosed by fields. There is that same knowledgeable intimacy between people, the same sense of forming a little universe, the same tacit conviction of durability that is questioned only when another world seems about to collide or a familiar landmark or villager is being taken away.

It is even arguable in the situation created by the flight of the middle classes to the suburbs and beyond, and the social isolation of the Negro and the poor in the core of so many American cities, that the traditional territorial distinctions between village and metropolis are in some sense being turned inside out. The impersonal transience of metropolitan life is being transferred to the outer rings of the cities, where cosmopolitanism assumes new forms and flourishes vicariously through television or some other means, and its social networks begin to transcend suburbia altogether. The close face-to-face relationships of the traditional village are often now more palpable in the self-contained and self-containing slums at the centre than in the distant villages submerged by their suburban newcomers, dead in the week and alive at the weekend.

3

There is here one long perspective of importance. The cities, which in some places have been losing their geographical tidiness for two or three generations, are now perhaps in the process of losing their separate identities altogether. The technologies of our own day are having a much more profound impact on the social ecology of cities and the quality of life within them than earlier advances of a more primitive kind once had. The structure of advanced economies with their increasing emphasis on services rather than products, communications systems that extend drastically the potential scope of many of the old business markets, the nationwide supply of power through electrical grid systems, the indefinite extension of the means of personal mobility – these are exercising one kind of influence, most noticeably of all in the United States. The urban repellent of acute congestion, incipient public violence, pollution of air and water, importunate social demands by the poor and deprived, increasing sensitivity to environment in whatever form or for whatever purpose – these are exercising influences of another kind. Between these positive and negative influences the physical artifact of the city is beginning to disintegrate. There are parallels here between physical form and social substance. The wider social networks that are bound to develop in a society making full use of its technological possibilities are now beginning to form on the regional, continental and intercontinental scale. For the members of such a society, personal relations have fewer and fewer territorial limits.

The sense of community, which has an almost tactile quality in village society, has not been eroded everywhere with equal force. Among the mining communities in the north-east of England, in places that have been purged of all other rusticity, the fierce loyalties that come from common disasters and unjust treatment by remote governments hold them together still. In other places, uncharacteristically urban events, like the August bank holiday walk by thousands together out of Leeds onto the moors, go on under their own momentum or a desire for a common identity. There are even signs among the urban poor of that kind of secret understanding between strangers that Tocqueville recalled in his *Souvenir* when he wrote of 'a kind of morality peculiar to times of disorder, and a special code for days of rebellion'. It would be a mistake to regard the sense of community as having been rendered entirely archaic even among the thoroughly blasé and urbane, much less among the urban villagers of the slums, where the disorientation of social life from more bourgeois styles has only been carried through by a complex organisation peculiar to their own (sometimes 'anti-social') needs.

It is clear all the same that *community* is a term which has been changing its meaning for a very long time, and in some contexts it now means very little beyond the old crowd at the pub or the regulars in the self-service laundries or the little adolescent groups that collect in the light of back-street fish-and-chip shops. The concentrative forces that produced the cities as we now see them have in some places already come to an end. The city, once the Renaissance state of its own, aloof from its surroundings except for purposes of provisioning, has ceased even to be a single component in the nation-state, a centre for administration of a wider whole, the locus of industry and trade. It has become instead its controlling mechanism and motive force, and its changing structure is perhaps already beginning to provide an entirely new social framework for entire nations, as it is certainly now putting new items onto the agenda of central and local governments. Urban problems, which once looked small-scale, fragmented, almost inert, now seem to have congealed – and not in the United States alone – into the 'problem of the cities', forbidding, intractable, volatile. The city is now history's looking glass and what it reflects are the conflicts of class and race and ideology that are the products in our time of historical processes far transcending it.

4

The chief dimension of the urban community is social distance. This is being felt more acutely now than it was during the formation of the first industrial cities, if only because basic conditions have improved somewhat. In Britain, for example, the housing problem had barely been perceived by the end of the nineteenth century, and the eight million people who were, according to Sidney Webb, being housed, washed and watered in them worse than horses, had scarcely begun to measure the distance that had to be closed. The middle classes had given that distance a physical dimension by their retreat to the suburbs. The physical residue they left behind helped to fix it more concretely, for the houses they vacated were normally ill-suited to multiple occupation and therefore deteriorated all the more readily when pressed into use by the lower classes. This not only meant that decaying neighbourhoods lacked the stability in local affairs which would have come had the middle classes remained, nor simply that their social problems tended to develop unseen, but that they were cursed by the poverty of their own rateable values. Schemes for equalising local rates, which tended to be regarded as one of those empty gestures that blessed neither givers nor receivers, did not develop anywhere to any marked degree until the very end of the nineteenth century.

It must be remembered, of course, that the mere juxtaposition of different living styles has never noticeably reduced their differences, not even when, as in ancient Athens, physical contact between them was almost inescapable and the living accommodation deemed fit for persons of high and low rank was barely distinguishable. What clearly did happen later was an accentuation of such differences as the growth of private property took place and was reinforced by the award of public honours. These developments proclaimed social differences among citizens in quite unequivocal ways. The range of common experience among town-dwellers seems to have diminished as the scope for private consumption opened up. A glance at the irresistibly widening gulf in modern Rio de Janeiro between the *favelas* of the squatter poor and the luxury flats of the rich, sometimes within range of the common fly below them, illustrates the point clearly enough. What has tended in relatively recent times to unbridle the frustrations of the poor in so many places has been a sustained awareness of differences in social conditions, in expectations of life and of advancement in the world, in degrees of hope – in a consciousness, one could almost say, of the removable differences in the quality of human life. Sooner or later cities have always enabled such things to be seen. Television cameras now ensure that they are demonstrated for the whole world to witness.

The historical process of dividing the urban ground plan into socially segregated compartments has not occurred in the same institutional setting everywhere nor produced identical results with equal speed. There is, for example, the obvious difference between the ecological patterns of cities north and south of the Rio Grande: in the former, the rich have tended to take to the suburbs; in the latter, they have kept their hold on the centre while the working classes and the poor suffer the inconveniences and miseries of life on the perimeter. The latter pattern also existed up to the eighteenth century in cities of the Old World large enough to have suburbs; then the merchants in particular, looking for the best of both worlds, urban and rural, within daily coaching distance of their London counting houses, began to leapfrog the suburban communities already sprawling beyond the ancient city limits. A number of familiar geometrical variations of the zones created by such tendencies can also be clearly seen in the ground plan. It is a geometry which simply exhibits the economic and cultural diversities to be found between cities which are no less varied than their age profiles and occupational structures.

The ground plan of a city is in truth a kind of effigy of the social system from which it has been struck. The benefits as well as the costs of pursuing particular ends, not to mention the social and legal disciplines that society accepts in distributing its rewards and penalities, show up vividly in the detail. Britain's pursuit of industrial power and overseas expansion in the nineteenth century, for example, was unimpeded by the constraints of investing heavily in the housing and welfare of the labour force at home. Little time was spent in maturing industrial workers and virtually none in superannuating them. One of the social costs accepted by the industrial pioneers was, therefore, poor housing for the ordinary people. This was a condition that might have been different had more capital been freed from more directly productive use – but perhaps not so radically different as might seem at first sight. Another way of putting this situation is that the quality of the lives of those still using these houses and neighbourhoods two or three generations later has been impaired in some degree by what was initially done. It is not until very much later that the historical implications of the building contracts which were first entered into, of the terms on which the capital used to meet them was raised, of the low standards of building tolerated, or of the imposts laid on building materials by the government, can be fully understood.

Wherever one looks, the forces of change have operated with peculiar subtlety and have produced constantly varying patterns on the ground. Neighbourhoods go up and come down in social status in ways that have seldom been subject to close historical examination. But it is clear that these mutations have always had real meaning for those involved. The signs were money lost or made by those on the move, neighbourliness increased or diminished among those left behind, local amenities enhanced or destroyed, and those indefinable nothings that might have gone on drawing people to the spot thrown unthinkingly away. Here, in fact, are some of the most mercurial qualitative changes of all. They suggest many more minutely significant historical perspectives to the quality of urban life than this brief essay can possibly reveal. They are overlaid by personal patterns of life that might change, or not, in phase with the neighbourhood. These aspects of the matter are a reminder that the quintessence of the quality of urban life is to be found, not in the general circumstances with which an essay like this must deal but in their particularity. The true dimensions are matters of detail. The nearest approach to them lies through their local history, especially in that nearly contemporary field, where historians are so ill at ease, in which the verbal testimony of old and young have to be attended to with even more care than the public-conscious written records of the administrators.

5

One of the implications of the discussion so far is that the most fundamental influences on the quality of urban life were often matters of quantity. The numbers of people in a given space, the speed at which they increased, and the extent to which this development occurred in isolation or in a system of cities combined to make the growth of cities beyond a certain size a different kind of human experience and to provide for a new sort of urban culture. However it be defined by the leading authorities, the urbanisation of the world's population has achieved a different order of magnitude over the last 150 years or so from that prevailing before. During the more than six thousands years since cities began, the isolated unstable pockets of human concentration that had formed around local potentates or regional markets were completely overwhelmed in number by people working the land. This was true even where rapid urban developments were about to occur, as in England in the early eighteenth century. By the beginning of the nineteenth century there were only seventeen towns of 20,000 inhabitants or more and only one of more than 100,000 – London – which was about to become the first city anywhere to contain a million people. Throughout the world there were probably no more than twenty places at that time with populations exceeding 100,000. By the middle of the next century the number was approaching 900 of which 50 held more than a million people. According to Kingsley Davis, the increase in the proportion of the human population living in cities of 100,000 or more is now accelerating, and in the decade 1950–1960 the rate of increase became twice that of the preceding half-century. Davis calculates that over a third of the world's inhabitants already live in urban places of some size and that the distribution of this population will, by the last decade of this century, be roughly comparable to that prevailing in the most highly urbanised country, Great Britain, in 1851, when about half the population lived in towns. The process of redistributing these human aggregates will then be within reach of its end, for the proportion of the population living in cities and their suburbs in the most advanced nations of the world already appears to have reached a ceiling at around 75 per cent of the total.

There is no need to amplify this familiar outline with local detail in order to make the point that the quality of human life in general is not on the verge of assuming an urban condition everywhere. The statistics are in some respects ahead of the qualitative changes involved in the process of transposing and modifying agrarian institutions to an urban setting. This is true not only for countries in which the process has been accompanied by industrialisation but in those still struggling to achieve it. In the latter, the speed of urbanisation is really a function of simple population growth, and the cities are now having to absorb the resulting numbers much faster than ever was the case among developing countries in the past. On the other hand, the more pervasive massing of human populations has already had two kinds of effect, the one demographic and the other aesthetic. It may also have had a number of psychotic effects of the kind observed in overcrowded populations of other primates. Edwin Chadwick, the social reformer of the nineteenth century, once came very near to saying that the violent tendencies of the lower classes of his day were related to their overcrowding, and told a story about one owner of a court of dwellings who had found it necessary to give it two entrances 'so that people in feud could avoid meeting each other'.

6

The most direct aesthetic effects of concentrated numbers, noise and smell have no historical dimension whatever. It is a matter of common observation that noise levels have almost certainly been rising everywhere within living memory despite the muting of road drills, the banning of motor horns after hours, or vague legislation about the number of decibels of sound to be emitted at any point. Even now there is hardly any scientific evidence about actual levels of noise and their impact on human life. Around the closes of selected cathedrals in England today, the simulated sounds of sonic booms are being let off, not to see whether anyone objects (which they will learn not to do) but to ensure that stained glass and eroded pinnacles are not actually brought down. Advertisements for double-glazing reinforce their appeal to customers wanting extra warmth with the bonus of quietness. It is a commodity now worth marketing, but it is doubtful whether the quality of urban life has been seriously reduced until fairly recently by the lack of it. It is the so-called beauty spot within reach of a million cars that is now more threatened by transistorised 'pop' and the deafening discothèque that offers for pleasure more noise than can be contained in any street.

What is less certain is whether the combined assault on the senses of a profusion of sights, smells, noises, crowds, moving objects, changing levels, constraints, commands, is an important source of disturbance to people. How widespread is that characteristically urban malady, agoraphobia – unidentified before 1873 – in its mild or its extreme forms? Some writers have argued that the urban scene has more sources of disturbance than is commonly thought. Kevin Lynch, for example, has reason for disquiet over what he calls the lack of visible identity that comes from overplanned spaces or excessively standardised components. Can one be certain whether he is leaving Blackpool or arriving in Chipping Sodbury? Rational answers to pressure of numbers and competing claims on spaces have tended to produce their own irrationalities and perplexities. The baffling tangles of street signs and other public paraphernalia, the concrete arteries that curtail human movement, the dissonances of colour and form which go with commercial eagerness (especially now that advertisers know we must be approached 'in depth'), the planing away of the coarse natural grain of individual places and the veneering of the surfaces in a plain monochrome – these have combined to create a habitat that differs markedly from the public centres of things of barely a generation ago. The most obvious historical factor here, of course, is the motor car, whose demands on social space have risen on an exponential curve that shows little sign of flattening out. The general failure to recognise the high social costs incurred in meeting this inordinate demand has to be explained, however, in terms of social ethics and political realities or even plain hedonism rather than transport economics. It seems fair to say that the automobile has been winning its claims for space because most people want it to win (for reasons that are far more inscrutable), and there are political penalties for denying the fulfilment of these desires. What the automobile has actually meant in terms of the quality of life can be assessed in part by reference to the figures for road casualties, but what it has meant aesthetically or emotionally is beyond historical reckoning. The historian, like anyone else, can but look at the multiple freeways converging on Los Angeles or at the arterial roads that meet in the new heart of Birmingham in England and wonder. The effect appears to have been disastrous in terms of human values since the circulation of traffic has become more important than the circulation of people.

The aesthetic aspects of the quality of urban life have something to do with the way in which the parts are put together. Among the chief historical changes that have occurred in this respect in modern times has been the introduction of discontinuities. It would be unduly romantic to insist that the fitting together of the old small towns of England – or of New England too – was always a comfort to contemporary observers, yet in many of their forms and settings they have an undeniable seemliness to modern eyes. This sense of aptness springs from the basic affinities in the purposes of the buildings on the main streets, the dimensions to which they were built and the character of the local materials. Within these overall conditions there usually developed a variety of buildings held together by a kind of rhythm of their own making which corresponded to the human stride. The size of the openings in the walls for doors or windows or between the buildings for squares or funnelled-out places for markets, the height of the structures, the pursuit of the natural contours by the streets, all played a part. It was almost as if the whole scene could have been composed by reference to cubits and spans.

In the course of the eighteenth century, the unity, though not the form of such developments, was disciplined and refined in Bath and Edinburgh, in the spas and watering places, and in the West End of London, to a degree that is cause for astonishment still, given the advance at the same time of ideas about the perfection of things in a state of natural growth. The unbroken stride of the Georgian terrace and the classical idiom of its Palladian counterpart, the suburban villa, were transmuted by means of builders' pattern books into innumerable doll house replicas of what were thought to be their essential features until they were modified almost out of existence. The archaeological evidence for this is recognisable still throughout the inner suburbs of London and in the older parts of Baltimore. The principal streets of Victorian towns were slow to put on any respectable uniform. The street improvements which were beginning to take place, more generally as a means of disinfecting a slum or arching over an offensive sewer than as an artery for traffic, did provide new opportunities for regular street fronts in some places, even though taste itself – in John Betjeman's phrase – was thickening so fast that the opportunity tended to be missed. No one could now pretend that the central parts of these towns, where the prevailing values and business interests of the community were both on show, were values of aesthetic harmony. The chatter of advertisement in every form, including giant-sized autographs and trade symbols across commercial buildings (seldom as a kind of architectural headgear, as in other parts of the English-speaking world), the greatly varying scale and modules of buildings that came with the wider substitution of iron for timber and the greater variety in warehousing and office needs, the use of building materials brought in by railway, and the growing volume of horse traffic on the streets, were none of them composing influences.

Yet composure of this kind is really an afterthought. It occurs to a generation that took over still grimier buildings and more tortuous streets in relation to their needs and looks back now across the waste land of the inter-war years, when mass unemployment in the older industrial towns meant a standstill for everything. What really mattered to those pre-Keynesian generations was work. To the working man, the quality of life in the towns depended entirely on a job; and artisans on the tramp or agricultural labourers turning their backs on the land were responding to the call of higher wages or the hope of them. It was their first lesson in the arithmetic of the city. In his brilliant exposure of the hidden forces of city life, Georg Simmel wrote of the urban economy as being imbued with a calculating quality: 'Only money economy has filled the days of so many people in weighing, calculating, with numerical determinations, with a reduction of qualitative values to quantitative ones.' The force of that inexorable process, alas, has not yet been spent. City life has always had a legendary intensiveness, a sense of things twice their size, an enticement, a reward for everyone somewhere between overstuffed charities and underused capital. The French sociologist Durkheim taught that the division of labour in urban society which created a greater variety of jobs was related not only to the massing of people but to the social attractiveness of it. He saw an inseparable connection between what he called moral density and material density, and which he stated in terms of a 'law of gravitation in the social world' – the social mass exercising an attraction by its own density.

There is no room here to test the truth of Durkheim's statement even were there the means. The simple picture that one must have of the nineteenth century in this regard is of movements by the million, most conspicuously transatlantic ones, virtually all of them wheeling on the cities, most of them ending there but others filtering through. The voracious appetites of the towns of Britain, gulping people in from the country or from other towns and disgorging them, or some of them, in successive bouts of prosperity and depression, was repeated within the entirely different orbits of the cities on the eastern seaboard of the United States and of the moving frontier to the west. The cities were bound to be marked by this huge drama, if only because they were nowhere ready to take in the numbers that came or to give breathing space to those that remained. The sharpest demographic effect of this was expressed in terms of mortality.

The high loss of life in the towns of the eighteenth century had been one of the most effective hindrances to their more rapid growth. London's reputation as a devourer of souls was borne out by its Bills of Mortality which told plainly of the great excess of deaths over births. 'London will not feel any want of recruits,' wrote Corbyn Morris in 1751, 'till there are no people in the country.' By the middle of the nineteenth century there were, in a contemporary phrase, other 'burial pits of the human species'. Liverpool, Leeds and Manchester each grew by 50 per cent in the 1820s, Bradford and West Bromwich at around 70 per cent, and Glasgow at 30 per cent or more for each decade between 1801 and 1841. During the 1830s, Glasgow's population was increasing twice as fast as its houses, while the ratio of typhus cases admitted to the Royal Infirmary (which had been under 10 per cent of total admissions from 1800 to 1815) reached 50 per cent. Typhus meant dirt and destitution, and its pronounced appearance at a time when the industrial towns were being packed so tight with people is significant. So also is the fact that the incidence of tuberculosis remained almost entirely urban throughout the nineteenth century. Cholera, which killed only in thousands while frightening tens of thousands more between the 1830s and 1860s, occurred in brief epidemics and did not correspond as closely with conditions of overcrowding, though it was yet another demonstration of the capacity of towns to waste human life. It is impossible to correlate statistically the density of these urban populations with the diseases they suffered because mortality depended on diet, occupation and age structure, as well as domestic conditions. There was, nonetheless, an impressive difference in the figures that were collected on the death expectations of the rich and the poor. One local doctor in Leeds, for example, calculated around 1840 that the mean age at death for the upper classes was forty-four, for the middle classes twenty-seven, and for the lower classes nineteen.

The tendency of urban death-rates to drive up national averages did not abate in Britain before the twentieth century, but urban birth-rates had long been moving the other way. As was the case more generally in the Western world, the age at which both sexes married was significantly lower in the towns than in the countryside and the proportion of the urban population marrying was greater. Yet both the size of completed families and the birth-rate were lower in the towns than in the countryside, a difference in fertility which appears to have stemmed from the deliberate limitation of families by the urban middle classes and, a generation or more later, by the urban working classes. J. A. Banks has argued that this democratisation of birth control became possible because of the opportunities which urban life gave to the working classes to make comparisons of living standards with their well-to-do neighbours. What certainly seems the case is that the position of women in society and of children in relation to the family have both undergone changes which have risen out of urban conditions. The impact of these changes on other social relations has also had a feedback effect on the quality of urban life itself – though we may only now be witnessing the culmination of this process in the changing role of adolescents in society.

The Victorian middle classes, as Asa Briggs has pointed out, saw the growth of their cities, and in some senses the quality of what went on in them, primarily in terms of numbers. They also recognised profoundly that both depended on technological achievements. Even their visions of utopia were based on these developments. They took their technologies as far as their own imaginations could reach or thought back to living conditions which dispensed with them in an unimaginable way. The city naturally occupied a central position in these speculations because the possibilities for controlling the environment had never drawn so close. In a purely technical sense, the short historical span that has occurred since then has made every one of these possibilities capable of being realised. There is little now that single-minded effort on a sufficient scale cannot achieve. What is difficult is for our imaginations to reach as far as our own technologies will allow.

The cities have become the special repositories of these ironies. The basic equipment of the home has come to include machinery and power on a scale sufficient at one time for a small factory, and the electrical consumption of a metropolis of ten million in a rich country has come to exceed that used in a poor nation of four hundred million. This material density of city life has been increasing sharply, particularly since the 1930s. The invention of the domestic version of industrial equipment of all kinds and the domestication of the means of entertainment have tended to give social life a new, more private focus while reducing the means of privacy in action as well as in the imagination. The space required for social life on every level has become more uniform, and social distinctions have come to depend less and less on the scale of domestic arrangements than on their style. Domestic servants, who were already giving the Victorian middle classes some trouble, have been disappearing at high speed, though a cheap substitute has been found in *au pair* girls from the Continent who are prepared to do most things in return for the opportunity of visiting the country for a prolonged period. Do-it-yourself appears to have become less of a slogan than a new kind of democracy. Yet appearances in these matters are deceptive. Despite all the technical possibilities, everyone knows that the enjoyments and miseries of city life still often depend on all kinds of trivial and unsophisticated circumstances. It has become something of a political joke to be living in Britain in the white heat of the technological revolution of the 1960s. What we need to do now, therefore, is to examine quite briefly some of the technological and administrative factors that have come to influence the quality of urban life at so many points.

7

What is immediately striking about so many of the basic inventions of the city is the recent date at which they were brought into widespread use. The water closet, for instance, the most urbane installation of all, though invented in the sixteenth century was not developed commercially before the end of the eighteenth. And substitutes for it – like the Moule patent earth closet, invented in 1860 and regarded as a great advance on the public middens of many of the manufacturing towns in the North – continued in use for generations yet. At the middle of the nineteenth century, London was still perforated with cesspits and had not completed its scheme for sewage disposal in the Thames estuary rather than its own tidal reach. Similarly, provincial towns had as great a variety of means of coping with their sewage as they continue to have in collecting household refuse. Bringing the water closet indoors has an even more recent history.

Drinking water tended to remain a scarce and rather complex fluid in British towns till the very end of the nineteenth century. Microbiology was in its infancy until the 1800s and water analysis was bound to remain rather unperceptive. The inclination in many towns to collect water from the local river grew annually more hazardous as waterborne sewage was carried as often as not to nearly identical points, and shallow surface wells received the percolations from cesspits, graveyards and industrial premises of all kinds. As late as 1872 a depot for processing dried dung still operated next door to the filter beds of a London water company. The supply of water was generally intermittent and the air space in the cisterns in which water was domestically stored often filled with noxious gases drawn in from nearby sewers and water closets. A continuous supply of water was unobtainable anywhere, even in London, much before 1900. According to the Milner-Holland report on the condition of housing in Greater London in the mid-1960s, only about a quarter of privately rented households had a fixed bath, a wash basin, a hot water supply and a water closet in or adjoining the house.

Most of the other improvements in domestic facilities that began to confer tangible advantages on city-dwellers have, in fact, occurred within living memory. Despite eye-catching displays at international exhibitions, gas lighting did not begin to supplant oil lamps in homes of all social classes in Britain until the penny-in-the-slot meter was invented in 1892; and kitchen ranges for cooking which had not come into general use until about 1870, were not replaced with gas cookers in any number until the Edwardian period. The triumph of electricity for either purpose followed much later still and belongs to the 1930s. Even in the United States at the beginning of that decade less than three per cent of families cooked by electricity. In Britain, where back-boilers to open grates in living rooms were first being installed in any numbers in the 1890s, the widespread adoption of domestic central heating, mainly fired by gas boiler within the home, is only just beginning. The inter-war period, it might also be noticed, was also the threshold for much of the domestic equipment now regarded as a necessity of one kind or another – the automobile, vacuum cleaner, refrigerator, washing machine, telephone. These helped to release time, and the gramophone, radio and cinema, which were then having their effective beginning, helped to fill it.

All these technological developments marked some kind of change in the condition of domestic life and presumably led to some enhancement of its quality. When considering the relationship between technology and the quality of the life of the urban community at large, it is difficult to be certain which is cause and which effect. The introduction of steam railways, for example, interconnected cities, enlarged their hinterlands, imposed a new sense of space and time on their economies and their social life, gave new tasks to their municipalities, and determined the whole chronology of their urban growth. To Mathew Arnold they banished feudalism forever. The demands of the urban communities in turn – for enlarged access to the suburbs and places of recreation for their own provisioning, and for a return on their investments – made a difference in the quality of the services that could be provided. Their ultimate contributions to the efficiency of household management, the welfare of suburban families, the emancipation of women from an all-absorbing commitment to the home, were given first to the middle classes and did not begin to affect the working classes to any marked extent before the very end of the nineteenth century. For the latter, the initial impact of the railway was more often a blow than a blessing. In Britain, the demand of the railways for satisfactory termini was unequivocal. To reach these points they often had to destroy houses and other premises on a tremendous scale. By dislodging their occupants this action tended to start a chain reaction which subsided only when the last ripples of migration set off in this way were absorbed in the suburbs. In the larger cities these demolitions were augmented by others for street-widening, office-building, public works, and by the persistent tendency of high land values at the centre to cause the population to disperse for cheaper living room. From the 1860s the populations of these central districts were beginning to decline almost everywhere. The 'haussmanization' of Paris and the building of the boulevards performed a similar operation during the Second Empire. The urban freeway programme in the United States at the present day provides another echo.

8

These upheavals are a reminder that some of the most pervasive influences on the quality of urban life have been acts of government. Some have had direct consequences, for good or ill, that could scarcely have flowed from any other source, such as the whole programme of social welfare legislation which has slowly been unravelling itself in Britain since 1906 without ever quite ensuring for everyone a minimum acceptable standard of living. No doubt pensions, sickness pay, unemployment relief, even the workhouse, sometimes made grim realities endurable a little longer or took the edge off more desperate acts by unhappy people. The quality of urban housing, however, has never been ensured by legislation, nor sanitary codes kept by regulations. Indeed, from what we know of housing reform in England before 1914, we are bound to ask whether it had not made things worse in many places by forcing up tiny islands of decent standards here and there at the expense of the quality of housing round about – not to say disturbing the social ecology of the area in such a way as to intensify its worst tendencies. Condemning unsanitary dwellings and turning people out of doors usually meant aggravating the overcrowding nearby, and rehousing them has been difficult to do until comparatively recently, in part because the new rents either could not be afforded by those displaced or were felt too excessive to be met. In times of inflation the quality of working-class housing tends to deteriorate if only because working-class concepts of a fair rent drag behind their actual movements and families make do with less space than they should have. In many of the cities of Latin America and India the attempt at urban improvement is regularly being frustrated in another way: by squatters taking over cleared ground before any housing can be erected, creating thereby a political presence as well as a human demand.

These are, of course, no more than faint hints of governmental influence as well as impotence in relation to the quality of urban life on its lowest levels. Similarly, they are no more than the barest suggestions of how acts of amelioration have not always had their expected results. The historical record of governmental arbitrariness is actually far more extensive and indirect. It has been conducted by means of budgetary and fiscal measures that have been assuming more comprehensive forms virtually everywhere. The ultimate controls on the advance in the quality of urban life are being determined within fairly wide limits by governments, not only explicitly by discrete grants to various cultural organisations or massive allocations of funds to public systems of education and the like, but implicitly by every other way in which public money is spent. The latter includes global strategies of defence and trade and the extent to which resources are being made available to help poor countries whose needs are so much more acute.

In a more domestic sense, the very performance of government helps to distribute the cultural prizes unevenly. In Britain, the great divide is between north and south, between the kingdom of the government in London, with its crowded south-eastern hinterland of rolling suburbia and coastal resorts, the sunniest, most prosperous, most expensive and most densely settled region of the country to which industry is now gravitating more naturally than ever, and the old centre of the industrial revolution on both sides of the Pennines in the north, a more frequently depressed, more intricately textured, more independent country with its own distinct cultures. These sprang from great diversities of social structure and sheer native wit that produced across the country a rich variety of thrusting or conservative or purely supine elected councils that either put money into things or did not, whether it was a town hall, a sewage farm, or a processional avenue that would give mayor-making more style. In the course of the nineteenth century the metropolitan influence of London gradually enthralled all of them, and they are no longer so clearly distinguishable. Yet what has not happened is any devolution of metropolitan institutions. Whitehall has stayed intact. London first became a centre of conspicuous consumption during the seventeenth century because it held the Crown, the Court, the law, the government, parliament and the largest single share of the country's industry and trade. All this it has retained, and to it has now been added the nation's richest hoard of cultural treasures and treats and the fattest cornucopia of pleasures in the world. In one way much of this has come about by the sheer force of being a world city, but the foundations for it were being laid on an imperial basis late in Victoria's reign. No government since has acted with any resolution to reverse the provincial flow. When, by a purposeless stroke of government, performed in 1961 in the teeth of every outraged body of artistic opinion in the country, the very gateway to the northern provinces – Hardwick's classic Doric arch at Euston – was destroyed, it was as if the process had all the unstoppability of a ritual murder. Let the provinces stand back.

Looked at from this provincial corner in which I write, the quality of urban life is beginning to be influenced by more subtle metropolitan influences. We have been witnessing during the last few years a marked growth in immigration from the British Commonwealth, a kind of tidal movement flowing back from territories taken long ago and lately released from colonial dependence. This migration has produced in a number of cities in the Midlands and the North, as well as London, a new kind of social mass that is beginning to infuse into local affairs a new kind of problem – race relations. The historical perspective here is a long one, co-ordinate in many ways to that by which Britain's industrial cities must be seen. Both stem from the nineteenth century when commercial expansion overseas began to yield its first rich harvest for the industrial pioneer; and it is now that the full implications of this enrichment and the unconscious collection of an empire under the British Crown can be realised. What this has meant in terms of qualitative change cannot yet be properly grasped, for every large and conspicuous inflow of people from abroad in modern times has produced in the country a certain amount of emotional noise while it was taking place.

For the cities that have received substantial numbers of migrants, the impact on their cultural life has profound meaning, a meaning which only begins to become clearer as these communities endeavour to work out in quite pragmatic terms how to make urban society in Britain a composedly multiracial one. Leicester is among their company. In a different direction altogether, the approach to a solution of another crucial issue facing this city – as it does others – might have been clarified a little since I began to write. The future quality of urban life is much embroiled with the automobile, and now Leicester's planning officer has published his vision of the city at the end of the century. It is based on the first scientifically devised traffic plan, for any city, that says 'no' to the automobile. We now must wait to see whether the motor car will obey.

PART TWO

Transport and Urban Transformation

5

The objects of street improvement
in Regency and early Victorian London

The gradual acceptance by politically influential people of the belief that deliberate control of town growth was both feasible and fruitful is a theme in the history of town planning which has many aspects. The transformation of nineteenth-century cities by means of street improvement was one of these; and David Pinkney has recently made a mature assessment of the range of motives underlying the sweeping changes wrought in the configuration of Parisian streets under the Second Empire.[1] By contrast with Paris under the prefecture of Baron Haussmann, the transformation of London was tentative, not to say hesitating, and not undertaken for all the same reasons. In Paris, Pinkney has shown that political and strategic aims were mixed with desires for aesthetic and social amelioration. 'In London', Napoleon III is reported as saying, 'they are concerned only with giving the best possible satisfaction to the needs of traffic.' But were they? It is the purpose of this brief essay to comment on the validity of this assertion, and in doing so to illustrate an early approach to matters of urban improvement which are still at the heart of some contemporary town-planning problems.

1

The most dramatic scenic transformation of London before mid-century had occurred in the West End in the cutting of Regent Street after 1814. This was as much the personal triumph of John Nash's indispensable patron, the Prince Regent – later George IV – as it was a consummate display of his own architectural virtuosity. Even in its uncompleted state, Nash's plan was an unparalleled achievement which inevitably dwarfed the modest achievements which followed. But it was also different in another way. For its genesis, which dated from the end of the eighteenth century, lay quite simply in the determination of John Fordyce, as Surveyor-General of Crown Lands, to augment the Crown's landed revenues.

It was for this reason that Fordyce had first proposed, in 1793, the compilation of an accurate map of 'Marybone Park' and district (being the greatest of the Crown's metropolitan estates), which should form the basis of an open competition for the future development of that area.[2] His Majesty's Commissioners of Woods, Forests, and Land Revenues clarified these intentions when, in employing their own departmental architects to prepare schemes, they observed that

the present distance, and, in many parts, mean and inconvenient access, from Marybone Park to the parts of Westminster between that and the Thames, are manifest drawbacks the value of the Estate; and a more direct and commodious line of communication, while it would enhance that value, would also improve to a great extent that of other property, both of the Crown and Individuals, situated in the above district.[3]

Nash himself expressed a similar view when he said,

The main object of the Crown, I conceive to be, the Improvement of their own Estate, to augment and not to diminish it, and not to sell any part of it; a magnificent and convenient Street for the Public will be the result, not the cause . . . . If the whole Street had passed through Property not belonging to the Crown, it might become a nicer question, whether the object in view was commensurate with the expense . . . but it fortunately happens that four out of five of the property through which the Street will pass belong to the Crown, and the greater part of the rest to the Duke of Portland, who will be as much benefited as the Crown itself; seeing that it leads into the very heart of his best property, Portland Place, to which there is, at present, no appropriate access. The Crown property consists, principally, of old ruinous Houses laid out in narrow streets, the greater part not worth repair, many of them in ruins, the Leases of which are continually falling in; independently, therefore, of considerations belonging to Marybone Park, it would be the interest of the Crown, instead of renewing the Leases of these old Houses, to take them down, form a better arrangement of wider streets, and let the Ground on Building Leases.[4]

What sparked the tinder of the Prince Regent's architectural aspirations was apparently the increasing demand for houses in a crowded metropolis which the rapidly expanding suburbs only partly met. And what largely determined the locality of Regency street improvements was the distribution of Crown property, for these improvements were conducted as normal estate development, paid for out of the ordinary landed revenues.[5]

The line the new Regent Street actually took was, as John Summerson has pointed out, an empirical solution 'designed to steer between the Scylla of compensation and the Charybdis of inconvenience',[6] but it was nevertheless one which was entirely consistent with contemporary social arrangements. For it consciously confirmed the separation of social classes which had been implicitly determined by the existing street pattern: Nash himself stressed that

the whole Communication from Charing Cross to Oxford Street will be a boundary and complete separation between the Streets and Squares occupied by the Nobility and Gentry, and the narrow Streets and meaner Houses occupied by mechanics and the trading part of the community.[7]

Nash, it is clear, had no sanitary zeal for the clearance of slums for its own sake; his avowed intention was, on the contrary, to contain and not to disperse them. When James Elmes published his eulogy on metropolitan improvements in 1828 and spoke of 'the conversion of dirty alleys, dingy courts and squalid dens of misery and crime . . . into "stately streets",'[8] he was not, therefore, identifying the main purpose of Regency street improvements but one of their incidental consequences.

2

The somewhat inconspicuous years coming between the death of both Nash and his patron in the early 1830s and the birth of the Metropolitan Board of Works in 1856 were not devoid of street improvement: Farringdon Road, Commercial Street, New Oxford Street, Victoria Street and New Cannon Street were the most notable schemes either begun or completed during these years. Moreover, this was a period of not inconsiderable industry in the preparation and examination of scores of concrete proposals for both trifling and dramatic changes in the street plan of central London. Between 1832 and 1851 a succession of parliamentary select committees issued between them some fifteen reports covering a wide variety of these schemes, of which twelve were ultimately carried through in modified form. This industrious planning involved the redevelopment of extensive areas, and although many schemes failed to pass the fine sieve of financial expediency, the evaluation of alternative proposals provides an adequate commentary on attitudes towards both the function and the mechanism of street improvement.

3

It is this evidence on the motivation of early Victorian street improvements which is at such variance with Napoleon's view. For even the most casual reading of these reports reveals the concern felt on all sides at the demonstrable relationship between housing conditions and public health; and, what is more, an examination of this evidence also shows the marked extent to which 'improvers' relied on street improvement as the adjusting mechanism.

The Commissioners of Sewers for Finsbury, for example, wrote to the Privy Council in 1835 to say that an extension of Farringdon Street would not only provide a trunk route right through Central London to St George's Fields in Southwark and thus provide an excellent means of communication between north and south London, but added that such an improvement was 'far more important as relating to the health of that part of the capital through which it would be made, by the removal of a description of buildings that have long been a hotbed of disease, misery and crime'.[9] Similar officials in Westminster evidently shared such views in respect of the proposed New Oxford Street through St Giles'.[10] As for the future Charing Cross Road, a resident of Bedford Square declared that its traversing Seven Dials 'appears so necessary that almost every person in London, who has submitted any plan of improvement in that part of the town, has adopted the same plan'.[11]

This general attitude was explicitly stated by the Select Committee of 1838 in its second report: the Committee did not 'confine themselves to the single purpose of obtaining increased facilities of communication' but considered that 'other public benefits might in some cases be derived simultaneously with that principal object',[12] in particular the partial clearance of the 'Rookery' of St Giles' by means of an extension of Oxford Street to Hart Street.[13] They based these conclusions on a mass of evidence they had taken on the desirability of promoting such street improvement schemes as improved both public health and morals, and they had been regaled by first-hand accounts of the brutish horrors of slum life in various parts of central London. It was hardly surprising, therefore, that they insisted that

the most important improvements . . . are in direct proportion to the degree in which they embrace all the great purposes of amendment in respect of health and morals . . . by the removal of congregations of vice and misery, and the introduction of a better police.[14]

The acceptance of this rough-and-ready criterion of desirability in street improvements naturally affected both the layout of new streets and the degrees of priority accorded to different schemes. Thus it was that when, for reasons of financial expediency,[15] the programme of improvements had to be drastically reduced, schemes were judged according to

several objects of public utility, viz. 1. The opening or enlarging of communications for the general convenience of public intercourse; 2. The improvement of certain districts, of which the present state is greatly injurious to the health of the inhabitants; 3. The melioration of the moral conditions of the labouring classes closely congregated in such districts.[16]

More than this, the line taken by new streets was generally determined by its effectiveness in clearing as many slum dwellings as possible. When James Pennethorne, whose early training had been under Nash, was being closely questioned by the Royal Commission on Metropolitan Improvements in 1845 on his choice of the line for the future Victoria Street, he was asked,

But you did not look to the means of local communication, or of architectural ornament or development?

His answer was,

No; I regarded solely the sanatory question. My object has only been to ascertain how best to improve the condition of the inhabitants of Westminster by improving the buildings, the levels, and the sewers, and by opening communications through the most crowded parts.[17]

The Commissioners evidently endorsed Pennethorne's proposals, for in justifying a slight modification of the memorialists' original scheme they pointed out that

its effect has been to divert the channel of communication in a direction further south, into a more imperfectly drained, a more densely peopled, and consequently a more objectionable portion of the district.[18]

4

The objects of street improvement in early Victorian London were seldom single, for street improvement during these years provided almost the only effective way of rectifying on a grand scale some of the worst features of urban growth.[19] The disjointed maze of streets in central London was not only inefficient for transport and frustrating for the police but prodigal of human life. Thus, street improvement became not merely a method of increasing the circulation of traffic but a blunt, though seemingly effective, instrument of slum clearance. The naïve expectation that, merely by redrawing the street map of London at key points, both the traffic and slum problems could be solved together had, it is true, a short life, while the problems themselves have had unwanted longevity. But while this hope prevailed schemes for street improvement were scrutinised for their effectiveness in ventilating the rookeries of central London.

What chiefly distinguished Parisian and London street improvements in this respect was not so much their sanitary aims, nor their conspicuous failure to obliterate slums (which were generally merely displaced, often in aggravated forms, to other localities),[20] but the size of the budgets available to each, and the powers exercised by the planning authorities. For, unlike the grandiose schemes of Napoleon III which, by importunate borrowing and dubious book-keeping, could tap not only the savings of private investors but the vast reservoir of imperial funds,[21] the schemes of early Victorian London had to be financed by borrowing on the open market, and not by subventions from the State. But the creation of an authority able to use the draconian measures of the Second Empire involved political decisions which were quite alien to the temperament which had produced the pusillanimous Metropolitan Board of Works.[22] *The Times*, envious of the Parisian street improvements, was apparently prepared in 1861 for the creation of an authority which 'would have strength enough to double the work of Hercules, and to cleanse not only the filthy stables, but the river which runs through them'.[23] Two cardinal tenets of contemporary Liberal faith were, however, the need for scrupulous governmental economy and the avoidance of transfer payments in all schemes of social reform.[24] Street improvement was, it is true, already forcing some people to re-examine their political axioms and to advocate principles of public finance and administration which would permit current social problems to be tackled realistically;[25] but, until these new concepts of social obligation had been fashioned and accepted, schemes for public betterment like street improvement were bound to be limited both financially and administratively. Commenting on the finance of Parisian street improvements, a legislator of the old school told the British Association in 1863:

The state has come to the assistance of the city in this matter; but it can only be by casting the burthen upon the taxpayers of the country generally – a course which may be tolerated in a highly centralized country, like France, where, in fact, Paris is everything, and the rest of the nation nothing in comparison with it – but which would hardly be tolerated in England, where we pride ourselves on making every place pay for its own improvements.[26]

5

Street improvement in early Victorian London had, therefore, to serve more than one end: the premium which financial expediency placed on proposals which were aimed solely at solving traffic problems, caused street improvement to be identified during these years in the twin role of improving both communications and public health.

6

Workmen's fares in south London, 1860–1914

'I am quite sure', Mr A. J. Balfour told the House of Commons in May 1900,

that the remedy for the great disease of overcrowding is not to be found in dealings, however drastic, with insanitary areas. If you can accommodate by raising the height of your buildings, a larger population on a given area, well and good. But if you cannot do that, then you must go outside the narrow area at the centre of your congested district, and you must trust to modern inventions and modern improvements in locomotion for abolishing time.[1]

Almost all the major problems confronting his generation of Londoners had arisen from the extremely rapid rate at which London had grown during the previous half-century. Not least among these was the problem of eradicating the teeming slums which bordered the central reaches of the Thames and sprawled, on its southern bank, over the flat alluvium areas of Bermondsey, Walworth, Kennington, North Lambeth, and beyond. It is in this context, as a corollary to the housing problem of Victorian London, that workmen's fares on trains and trams should be viewed. They played perhaps the most significant role of all in the solution of these difficulties, and in contributing markedly to the pace and direction taken by suburban development in the generation before 1914. It is the purpose of this essay to examine the origins and extension of workmen's fares in south London in Victorian and Edwardian times, and to suggest the part played by them in these wider developments.[2]

1

By the end of the century few illusions lingered on the inappropriateness of the remedies so far applied to the housing problem. There had been, for example, the phase of 5 per cent philanthropy, when model dwellings – the Model Industrial Dwellings which General Booth had roundly condemned as being 'only a slight advance upon the Union Bastille'[3] – were run, in 1875, by some twenty-eight different organisations and individuals. In south London, six separate groups did much to alleviate conditions here and there.[4] The tenement blocks administered by these organisations had admittedly quadrupled average population densities on their sites and introduced more healthy living conditions.[5] These charitable efforts had been supplemented since the early 1850s by a string of acts regulating overcrowding, cellar dwellings and other insanitary property.[6] Municipal authorities, too, had attempted to rehouse the inhabitants of slums which had been split open by new thoroughfares and railway clearances in central London.[7] This had been in response to the pleas of men of responsibility like George Godwin, the first editor of *The Builder*, who had asked as early as 1845 for more 'doing' and less talking about rehousing dispossessed inhabitants.[8] At about the same time, Charles Knight could not resist the succinct comment, when describing Elizabethan suburban slums, '*We* occasionally sweep away the wretched dens, hidden in back courts and alleys, where the poor are smothered; but far too rarely do we make any provision for them.'[9] Lord Derby, Lord Shaftesbury and the Bishop of London each made eloquent speeches on the results of street demolitions in the Lords' debate on metropolitan railways in February 1861.[10] And, as the inhabitants of notorious districts like Seven Dials and Clare Market spilled over into the surrounding neighbourhoods and aggravated the congestion there, the evidence of the Blue Books and the writings of sympathisers brought to light the pernicious effects of an inadequate approach to the problems of congestion, which had been multiplied by street improvements and railway clearances.[11] The problem reached a wide audience. Léon Faucher, at one extreme, brought a foreigner's perspicacity to bear on the matter in his *Études sur l'Angleterre*, published in 1856. Arthur Morrison, at the other extreme, set fictitious events in scenes of awful reality to show, in his *Child of the Jago*, which appeared in 1896, how new slums rivalling the old sprang up when areas were only partially cleared. In fact, the building of blocks of model dwellings aggravated overcrowding in adjoining neighbourhoods because the displaced inhabitants merely moved into nearby streets.

Clearly, these voluntary and municipal remedies for the housing congestion of central London were mere palliatives, and the great and charitable efforts of these bodies inevitably enjoyed only limited success. At best, they diminished the discomforts of overcrowding,[12] but even this was achieved only with increasing difficulty as the cost of rehousing in central London was forced up to prohibitive levels by the competition of business firms and government offices for the limited and increasingly valuable ground space. In effect, no real solution of the housing question had been found, since there was little, if any, increase in the accommodation provided.[13] A spokesman for the London working class asked, in 1883, 'Would it not be far wiser and more judicious to encourage migration and emigration from districts where there is a congestion of labour, rather than attempt to improve the surroundings of the latter?'[14] The solution which he was proposing to the housing problem was in reality an improvement in suburban transport facilities. This was an approach to the question which, though not new,[15] became increasingly obvious as alternative solutions were tried and failed. Mr Balfour was in fact echoing an idea which was by 1900 winning increasing support on all sides. In 1902, the Sub-Committee on Locomotion of the Browning Hall Conference, for example, made the case of south London quite plain when it reported that

If a comparison be made it would seem that the needs of South London are greater than those of the North. Central South London offers the worst examples of over-population; and, nevertheless, the remedy is near at hand, for there is much available building space in Outer South London which might take the surplus population.[16]

2

The history of the 'parliamentary train' after Gladstone's Act of 1844 is well known.[17] The requirement of Section 6 was that all passenger railway companies should every weekday run at least one train over the whole length of their lines at a speed of not less than twelve miles in the hour, including stops at all stations, at the maximum fare of a penny a mile. There were also certain stipulations about passenger accommodation and luggage. In return for these concessions, companies were relieved under Section 9 of the passenger tax on all third-class journeys on 'parliamentary trains'. Between 1832 and 1842 this tax had been at the rate of a halfpenny a mile for every four passengers, amounting to an eighth of a penny per passenger mile; and for the next two years was at the rate of 5 per cent on all fares,[18] a tax which Sir Robert Peel admitted to introducing 'with a sense of humiliation'.[19] The Board of Trade had been authorised at the same time to dispense at its own discretion with any of the requirements for third-class travel, but was not allowed to alter the mileage rate. It had accordingly dispensed with the stopping requirement, though this was challenged in the courts and overruled.[20]

The provision of third-class fares at penny-a-mile rates was not sufficient impetus, however, for the outward migration of the inhabitants of the congested central districts. The working classes remained firmly rooted to the old areas of settlement near the river, for a number of good reasons. It was not that charity or rehousing schemes materially hindered their migration to the suburbs, as the Metropolitan Board of Works and others had believed,[21] for the people who occupied the model dwellings on the site of demolished slums were very seldom the same as those originally displaced.[22] Suburban life was not an unmitigated blessing. Expensive meals away from home, longer working hours, the absence of cheap suburban sales of fish and meat as at Smithfield and Billingsgate,[23] the loss of the society of friends in a community where length of residence increased the chances of help in times of trouble,[24] and the lack of congenial company and amusements,[25] all lessened the recognised advantages of improved health and better housing in the suburbs. According to Lord Shaftesbury, wives were far less inclined to remove a distance than men, since by doing so they forfeited extra earnings from charring and washing which usually amounted to three or four shillings a week.[26] A family which moved only two miles lost these tangible advantages: correspondence was cumbersome and visiting an extravagance on a twenty-shillings-a-week budget, out of which one-third was earmarked for rent. Thus, even the strongest ties soon weakened and old associations were forgotten.[27] Above all, the imperative necessity of men living near their work when this was casually obtained had long been recognised.[28] Finally, the cost of the daily journey to work was too high at penny-a-mile rates for most of the working class. Of those who had migrated to the suburbs, large numbers in the 1880s wished to return to their old areas.[29] A painter who had migrated to Battersea at this time for the health of his family found himself decidedly worse off after four months and had to return.[30] Miss Octavia Hill considered that substantial numbers wished to return because of travelling expenses.[31] Clearly, a mass movement of the working classes into the suburbs, without which no real solution to the problem of central London slums could be worked out, awaited the wide adoption of really cheap fares.

The daily fare to and from work had to be a matter of a very few pence at the most. Workmen's trains which met this condition were being operated in the North from as early as 1852 on a section of the Stockton and Darlington Railway, and special concessionary rates were not uncommon in some mining districts.[32] In London, the Metropolitan Railway Company voluntarily introduced workmen's fares in 1864, over eighteen months before it was statutorily compelled to do so, on its Moorgate extension which was opened in 1865.[33] It thus had the distinction of being the first London line to introduce workmen's fares, for the workmen's trains on the Metropolitan Extension of the London, Chatham, and Dover Railway were not running until February 1865.[34] In fact, an act authorising these lines had been passed in 1860, and this provided for workmen's fares on services between Victoria and Ludgate Hill.[35] When services began in 1864, a daily train was provided from each terminus, starting at 4.55 a.m., and finishing the journey by 6.0 a.m.; a return train left at 6.15 p.m., and on Saturdays at 2.30 p.m. A rigid requirement was that only artisans, mechanics and daily labourers, both male and female, were to be carried, whose shilling weekly tickets were to show the name and address of the employer. Another early cheap fares concession by this company was granted to the Penge tenants of the Metropolitan Association for Improving Dwellings of Industrious Classes, who were able to make the daily journey to work in London for two shillings a week.[36] Under Section 134 of the London, Chatham, and Dover Railway (New Lines) Act of 1864,[37] the company was also required to run one train daily from Loughborough and Peckham Junctions to Ludgate Hill, the up journey to take place before 7 a.m., and the return to be permitted after 6 p.m.; the fare was a penny in each direction. The London, Brighton, and South Coast Railway, as lessees of the East London Railway line to New Cross, were required by the East London Railway Act, 1865,[38] to run a daily train on similar conditions between New Cross and Liverpool Street when this line was opened.[39] The South Eastern Railway voluntarily issued workmen's tickets on the Woolwich line before the end of 1868.[40] North of the Thames the Great Eastern Railway issued workmen's tickets from Bethnal Green Junction to Stoke Newington from 1872, and from Liverpool Street on its opening in 1874.[41]

All this preceded the passage of the Cheap Trains Act in 1883, which repealed the passenger duty on all penny-a-mile fares, and at the same time compelled the railway companies to introduce workmen's fares as and when required by the Board of Trade. At the time when these general and compulsory powers were enacted, six companies in London were already required to run workmen's trains at specially cheap fares. Although the statutory requirements amounted to only eleven trains at that date, ten times that number were actually running. Thirteen workmen's trains were being run by the London, Chatham, and Dover Railway, and thirty-two by the London, Brighton, and South Coast Railway, although the statutory requirements were only one in each case; while the London and South Western Railway was operating twelve and the South Eastern Railway two workmen's trains, without any statutory requirements at all.[42] Some idea of the traffic volume of workmen's trains before the passage of the Cheap Trains Act can be obtained from the figure of 182,513 workmen's tickets issued during 1882 on the South Eastern Railway alone. The total number of daily return workmen's tickets issued in London in 1882 was 7,152,923,[43] representing an average daily rate of 25,671.[44]

The Cheap Trains Act was undoubtedly designed, as the LCC Committee on Public Health and Housing put it in 1891, for 'further encouraging the migration of the working classes into the suburbs' in order to relieve the central housing congestion.[45] Although it was in a sense directly due to the recommendations of the Select Committee on Artizans' and Labourers' Dwellings Improvement Act in 1882, which recommended that similar conditions to those then in operation on the Great Eastern Railway should be enforced as the opportunities presented themselves,[46] it was also the product of the Travelling Tax Abolition Committee.[47] This body, which was formed under the leadership of G. J. Holyoake[48] in 1877, vigorously pursued the object of rectifying the inconsistency that the passenger tax still applied to all trains other than those which complied with the stopping requirement, even though it may have been possible to travel on them at penny-a-mile fares. The committee was formed in response to an observation made in parliament that no committee representing the working class had asked for the repeal of this tax, whose burden fell heavily on them. It organised memorials, arranged interviews with ministers, petitioned parliament, held public meetings and published a stream of pamphlets and other literature, including a *Gazette*,[49] and continued its activities for some years after 1883 in the hope of ridding the railways of all taxation.[50]

The extension of workmen's fares after the passage of the Cheap Trains Act came to depend on the degree of pressure which various groups were able to bring to bear on the Board of Trade, which, with the Railway and Canal Commission, had been given powers by the act to fix reasonable fares, and on the attitude adopted by these departments towards the railway companies themselves. There were two objects of criticism. The first and more easily sustained criticisms were levelled at the time and scope of the services and some of the conditions of issue. The second, which met considerable opposition from the railway companies themselves, was aimed at the level of fares.

Nine years after 1883 many more workmen's trains were being provided than had been available before the requirement to run these services had become general. By 1892,[51] the London and South Western Railway was issuing tickets from thirty-six stations, the most distant of which was Weybridge, nineteen miles from Waterloo. Workmen's trains on this line were generally punctual, and the intervals of service and time limits were varied skilfully to suit local requirements. Tickets were issued either daily or weekly, according to the zone, the latter type being confined to the more distant stations: these return or weekly season tickets on workmen's trains were not optional alternatives, and these conditions of issue were sharply criticised by weekly-ticket holders who were occasionally prevented from making regular daily journeys.[52] Third-class season tickets were also issued at many stations on this line, and were often preferred by workmen since they were usually as cheap as, and sometimes cheaper than, workmen's tickets themselves. They were, however, not as popular as they might have been because half a crown had to be deposited on issue. The South Eastern Railway issued workmen's tickets from seventeen stations on its lines out as far as Dartford, seventeen miles from the terminus. But the Public Health and Housing Committee of the LCC considered these services to be inadequate and unsatisfactory. Only four up trains and only one down were provided; a single train started outside the LCC area. One good feature of cheap travel on this line was the extent to which third-class season tickets were issued. The daily rates of such tickets were not infrequently lower than workmen's fares, and in the case of Dartford the workmen's ticket actually cost 17 per cent more than the daily rate for the quarterly third-class season ticket.

The London, Chatham, and Dover Railway ran workmen's services to twenty stations, the most distant being Penge, seven and a quarter miles from Ludgate Hill Station. The rates per mile were high when compared with other lines: for example, tickets issued to and from Elephant and Castle were at the mileage rate of 8d, and to Borough Road at the rate of 1.33d, the latter actually exceeding the Parliamentary rate. This company was the only one still insisting in 1892 on *bona fide* workmen, who were liable to be required to give the name and address of their employers when applying for tickets. The most liberal provision of workmen's trains was made by the London, Brighton, and South Coast Railway, which issued workmen's tickets from thirty-seven stations, as far south as South Croydon, eleven and a half miles from London Bridge. Forty-six stations were interconnected locally for workmen's trains. The LCC, which was intimately concerned with the spreading of the working-class area farther afield, was understandably critical of the overall provision of workmen's tickets in south London. It recommended the setting up of a fare zone system covering radii of five, ten and fifteen miles, in order that the housing congestion in the central area should be dissipated as speedily as possible.[53] The Public Health and Housing Committee of the Council made the same point the following year, and resolved that

having regard to the urgent necessity which exists for further encouraging the migration of the working classes into the suburbs, the Committee be authorized to select the most suitable instances in which they think action is desirable, and to address a letter to the Board of Trade on the lines of the report, asking that Board to use its power to obtain an increase in the number of trains, a prolongation of the hours during which the trains run, increased uniformity of fares, and a more convenient and uniform system of tickets.[54]

James Hole, the celebrated writer on working-class housing problems, was, in contrast, less moderate and stated in the same year that he saw no reason why all trains should not be workmen's trains.[55]

Nevertheless, by 1894 a considerable expansion in workmen's services had taken place, as the table shows on page 94. A notable improvement in workmen's facilities by this date was the fact that workmen's tickets were available on any train before 7.30 a.m. on the London and South Western Railway and the City and South London Railway.

The LCC was was not yet satisfied that sufficient services were being run to encourage rapid working-class migration to the suburbs. Workmen themselves joined with the LCC in pressing the Board of Trade to be more vigorous in its demands on the railway companies. In 1896 the Board of Trade therefore circularised the railway companies to discover what new facilities had been provided. Their replies revealed that very little had been done by some of the companies. Workmen could now generally return by any train on the day of issue, and the London and South Western Railway had gone so far as to allow workmen's fares on trains arriving up to 8 o'clock,[56] though the London, Brighton, and South Coast Railway had

Company	Workmen's tickets issued, 1893	Numbers of up trains 1894	1890
LC & D Railway	1,563,850	21	17
Met. & Dist. Railway	55,512 (est)[1]	8	5
LB & SC Railway	2,145,115[2]	43	36
L & SW Railway	1,924,830[3]	126	86
SE Railway	584,804	10	6
City & S London Railway	unavailable	23	–
Totals	6,772,899	231	150

Notes:
1. During September and October 1893 the figures for traffic on the sections of the line south of the river were 15,763 out of a total of 284,901. The proportion of 4.5% has been assumed to be true in relation to the total traffic volume of 1,223,700 for the whole year.
2. The original figure has been halved to bring it to the common denominator of tickets issued rather than double journeys completed.
3. 65,329 weekly tickets have been multiplied by six to give daily equivalent. 470,861 daily tickets out of a total of 1,532,856 were issued from Clapham Junction to Waterloo alone.

Source: *Parliamentary Papers*, 1894, LXXV (C. 7541). This return gives workmen's fares and number of trains available from each station at which workmen's tickets were issued.

rejected this innovation as likely to lead to big losses in revenue. They may have been justified on this point, for when, in 1900, the South Eastern and Chatham Railway introduced workmen's tickets on the North Kent, Mid-Kent and Greenwich lines, ordinary passenger bookings fell by £4,000: it is true that this was compensated by workmen's tickets receipts of £4,500, but the extra operating costs in conveying the additional 800,000 passengers may easily have offset this.[57]

Although organised labour then represented only a fraction of total workmen passengers, a survey of their travel requirements by the LCC in 1897 clearly indicated how inadequate workmen's services were on the main line railways in south London at that time. One hundred and sixty-seven trade societies or branches with nearly 160,000 members were approached. It was estimated that the total number of workers in the area was about 330,000. Assuming the same proportion of these made daily journeys as did the members of the unions approached (25.3 per cent), some 105,000 travelled daily, for whom ninety-nine daily workmen's trains with seating accommodation for 43,000 actually ran.[58] On this estimate, double the accommodation provided was actually required, a situation which appears to have been more or less true in all areas served by the main line companies. There were, inevitably, complaints of overcrowding in carriages as a result of this situation.[59] The Statistical Officer to the LCC pointed out that, although accommodation provided by workmen's trains was increasing, more and more workers were settling around Vauxhall, Queen's Road, Battersea and Clapham Junction, because fares were still too high for them to be able to afford to live farther out.[60] A general extension of the hours of service to 8 o'clock was also considered likely to promote an extension of the suburban area by permitting other classes of workers to take advantage of the services: Section 3, Sub-section (*b*), of the 1883 Act had provided for this change where a real need existed, and a Board of Trade report issued before the passage of the act had also referred to the need for it.[61] It was with this idea that a Cheap Trains (London) Bill was promoted in 1889 to force all railway companies having central London termini to issue workmen's tickets at halfpenny-a-mile rates on trains arriving up to 8 a.m. from all stations within a twelve-mile radius; but the bill was lost on the second reading the following year.[62] The idea of workmen's tickets being generally available on trains up to 8 o'clock was not altogether lost, however, and the Battersea Vestry, prompted by the London Committee for the Extension of Workmen's Trains, was one of several local bodies which urged the case.[63] The special case of women workers who had to wait long periods before admission to their workplaces was taken up in order to secure for them accommodation on trains up to 8.30 a.m., but this was unsuccessful.[64]

In 1898 and 1899, numerous applications were made by individuals, reform associations and municipal authorities for improved facilities.[65] In particular, the London Reform Union, led by Sydney Buxton, conducted a vigorous campaign for the meeting of workmen's needs, and brought a number of successful cases in the courts to compel the railway companies to increase workmen's facilities. Sometimes, voluntary concessions were obtained and, at other times, public inquiries were held by the Railway and Canal Commission.[66] General concessions were obtained on services from Penge, Greenwich, Maze Hill, Plumstead and Blackheath, and between Ludgate Hill and Victoria. The National Association for the Extension of Workmen's Fares also successfully campaigned for reductions in fares from Earlsfield, Southfields and Putney to Waterloo, and for other concessions on the East Dulwich line from London Bridge. The Fawcett Association represented the special demands of the Post Office workers and employees in the London markets, particularly on the line from Croydon to Victoria. The Postmen's Federation, too, made special demands, particularly for an early train from Kennington Oval on the City and South London Line to King William Street: this was at first refused on the grounds that the line had to be closed for repairs, but was afterwards allowed.[67]

A number of private individuals and M.P.s also made specific requests for the extension of workmen's services. A memorial from workmen in 1884 requesting an improved service from Penge resulted in a further train being put on, while a similar result followed the complaint of a Woolwich inhabitant the following year. The London, Brighton, and South Coast Railway agreed to run two extra trains from Thornton Heath in 1898 and five years later another from Thornton Heath, Selhurst and Norwood Junction. Bromley, Bickley and Kent House services were provided by the London, Chatham, and Dover Railway, and services to Clock House by the South Eastern Railway on the representations of the local MP and the Beckenham UDC. An outlying service between Gravesend and Dartford was agreed to by the South Eastern Railway on the application of a private individual in 1898. Typical of municipal action of this kind was the resolution forwarded to the Board of Trade as the outcome of a conference on the subject convened by the Fulham Vestry, and widely attended by delegates from south of the Thames. Here the request was for later workmen's trains.[68]

Despite the south London railway companies' apparent readiness to comply with most reasonable requests, the unequal provision of cheap trains was by 1904 beginning to lead to uneven population densities, and complaints were heard that the Cheap Trains Act had failed to fulfil its purpose.[69] The recommendation that workmen's trains should be provided to encourage suburban settlement[70] was hardly favoured by the railway companies who were already sustaining heavy losses in many well-established districts. The London, Brighton, and South Coast Railway, for example, calculated that the average running cost per workmen's train mile was 4s 3d against the average receipts of 3s 1¼d.[71] The suggestion that workmen's trains should be subsidised by the municipality in order to encourage suburban migration was also unpopular in another quarter.[72] In 1905, a select committee recommended that where insufficient traffic existed for the normal provision of workmen's trains in a new locality, powers should be given to a statutory tribunal to compel the issue of workmen's tickets in selected trains.[73]

The readiness with which railway companies in south London generally met demands for more workmen's trains or for small alterations in running arrangements was not matched by their willingness to lower fares or to alter their rates, as the Public Health and Housing Committee of the LCC concluded in 1896.[74] An MP in the debate on an amending Cheap Trains Bill in 1900 asked,

If you do not provide cheap workmen's trains in order to carry them to and from their place of residence, how are they to travel? It has never been taken into consideration what is the rate of wages of the men who have to travel by these trains. Many of these workmen do not earn more than 16s. a week, and out of that they have to pay 3s., 4s., or 5s. a week for travelling.[75]

This was an exaggeration, but it could easily be shown that, despite the extension of services, the aim of scattering the working classes over a wider area had not yet been achieved. It had been recognised by the Royal

Commission on the Housing of the Working Classes of 1884–5 that workmen's fares should not be greater than the difference between rents of working-class homes in London and the suburbs.[76] More accurately, the money spent by the suburban worker on fares had to amount to something less than the difference between urban and suburban costs of living, including rent. In 1908, it was estimated that the combined rent and retail price index for the Central Area of London was 99, for the Middle Area (south-west) 99 and (south-east) 97, and for the Outer Area 100; Croydon was 99.[77] When the margin was so small as this, it was imperative that workmen's fares should be very low indeed if they were to have the effect of encouraging working-class migration into the suburbs. By 1906, cheap fares were clearly recognised as the most effective measure for getting the working classes out of the congested districts, but none of the experiments so far had succeeded to any appreciable extent, except in the case of the twopenny workmen's, for example on the South London Line from London Bridge via Brixton and Battersea to Victoria.[78]

This is quite clear from the concentration of working-class inhabitants round railway stations on the London, Brighton, and South Coast Railway. The Workmen's Trains Inquiry of the LCC, which reported in 1898, clearly showed how the working classes were then concentrated mostly within the orbit of the South London line, and more thinly in districts served by the line through New Cross, Forest Hill, West Norwood, Balham and Clapham Junction. A third route through East Dulwich, Streatham, Penge and Anerley served areas in which the working classes were far less numerous.[79] In view of the tendency for rents to rise when transport developments reached the point at which suburban migration had been accelerated, it is significant that the lowest average rents ruled in the south-western and south-eastern districts, which were not served by workmen's trains at all.[80] That the development of these suburbs was retarded may partly be explained by the relatively limited scope of the twopenny fare in south London. In north London, the distance which could be travelled on workmen's trains in 1905 at this fare was about eleven miles, in west London nearly twelve miles, in east London well over twenty-one miles. In south-east London the comparable distance was about eight and a half miles, and in south-west London under eight miles. There was little doubt that the working man was not likely to migrate to the suburbs for the sake of the amenities alone, but needed an economic incentive in the form of cheaper fares.[81] The Statistical Officer to the LCC was undoubtedly right when he pointed out that existing workmen's train services could not be regarded as giving free play to migrational tendencies when fares were, in fact, very close to ordinary third-class rates, which held out no special inducements to working men.[82] He strongly recommended offering the same inducements, in lower fares all round, as existed in north-east London.[83] When he spoke of the negative effect of merely cheap fares in the distribution of population, this is the consideration he clearly had in mind.[84]

The use to which differential fares rates might be put had been recognised by the LCC a few years before.[85] It was observed in 1902 that unequal rates had had the effect of guiding the outward flow of suburban migrants into the cheapest channels instead of diffusing them equally in all desirable directions.[86] This had resulted in traffic congestion and overcrowding appearing in the suburbs themselves. Cheap fares, if of less than universal application, merely contributed to displaced congestion. The natural desire to control the level of fares in order to exert a qualitative control on suburban expansion was a new departure in town planning.[87]

By 1912, the cheap fare was clearly recognised as a factor of outstanding importance in governing the distribution of the population. The twopenny return fare was then regarded as being within the reach of the largest body of workers, while fourpence was regarded as the maximum.[88] The geographical limits to these fares tended to remain fairly stable. Describing an imaginary arc from west to east, the limits of the twopenny return workmen's fare in 1912 were: Battersea Park Road (SE & CR), Clapham Junction (L & SWR), Clapham Common (C & SLR), Herne Hill (SE & CR), South Bermondsey (LB & SCR), Southwark Park (SE & CR) and Surrey Docks (ELR). The limits of the fourpenny return took in a much larger area: Battersea Park, Clapham Junction, Tooting Junction, Selhurst, Crystal Palace (LB & SCR); Putney and Southfields (L & SWR); Crystal Palace, Woodside, Kent House, Catford, Greenwich Park and Plumstead (SE & CR).

The proportion of workmen's trains passengers to total ordinary passengers had, by 1912, reached a comparatively high figure in the London area. These proportions were, respectively, 25.1 per cent on the South-Eastern and Chatham Railway, 18.2 per cent on the London, Brighton, and South Coast Railway, and 25.6 per cent on the London and South Western Railway. Workmen's tickets were at that date most numerous in the six-to-eight mile and eight-to-ten mile zones, being here nearly 40 per cent and 35 per cent of the total tickets issued respectively. Although the numbers of ordinary tickets and workmen's tickets issued were increasing most rapidly in the twelve-to-fifteen mile zone between 1907 and 1911, ordinary tickets there outnumbered workmen's by nearly five to one.[89]

Finally, it is necessary to recognise that the tramways had been operating workmen's services of considerable importance since their inception, both inside and outside the county boundary. In short, they had always been statutorily obliged to run certain workmen's trams, and when their operation was taken over by the LCC,[90] workmen's fares were used to encourage suburban migration of the working classes still more. By 1895, workmen's trams were, in general, operating smoothly and adequately throughout most of south London, complaints of overcrowding were not frequent on most routes, and ten years later almost 300 workmen's trams made daily journeys.[91] In 1895, the most frequent services were on the route from North Street, Wandsworth, to the Hop Exchange and to Westminster Bridge, both of which were usually seriously overcrowded. By 1905 the heaviest workmen's trams traffic was on the routes from New Cross Gate and Tooting to Blackfriars Bridge. It is significant to note that passengers were not always more numerous on the morning up journeys. For example, the Rye Lane to St George's Church service took only nine passengers up but returned with twenty, on the average, while the service from the 'Lord Wellington' to St George's Church carried sixty-five passengers up and seventy-eight down. These figures serve to show the important fact that not all traffic, by any means, went up from the outer suburbs, but that there was, too, a considerable volume of cross-traffic and down-traffic. Some of the latter was, no doubt, merely the continuation of journeys begun on the north side of the river, but some was attributable to working-class concentrations still in existence in the central areas. Workmen's fares on trams were generally much lower than those on railways: by 1912 the limit of the twopenny workmen's tram fare was the county boundary itself.

3

It has not been possible within the scope of this essay to do more than suggest the kind of contribution which cheap fares made to south London's suburban development within the fifty or more years under review. There is an obvious enough correspondence between the perceptible quickening of the pace of suburban development from the 1880s and the general and compulsory introduction of workmen's fares on the railways in 1883. The population of central London, which had been declining since 1861, fell particularly rapidly from the 1880s,[92] a fact which a contemporary statistician[93] and numerous witnesses at parliamentary inquiries[94] related to the growth of the surrounding districts. Unfortunately, it is not possible to assess quantitatively the contribution which workmen's fares made to this migration of south Londoners, for two main reasons. First, the Registration Districts on which the census returns were based are too large, straddling any useful boundaries which might be drawn, to study narrow regional developments; the decennial figures, too, are awkward data for testing the effects of the gradual extension of workmen's fares which we have been examining. Secondly, although it is possible to identify the chief factors affecting suburban migration, it is not possible in each case to isolate them for separate study. The effects of workmen's fares mingled with those of the general development of suburban transport, and with those of the decline in the central market for casual labour, the shortening of working hours from the 1870s onwards, which permitted the suburban dweller to enjoy the amenities of a suburban house at the cost of extra travelling time, and the general rise in working-class incomes out of which additional fares could be met. But it is still possible to recognise in workmen's fares a most significant factor in the southern expansion of London. Indeed, it has been pointed out that, by 1912, about a quarter of all suburban rail passengers were workmen's ticket holders, and that in the six-to-eight mile zone 40 per cent of all tickets issued were workmen's. It seems reasonable to conclude that workmen's fares broke down at least some of the economic obstacles to working-class suburban migration, and thus helped to provide a solution to London's more pressing housing problems, which had become particularly acute in the last quarter of the nineteenth century.

It is also clear that in contributing to rapid suburban growth, particularly after the First World War, workmen's fares helped to create fresh problems, both in the new areas and in the old. These were of two kinds. First, the very speed at which suburban expansion occurred accelerated the rate at which the older, central areas deteriorated. Since railways had first made their mid-Victorian contribution to spacious suburban living there had been a marked tendency towards social segregation. The retreat of the rich, or, more accurately, of the middle classes, and the unfortunate effects of the isolation of the poor, were clear enough to many contemporaries, from Disraeli in *Sybil* (1845) to C. F. G. Masterman in *The Condition of England* (1909).[95] The constant migration of the middle classes towards the outer suburbs led to a gradual deterioration of the districts which they left, which were no longer on the frontier between town and country. Slum conditions, in a word, were allowed to develop in some of the central suburbs, partly as a result of the flight of residents who might, had they remained, have stabilised the conditions of growth and maintained reasonable standards. As it was, the problem of slum clearance after 1918 was left to municipal authorities to solve by rehousing schemes. Among the factors causing the outward migration of the 'better-off' was the desire to maintain the exclusiveness which workmen's trains clearly threatened.

In addition to these social problems in the inner suburbs, there were the problems which arose as a result of the great distances which suburban workers had to travel. By 1914 the rate at which London's surrounding countryside was being engulfed was accelerating, and longer travelling times ate into leisure hours. The problems of growth and size then put to town and country planners had arisen, at least in part, as a result of one of the chief solutions adopted for the problem of Victorian slums, namely workmen's fares.

7

Railways and housing in Victorian London

Who builds? Who builds? Alas, ye poor!
If London day by day 'improves',
Where shall ye find a friendly door,
When every day a home removes?

The Builder, IX (1851), 395

Show these men cottages in the country, such as I have supposed, readily accessible, and combined with an increase, not a diminution, of the other necessaries of life, and I am persuaded they would take advantage of them.

J.T. Danson: *J. Stat. Soc.*, XXII (1859), 377

The social history of Britain's railways is still largely unwritten. Yet it is probably true to say that railways had more radical consequences for the anatomy of the large mid-Victorian towns than any other single factor. Apart from increasing both their growth and prosperity, railways caused drastic changes in the configuration of many of their existing streets and in their internal communications. The changes they brought were not, however, confined to the physical layout of the urban landscape. Railways also influenced the daily lives of the townspeople themselves. It is the purpose of this essay to assess the impact which the building of railways had on one aspect of the lives of London workers a century ago, namely the condition and location of their homes.[1] First, we shall examine the progress and extent of the housing demolitions which had to be made for new railways, and trace their immediate effects. Then we shall examine their long-run consequences, and the question of compensation of weekly tenants and others. In conclusion, it will be possible to suggest very briefly the part which these events played in the evolution of an effective social policy for the peculiar housing problems of Victorian London.

1

The demolition of London streets did not, of course, begin in 1837, for many hundreds of houses had already been destroyed before that date for bridges, docks, private estate development, and some street improvements. But as railways penetrated as close to the heart of London as either the Metropolitan Railway Commission recommended[2] or the Corporation of the City of London would allow,[3] they soon increased the scale of these demolitions.

Their general character naturally excited considerable comment, for private property had seldom been more seriously threatened. Railways, to judge by a piece of *Punch* satire in 1842,[4] exercised even then undeniable authority to amend the map of London: St Paul's itself was not above being sacrificed to them – 'should the Bishop of London, however, object, an application will immediately be made to Parliament on the subject, when, of course, the church will at once be placed at the disposal of the Company'. Lesser property was hardly more immune. And Dickens was quick to recognise the drama of these events and to publicise them. The shocks of the 'Railway Mania' had hardly subsided before his readers were regaled, in a familiar passage in *Dombey and Son* (1848), with a vivid and authentic account of a metamorphosis which erased all but the disreputable memory of Staggs's Gardens in the practically fictitious north London suburb of Camberling Town. Charles Manby Smith, too, had watched the building of London's railways for many years before he published his impressions of their social consequences in his *Curiosities of London Life* in 1853. He then wrote (p. 361) of 'the deep gorge of a railway cutting, which has ploughed its way right through the centre of the market-gardens, and burrowing beneath the carriage-road, and knocking a thousand houses out of its path, pursues its circuitous course to the city'.

Stray but more precise estimates of the numbers of working-class people actually turned out of doors by particular railway schemes were also made at the time. For example, George Godwin, editor of *The Builder*, whose first youthful appearance in print in the 1830s had been to vindicate the multiplication of railways,[5] later qualified his unreserved enthusiasm when, in 1854, he saw for himself how 'hundreds' of houses had been destroyed by them in the 'last few years' in the City Liberties, Marylebone and St Clement Danes;[6] and he wrote of the process which was still going on ten years later when about 1,000 houses in the Fleet Valley, estimated to have housed 12,000 persons, were destroyed.[7] A contributor to the *Fortnightly Review* in 1866[8] stated that the North London Railway Company had already destroyed 900 houses, mostly occupied by working-class families, in building a mere two miles of track from Kingsland to Finsbury, and 'in preparing the Chatham and Dover Railway Extension to Farringdon, courts and lanes have been literally swept through by dozens'. In the same year, demolitions in Somers, Camden and Agar Towns for the metropolitan extensions of the Midland Railway Company totalled, according to *The Working Man*, 4,000 houses, in which about 32,000 persons, almost all the families of working men, had lived.[9] This doughty champion of working-class interests strove to keep its readers tolerably well informed of at least the major clearances: 20,000 people, it reported, were involved in the demolitions by the Midland Railway Company for their intended terminus in the Euston Road.[10] When building operations began in 1865 on Broad Street Station, so it was claimed, 2,000 persons became temporarily homeless.[11]

Estimates of proposed demolitions give the same impression of their general scale. 2,850 people were threatened in 1836 by the London and Blackwall Railway[12] when it applied for powers to build its line from Blackwall to the Minories through crowded districts.[13] In the Lords' debates, figures of impending demolitions were freely quoted to strengthen the case for a partial retreat from a *laissez-faire* attitude towards the consequences of railway building, whether this was conducted on a unified plan or not.[14] Lord Shaftesbury, for example, drew attention in 1853 to the London Dock Company's proposal to pull down 500 houses and displace 5,000 people. Lord Derby, in the debate on metropolitan railways in 1861, spoke of the plight of the parish of St Bartholomew's, nearly half of whose 5,000 working-class inhabitants were threatened by some of the fifteen different railway schemes then before parliament; and most of these were already under notice to quit.[15]

What can we make of these various figures? Those used as parliamentary ammunition were probably rather more of a challenge to government to produce better ones than an accurate testimony of verified facts. And it is unlikely that the printed estimates – many more of which must still be buried in the materials for the social history of Victorian London – were, before 1853, any more reliable. It is hard to see how contemporaries could have been at all well informed on these matters when the volume of displacements was so large and the amount officially recorded so small. At first, railway companies were neither compelled nor inclined to publish details of their street demolitions; nor were their extent and consequences methodically assessed by central or local government. Until the early 1850s the real costs of metropolitan improvements were therefore unknown, for the displaced persons of early Victorian London remained uncounted and their migrations uncharted. It is not possible, therefore, to reach any very definite conclusions from these estimates alone. But even though they cannot be said to inform us with precision they do indicate the approximate volume of displacements. They seem to show that the figure of 20,000 persons displaced by 'metropolitan engineering works', including railways, before 1864,[16] or even that of 50,000 by 1867,[17] are both too low.

Fortunately, some other unpublished figures are available to supplement these imprecise data. In 1853 Lord Shaftesbury secured the adoption by the House of Lords of a new standing order requiring promoters of all private bills which involved the demolition of thirty or more houses in the same parish occupied by the 'labouring classes', to make a return of their number and occupants, and of any measures they proposed for remedying 'the inconvenience likely to arise'.[18] This was, incidentally, the first of a long string of requirements affecting not only private bill procedure[19] but the course of public bill legislation as well.[20] And it is on these demolition statements that, despite their shortcomings, we have to rely for any comprehensive picture of the extent of housing demolitions for railways. No one has ever contended that these statements are a meticulous record of the facts of working-class housing demolitions. Indeed, some contemporaries treated them with scant respect.[21] But, for reasons which are indicated in a note at the end of this essay, there are good grounds for believing that they are, if anything, rather conservative documents; that there are some known and, probably, some unknown omissions, strengthens this view.

There were in all sixty-nine separate schemes, involving the displacement of over 76,000 persons, between 1853 and 1901. Fifty-one of these schemes, affecting over 56,000 persons, occurred in the period before 1885, during which no provision was made for rehousing those displaced. The rate at which these displacements occurred from year to year was, not surprisingly, uneven, and almost 70 per cent of them were concentrated in the twenty years following 1859; the period of most intense activity was, in fact, a comparatively short one, for nearly 37,000 displacements occurred in the period from 1859 to 1867 alone. The impact of these displacements was as a consequence all the more keenly felt, and it is clear from these figures that there is a *prima facie* case for supposing that the building of railways in Victorian London was not completed without incurring certain social costs. It is now necessary, therefore, to examine the nature of these costs[22] and the identity of those that met them.

2

The social consequences of these housing demolitions are not hard to discover. They were both immediate and delayed, and were governed to some extent by the stringency with which rehousing requirements were enforced after 1885.

The immediate effects of both conditional and unconditional demolitions were soon plain to most observers. But not to all. Some welcomed such improvements unreservedly, in the buoyant hope that they would revitalise decaying central areas. More crudely, this was to be a technique for 'shovelling out the poor', for local bodies could not easily resist the temptation to support such schemes, both to increase rateable values by a change in land use, and to shed some of the burden of poor relief.[23] Demolitions had for these the unmitigated blessing of sweeping away, for example, the 'ill-ventilated *culs de sac* and dens of wretchedness in the vicinity of Shoe Lane and Saffron Hill – the nurseries of vice, the nuclei of filth and disease'.[24] Not all vestrymen were schooled in these sophistications of local finance, however, nor did they convince more disinterested authorities. Canning's Metropolitan Railway Commission was a case in point: densely populated districts were not always 'sensibly improved' by railway clearances, it argued; and demonstrated how some metropolitan lines had actually thwarted the street improvements by which slums might have been cleared. A good example of this was the London and Blackwall Railway which, by crossing White Lion Street, had interfered with the formation of the new street from London Docks to Commercial Road.[25]

It was sometimes argued that those evicted migrated to the suburbs. This was a process to be encouraged, not hindered, according to *The Times* (2 March 1861):

As we cut nicks through our woods, and roads through our forests, so it should be our policy to divide these thick jungles of crime and misery. Much has already been done to tempt these people to purer air and better habits. Thousands of cottages are springing up yearly in the suburbs.

And it was often assumed that the general effect of these clearances, 'though attended with the present inconvenience of disturbing the occupants, is ultimately of unmixed advantage, by driving them into new and better tenements in the suburbs'.[26] A number of railway bills were, indeed, drafted on this principle, though the argument that those displaced would migrate to the suburbs was more convincing to those content with inaction than to those who genuinely desired this solution.[27] To many working men, London was, as to Kingsley's Alton Locke, 'the City of Destruction', and their 'Wicket of the Way of Life was strangely identified with the turnpike at Battersea Bridge end, and the rising ground of Mortlake and Wimbledon was the Land of Beulah'. But that was all. In fact, the working classes vigorously resisted any tendency to be moved from their homes in the very heart of London before the 1880s, for not only would even the shortest removal involve the loss of tangible benefits, but it would endanger their very livelihoods as well. It was estimated, when metropolitan railway building was at its height in the middle 1860s, that about 680,000 workers in central London depended upon casual labour,[28] and for these, whose employment was daily or hourly, distant lodgings would have been a crippling handicap.

In these circumstances, it was only a matter of time before the theory that railway clearances were accelerating a general working-class exodus from central London was discredited. Those who saw their homes reduced to rubble well knew the immediate consequences of the demolition of houses for new railways.[29] Not surprisingly, an Evicted Tenants' Aid Association came into being in the 1860s and busily agitated for remedies to allay the miserable consequences of these demolitions.[30] Their deputation told Lord Derby, then Prime Minister, that although urban living conditions were bad enough before the railways came, these evils had been 'vastly increased by the extensive railway ramifications in all parts of the metropolis'.[31] And, as the clearances increased, social observers of all kinds showed how over-crowding grew worse in adjoining districts when houses were knocked down for railways and miscellaneous improvements. The destinations of those displaced in a typical clearance were given by one onlooker to the reporter of *The Working Man* in 1866[32] in words which had an authentic ring: 'Where are they all gone, sir? Why, some's gone down Whitechapel way; some's gone in the Dials; some's gone to Kentish Town; and some's gone to the Workus.' And in the same year, in an article bitterly entitled 'Attila in London', Charles Dickens's famous weekly, *All the Year Round*, exposed to its readers some of the sordid details of these demolitions:

Pigsties, dung-heaps, dogs, children, and costermongers' refuse, jammed together into a heterogeneous and inextricably confused mass, fringe all the squalid homes . . . [But] standing with your back to the entrance of any of these courts, you look far away across the line of railway over a vast and desolate waste.[33]

For almost all those involved, these evictions meant a change for the worse – higher rents and less room. Naturally, the supply of house-room could not immediately adjust itself to the increased demand, and rents reacted accordingly. Nor was this a passing phase, for railway connections helped to raise land and property values in proportion to the changes in use consequent upon the improved amenities, and former rents were never regained.[34] Moreover, the effects of a sharp decline in the supply of house-room were not confined to those actually displaced, any more than they were to the very poor. All ranks of the City Police, for example, memorialised the Commissioner in the early 1860s and blamed for the increasing 'difficulties we experience . . . the alterations and improvements made for railways, new streets, and buildings'.[35] A representative of another section of the working classes whose living conditions were changed by railway demolitions was Thomas Wright, working-class *littérateur* and self-styled 'Journeyman Engineer'. His first book, *Some Habits and Customs of the Working Classes* (1867), had established an almost unique reputation, for probably none knew better how the working classes lived. For this reason his personal diary of events while being evicted for the 'City and Suburban Company's line' – it appeared in his classic, *The Great Unwashed*, the following year – was specially noteworthy: it not only illustrated in unaccustomed detail the acute shortage of house-room in central London and the social descent which demolitions often entailed, but helped to make the process of eviction more graphic to a wider public.

To educate the literate in social cause and effect was a slow process. The immediate consequences of unconditional demolitions were, it is true, not left greatly to mid-Victorians' imaginations. Builders and architects,[36] local and national administrators,[37] clergymen,[38] the working classes themselves,[39] and a whole range of social observers[40] produced such a volume of fact and interpretation as could not apparently have failed to dislodge even the most stubborn convictions that railways were unmixed public benefits. All stressed the increased overcrowding in nearby districts which these demolitions caused. But deliberate control of these social consequences did not come with mere observation. For it was still possible to pick one's way past labyrinthine rookeries and to gaze, not on a 'wilderness of howling humanity',[41] but on magnificent 'improved' façades and the awesome vitality of the locomotive. To the faintly patronising *The Workman's Friend*, for example,[42] these civil engineering works were objects of civic pride and not of suspicion, and this was how these dramatic transformations must have appeared to many Londoners. Most of them were enormously impressed by Baron Haussmann's spectacular replanning of Paris since 1853,[43] but few realised that to his own countrymen 'haussmanisation' was a by-word for ruthless destruction by unscrupulous methods, and that the Parisian mob, hounded from the centre, had merely been displaced to Belleville and Montmartre.[44] Thus, when the Lords debated metropolitan railways in February 1861, warnings of their social implications were greeted in the influential press with impatience and ridicule. 'An old lounger at the bar of the House', thundered *The Times* on 2 March,

might have supposed that he had gone back thirty years, and was listening again to the old nonsense which vexed the ears of the nation in the days of his boyhood... Two noble Peers ... were repeating the commonplaces against Railways. Nothing, however, is too foolish not come into fashion again . . . we can see nothing but unmixed good in the evils denounced by Lord Derby and Lord Shaftesbury.

And *Punch* echoed this comment with faint satire and a crude pun. But its readers, one gathers, were resolved not to be seduced by 'the god Terminus' for a different reason, for they were more concerned to preserve architectural vistas from the vulgarities of 'The Goths and Vandals Railway' than they were to minimise the consequences of their demolitions.[45]

So far as a remedy for the social consequences of housing demolitions was concerned, the majority of contemporary opinion was undoubtedly at first on the side of some brand of *laissez-faire*. But the various social mechanisms on which those who held such opinions relied failed to adjust the housing situation in central London. The physical gaps created by metropolitan railways among the dwellings of the poor were not automatically filled, either by philanthropic or profit-seeking effort: to James Hole, speaking in 1853, their contributions to the housing shortages caused by railways and other improvements were 'like drops in the ocean'.[46] Thirteen years later this was equally true and the situation much more urgent: 'The most zealous worshippers of that political idol – *Laissez-faire* – are obliged to confess', declared one observer, 'that in this matter voluntary effort has been fairly tried, and has failed to provide for more than a small fraction of the great emergency.'[47] This opinion was admittedly slow to take root, but ultimately it led to uncompromising government intervention to compel railway companies to rehouse those they displaced.

When, in 1853, Lord Shaftesbury first raised the matter of displaced occupiers, he had wanted to compel promoters of bills to provide other homes for those displaced within three years and at a 'convenient distance'.[48] He claimed that his proposal, which was not new,[49] had already won the support of Mr Morton Peto, the railway contractor, who was by that time MP for Norwich,[50] but his hopes of having it adopted as a standing order by the Lords were dashed by their criticisms of its impracticability. As it was, a select committee was appointed to consider how best 'to remedy the Evils produced by such displacement of the Population', but its perfunctory minutes gave no clue – unless their terse formality told its own tale – to the factors which influenced it in recommending the adoption of the much less restrictive standing order already mentioned.[51] State intervention in these matters must have appeared a delicate business and hedged with dilemmas. It was probably one of these, produced by the Earl of Wicklow, which clinched the matter:

Would the House, if they required the same number of houses that had been pulled down to be rebuilt, require also that the proprietors should receive the old tenants back into the new houses? If they did not, they would do nothing for the tenants; while if they did they might compel the landlords to receive tenants whom they did not wish to have.[52]

The Times (24 March 1853), bridling at an implied recognition of 'tenant-right' which was inimical to 'our notions of property', also queried the practicability of compulsory rehousing:

If the time given is short, the obligation may be unduly onerous on the promoters of what, after all, is assumed to be an 'improvement'; if long, all the evil consequences of the ejectment would be suffered and exhausted before the remedy was applied.

It was partly as a result of these apparent difficulties, and partly because reformers' hopes were pinned instead to more general solutions of London's housing problem – particularly to the Lodging Houses and the Torrens and Cross Acts – that promoters were unhampered by rehousing requirements for at least twenty years. Nothing shows this more clearly than the demolition statements themselves, which needed no justification for unconditional displacements. In the column for action to be taken appeared noncommittally, 'none', 'no inconvenience anticipated', 'persons displaced will easily find accommodation', and similar remarks.

It was not, therefore, until 1874 that a real approach was made to compulsory rehousing. In that year, the Council of the Charity Organization Society formed a committee of MPs and others under the chairmanship of Sir Sydney Waterlow, then Lord Mayor, to consider suitable action to improve working-class dwellings, and this led, after a deputation to the Home Office and some support from Sir James Kay-Shuttleworth in the

House,[53] to the formulation of some new standing orders which placed special requirements on promoters of bills causing displacements: the principal ones were the giving of eight weeks' notice of taking houses of the 'labouring classes' and the provision of alternative accommodation.[54] Despite these provisions, which were embodied in several acts involving displacements in London,[55] railway companies successfully evaded them all for a further nine years. The evidence which the Royal Commission on the Housing of the Working Classes collected in 1884–5 was emphatic on this point: no rehousing scheme was carried out by any railway company in London before this time. The probing of the commissioners revealed a most confused situation. Some companies had appeared to have contracted earlier, even voluntarily, to rehouse those displaced, but later were found to have avoided doing so. In 1859, for example, the Metropolitan Railway bought and converted a court in St Bartholomew's to demonstrate to its sharpest critics how the company could rehouse more people than it displaced; but within two years, when these 'model' dwellings had served their purpose of allaying opposition to the company's bill, they were converted into warehouses and their occupants evicted. Statutory requirements were most commonly evaded between 1874 and 1885 by acquiring the property and emptying it of its inhabitants before 15 December in any given year, the date on which the number of inhabitants was reckoned; another method was for railway companies to conclude private agreements with landlords to do this for them.[56]

It is clear from this that the rehousing requirements originally imposed on the railway companies made no marked difference to the immediate consequences of railway demolitions. Nor were they effective when they were strictly enforced after 1885. The main reason for this was that alternative accommodation was seldom available before houses were demolished. Hence, so long as ample vacant accommodation was not available locally there was nothing to prevent the same overcrowding as would have occurred without statutory provision having been made. When the Great Central Railway Company, for example, displaced in 1898 about 1,750 people on the site of Marylebone Station, these people immediately increased overcrowding in Lisson Grove[57] because the company had not yet prepared a rehousing scheme.[58]

There was, however, an additional reason to explain why the period of compulsory rehousing did not see any very marked improvement in the plight of families evicted for railway-building. The invariable time-lag between demolition and the provision of alternative accommodation ensured that its ultimate occupants were seldom, if ever, the same persons as those originally displaced. Naturally, the high cost of rehousing, which was much greater in central London than in the suburbs, forced up rents for the new accommodation, and wage-earners of different status moved in.[59] In this way, the character of these areas was transformed socially as well as scenically, and that of the surrounding districts which received the displaced poor deteriorated still further. Nor was this all, for the pressure on the available living accommodation in the central area soon overcame its absolute capacity, and the overcrowded areas sprawled farther afield.

3

So far we have been considering only the immediate effects of the demolitions for railways. The chief of these was the aggravation of overcrowding in the central areas where most displacements occurred. But this congestion could not be contained within that area, and the delayed social consequences of railway building arose from the centrifugal migration of the population of central London, to which it ultimately contributed. Charles Booth and his team of social investigators traced the causes of this in the 1890s to the fact that even densely packed slums had a limit to their capacity. By then, the rate at which working-class dwellings were being destroyed for warehouses, factories, offices, street improvements and private estate development had quickened, and the consequent 'over-spill' affected wide areas. Thus, for example, the ripples of migration set up by displacements around Lisson Grove finally lapped the streets of Kensal New Town; and those of Hoxton and Shoreditch were perceptible in Tottenham and Walthamstow.[60]

Forty or more years before Booth wrote, a similar trend had been initiated by the railway clearances of that day. An illustration of this was the effect of the building of the North London Railway Company's extension soon after 1861 from Kingsland to Broad Street. Some 5,000 persons were probably displaced, about half of whom were in the parish of Bishopsgate, which had a total population of about 10,000. According to the Rector, the migration of most of those displaced to Shoreditch and elsewhere was an indication that an absolute limit had been reached in the capacity of existing accommodation within the parish, for the annual charitable disbursements of over £2,000 were prizes which were not lightly forgone.[61] Confirmation that a shortage of accommodation had already had similar effects in this part of London was given by the Secretary to the company when, in supporting his own 'traffic case', he revealed that some twenty-shillings-a-week labourers in Blackwall and the West India Docks already lodged their families at Kingsland, with whom they stayed for the weekends only, remaining themselves in the City for the whole of the working week.[62]

The intensification of congestion in central London which railway demolitions helped to bring about also had the consequence of accelerating middle-class migration to the suburbs. The revulsion of this class from an increasingly sordid environment was by no means new, but first-class railway season tickets and the ubiquitous horse-bus were fresh means to the end of suburban migration, and the middle classes seized them eagerly.[63] These consequences of railway demolitions did not, of course, operate in a vacuum, and it is therefore impossible to attribute them specifically to a single chain of events. But it is clear that railway demolitions made no insignificant contribution to this redistribution of social classes by detonating a kind of social chain reaction: the poor, who were displaced by railways and other improvements, displaced the artisan, who dislodged the lower-middle and middle classes from the exclusive suburbs to which they had retreated.

This was, indeed, the real measure of the impact of railway demolitions on the social characteristics of the suburbs, for they led by means of workmen's fares to a mass migration thither of the working classes. Rapid suburban growth was, it is true, no novelty when the Railway Age dawned, but its earlier social characteristics had been different.[64] Sydney Smirke, antiquarian and architect, had some notions of the new pattern of suburban development in 1834 when, in his prophetic *Suggestions for the Architectural Improvement of the Western Part of London*, he coupled with a vigorous appeal for slum clearance and rehousing the suggestion that 'portions of unoccupied ground should be taken in the skirts of the town . . . and let a village, expressly dedicated to the working classes be there erected'. And the second burst of railway building had hardly begun when, in 1845, an early number of one of those ephemeral periodicals so characteristic of the 'Mania' – Hyde Clarke's *Railway Register* – not only saw the practical value of the railway to develop the suburbs, but hailed it as the fairy godmother to the wretched tenants of the houses strewn in its metropolitan path. In the second of a series of articles on 'Metropolitan Improvements' it confidently declared:

Towns need no longer to be fortresses, or densely packed hives of death or pestilence . . . London may, and ought to be diffused . . . to be *spread out* over an area of five hundred in place of fifty square miles . . . WHAT IS TO BE DONE WITH THE POOR OF LONDON? They are being expelled from their haunts – rookeries, they are called – by the restless foot of local improvement.

A few pages later the solution was proposed:

When the locomotive agency of the metropolis and neighbourhood has been completed, and the legislature has exercized its power in *minimizing* the charges of the parliamentary train, workpeople, like their employers, will be free to roam; like them they will not be compelled to live near the shop, warehouse, factory, or office, but may seek rural abodes.

Indeed, an exciting new prospect of planned towns seemed possible –

poleonomy, or the laying out of towns . . . with a regard to the health, comfort, and convenience of their inhabitants . . . a new science.[65]

The Health of Towns Association, too, contended that cheap fares were one factor in the relief of central overcrowding.[66]

A more specific proposal of this kind was made at about the same time by the Solicitor to the City Corporation, Charles Pearson, when giving his evidence to the Metropolitan Railway Commission. He could see no other solution to the problem than that of dispersing the working classes by very cheap trains so as to get 'the better order of mechanics' into suburban 'colonies' of his own severely practical design.[67] He boldly contended that mechanics and clerks could profitably be carried at a penny per ton-mile, whereas conventional passenger rates were then based on a single passenger equalling a ton of goods.[68] Nine years later, he urged on the Cabinet[69] and the Select Committee on Metropolitan Communications[70] a similar solution for population displacements, and reiterated it many times over the next few years.[71] His suggestion was far-reaching, and one interesting outcome of it was a proposal in 1858, from the Lord Mayor's committee which had been formed to re-examine it, for an underground railway which would 'provide cheap trains for the working classes at reasonable hours'.[72]

Specially cheap fares as a solution to mid-Victorian London's housing problems soon attracted considerable support. In 1859, *Household Words* solemnly indicated to the railway companies, in an article suggestively entitled 'Rustic Townsmen', 'the social duty which they now have to perform'.[73] And by the 1860s this particular solution had even more point, though it was not without its critics.[74] Campaigners for cheap fares and suburban development to cure urban ills put their case, however, as often as the opportunity presented itself – in Parliament,[75] to the National Association for the Promotion of Social Science,[76] and in a stream of books, pamphlets and periodicals. It was a focus of interest for a surprising medley of writers. William Bridges Adams, for example, revealed himself as no less of a visionary than an engineer in his encyclopaedic and undeservedly neglected work, *Roads and Rails* (1862): 'facile transit' was the key to his planner's dream of deploying south London on the healthy suburban slopes of the Surrey hills, and cultivating its existing low-lying tracts as orchards, gardens and meadows.[77] Ebenezer Clarke, member of the council of the Central Cottage Improvement Society, was another who urged, in his curious and informative manual of self-help, *The Hovel and the Home*, 'suitable semi-detached cottages, a short distance from London', as the best plan for 'displaced persons'.[78] He noted approvingly a suggestion made in *The Builder* that some industrial decentralisation would help this process.[79] George Godwin, too, hoped that eventually the homeless nomads whose wanderings he had pursued when their homes had been destroyed would become suburban dwellers 'with the aid of the locomotive and far-seeing railway directors',[80] and he stressed the need for a comprehensive plan to solve the problems of this greater London which he visualised.[81] Others had had hopes that private philanthropy might have promoted the same end: George Peabody's gift was vainly looked to as the fund to finance suburban development over a ten-mile radius 'where the railways will give facilities for the cheap daily conveyance of workmen'.[82] Another writer enlarged on

Pearson's scheme for those evicted by railways and metropolitan improvements, and suggested suburban boulevards providing four lines of rails for 'traction engines', toll-roads for private carriages and free footpaths for pedestrians, with sufficient ground on each side for houses.[83] To James Hole, writing in 1866, 'model' suburbs and cheap fares for working men were not only eminent solutions to a pressing problem, but due retribution for wholesale displacements of the poor.[84] *The Working Man* underlined this point in a blunt editorial as Hole's book appeared,[85] and from its columns at the end of the summer came the almost plaintive plea of one of its proletarian contributors whose Rotherhithe home had been pulled down by the East London Railway: 'Why don't they build us a great village or town out Epping way . . . and then let the railways bring us backwards and forwards for a trifle? They take our homes; let them give us something in return.'[86] Cheap trains alone, it was claimed, 'could convert the curse of forcible removal into the blessing of a suburban residence within reach of work'.[87] How little the railway had yet directly influenced the future holders of workmen's tickets is hard to visualise. As late as 1873 a contributor to *The Workman's Magazine* declared that many of the working classes never travelled by rail.[88] Indeed, the denizens of Field Lane, Cow Cross, Jacob's Island, Rose Alley and Tiger Bay – addresses which were so many parodies on their squalid actuality – had as yet hardly sampled even the excursion train, cheap as that was, and journeyed for most rare treats to Epping by greengrocer's cart hired on an instalment plan.[89]

The deliberate choice of workmen's trains as a remedy for the housing problems of Victorian London was, therefore, of almost incalculable effect. The first ever run in London were all intended to mitigate the consequences of displacements caused by the building of new lines:[90] clauses to this effect were inserted, for example, into the North London Railway (City Branch) Act of 1861[91] as a consequence of the demolitions for the line from Broad Street to Kingsland, and into the Metropolitan Railway (Finsbury Circus Extension) Act of the same year[92] as a result of the demolitions for the building of this line from Paddington; this tended to become a general practice. Some railway rehousing there certainly was, but the railways had in workmen's fares an effective alternative, whose advantages were not lost on Home Secretaries. Not surprisingly, therefore, a Select Committee on Workmen's Trains could recommend in 1905 that railway companies should be relieved altogether from rehousing persons displaced by railway improvements so long as they made adequate concessions in fares to encourage suburban migration.[93] What is more, the expedient later became a chosen instrument, for workmen's fares were also used to facilitate slum clearance by means of suburban rehousing.

It would, of course, be fanciful to suggest that metropolitan railway building alone produced the conditions which led to this particular solution.

But it is clear that these housing demolitions certainly hastened the general adoption of workmen's fares in London, not least by demonstrating the inconsistency of the passenger duty which persons displaced by railways and new streets had to pay if they were not to aggravate the housing problem.[94] And they did more. For it was in order to improve working-class living conditions which had been so much aggravated by these housing demolitions that, under the chairmanship of Edwin Chadwick, the Department of Economy and Trade of the National Association for the Promotion of Social Science appointed, in 1866, a committee of MPs and others[95] which that year resulted in McCullagh Torrens's original bill to promote slum clearance.[96] The *Railway Register*, it is worth recalling, had expressed the matter succinctly over twenty years before: 'Two courses are manifestly open for dealing with London: either we may *plant out* in the vicinage, or try to make the existing site more fit and commodious.'[97] Demolitions for railways had helped to put both of them on trial.

4

Punch's facetious prospectus of 1845 for a 'Grand Railway from England to China', with its terminus on the demolished site of St Paul's, was not an entirely fanciful project. As a comment on the extravagant schemes of the day it illustrated better than cold facts both the feverish excitement of visionary speculators and the wild conception of some of their plans.

It is easy, therefore, to understand why railways were not restricted by the special covenants which would have been necessary to ensure fair treatment for the affected property-owners and tenants alike. It is certainly true that the former had obtained their charter in the Lands Clauses Consolidation Act of 1845,[98] which established the legal basis for compulsory acquisition of land in place of the piecemeal and flimsy compensation clauses found in earlier bills.[99] But the principles of assessment remained undefined, and these had to be elaborated in a long string of judicial decisions: the principal issues were the interpretation of the sections covering compensation for the land taken and its severance from other lands of the same owner, and for injury to other owners whose land was not actually taken for the works.[100] The outcome of these judgments was that the basis for compensation was the value of the land to the vendor at the time of serving notice to treat, and not necessarily its current market price,[101] and that compensation should also be paid for any loss incurred by the expulsion.[102] In general, it could be said that the courts interpreted the compensation requirements of the 1845 act very generously in favour of landowners.[103] Indeed, it is arguable that the scale of compensation was far too high, for it is probable that the huge bill for the compensation of land and property owners was a powerful reason, apart from legal complexities, why tenants were not better treated.

As for tenants, there were two ways in which the real costs to them of moving house or business could have been compensated: by provision of equivalent alternative accommodation, or by payment of adequate financial remuneration. We have already seen how the former was never realised, at least during the main wave of railway construction before the end of the 1870s, and it is now necessary, if we are to assess in real terms the cost of railway building in Victorian London, to take account of the uncompensated burden borne by many evicted tenants of small business premises and dwelling-houses.

Arbitrary money awards for enforced removal undoubtedly had an attraction for both givers and receivers. So far as weekly tenants were concerned, they had no legal claim to compensation whatever, and even small sums were therefore very welcome. The weakness of their legal position was forcibly demonstrated when a case was brought by a number of them against the Midland Railway Company in 1865, following the extension of the line from Somers Town: the judgment delivered in Bloomsbury County Court was that although hardship was sympathetically recognised nothing could be done to compensate those evicted:[104] 'The custom has been to consider only the interests of those, whose premises being taken for the works, are obviously entitled to compensation,' ran the annual report of the Westminster District Board of Works for 1869,[105] in describing the completion of the Metropolitan District Railway. 'Even in this class, however, a very large amount of injury is frequently sustained for which compensation is not obtainable, while beyond this class the amount of injury inflicted without any possible remedy is very large and far in excess of what is usually supposed.' It may be added that this was probably far larger than it would have been had railway companies not had – all the protestations of *The Times* to the contrary[106] – a definite financial and legal interest in taking their lines through poor property rather than wealthy, for weekly tenants never opposed railway bills.[107] Lord Derby, for example, had insisted that the original Metropolitan Railway Bill had been virtually unopposed because there was not a single person of sufficient means to petition against it.[108] Now it may appear that one of the best protections afforded the tenant was probably the threat which demolitions constituted to the incomes of parishes and district boards of works, on the assumption that lowering gross rateable values placed extra burdens on the rest of the ratepayers. Indeed, there is no doubt that local opposition to railway schemes was occasionally adamant on these very grounds. But it is clear that schemes involving the demolition of the poorest property were less likely to raise local opposition, for these wiped off more liabilities than assets.

The attraction of lump-sum payments to promoters of bills involving displacements is equally clear, for they both eased the process of eviction and settled obligations outright. Several witnesses – architects and surveyors – to the Lords' Select Committee on the North London Railway Bill (1861) described their long experience in 'valuing out' working-class tenants for railways and new streets: 'a sovereign or two to go out' appears to have been one successful inducement; another was to pay arrears of rent.[109] But the treatment which an individual might expect – to judge by the sharply conflicting evidence – was not predictable, for this depended as much as anything, apparently, on the self-interest and disposition of the promoters of the bill. Railway companies, it was said, 'pay, adequately or inadequately, and then wash their hands of any responsibility'.[110] At one extreme, the curate of St Bartholomew's, Cripplegate, contended that compensation could be as low as eighteen pence per family; at the other, railway officials mentioned aggregate sums like £7,500 being paid out in cash to weekly tenants evicted from the site of Liverpool Street Station, and individual amounts varying between £2 and £3 per tenant on the Metropolitan line between Aldgate and Trinity Square.[111] The agents of some railway promoters were apparently convinced that compensation to weekly tenants was quite adequate, for they argued that those evicted actually welcomed the process to get the lump-sum payment.[112] It is clear, of course, that this eagerness was in reality an indication of the degree of poverty and not of the real costs involved: working-class households notoriously overcrowded themselves with lodgers for the same reason without reckoning the hidden real costs of cramped accommodation.

5

To sum up. It is clear from this brief examination of railway building in Victorian London that it involved social costs which were nonetheless real for being half-hidden and difficult to assess. As to their quantitative aspects, it may be said that during the last fifty years of the Victorian era, something like 80,000 men, women and children were involved in varying degrees in these disturbances, rather more of them in the first half of the period than in the second. Of the actual numbers involved it is not possible to say with certainty more than this. Of the social costs met by those evicted it is, however, possible to be more definite. During the later period they were smaller by a much larger margin than the difference in the figures suggests, for the total housing accommodation in the area of the demolitions fell only slightly because of the stringent application of rehousing requirements; and although the new accommodation did not directly benefit those actually displaced, this class was not compelled to crowd into already overcrowded rooms as the persons displaced by earlier clearances had had to do, but many of them became the incoming tenants of the houses vacated by the class which could afford the higher rents of the new accommodation.

On the qualitative aspects of these demolitions it is possible to be more specific. It has been clear in the course of this study that the whole of the real costs of improved communications were not met by the promoters themselves, but that some of them were distributed among many thousands of London's poorer classes. This deserves emphasis. Men of property had, if not more tangible, then more enforceable, claims to compensation for compulsory acquisition, and these were generally adequately met by the railway companies. The incidence of the uncompensated costs borne by weekly tenants varied, however, according to local circumstance and the social consciences of promoters and legislators. Where adequate vacant house-room was available for those displaced, and they received sufficient cash to cover their removal, the cost of the upheaval was limited to the inconvenience of the disturbance and the break-up of their community ties. These could be serious enough. But at the other extreme were families who received no cash compensation, however nominal, and had to squeeze their homes into already overcrowded accommodation because their livings – men's, women's and children's – depended on casual employment of all kinds in the heart of London. It was of these that Dr Letheby once wrote, 'The spirit of improvement which has led to the destruction of the poor man's haunts, has had but little regard for the poor man's wants; and after all, the majesty of a great city may be but the glittering diadem upon the front of death.'[113] These social costs have, then, no precise magnitude, for they were simply one item among many which lowered in countless ways, not only the expectation of life of thousands of dwellers in the rookeries of Victorian London, but all their other standards as well.

The real explanation of why London's poor bore the brunt of the social costs of these railway extensions cannot be given, however, solely in these terms. The truth of the matter appears to be that during the early part of the period the ideas of most of the 'improvers', of the champions of the interests of the poor, and of railway promoters, temporarily complemented each other. Slums were both eye-sores which offended the aesthetic planners of the urban landscape and a series of challenges to the handful of men who saw their social responsibilities more clearly than their contemporaries did. As for the architects of metropolitan railway communications, they mainly pursued their own interests in a highly competitive field, but their role was one which must have appeared to come very near to justifying the assumptions of mid-Victorian *laissez-faire*. As Sir George Clark has pointed out,[114] the absence of state intervention could be justified not only on grounds of present expediency, but on those of the ultimate welfare of the very classes who appeared to be most threatened by the self-interested actions of others. Thus, it appeared that the demolitions not only served to expunge the stain of the slums but provided the means of evacuating their inhabitants to healthier surroundings. This was the theme to which *The Times* devoted its editorials again and again. 'If the working people of the city are compelled to find room at a greater distance from their work,' it declared in one of these avowals of faith, there will be builders and speculators ready to supply their wants. This is not an affair for railway companies . . . Government has nothing to do with providing dwellings for the poor, and has no more right to impose an obligation of this sort on railways than anybody else who pulls down a dwelling-house to build something else – a church, for example – in its place. The interference is both idle and contrary to the usages of this country. It can end in no good. We accept railways with their consequences, and we don't think the worse of them for ventilating the City of London . . . . You can never make these wretched alleys really habitable, do what you will; but bring a railway to them, and the whole problem is solved.[115]

In fact, in the absence of other powers, railways and other improvements provided the only means of obliterating insanitary neighbourhoods.

But the fragility of these arguments for non-intervention by government appeared only with the passage of time. The far-reaching social consequences of unconditional demolitions were merely illustrations of the economic and social interdependencies then being wrought in Britain's national life by the conditions of her expanding economy. And instruments for a social policy which were more adequate to London's housing problem had to be fashioned as the older piecemeal methods revealed their own inadequacy, and as the demolitions themselves generated both a new sensitivity to urban conditions and an increasingly articulate criticism of them. 'That we raise a "bitter cry"', insisted one social commentator at a time when this awareness was being expressed for the first time in effective state intervention, 'does not mean that we are worse than we have been; it rather means that we are realizing more fully that we might be better.'[116] It was in a sense natural, therefore, that the twisting of this particular thread in social policy, like the whole skein, should have been a slow, erratic process. 'It is one of the paradoxes of mid-Victorian history', H. L. Beales once remarked, 'that expanding economic unity – symbolized by railways as a really effective agent of integration – went with social little-mindedness in the parliaments of the time.'[117]

Thus the advocates of state intervention to solve the problem of rehousing the evicted tenants of houses taken for railways did not, at first, get a hearing any more sympathetic than did that hustling general contractor of such a large part of the programme of collectivist works, Edwin Chadwick, in 1854. The new economic and political interests thrown up by Britain's industrial-isation had certainly been successful in gaining both freedom from old controls and legislative warrant for new enterprise. The measure of their success in resisting state intervention in the field of rehousing clearly lies in the fact that it was not until 1885, when most of the damage had been done, that the long debate as to how and to what extent the uprooted should be rehoused was settled by enforcing the requirements which had for some time been written into private acts, and had been evaded. Then, the question became: where should the displaced persons' new addresses be? This verged on the broadest issues of the conscious planning of Greater London, in which the suburban railways would have a major role to play.

8

Some social costs of railway-building in London

The full impact of railways on Victorian society is undoubtedly beyond all the devices of strict social accounting. What is more, precise quantitative assessment of subtle social changes can frequently be quite meaningless. This is not, however, entirely the case with one category of measurable data which has hitherto been ignored in computing the costs of railway construction in Britain. This is the series of figures available from 1853 in the demolition statements which were furnished by railway promoters all over the country before the first reading of bills involving the displacement of thirty or more houses in the same parish occupied by the 'labouring classes'. An illustration of the use to which this class of record may be put in depicting the consequences of the building of particular lines, and an indication of where these statements may be found, have already been given.[1] The purpose of this essay is to comment upon the nature of this historical material, and to append the details for the London railways between 1853 and 1901.[2]

The historical validity of these records is not strictly in direct proportion to the accuracy of the figures they contain. Quite clearly few of these statements – if any – were accurate in the sense that they corresponded minutely with the actual clearances. Indeed, there are good reasons for supposing that not all were even accurate estimates of proposed demolitions.

First, although the statements have a facile meticulousness, no one was originally responsible for checking them.[3] The Examiners of Standing Orders do not appear, from those minute books which I have read, to have examined the accuracy of the statements; they simply confirmed their deposit. Nor was such testing within the terms of reference of select committees on private bills;[4] and from the proceedings of several select committees which I have examined, none appear to have exceeded these. Indeed, elaborate checking was purposeless so long as promoters could not be compelled to rehouse those displaced or to provide for them in some other way.

Secondly, the practice in drafting these statements varied among promoters in two important respects. As to the area included, the most usual

119

basis was to include all property within the lines of deviation,[5] and most promoters stressed this, claiming that the actual numbers to be displaced would be, generally, only between a fifth and a third of this figure. Several promoters did not do this, however, and one cannot be sure whether they neglected to enter the usual rider because they were careless of the bad impression which high returns created in parliament, or because they had anticipated this by entering the numbers which would actually be displaced on the land finally taken. As to the persons involved, it is very doubtful whether the term 'labouring classes' meant the same thing to all promoters. It has been a curious tradition of housing legislation – which the consequences of railway displacements soon markedly affected – that parliament has avoided exact definitions of this and similar terms in that context in order to retain the utmost flexibility in their use;[6] it is not without significance, moreover, that the earliest attempts at definition were made in drafting the rehousing clauses considered in an earlier essay.[7] Incidentally, there is an interesting parallel worth mentioning here between the gradual extension of rehousing requirements under the housing acts and the widening connotation of the term 'labouring classes' and its final abandonment in the development of workmen's trains.

Thirdly, there were defects in the drafting of these statements which were common to all promoters. They were generally abstracted from the Books of Reference, which gave details of owners, lessees and occupiers of property within the lines of deviation, but did not record members of families, lodgers or casual occupiers. This, and the unsatisfactory nature of door-to-door visits to supplement documentary information, meant that promoters were able to interpret the Lords' Standing Order 191, which required the demolition statements to be supplied, according to their own standards. Thus, the test of a working-class dwelling to some promoters was whether it was occupied by several small tenants; to other promoters, the criterion was an arbitrary financial one, whether the head of the family earned a pound a week or less; to others, the borderline was finely drawn between the artisan and the labourer.

There were also differences between the estimates of displacements and their actual volume. Obviously, some of these occurred because of defective estimates, as already shown. A single instance is an adequate illustration of this: the original statement furnished by the North London Railway Company for its proposed branch line from Kingsland to the City showed 1,066 persons occupying 492 houses, but it was later admitted that only heads of families had been counted, and that between 4,000 and 5,000 persons were actually involved.[8] There were, too, differences which arose because some railway companies acquired land by private treaty before launching by parliamentary bill a scheme involving compulsory acquisition, and an examination of a number of Books of Reference confirms this:[9] it was partly as a result of this device that the Commons adopted their original Standing Order 49 in 1874, and that the government promised to tighten up this aspect of private bill procedure.[10] In other cases, as shown earlier,[11] some companies obviated the necessity of publicising their intentions by inducing landlords to empty property which was later to be demolished. It should also be remembered that the total displacement was larger than appeared in the statements by the unrecorded volume of small demolitions, for there were many acts for railway construction, including large works like the Victoria Station and Pimlico Railway, for which no statements were made or, presumably, required. Moreover, although the term 'house' had had an accepted usage by the Registrar-General since 1851, it had not been defined for the purposes of assessing the magnitude of railway demolitions, and its use may have been, at its best, as unrealistic as the census 'house'[12] and, at its worst, as loose as that of the term 'labouring classes': even twenty-nine separate tenements could easily have contained ten times that number of inhabitants, while twenty-nine tenement buildings might have held hundreds more.

If these considerations show that the demolition statements do not contain verified statistical data, they nevertheless do not invalidate them as evidence – probably an understatement – of the approximate numbers of nameless and propertyless people whom the railways displaced after 1853. Naturally, to assess the social costs of railway-building to the uprooted members of the intricate local communities of either Victorian London or the provincial cities, it is necessary to supplement the bald declarations of these statements by all kinds of other evidence. Some of the sources of such information have already been used to illustrate the effects of these railway upheavals on the condition and location of working-class homes. But what were the fortunes of the small local traders whose markets collapsed in the rubble? Their involuntary migrations were often logged, it is true, not only in the compensation ledgers of the railway companies, but in rate-books and street directories; but others disappeared without trace. How many, one wonders, were like the chimney-sweeps of Marylebone, who successfully organised a claim for compensation on the loss of their trade, and how many were like the pathetic charwoman who hanged herself when her clients were driven away, in the Marylebone Station demolitions about 1895?[13] The demolition statements alone cannot answer such specific questions as these. But they do both focus attention on the complexity of the social repercussions of railway building, and add another human dimension to the cross-section of society which the Books of Reference reveal. In doing this, they provide valuable data for the study of local and transport history alike.

Period of operations*	Act	Promoter	Principal works	Persons displaced†
1854–63	17–18 Vict., C. CCXXI	Met. R	Exts to GPO and to Paddington; juncts. with L & NWR and GNR	307
1859	22 Vict., C. XXXV	GNR	Junct. with NLR	440
1859–64	22–3 Vict., C. LXXXI	Charing Cross R	Junct. with N Kent & Greenwich Lines of SER; and line London Bdg to Charing Cross	4,580
1860–4	23–4 Vict., C. CLXXVII	LC & DR	Met. Exts: Herne Hill to Farringdon St and junct. with Met. R; and Herne Hill to Victoria Stn & Pimlico R	3,150
1860–	23–4 Vict., C. CXXIII	London & Blackwall R	Branches to St Katharine's and London Docks	173
1860–3	23–4 Vict., C. CLXVIII	GNR	Junct. between GNR at Regent's Canal and Met. R at King's Cross	430
1861–4	24–5 Vict., C. CLXIV	Hammersmith & City R (GW & Met. Jt)	Green Lane Bridge, Westbourne Park, to Hammersmith	400
1861–6	24–5 Vict., C. XCIII	Charing Cross R	Junct. nr Red Cross St and ext. to Cannon St	557
1861–5	24–5 Vict., C. CXCVI	NLR	Ext. Kingsland to Broad St	4–5,000
1861–5	24–5 Vict., C. CCXXXIII	Met. R	Ext. Smithfield to Finsbury Circus	1,100
1862–	25–6 Vict., C. XCVI	SER	Widening N Kent Line at Deptford	208
1862–	25–6 Vict., C. LXVIII	LB & SCR	Enlargement of London Bridge and Bricklayers' Arms stations	398
1863–6	26–7 Vict., C. CXLIII	LB & SCR`	E Brixton to London Bridge	66
1863–71 (–88)	26–7 Vict., C. CCIV	LC & DR	Line Peckham Rye to Greenwich Park	367
1863–7	26–7 Vict., C. LXXIV	MR	Met. Ext. from Bedford	3,167
1864–74	27–8 Vict., C. CCCXIII	GER	Liverpool St Stn and lines to Enfield, etc.	1,071
1864–8	27–8 Vict., C. CCXXXI	MR	St Pancras Branch (junct. with Met. R)	1,180

Period of operations*	Act	Promoter	Principal Works	Persons displaced†
1864–84	27–8 Vict., C. CCCXXII	Met. Dist. R	Line W Brompton to nr Fenchurch St	2,246
1865–76	28–9 Vict., C. LI	E Lond R	Line New Cross to Shoreditch	4,645 §
1865–	28–9 Vict., C. CXVII	GER	Junctions at Stratford, Seven Sisters Rd, Bethnal Green, White-chapel	548
1866–78	29–30 Vict., C. CCLV	GER	Alterations between Hanger Lane and West Green Road, Tottenham	361
1866–	29–30 Vict., C. CLXXX	E Lond. R	Juncts. at Bethnal Green	207
1866–	29–30 Vict., C. CCCLXIII	LC & DR	Enlargement of Ludgate Stn	650
1866–84	29–30 Vict., C. CLX	Met. R	Additional works in Paddington, St Marylebone, St Pancras and City	1,510
1866–8	29–30 Vict., C. CLXXVIII	Met. Dist. R	Additional works in Kensington, Westminster and City	1,180
1866–78	29–30 Vict., C. CCXXVII	SER	Line Charlton to Deptford	165
1867–9	30–1 Vict., C. LXXVIII	NLR	Widening City Branch between Shoreditch and Islington; branch between Bow and junction at Bromley with London, Tilbury & Southend R	1,440
1872–8	35–6 Vict., C. CLIII	SER	Junct. of Cannon St & Charing Cross R with LC & DR	2,118
1875–7	38–9 Vict., C. CCVIII	Met. Dist. R	Junct. with Kensington & Richmond line of L & SWR at Hammersmith	350
1875–	38–9 Vict., C. CXI	MR	St Pancras connecting line (Somers Town gds) and Brixton Stn branch	2,942
1876–	39–40 Vict., C. LIV	Lond. & Blackwall R	Enlargements at Fenchurch St Stn	417
1876–	39–40 Vict., C. LXXXIV	LC & DR	Widening viaduct over Denmark Rd, Camberwell, etc.	126

Appendix (cont.)

Period of operations*	Act	Promoter	Principal works	Persons displaced†
1876–	39–40 Vict., C. LII	E Lond. R	Junct. with GER at Bethnal Green	2,016
1876–	39–40 Vict., C. CXLV	MR	Junct. with Lond. & Blackwall R at Preston Rd, Poplar	1,471
1877–	40–1 Vict., C. LXXXV	Met. R	Enlargements nr Aldgate Stn, etc.	505
1877–	40–1 Vict., C. LXIII	Lond. & Blackwall R	Junct. with Stepney-Bow ext. at Regent's Canal and with Blackwall line at Island Row	634
1877–	40–1 Vict., C. CVIII	L & SWR	Enlargements in St Mary's, Lambeth	560
1877–	40–1 Vict., C. XCI	L & NW & GW Jt R	Widening of West Lond. R at Hammersmith	614
1877–	40–1 Vict., C. XLV	L & NWR	Works at Chalk Farm Bridge, St Pancras, etc.	273
1878–80 (–99)	41–2 Vict., C. CLIV	Met. Dist. R	Ext. West Brompton Stn to Fulham (Willow Bank); junct. with N & SW Junct. R at Acton	797
1878–	41–2 Vict., C. XCVI	MR	Junct. with Met. and Met. Dist. R at High Street, Kensington Stn	257
1879–84	42–3 Vict., C. CCI	Met. and Met. Dist. R	City lines and extensions and junct. with E Lond. R	1,195
1879–	42–3 Vict., C. CL	GER	Junct. with Tottenham & Hampstead Junct. R at Tottenham, etc.	179
1879–	42–3 Vict., C. XLIX	E Lond. R	Enlargements in St Paul's, Deptford	840
1881–	44–5 Vict., C. CXCVIII	SER	Greenwich Dock & R	468
1883–	46–7 Vict., C. XXV	N Lond. R	Works in St Leonard's Bromley, Mdx, at Limehouse Cut of R. Lee	1,372
1885–90	48–9 Vict., C XCIII	GER	Enlargement of Liverpool St Stn	737
1885–91	48–9 Vict., C. CXIV	London & Blackwall R	Widenings on north side	1,063
1890–2	53–4 Vict., C. CVIII	GER	Widening between Bethnal Green and Hackney Downs	382

Period of operations*	Act	Promoter	Principal works	Persons displaced†
1890–1900	53–4 Vict., C. CXLVIII	LB & SCR	Enlargement Willow Walk Goods Stn	1,962
1890–4	53–4 Vict., C. CXXXVIII	MR	Enlargements at St Pancras	1,376
1890–4	53–4 Vict., C. LIII	L & SWR	Widenings between Waterloo and Nine Elms	1,041
1893–1902	56–7 Vict., C. LXXXVII	Waterloo & City R	Clearances in St Mary's, Lambeth	90
1893–7	56–7 Vict., C. I	Manchester, Sheffield & Lincolnshire R	Metropolitan extension and Marylebone Stn	4,448
1896–8	59–60 Vict., C. CXXVI	SER	Widenings at Lambeth, Rotherhithe, Deptford	1,492
1897–1902	60–1 Vict., C. CCLVII	Whitechapel & Bow R (Met. Dist. & London, Tilbury & Southend Rs)	Displacement in St Leonard's, Bromley	742
1897–	60–1 Vict., C. CCXXVII	SER	Widening in Horselydown and Bermondsey, etc.	1,120
1898–	61–2 Vict., C. CIII	L & SWR	Widenings in Lambeth, Wandsworth, and enlargement of Waterloo Stn	2,500
1898–	61–2 Vict., C. CCLIII	GCR	Enlargements at Marylebone	1,750
1898–	61–2 Vict., C. CCXXXIV	L & NWR	Widening nr Regent's Park	400
1900–	63–4 Vict., C. CX	GER	Extensions in Whitechapel	720

Notes: *The earlier date in each case indicates the year of the act, and the later the year in which the works were completed and the line or station opened to traffic – if that is known. The dates or periods of actual demolitions can be established for certain in very few cases because construction dates are unfortunately rarely available, but the presumption must be that as clearances were invariably in the first stage of the works, these generally began shortly after the passage of the act.

†The figures for persons displaced have been obtained either from the demolition statements themselves or, where these are unobtainable, from reports of select committees on bills, or, for the period after 1885, from *Report of Joint S.C. on Housing of the Working Classes, Parl. Papers*, 1902, V, Appendix H (2). Schemes which involved displacements but for which no statistical data are available have been excluded.

§6,713 was the figure given for this displacement in *The Builder*, XXII (1864), 241.

PART THREE

The Urban Fabric

9

The slums of Victorian London*

How much do we know about what it meant to be alive in a Victorian slum? How much *can* we know about an experience which was remote from almost all those who wrote about life in the towns or took oral evidence about it for various commissions of inquiry? Perhaps nothing reveals more ruthlessly how little we do know about urban culture in Victorian England than a survey of the secondary sources from which its slumminess may be discerned, nor makes that evidence more fragile than reflecting on what it is bound to omit. The sheer bodily sensations to be had from the daily round of slum life, the emotional demands it made and the responses it evoked, the mental reactions to the special miseries and the gaieties of living in the gutters of urban society – the real meaning, indeed, of life at certain levels – are not contained now to any extent even in the archaeological remains of the slums of Victorian London, much less in any well-calendared archives. They have almost all gone. Smell – to take but one of the most evocative elements of the slums – has no historical dimension; yet it has always been one of their chief ingredients, a factor potent enough in the end to drive George Orwell from the ferret's cage he once occupied in a post-Victorian generation,[1] or to put George Augustus Sala back on the streets – his nostrils filled beyond endurance with the stench of the bugs – after his attempt to doss down for the night in a slum eighty years before Orwell.[2]

It is surprising enough that little sustained work has been done on London itself, let alone its nether side. The last thoroughgoing study of its history as a whole was published long before Victoria's Golden Jubilee, and it is lamentably true that no comprehensive history of London has yet been written.[3] It is equally true that, despite the enormous demand that seems to have existed for local histories of London's villages and boroughs, especially

* This paper is a development of one read to the fourth annual conference of the Victorian Society, held in London, 30 Sept.–2 Oct. 1966. It was included in an abbreviated form in *The Victorian Poor*, ed. Paul Thompson (1967). It has also benefited from comments made by members of historical societies to whom it has been read at Glasgow and Exeter Universities and from those of the Victorian Studies Group at Leicester.

towards the close of the Victorian period, very few of them kept antiquarianism at bay long enough to give historical significance to lives and to landscapes that had so lately been contemporary.[4] Nor has this gap been closed at all effectively since, for reasons which I considered once before.[5] All this is the more surprising because this is a period which includes some of the great social investigations of the urban scene, particularly those of Mayhew and Booth, and which is incomparably rich in municipal and parliamentary records.[6] Their sheer weight and catholicity do something to preserve them from historians but this may one day incur a double penalty and make them as prone to space-saving operations in overcrowded offices as those belonging to industry and the professions have already been for a long time.

The fact is that the annals of the urban poor are buried deeper than those of the rural poor and the London poor perhaps deepest of all. Walter Bagehot's remark that the character of the poor was an unfit topic for continuous art gives only one of the many reasons why nearly contemporary historians should not have dug for them to any extent; but it is remarkable that there should have been so little historical investigation since then. Apart from the more general researches of E. R. Dewsnup[7] and William Ashworth,[8] and three or four unpublished theses completed more recently,[9] hardly anything has been done to extract from the hundreds of accounts of the beginnings, growth and destruction of slums in Victorian London an historical explanation of how these things happened, or any dispassionate analysis of the way in which life in the slums was carried on.[10]

We still have no comprehensive and balanced view of the Victorian phase of slum clearance, nor of the leading figures in that movement, nor even of its vast printed annals, let alone those pulpy pieces of cheap literature that once poured so liberally from slum presses for sale on the streets.[11] This half-hidden world will never be fully rediscovered, I suppose, and its mysteries may in the end be found to be as empty as Bagehot insisted they were, but our ignorance of how life went on in the slums ought to goad us a little more. By concentrating so much on the administrative rather than the sociological aspects of the slums we have, I think, tended to take rather a narrow view of them, of how they came about, why they should have rankled one generation and not another.

This essay has therefore two main aims: to review as briefly as possible the printed materials that are available on the experience of slum life and of attitudes towards the slums of Victorian London; and to examine, again fairly briefly, the reasons for the existence and survival of those slums. But first there is a question of definition.

1

What is a slum? According to J. H. Vaux's *Flash Dictionary* (1812), 'slum' was little more than a name for a room, though by the 1820s the word had three distinct meanings as a slang expression for various kinds of tavern and eating house, for loose talk and gipsy language, and, more vaguely, for a room in which low goings-on occurred.[12] It was this last root from which the modern meaning of the word has developed to include whole houses and districts in town and country. Pierce Egan began using it in this way in his *Life in London* in following the antics of Corinthian Tom in the 'back slums' of the Holy Lane, or St Giles, and defined the term in a footnote in one place as 'low, unfrequented parts of the town'.[13] Dickens was using the term in this sense in a letter of November 1840 when he wrote, 'I mean to take a great, London, back-slums kind of walk tonight.'[14] He did not, so far as I know, use it in print in any of his novels or other writings of the 1840s, though one of the older meanings of the word was certainly carried on by Mr. Slum in *The Old Curiosity Shop*, and Henry Mayhew discovered some actual writers of slums, or what one dictionary so graphically called *fakements*.[15]

As a straightforward term for bad housing, its form had evidently soon started to change simply to 'slums', as it appeared in a letter to *The Times* in January 1845,[16] and from this time it passed into very general use as a semi-slang expression, a synonym for 'rookeries', 'fever-dens', 'little hells', 'devil's acres', 'dark purlieus', until eventually the inverted commas disappeared.[17] This took a surprisingly long time to happen and some writers in the 1880s were still using the term in this tentative way. By then, certainly, it had also become a verb, and slumming was already the word to describe the inquisitive, charitable or conscience-salving act of 'poor-peopling' – the kind of thing, attributed to Lady Aurora Languish, for example, in Henry James's *The Princess Casamassima* (1886).

These semantic adjustments may be significant, for the lack of a word for such a common phenomenon does not necessarily correspond with an experience too esoteric for ordinary speech, but with one too readily accepted to require a pejorative term. Did those living in the slums ever use the term as readily as those that did not? What was being overlooked, I think, before 'slum' was properly coined was the existence of a housing problem – itself not normally referred to as such until nearly the end of the century – as distinct from one of sanitation or public health. The changing meaning of this term seems to reveal a changing attitude to the phenomenon itself.

Precisely what it ever meant on the ground has never been clear, partly because it has not developed that kind of technical meaning which definition in an act of parliament would have given it: indeed, it still lacks this kind of precision and tends to be defined even nowadays in terms of the *number* of obsolescent houses which a local authority can clear rather than the kind of houses involved.[18] This vagueness in practice has been aggravated by the failure of parliament or the courts to define at all clearly the chief characteristic of a slum, namely its overcrowding, or the actual basis of the medical judgment that a house was 'unfit for human habitation'.[19]

The implication of this is that, like poverty itself, slums have always been, as they now are, relative things, both in terms of neighbouring affluence and in terms of what is intolerable or accepted by those living in or near them. Such a term has no fixity. The study of it requires a sociology of language,[20] for it was being applied with varying force over the period and with different emphasis at any one time by different social classes; it was being used in effect for a whole range of social and political purposes; and the very districts which were liable to be labelled with it were approaching that condition at different speeds and for various reasons. It is not possible now to invent a satisfactory definition of a slum, even a London one, in the nineteenth century. 'It may be one house', wrote Robert Williams in his *London Rookeries and Colliers' Slums* (1893),

but it generally is a cluster of houses, or of blocks of dwellings, not necessarily dilapidated, or badly drained, or old, but usually all this and small-roomed, and, further, so hemmed in by other houses, so wanting in light and air, and therefore cleanliness, as to be wholly unfit for human habitation.

Slums are three-dimensional obscenities, whether in bricks and mortar, wattle and mud, timber and corrugated iron, or asbestos; and they have rightly been regarded by the many writers who have dwelt on them as the great stains on civilisation. Yet there is no definition that is applicable to historical evidence that can translate this into some handy yardstick.[21]

2

What, then, is the historical evidence for life in the slums of Victorian London? We might begin by noticing that although the slum has nowhere yet been defined historically, its universality and the attempt to recognise its place in the life cycle of twentieth-century cities, have produced a sociological literature of considerable importance. In one sense this tradition provides the closest link we have with the phenomenon in its nineteenth-century aspect because it originated in the protest literature of the last two decades of that century, and has since been reinforced by a sporadic interest in the condition both of Victorian slums that have survived the period and of Victorian housing developments that have more recently subsided into slumdom. Nothing published in Britain has generated quite the same response as the pathological approach of the Chicago school of sociologists in the 1920s, itself much influenced by the work of earlier reformers like Jacob Riis, Robert A. Woods, and a number of others.[22] Yet the studies of slum communities and slum tendencies which have been undertaken since then have, despite their own conflicts on the interpretative level, a cross-cultural significance that has hardly been realised.[23] One or two recent studies in particular have hinted very interestingly at the scope that exists for interpreting slums in almost ahistorical terms, and their role in town planning and urban renewal is tending to keep their nineteenth-century phase of development very much in view in finding twentieth-century solutions for the problems they have raised.[24]

In Britain, where the growth of the social sciences was markedly less rapid immediately following the close of the Victorian period, there has been less carry-over from the protest literature to a scholarly appraisal either of this writing or of the phenomenon itself. Booth,[25] it is true, was followed up methodically by H. W. Llewellyn-Smith,[26] and there were some flashes of protest in the 1920s and 1930s that echoed the earlier outbursts,[27] but the issue had apparently already become an administrative one and the retrospective writing of the inter-war years (with one or two exceptions) did not rise much above this level. To Patrick Geddes, the process of city-building in the nineteenth century was a lamentable episode: 'slum, semi-slum and super slum', he wrote, 'to this has come the Evolution of Cities'.[28] The slums, like the poor that occupied them, now began to appear immutable and there was little sense of discovery to be had from gathering any fresh evidence about them. It is the fact that so many familiar slums did survive in the different circumstances of the 1950s – coupled with the post-war resurgence of the social sciences, perhaps – that made their discovery possible once more. The coming and going of ideas in Britain about the aberrations of urban life, as about urbanism itself, need altogether much more thorough investigation.

The facts about the slums that had become merely unpalatable in the twentieth century were often shockingly fresh or simply incredible to those that gathered or digested them in the nineteenth. The passion for exact knowledge about the condition of society probably was aroused a good deal less by scientific curiosity than it was by the desire to remove the dangers that were on the doorsteps of the respectable classes in the 1840s. The reports of poor law commissioners, select committees and royal commissions which built up the public indictment of squalor of all kinds, naturally embodied a great volume of data about the slums of London, and the scope of that material is already familiar to anyone who has studied its sanitary history.[29] One of the commissioners involved in these investigations, Hector Gavin, published in 1848 a remarkably perceptive house-by-house survey of classic dimensions on the slums of Bethnal Green, which he entitled *Sanitary Ramblings*;[30] and several members of the Statistical Society of London read papers to its meetings on the condition of other parts of London which fell below Gavin's level of detail and objectivity to only a minor degree.[31] Not the least remarkable fact, however, about the next thirty or forty years was the failure of any researcher to maintain the systematised curiosity about the slums displayed by these early investigators. For all their definition, colour and humanity, Henry Mayhew's more celebrated findings, made in the first place for the *Morning Chronicle* inquiries of 1849–50, provided little more than a panorama of the poverty – and of the itinerant

employment – to be seen on the streets.[32] It is possible to say that they
suffered from his under-disciplined curiosity and his spontaneous desire to
make the poor known to the rich: the theme which had first been so
dramatically drawn out by Carlyle in his article 'Signs of the Times' in the
Edinburgh Review in 1829 and more recently by Disraeli in *Sybil* (1845)
appears as commonplace only in retrospect.[33] Strictly speaking, Mayhew's
work was essentially a form of higher journalism, not of social analysis; and
his reports did not in any case take the reader very far off the streets into the
choking wilderness of the slums themselves.

The bulk of the annals of the slums between the 1840s and the beginning
of the 1880s are basically of this type, social reportage that was meant to
supply unpleasant facts to those unlikely to obtain them for themselves. Not
surprisingly, they were often a thin camouflage for other things, like the
accelerating alarm felt at the approach of dangers such as spiritual and moral
destitution or 'gore-faced revolution'; they could also merely serve the ends
of the popular journalism which was fastening just then with such relish on
the mysteries of the metropolis.[34] It was rare for such writing to avoid the
anti-urban bias which a contemplation of the evils of the city could scarcely
avoid conjuring up.

When we look at this great city [of London], with all its pomp and splendor – its wealth,
power, and greatness – its palaces, cathedrals, and mansions – its courts of justice,
academies of science, and institutions of philanthropy – surely we mourn that such a city
has so much wickedness, degradation, infidelity, heathenism, and profligacy . . . . The
swarms of wretched, filthy, haggard, dissolute, profligate, care-worn, outcast masses who
inhabit the dingy courts, dingy cellars, and miserable garrets of our great towns, call loudly
upon us to go and carry the message of peace to their benighted homes . . . . Christians!
arouse yourselves to work! Thrust in the sickle and reap, for the harvest of the earth is
ripe.[35]

Understandably enough, an anonymous pamphleteer advised would-be
servant girls to avoid this harvest field:

O, ye happy village girls! whom a wise and bountiful Providence has set at a distance from
these suffocating towns and cities which are the cemeteries of nature . . . . Cling to your
country homes as the nearest representation this world affords of that Paradise recorded
in your Bibles.[36]

These remarks epitomise one set of attitudes, but another note had also
been struck. This was sounded by R. A. Vaughan, a Congregational
minister, whose *The Age of Great Cities* declared with equal fervour the
possibilities of urban progress in an industrial age, despite the signs of
retrogression that were already visible.[37] There were, unfortunately, few
men, if any, in the years that followed who could combine vision of this order
with the political and administrative capacity needed to avoid the calamity
of the slums whose growth was surpassed in some places only by that of the
suburbs.[38]

It must be remembered that very little indeed had been written so far on the living conditions of the metropolitan poor. Even so finely observed a work as John Hogg's *London As It Is* (1837),[39] or Richard Seeley's more subtle reproach, *The Perils of the Nation* (1843),[40] had virtually ignored housing conditions altogether. One of the earliest specific literary references to slum conditions does not come till 1842, when James Grant described in his third account of London life how 'whole families mess together as if they were so many pigs' in St Giles's, Drury Lane and the East End, and regretted that no association existed to discover the facts and provide the remedies. 'The great mass of the metroplitan community', he wrote, 'are as ignorant of the destitution and distress which prevail in large districts of London . . . as if the wretched creatures were living in the very centre of Africa.'[41]

Probably the first work given entirely to slum housing was the Rev. Thomas Beames's *The Rookeries of London*, which appeared in the very wake of the *Morning Chronicle* articles and offered an astonishingly sober appraisal of the dynamics of slum-making in central and south London.[42] Yet there was in general an understandable touch of sensationalism as well as naïveté in a good deal of the writing about the slums over the next twenty years. One thinks of Henry Morley's horror at the cartloads of filth being dug and scraped from the thirteen once fashionable houses in Wild Court off Drury Lane in 1855 – 150 cartloads from cesspools, 350 from the basements, a ton of bugs alone – and can understand how his thankfulness for the new hope being given to the hundred families coming in should have been virtually undimmed at the sight of four hundred families being driven hopelessly out.[43] Yet thirty years and innumerable philanthropic acts later the whole district of Great Wild Street was still firmly held by the poorest of the poor. Razing a slum was not a final act of reparation. This kind of knowledge was accumulated slowly. In the meantime journalists who were prepared to go into the slums were building up factual dossiers that were better than stark ignorance. Among them George Godwin, editor of *The Builder* since 1844, and John Hollingshead (who, almost more than anyone, aimed at quantifying his data as far as he could) were probably the most authoritative;[44] there were also George Augustus Sala, Henry Morley, James Greenwood, and others. Many of their forays into the slums were to get copy for *Household Words*, *All the Year Round*, and other newspapers and magazines, and some of their reports were subsequently collected, interspersed with less horrifying items, into separate volumes.[45] It is a little surprising in view of this journalism to find the illustrated papers, such as *Punch* and *Illustrated London News*, so short of material relating to the slums in this period.[46]

One effect of these writings was not only to begin to turn the slums into a public spectacle, perhaps even a public entertainment, but to enlarge the scope both for private charity and public social policy. For example, one clergyman in the East End, noticing the unevenness in the distribution of the slums and the big differences in the cost of relieving the poor among the poor law unions of London, argued very cogently as early as 1858 for some equalisation of the poor rate.[47] On a more practical level, Mrs Lydia Ranyard had already published her account of the Bible-women she had set to work, dispensing not only the scriptures but practical charity of every kind in the worst slums of London.[48] C. B. P. Bosanquet, writing at the end of the 1860s, was able to describe the opportunities that were already being used by the charitably inclined in visiting the slums to dole out soup, clothes, bedding and Bibles, and cautionary advice to anyone inclined to follow in their footsteps.[49] From this time, too, slum clergymen, wanting cash or help in performing functions that had much more in common with what is now described as social work than it had with the activities of the clergy in less destitute parishes, were becoming almost voluble in publishing information and anecdotes of their successes in lighting up dark corners and sermons on those that still lay beyond the light.[50]

A second effect of this kind of writing was to reveal a new kind of social hierarchy. 'On the dunghill of poverty', observed Douglas Jerrold in his novel, *St Giles and St James*, 'how great is the distinction between the layers of straw.'[51] That there was 'an aristocracy of rags' was demonstrably so from the strictly non-fictional interpretation of the working classes that was given presently by Thomas Wright in his classic *The Great Unwashed* (1868) and *Some Customs and Habits of the Working Classes* (1867).[52] The slums were not confined to particular levels of this hierarchy, but it was becoming clear that there was a certain level below which neither charity nor any public authority was accustomed to go. Henry Morley on another of his sallies into the slums in the 1850s reckoned to have discovered in one part of Bethnal Green, not the workhouse, criminal or begging poor, but the 'quiet poor' – a stagnant and politically supine community of some fourteen thousand weavers and hawkers, sunk below the level even of discontent, each family occupying with dreadful respectability its own little room in which the people outnumbered all the other objects in it.[53]

This kind of 'deserving poor', standing above a line of low-grade respectability, giving little trouble and keeping mostly out of sight, could conceivably be raised by degrees, their finer feelings – brutalised though they were – could be aroused, and something could be done to 'raise them a rung in life'. The sense of discovery displayed by many writers on Victorian slums, clergymen included, when recounting the human qualities that moved below the dirt and crime, reveals a prevalent conviction that this could hardly be so. 'We have started to learn', one contributor to the *Ragged School Union Magazine* wrote in 1851, 'that boundless opulence and wretchedness the most extreme dwell side by side. . . . Such discoveries are at once painful and alarming, but if they be realities, it is essential that they be widely known.'[54] One is reminded of Sir Francis Burdett's impressions on first looking into Dickens's *Oliver Twist* – pain and doubt.[55] The sense of novelty did not seem to disappear till the 1890s, the disbelief and the awful anonymity and imperviousness of the problem of where and how to house the poor did not go until long after that.

Below this level of 'deserving poor' were what were generally known as 'the criminal classes', potentially if not actually violent, undeserving of consideration and help, sub-human almost: it was a future Archbishop of Canterbury who could write of his first slum parishioners in the early 1890s, 'my first flock contained 2,000 human (?) beings'.[56] 'Looking at the foul houses, hearing the foul language, seeing the poor women with black eyes, watching the multitudinous children in the mud', wrote Walter Besant of what was one of the least fashionably miserable parts of London in 1893, Rotherhithe, 'one wonders whether these agencies are enough to prevent this mass of people from falling lower still into the hell of savagery.'[57] It is this underworld of the mere dosser, shifting in and out of work and crime, which has tended to fall right out of sight in the history of housing as distinct from the history of house demolition.

It was certainly getting into print at the time. By the 1880s not only were the monthlies and quarterlies – like *Nineteenth Century, National Review, Contemporary Review, Fraser's Magazine, Quiver, Pall Mall Gazette* and *Quarterly Review* – publishing articles on various aspects of slum life, but so too were the daily and weekly presses: *The Times, Daily News, Pictorial World, Echo, Globe* and *Graphic* were some of the principal avenues for this new surge of social reporting. One series of reports in particular, which appeared in the *Daily News* and *Pictorial World*, had unusually far-reaching effect, even though they were not all collected together in a single volume before 1889. These were the contributions of George R. Sims, of whom it was said by the *Contemporary Review* in its retrospective survey of the literature of 1880 that he was doing for London and its slums what Bret Harte had done for the American backwoods:[58] *How the Poor Live and Horrible London*,[59] somewhat overdramatised though that volume appears now, stimulated wide interest in the whole question of what should be done about the slums, and was the germ of the idea that presently erupted as *The Bitter Cry of Outcast London*.

This anonymous twenty-page penny pamphlet commonly attributed to the Secretary to the London Congregational Union, described, somewhat more phlegmatically than a good many recent utterances, the activities of a mission then being run in Collier's Rents in Bermondsey.[60] Neither the environment nor the missionary efforts that were bent on winning it over from the devils of the slums were peculiar. The title, the price, the direct language and the visibility of the target, help to explain why it should so aptly have hit the mark.

Whilst we have been building our churches and solacing ourselves with our religion and dreaming that the millenium was coming, the poor have been growing poorer, the wretched more miserable, and the immoral more corrupt. . . . Few who will read these pages have any conception of what these pestilential rookeries are. . . . To get into them you have to penetrate courts reeking with poisonous and malodorous gases arising from accumulations of sewage and refuse scattered in all directions. . . . You have to grope your way along dark and filthy passages swarming with vermin. Then, if you are not driven back by the intolerable stench, you may gain admittance to the dens in which these thousands of beings, who belong, as much as you, to the race for whom Christ died, herd together.

Specific addresses and the families occupying them were described, especially Collier's Rents; 'and we are told', the author observed, 'that the owner is getting from 50 to 60 per cent upon his money'. It was this remark that *Punch* immediately seized on with its cartoon 'Mammon's Rents' and the accompanying poem mordantly reflecting on its theme. For some weeks it pilloried the rookery landlords and finally broke off its campaign the following May (after a Royal Commission had been appointed to inquire into the housing of the working classes) with a cartoon of a clergyman getting a ribald reception for his over-dressed safari into the slums.[61] The public conscience, made uneasy perhaps less by the slum journalism of the preceding decades than by the onset of commercial distress and signs of popular agitation, was thus made ready not only for a redoubled output of books, pamphlets and articles on the slums and the housing problem, as it was now coming to be known, but for the serious discussion of the steps that were needed to make a policy towards the slums effective.[62]

The whole history of the implementation of housing legislation to this date needs more searching examination from the standpoint of the slums themselves, for it is by no means clear that the more and more imperative requirements it embodied actually improved rather than worsened the situation in all places and in every respect. It would not be unfair to suggest that at best it was achieving from the 1870s onwards a marginal improvement in the physical stock of lowest grade housing; that at worst it was merely interfering with the social ecology of these areas in ways which may even have aggravated their criminal and retrogressive tendencies. Did the Nuisances Removal Acts of 1846–66 or the Labourers' Dwellings Act of 1855–75 achieve, on balance, a real improvement in the lives of the slum-dwellers themselves?[63] The question was not put in that way, of course, to the Royal Commission on the Housing of the Working Classes which was appointed in 1884 as the most tangible result of the *Bitter Cry* and of the fusillades of pamphlets which it sparked off. (Ironically enough, these came more readily from slum missionaries of other denominations who feared being overlooked than they did from those wanting to corroborate it.) The disclosures that had been made were shocking enough, but there was the quite unsensational question to be answered of where and how to house the workers and how to stop the situation they were in from going wrong. The suggestion that some kind of retreat from the city was necessary – into the suburbs, the country or abroad – was never made more often.[64] Nor was the question whether satisfactory housing for the families of ordinary working men could be provided at a profit under prevailing by-laws more anxiously examined. Did the government have more of a role than it had so far played?[65]

There was coming into view now a striking difference between the somewhat pietistic literature and the altogether more pragmatic discussion of the questions that were seen to be forcing themselves on parliament and municipal government and crystallising rapidly into election issues.[66] This was also the point at which the need for more systematically derived data on the extent and character of the problem became more emphatic than at any time since the 1840s. It was not merely coincidental that Charles Booth should now have mounted his great exploration of the condition of the London poor in relation to the whole community around them. Perhaps it was also no coincidence that the most impressive empirically derived document of the age, after such a spate of impressionistic writing in the preceding decades, should have been almost dizzy with facts. Booth had no hypotheses that he wanted to test, only a desire to gather information that might help social reform. His seventeen volumes are not easy to use and were probably read much less at the time than they have been admired since.[67] The street-by-street descriptions and appraisal of general social characteristics are probably more valuable now than many of the statistics; his own pencilled notes describing people he interviewed himself, written with a novelist's flair for words that catch the human detail, make these accounts more credible still.[68]

It is worth noting here that the attempt Booth was making to be objective about social conditions was reflected by the efforts of novelists to bring social realism into their work, and the authentic literature of the slums of the last few years of the nineteenth century includes a certain output of this kind which is valuable for two reasons. First, the best of it seems to have embodied, if not the brute facts, then something of the rhetoric of both the dignity and the degradation of life in the slums. The second reason for historians to read this literature is to be prone to influences which were at work on the social conscience of the time. The sheer sentimentalism that made most novels set in the slums between Charles Kingsley and George Gissing[69] (though neither wrote directly on them) so unconvincing on one if not both of these counts was poles apart from the work of Arthur Morrison in *Tales of Mean Streets* (1894) or *A Child of the Jago* (1896), which were topographically and emotionally located with complete authenticity in the East End.[70] Israel Zangwill's *Children of the Ghetto* (1892), which had four editions in the first twelve months, told movingly and with a certain detachment a story that seems to have been woven into the very culture of the impoverished Jewish stronghold in and around Petticoat Lane.[71] St John Adcock's stories – particularly *Beyond Atonement* (1896) and *East End Idylls* (1897) – though uninformative in detail, are saddening still; Richard Whiteing's *No. 5 John Street* (1899) sardonically turned the social contrasts of the West End into a highly effective piece of reformative propaganda.

It was something of a paradox that these writers, like the great bulk of commentators on the slums in the previous half-century, should be dealing with such desolation in a spirit of such optimism, and that in a society still so sharply divided in many ways it was possible for them to get so involved with issues that were seldom personal to them. The imprint of these attitudes in relation to the problems of urban life and the actual circumstances in which they were formed clearly deserve to be studied more. However, the rest of this essay must have a more obvious aim.

3

Why did this street become a slum and not that one? At what point was its metamorphosis complete? What were its architectural elements? What changes took place among the inhabitants as this happened, in terms of numbers, households, social class, behaviour? At what point was this or that street redeemed, and how did this happen, in terms of general legislation, local initiative, landlord opportunism, charity? The answers are bound to be complex when one considers a particular case – what one reviewer of Mayhew called 'this localicity of pauperization'.[72] There is no room here to examine all 'The Reasons for Granby Street', in the manner of Michael Sadleir's authentic explanation in his *Forlorn Sunset* (1947) of the social descent of the region round the southern end of Waterloo Bridge in the 1840s. There is one piece of south London that I want to examine in a moment, but my main purpose is to argue that, apart from relatively trivial influences helping to settle the precise location of the slums, the major factors at work can simply be described in terms of the supply of and the demand for housing. The slums were the residue left on the market, the last bits and pieces to command a price. So I want to look at them more as products of general economic and social processes than as entities that can be examined at all satisfactorily in isolation.

The most general explanation for slum tendencies in particular places is that, without the kind of general control on the spatial development of the city that might have been given, say, by a rectilinear grid, there were bound to be innumerable deadends and backwaters in the street plan. A glance at Booth's maps shows how often these introspective places were seized by the 'criminal classes', whose professional requirements were isolation, an entrance that could be watched and a back exit kept exclusively for the getaway. They were not difficult to fulfil in scores of places in every part of

Victorian London. A more careful reading of Booth's maps would show how some additions to the street plan – a dock, say, or a canal, a railway line or a new street – frequently reinforced these tendencies. What often made them more emphatic still was the incense of some foul factory, a gas-works, the debris of a street market or an open sewer. They all acted like tourniquets applied too long, and below them a gangrene almost invariably set in. The actual age of houses seldom had much to do with it, and it was sometimes possible to run through the complete declension from meadow to slum in a single generation, or even less. Animal husbandry survived, of course, in caricature in some of these places, where pigs, sheep, cows and other livestock were still being slowly cleared in the 1870s from the slums they had helped to create. One man who had spent twenty years visiting the poor of a riverside parish could write as late as 1892 of the donkeys, goats and chickens which had as free a run of some of the houses by night as they had of the streets by day.[73]

It is possible, too, to trace the origins of slumminess in scamped buildings, whether legally done or not, on inadequately settled 'made ground' or by virtue of some builder's sanitary blunder. The history of building regulations is an unsatisfactory and badly told tale of the regulators never quite catching up with the builders, and of the piecemeal enlarging of the statutory code so as to reduce risks from fire and to health. The machinery for approving street plans and drainage levels took time to evolve and an incorruptible corps of local government officers to administer it.[74] No one can say with real confidence that the many hands required in building and rebuilding slum-prone neighbourhoods were under full and proper control in the public interest before the last decade of the century. Whatever was substandard physically was inclined to become socially inferior, too: the slummers themselves, though often adding the penalty of their own personal habits to the descending scale, seldom *created* such slums as often as they confirmed the builders' and others' mistakes. When this social descent began it was seldom, if ever, reversed, but went inexorably on, respectability taking itself a little further off, the sheer durability of such houses visiting the sins of their builders on the third and fourth generations of those that occupied them.

By a special irony the large houses vacated by the middle classes in their trek to the suburbs were capable of declining fastest after they had been given up, for they were far too large for any class but that for which they had been built and could be occupied economically only by being turned into tenements, for which they were not always at all well adapted. No slum was worse than property transferred in this way. The quite normal process of bringing land once settled at a low density into heavier occupation some-times got badly out of control; and back gardens, often quite small ones, were divided and sub-divided into alleys and courts which could scarcely avoid going badly wrong once rot had set in. There were, in fact, a hundred things that could go wrong: these hells were a collective act and their whereabouts were fixed by the same kind of concatenation of local influences that settled the circumstances of life anywhere.

Yet the making of the slums of Victorian London, like the grooming of jalopies for the American Deep South, was a process that began far beyond the reach of the slummers who packed into them. It is important to recognise that these unfortunates were more than anything else merely the residuary legatees of a kind of house-processing operation which was started by another social class with little or no idea of how it would end. It is also clear that the distribution of personal incomes and social disabilities in any society help to determine not only the way in which power is used at the top but the way in which weaknesses are shared at the bottom. The condition of the houses of the poor, far from being a quaint expression of their own debased tastes – a view widely held among the ruling classes of Victorian England[75] – was a reflex of the allocation of political power and economic resources in society at large.

One of the most general reasons for the slums of Victorian England simply was that the capital which might have wrought a change was being ploughed heavily back into the commercial machine instead of being distributed in higher wages, and its earnings benefited particular social classes differentially. If better houses had been built to house the workers during the nineteenth century, the higher wages paid out to make this possible would probably have raised the costs of exports and reduced the capital being sent abroad, which would in turn have held back the growth of exports. Another way of putting this would be that slums were necessary so as not to dissipate too many resources in housing, and that while labour was abundant, cheap and docile this was economically justifiable. The logic of this, tacitly accepted at the time, is that the slums helped to underpin Victorian prosperity. Yet it is hard to escape the view that one of the real costs of industrial expansion was the making of slums, then and since. Indeed, the wealth that was created in this process first benefited the middle classes, who used it quite literally to put a distance between themselves and the workers. The middle-class Victorian suburb was both an invention for accentuating these social distinctions and a means of putting off for a generation or two the full realisation of what was entailed in living in a slum. C. F. G. Masterman's powerful imagery of the nether world across which the middle classes were carried on their railway viaducts towards the heart of the commercial metropolis conveys this well.[76] These repercussions were all the more to be felt in a society in which landed wealth, drawn though it increasingly was from urban revenues, was still underpinning great embankments of privilege and political leverage, and in which economic forces were being allowed to spend themselves, within limits set by legislation for the public health, almost unrestrainedly. The housing of the poor, as of any other class, was an item of real property, capable of providing titles to wealth for a whole series of property-holders; it was expected to yield profits commensurate with whatever was regarded as the risks of investing in it; and it was held to be quite as much subject to the ordinary pressures of the market as any other commodity put up for sale.

Take demand first. The level of demand for living room in London, then as now, was basically a function of the expansion of the urban economy; and the capacity of an individual tenant to pay a given rent was governed by his personal income and regularity of employment. Though it had not yet completely magnetised England, London had already become, not merely the country's capital, but the centre for most of the big commodity markets and financial houses, the country's chief port and industrial area. This commercial metropolis was being made more impregnable still by the concentrative power of the railways at home and the gains of economic imperialism abroad. From just under a million inhabitants at the beginning of the century, these functions required the concentration of about four and one-half millions within the Administration County of London alone at its close, and of a further two millions distributed less congestedly in an outer belt of the conurbation. London therefore sucked up provincial migrants because jobs were either better paid there or thought to be so; it also offered a more liberal array of charities, richer rewards for crime, a more persuasive legend of opportunity than could be found anywhere in the country. So the net migration into London during the 1840s resulted in the addition of about 250,000 inhabitants, or almost a fifth of its mean population for the decade – a rate of intake which declined appreciably over the next two decades while its absolute level continued to climb, but which surged up again in the 1870s, when almost 500,000 or over fifteen per cent, were added to the natural increase.

The link between this immigration and the growth of the slums might be thought to have been a close one, for the newcomers presumably moved on the central areas like an avalanche, or, what sometimes appeared to be the same thing, like the Irish. In the 1840s they were swarming on the cheapest and therefore worst and most overcrowded districts from the very beginning. Were the inhabitants of London's slums, in fact, provincial in origin, drawn at different times from overmanned farms and under-employed industrial towns? We know too little still about the paths of migration into Victorian London to answer this question with real certainty. The censuses reveal merely the frozen climax to a decade of movement, but to judge by the birthplaces of those held in place, on census night in April 1881,[77] the evidence gives every appearance of going the other way and suggests that during the preceding decade, when not much over a third of London's population had been born elsewhere, the movement into London was concentrating on the most rapidly expanding suburbs and progressively less on the districts nearer the centre. Mayfair was an exception in drawing practically sixty per cent of its population from outside London. Bethnal Green, by contrast, which had been three parts slum when Hector Gavin had rambled over it in the late 1840s, and was by now one of the most extensive congeries of slum in London, contained little more than twelve per cent who had been born outside London, and the whole area of Whitechapel and St George's-in-the-East surrounding it did not raise the figure above twenty per cent; Seven Dials itself, plumb centre, had less than half as many inhabitants born outside London as had the most affluent parts of the same West End.

Booth's calculations suggest that there was an inverse ratio between the proportion of provincial immigrants and the poverty of the district. It may be that his statistical aggregates obscured the slums and potential slums that had insinuated themselves to some degree into almost every part of London at some time or other; St James's, as we have seen, was never so sylvan in the 1850s that its back-street slums could fail to transfix quite hardened observers with horror and nausea, nor were the Palace and Abbey at Westminster more than a stately veneer for the hovels crouching behind.[78] When one gets down to street level and looks at the proportions of cockneys to provincials in particular slums – particularly suburban ones – during the thirty years before Booth, the proportion of Londoners to the rest is considerably above that in London at large.

Take Sultan Street in the north-west tip of Camberwell, which Booth recognised as one of the vilest slums in the whole of London.[79] The birthplaces of the heads of the 104 households and their wives, enumerated there in 1871, when the whole area had just started its social descent, divided in the proportion of six Londoners to four provincials and Irish, a ratio which widened considerably over the next three censuses: in 1881 36 per cent of heads and wives were born outside London; by 1901 the figure had fallen as low as 26 per cent. Interestingly enough, the ratio of London-born in Sultan Street increased very markedly during this period as compared with that in Camberwell as a whole, even though by 1901 this larger community was showing signs of deterioration in social class and, along with this, an increase in the proportion of Londoners to the rest. That only 8 per cent of the children enumerated in Sultan Street in 1871 should have been born outside London (and less than 2 per cent in 1901) supports the evidence of the more general statistics that the slums of Victorian London were mostly occupied by second or later generation Londoners.[80] It is clear that the connection between heavy provincial immigration and the slums was not a direct one. The slums of Victorian London are more properly thought of as settlement tanks for submerged Londoners than as settlement areas for provincial immigrants to the city.

This centripetal and downward movement suggests another theme in the study of Victorian London that needs to be put in relation to the more familiar one of the centrifugal deployment of another section of the population into the suburbs. Here are two social gradients: one leading upwards and outwards; the other leading downwards, if not inwards. It raises some interesting general questions about the mechanics of urban growth, and suggests some of the social costs which were involved in them. Consider, for example, the question whether the slums were being occupied by a settled population or a rapidly changing one. Booth gives the impression that slummers were nomads, always on the move to find cheaper rooms, to tap fresh credit, to escape the rent-collector, or the police.

What happened in Sultan Street as its slumminess intensified? It was a street of around seventy six-roomed stock brick houses arranged on three floors, which had been virtually completed between 1868 and 1871.[81] It was built, with an adjoining street, on a small plot of cow-pasture which for forty years had been completely enclosed by a heap of clap-boarded cottages on two sides, a row of modest villas on another, and by the long back gardens of a decent Georgian terrace (row housing) on the fourth. What gave to this ineligible building land still greater insularity was a railway viaduct, pierced by two bridges. The Herne Hill & City Branch of the London, Chatham, & Dover Railway was taken clean across the back-gardens of the terrace between 1860 and 1864 as part of the larger strategy that that company was using to get the better of its rival, the South Eastern Railway, in its drive for the continental traffic to Dover: the tourniquet was in place. The building of Sultan Street was therefore specially speculative, as nothing makes plainer than the speed with which the improved ground rents[82] were passed from hand to hand. The local influences at work on this place correspond closely with what was said earlier. Cow-sheds and piggeries squeezed up with the surrounding houses, and a glue factory, a linoleum factory, a brewery, haddock-smokers, tallow-melters, costermongers keeping their good stuff indoors with them while leaving rotting cabbage-stalks, bad oranges and the like on the street, created between them an atmosphere which, mingled with household odours, kept all but the locals at bay.

Sultan Street itself was *not* badly built but some of its houses became slums almost at once and the rest followed inexorably. By 1871 these seventy or so houses were packed out by 661 persons, and almost a quarter of them were being made to hold between thirteen and eighteen occupants each, or more than two to a room. However, just over half of all the houses contained in 1871 between seven and twelve occupants apiece, a situation which could not be described as one of overcrowding. In ten years the whole spectrum had shifted. The total number living in the street had grown by more than half as much again (57.4 per cent) to 1,038, over half of whom were now to be found thirteen to eighteen per house, while a further 14 per cent were living nineteen or more per house; only a third of the inhabitants of the street were

145

living, on the average, less than two to a room. The net effect of what had happened, was that another forty-three families (197 persons) had come in and lifted the mean figure of persons per house from about nine in 1871 to fifteen in 1881. How many families had come and gone in the interval there is no way of telling precisely, but it seems clear enough from a statistical analysis of age-patterns at successive censuses that there was a big turnover in inhabitants, a process that produced by the 1890s a community that was distinctly older than it would have been if the younger people who had gone there at the start had stayed: the tendency was for older people to move in as the houses themselves aged.

As this was happening the structure of households was changing appreciably. One noticeable feature was that relatives and lodgers were disappearing from the street. That lodgers should be declining is probably more revealing than that relatives should be growing scarcer, because families too poor to put up a nephew or a parent might be supposed to have taken in a lodger provided room could be found: few indexes of poverty and overcrowding could conceivably be more significant than the inability to sub-let even sleeping room. In 1871 the proportion of households with lodgers, almost 15 per cent, had been practically the same as the average for Camberwell as a whole, but by 1881 it had fallen to just over 4 per cent. By this date the whole pattern of Sultan Street society was beginning to diverge significantly from that of the surrounding population in Camberwell as a whole. Three features make this plain: the marital status of the heads of households; the size of families; the occupational and industrial distribution of wage-earners. In all three respects Sultan Street society had in 1871 corresponded quite closely with that of Camberwell as a whole. By 1881, and still more markedly by 1891, there were signs that it was tending to become more matriarchal: relatively more widows, more married women whose husbands were away, and more single women as heads of households. So far as the size of both the household and the family are concerned, there was again virtually no difference between Sultan Street and Camberwell in 1871. By 1881 the average size of household had begun to diverge appreciably and before long the same was true of the size of families: both were larger in Sultan Street.

Rather interestingly, although there seem to have been no significant differences in the number of children to be found in families of the different social groups in Sultan Street or outside it in 1871, both skilled and unskilled workers in Sultan Street in 1901 had appreciably more children than the average for their class in Camberwell as a whole. The street seemed to be somewhat deficient in fathers and abundant in children! So far as jobs are concerned, the Sultan Street community already had many more labourers and domestic servants in 1871 than were to be found in Camberwell as a whole (80 per cent against 44 per cent), though the distribution between skilled and unskilled scarcely varied. It was this distribution which now proceeded to vary: the proportion of skilled to all labourers in Camberwell fell only slightly (62 per cent to 54 per cent between 1871–1901), but in Sultan Street it was halved in these thirty years (62 per cent, 46 per cent, 29 per cent, 32 per cent); actually the disparity was at its greatest between 1881 and 1891, for Sultan Street was slightly redeemed in the 1890s whereas Camberwell at large deteriorated a little more rapidly than it had become accustomed to do.

The newcomers to Sultan Street, which was on the edge of working-class London in the 1870s and 1880s, in this period came (to a much greater extent than was so of Camberwell as a whole) from the area lying immediately to the north of it and south of the Thames. As a suburban trend this was conspicuously sluggish. Why was it that the working classes did not move further afield? The reasons were almost entirely economic. Though we know far too little about family budgets it is possible to relate poor housing to low and irregular incomes in a very general way. It is clear, for example, from a survey taken by the Registrar-General of about thirty thousand working men in different parts of London in March 1887,[83] that the scantiest living accommodation was occupied by the families of the lowest paid and most irregularly employed men and that this increased roughly in step with money wages and security of employment: half the dock labourers, at one extreme, occupied a single room or part of one, while only one per cent of policemen occupied less than two rooms. As the proportion of men who were married did not vary significantly between occupational groups – the mean was 82 per cent – and the size of families appears to have been pretty constant, it seems reasonable to connect type of employment directly with room density. It is also fairly clear that in general the less a man earned the lower the rent he paid, the two sums bearing a rather surprisingly fixed relationship to each other, with rent coming out at around a fifth of the income of the head of the family. The picture is made still sharper by taking account of liability to unemployment in different groups. Very roughly, one may say that at one extreme (St George's-in-the-East) was a situation in which almost half the working men and their families in a whole parish occupied single rooms or less, with over a third out of work and over a quarter earning less than nineteen shillings a week; at the other extreme (Battersea) less than a fifth were unemployed, and around two-thirds occupied three rooms or more and earned over twenty-five shillings a week. This suggests that crowded living conditions were related to the general structure of the labour market.

So long as employment remained on a casual basis, with the number of jobs going fluctuating violently from day to day or hour to hour, not only for unskilled but also for some of the most skilled trades, working men were obliged to live within reasonably close walking distance of their work. The distance considered practicable varied between trades and might stretch to three or four miles, but there are many signs that working men often felt chained more closely to their workplaces than that.[84] The circle of knowledge of what work was going was a narrow one, and the prospect of making a journey for, rather than to, work shortened the commuting radius. Sometimes it was vital to be literally on call. In the docks or some of the East End trades, the connection between the worker's home and workplace sometimes had to be more intimate still, and it was in these circumstances of sweated labour and of insecure and poorly paid employment that creeping congestion either made a district ready for the complete descent into slum or more indelibly confirmed a condition that had already been sketched in. 'A slum', in a word, 'represents the presence of a market for local, casual labour.'[85]

The demand for working-class housing where it was needed in the centre of London was, it is clear, chronically inadequate because working men could not afford to pay higher rents. This also helps to explain why its supply could not be increased there, for this was also being curtailed by the high cost of land wherever more powerful bidders for it were capable of forcing up its price. The housing industry had come to be oriented almost entirely on speculative building in the suburbs because there land could be had cheaply and profits made relatively easily by improving its rental on the basis of an almost implacable flow of capital going into it. It is an interesting question whether the flow of private capital into suburban house-building has not always tended to be at the expense of investment in lower grade housing, unless moderated by public subsidies for working-class housing. The whole ethos of the five per cent philanthropy idea which was developed in the 1850s and 1860s to get private capital for this type of investment really evolved from a situation in which the returns on suburban house-building were not only setting the pace but making the *idea* of securing comparable returns on housing the lower working classes, as distinct from their 'aristocracy', largely nugatory.[86] It is arguable that one of the indirect effects of the growth of the population of London by provincial immigration was to divert some economic resources to the suburbs and, in a sense, to turn the 'terms of trade' between them and the working-class districts at the centre in their own favour.

There were numerous other factors working with this. Apart from the economic and technical limits to building really high blocks of dwellings on restricted sites at the centre during that period, the very structure of the housing industry, the shyness of private capital in financing the building of flats for the 'lower orders', the instinctive dislike of the potential occupants themselves to streets turned on their ends – all put an end to any real possibility of enlarging the housing capacity of the central districts.

Not only so; the supply curve appeared to be backward-sloping, for the higher went ground rents the more inadequate became the supply of houses at the centre: that is, instead of disproportionately more being supplied if the price of living room and rents rose a little, the very reverse tended to happen. Their number was shrinking constantly. The most draconian changes in London have always been to make way for a greater traffic in merchandise and fare-paying passengers, whether by sea, road or rail; and the docks, street improvements and railways being built in this period set off a whole series of detonations which could be felt not only on the spot but in long chains of reactions which reached even to the suburbs.[87] The connections between all this activity and the supply of living room became a commonplace among common people even though the scale of operations was never – nor perhaps ever can be – measured with real accuracy. In the history of the slums of London these 'improvements' – to use the generic term – had a special irony. They had always been hailed as the means of clearing the slums, though they had hardly ever failed to aggravate them, for their effect always was to reduce the supply of working-class housing either absolutely or in terms of the kind of houses which those turned out of doors by their operations could afford or wish to occupy. 'Here was a continual pushing back, back, and down, down, of the poor,' one slum clergyman told his lecture audience in 1862, 'till they were forced into the very places which were already reeking with corruption.'[88] This had been so, long before the Victorian period. It is possible to see allied to the commercial zeal for wider streets and larger openings in the City since the eighteenth century a restless opportunism for the demolition of the ugly, unhealthy, overcrowded – above all, commercially unjustifiable – bits of the ancient city.

Street improvement could even be justified on such grounds alone for the 'perforation of every such nest', wrote one enthusiast for improvement in 1800, 'by carrying through the midst of it a free and open street with buildings suitable for the industrious and reputable orders of the people, would let in that *Eye* and observation which would effectually break up their combinations'.[89] Such a point of view was executed literally over forty years later when James Pennethorne pushed Victoria Street through the back-streets of Westminster along a line he chose solely for its effectiveness in puncturing Pye Street and its neighbouring slums, known locally as Devil's Acre.[90] Not every pair of dividers that stepped across the map of London in this long age of street improvement between the 1780s and 1840s was guided solely by the topography of the slums: the Temple Bar improvers seem to have been practically oblivious of them, John Nash deliberately skirted them with his Regent Street, and to the arch-improver, James Elmes, the rightness of the line was settled primarily by reference to architectural principles.[91] Yet by 1840 no stronger supporting claim for a scheme could be made than that it improved an unhealthy district; of marginally slighter importance only was the aim of the 'melioration of the moral conditions of the labouring classes closely congregated in such districts'. Scarcely a scheme of street improvement in London failed to respond in some degree to this call of duty, or expediency, over the next sixty years. 'Courts, close, crooked, and ill-looking are in plenty; swarms of children ... costermongers ... the low night lodging-houses and ugly dens of Golden Lane,' was how one man saw such an opportunity as late as 1877. 'Let a good, broad, straight throughfare be cut through it from North to South: the whole district is at once opened up and plenty of elbow room given to the City.' It was a deepening and pitiless irony that the 'moral condition' of those affected tended to deteriorate in processes like these.

London was being dug and re-dug with restless thoroughness by railway navvies, too, and would have been even more trenched by them, especially during the 1860s, if the struggle between the railway companies had not cancelled some of them out. It was above all the railway's demand for land to carry their lines into or under the central districts that had the most direct effect on the dwindling supply of living room there, especially as they had, like the street improvers, every financial reason for choosing the poorest districts for their lines wherever they could. Until the 1870s or even the 1880s their demolitions tended to evoke a mixture of barely modified censure and almost unstinted praise, except on the part of those directly affected, or their few champions. Scores of writers described what happened as the railways burrowed their way into the centre and swept aside whole neighbourhoods of densely packed houses: some were merely stupefied by engineering marvels or the new vandalism; some reflected on their unerring aim at working-class districts; some thankfully remarked on the supposed benefits of destroying slums so efficiently; some tried to tot up the real costs of operations which defied all normal accounting methods. Watching the trains come by became an almost routine assignment for journalists, ticking off the days 'to get out', picking their way over the rubble, counting the houses that had come down, following in the footsteps of those turned out of doors to see where they had gone, estimating the further overcrowding of the already overcrowded. From the 1850s to the 1870s the press was full of it.[92]

It is almost impossible to believe that the repercussions of all this random slum clearance were not recognised at the time. 'Carts of refuse turn down one street and dirty families another,' explained one observer in the early 1860s in a book suggestively entitled *The Hovel and the Home*,[93] 'the one to some chasm where rubbish may be shot, the others to some courts or fallen streets, making them worse than they were before.' The notion that slummers turned out of doors could take flight for the suburbs or that the shock of flattening acres of crowded houses could be absorbed by the surrounding areas without difficulty was contradicted by brute facts so often, in every kind of newspaper, periodical, pamphlet and public utterance, that one is driven to conclude that there was some deliberation in this kind of permissiveness. Dr Acton wrote: 'This packing of the lower classes is clearly not yet under control.'[94]

That is clear from the more or less bland acceptance by select committees on railway bills and street improvement schemes before the late 1870s of easy assurances by the promoters that no difficulty would be encountered by those displaced, and of arguments which hinged on the facility of taking slum houses rather than factories or warehouses. At the back of this lay an over-tender but sharply legal regard for property compulsorily acquired, and a readiness of the courts to settle handsomely for property owners. Thus their lordships were told by the Metropolitan Board of Works' Superintending Architect when examining the bill for Southwark Street in 1857 that the course given to it enabled them to skirt several expensive properties (including Barclay Perkins' Brewery – 'That was a property which it was desirable to avoid') and save £200,000, while displacing fourteen hundred people living in the slums of Christchurch and St Saviour's.

No inconvenience is anticipated and the Bill does not contain any provisions [ran the written statement]. The surrounding district is much peopled with workmen engaged in the different factories and the Artizans are migratory and there is great accommodation for Artizans in the Borough – but the houses are dense and mostly too crowded for health, comfort and convenience.[95]

Demolitions for docks, railways and new streets added immeasurably to the slums that were spared, and exacerbated a problem they were powerless to solve without the most elaborate rehousing. The complete failure to do this was the prime reason why the West End Improvements designed to carry Charing Cross Road and Shaftesbury Avenue, among other streets, through some of the worst slums at the centre should nearly have been frustrated by a parliament which was coming to realise it. This was the first major scheme of its kind outside the City in which a proper attempt was made to prevent the multiplication of slums by the provision of alternative housing for those displaced, or at least for others who could afford the higher rents. The failure even here to give permanent homes to the lowest grades of slummers displaced was also the major defect in the activities of the numerous charitable bodies which laboured to increase the supply of working-class housing in or near former slums. Their activities, puny as they were in relation to the problem, scarcely touched the principal classes involved.[96]

4

There are two particular obscurities about the slums of Victorian London that need finally to be noticed. One is the statistics of overcrowding. The London County Council did better in its laborious collection of data than did the Registrar-General.[97] Yet in the authentic slum there was often a diurnal cycle of occupation which defeated almost any compilation. Such a cycle varied from place to place according to the extent to which night- and day-work matched well enough to keep bedding in use right round the clock, or the streets of the district sustained a vagrant population which drifted indoors to occupy staircases and landings for the night. The census 'house' is too much of a concertina for measurement of volume. Rooms themselves have always had elastic shapes, whether given to them by lath partitions or sacking screens dividing the occupants by night if not by day, or merely by a foot of no-man's land. The very numbers alleged by the censuses to have been contained by particular slums must be treated with suspicion, and virtually all large aggregates are practically meaningless. Journalists' arithmetic was notoriously faulty and still more difficult to interpret.[98] In one reckoning, based mainly on the Registrar-General's data pertaining to some of the worst of London's slums in the early 1890s, perhaps seven hundred to one thousand acres of them, the density was calculated by one amateur statistician to be of the order of 3,600 persons to the acre, with death-rates rising to forty per thousand; the average for London and its suburbs was under sixty persons per acre and a mortality of about twenty per thousand.[99] What such figures really mean, if anything, is difficult to see (except in propaganda terms) and they are quoted here to give an upper limit on an extreme experience.

The other point of obscurity concerns the great and little landlords of London. We know too little about who they were to be able to discover much of the truth about them.[100] To most contemporaries, the ground landlord was, however, the *diabolus ex machina* – as he was made to appear to some extent in *The Bitter Cry*. Henry Lazarus, in perhaps the most vitriolic pamphlet to have been uttered in the whole literature of the slums, *Landlordism* (1892), blamed the degradation of the slums on landlords who neglected to provide the basic amenities their estates required. 'Absentee-landlordism, subleases, rack-rents', he wrote, 'here is the trinity of England's land curse,'[101] the principal source of the slums. In one limited sense he was right. Under the London leasehold system the legal conditions for the development of urban land, and by implication the type of housing, even the social characteristics of a neighbourhood, were ultimately the responsibility of the lessor. What happened in practice as everyone now knows who has read the Milner-Holland report,[102] was that landlords did not normally succeed in establishing conditions which would prevail throughout the lease, either because the leases themselves were badly drawn or because a whole string of sub-leases stretched between them and the tenant, dividing responsibilities and inflating rents.

The truth of the matter is that the slums were no respecters of persons, and that they came about under the noses of the small as well as the large landowners for reasons that are not evident by looking at the slums alone. The responsibility for them was widely shared and would only be discharged by widely shared resources that included raising the incomes of the very poor, keeping them at work, and using humane means of helping the people who in spite of this failed to keep up decent standards. Can this be why slums should still seem immortal?

10

The speculative builders and developers
of Victorian London*

It seems strange that we should know so little about how Victorian cities were actually made. We know far more about the total effort that went into making them and the impact this had on the course of investment – perhaps on the very growth of the national income – than we do about the way in which these cities were literally pieced together.[1] It is true, just the same, that no one has yet been able to say with real conviction whether, or to what extent, the growth of her cities in the nineteenth century of itself stimulated or retarded Britain's general economic expansion. Yet what seems in some ways more remarkable than our ignorance on these bigger questions is the smallness of our knowledge about a number of little things, especially those involved in the basic developmental processes of converting open country into closed-up streets and of the business operations that carried them through. Here is an industry – to consider it for a moment at large – which in the first Census of Production in 1907 accounted for about £80 million output per annum, or nearly as much as the whole of the clothing industry, appreciably more than that of gas, water and electricity undertakings combined. We know more about the movements of some of the prices of the factors involved in the productivity of the house-building industry itself than we do about its structure and its ways of working.[2] No single builder, apart from a number of railway contractors, has been treated at length, though a number have been examined in relation to specific estate developments; and there are several unpublished studies of cities and towns which contain information of this kind.[3]

This essay is not intended to repair these omissions in one swoop. Too little detailed research has so far been done on the operations of builders and

* Much of the research on which the first part of this paper is based was helped financially by grants from the University of Leicester, and I am grateful to acknowledge these. It is also pleasant to be able to thank a former student, Dr D. A. Reeder, for his comments on a draft of this paper and for permission to quote from his thesis, 'Capital Investment in the Western Suburbs of Victorian London' (Ph.D., University of Leicester, 1965).

developers up and down the country, even in London, to make this possible. The logistics and finance of house-building, I suspect, do not have a standard form everywhere, any more than their cyclical fluctuations may be said to have coincided with each other. All that I can do here, therefore, is to say something about the general nature of these house-building operations in London, to offer a tentative outline of the structure of the housing industry, to describe some of the responses it made to the demand for small houses in the suburbs, and to begin to explore the ways in which these operations were financed. This means an encounter not only with that confidently bowler-hatted field-marshal, the speculative builder, whose forays into the country-side were never reversed or hardly ever interrupted, but with that discreet civilian figure, the solicitor, whose financial operations were sometimes vital in maintaining him at the front.

1

One would think that it ought to be possible to distinguish fairly sharply between the different functions that were performed in putting new suburban houses on the market: the supply of building land; its initial development; the construction of the houses; the provision of social overhead capital in terms of drainage schemes, gas-and-water undertakings, shops, schools, churches, pubs, music-halls, parks; and the means of transport which permitted and then sustained the whole operation.

The role of the landowner of a rural estate coming onto the suburban market would thus appear to be to give up the use of his land on terms which made its development for building practicable. He might simply sell the freehold outright to the developer. In and around London the normal reaction to the opportunity to develop land was to grant a lease which by Victorian times was never less than 60 years and could be on the semi-perpetual basis of 999 years: the short or London building lease, as it came to be known, was of 99 years, and this was the normal length by the last quarter of the century. What this meant was that the landowner was prepared to take a ground rent very markedly below the net income that would ultimately accrue to the estate once the land had been built over, and to rely on recouping himself for giving up the use of the land during the lease by taking the full improvement value of the development, which he could then rack-rent, when the land reverted to him at the end of it.[4] The developer performed the function of assessing the possibilities of development and setting it in operation. This usually meant finding much of the finance, making agreements with builders, securing one way or another such facilities – roads, drains, water supply, licensed premises, spiritual sustenance – as would make an estate 'go' – that is to say, be built over without a significant break and get occupied by the right class of tenant. The builders would put up the houses and find occupiers for them. Yet another array of commercial interests would supply the means of activating the estate with the shops and other facilities. These were the basic functions.

In practice nothing was so clear-cut. Meeting an anticipated demand for houses made every function a speculative one. Building land did not come on the market entirely smoothly; the capital needed to sustain the whole operation was capable to some extent of being put to other uses; the demand for houses, though appearing to grow inexorably under the pressure of population growth and metropolitan migration, was not entirely predictable in any particular place; the whole timing of the operation was liable to be disturbed by large and small dislocations to other investment programmes, particularly those relating to transport; nor was the whole process completed in one operation, but it was susceptible to redevelopment. What is more, the financial sources that were used were to a certain extent already involved in the operation and were not independent agencies. This was so in the general sense that the savings which formed the capital for estate development were made principally by the middle classes whose suburban migration was made possible by it. There was indeed an element of self-financing here, though suburban building was supported by savings drawn from the provinces, too. It ought also to be noticed that there was a good deal of reinvestment of the earnings of these business operations, either in the very suburbs in which they had been made or in neighbouring ones to which the process of suburban development was being newly applied.

Victorian London, in other words, was a commercial metropolis giving daily demonstrations of the gains of speculative enterprise of every kind, and these lessons had plenty of applications in the suburbs. The opportunities were in fact far too numerous and diverse for a standard response. The situation that had once existed – not long before the nineteenth century – in which landowners were almost literally overtaken in their sleep by the sprawling suburbs, no longer prevailed. Land let on loose tenancies had time and time again been made the subject of building agreements that deprived landowners of all but the reversionary value of their estates while allowing their lessees to pocket handsome speculative gains.[5] Since the close of the French wars in 1815, however, not only had the speed at which farmland was coming under the shadow of the built-up area accelerated, but it had become an almost calculable factor. The owners of this land were no longer prone to let it on terms which allowed others to scoop up the gains to be had from the new value put upon it in this way.[6] Yet, as the irresistible growth of London became one of the facts of life, the idea of participating in the business caught on not only among men of capital but among men of enterprise but no capital. At certain times and in particular places the suburbs became a bonanza which gave every capitalistic temperament its head. Lending on mortgage was the passive, safe-as-houses, five per cent, way of taking part; going into the land market, getting some suburban land ripe for development, making it go, was the active, speculative, all-or-nothing way of doing so.

The roughest calculations seemed to show that most of the money to be made out of this process went to the men who were first on the scene, who leased or bought land before its rise, and developed or sold it on the very top of the tide. The biggest profits came from speculating in building land, not from the building operations themselves, though putting up the houses was sometimes as necessary to the realisation of these gains as was the building of a suburban railway or the creation of a fashionable image for the suburb that had nothing else to commend it.

Here were innumerable situations in which the functions that were involved in developing building estates, and which are capable of being identified in isolation, actually overlapped. It was not the custom of landowners, for example, to stick merely at supplying land against ground rents; developers did not stop short when they had pegged out building plots; the suppliers of finance were not always prepared to keep strictly to their financial operations; nor were the business operations needed to open up an area by transport developments kept strictly separate from the building spree. In fact, situations became very quickly confused, the more so because the creation of titles to wealth in new districts – improved ground rents as well as commercial property – were passed rapidly from hand to hand. Few districts matured so fast that these complicating factors remained insignificant.

The pragmatic character of much of this suburban enterprise may be made clearer by the case of a man who acted primarily as developer but also as landowner, financier and builder in the Notting Hill district of west London in the 1850s and 1860s. This was Charles Henry Blake, a retired Indian civil servant, who found himself involved in these operations when his solicitor, using money that he had sent home from India in 1851, financed some of the builders at work on an ambitious development known as the Kensington Park Estate.[7] Returning home almost at once, Blake put in more capital, some of which he had borrowed for the purpose, and laid out in his first five years' operations £116,000, some of which he lent to a range of small builders, and some of which he used to put up 36 houses on his own account with the help of a builder whom he hired. The real entrepreneur in this enterprise had apparently been Blake's solicitor, and Blake himself fumbled with it so badly during the depression of that decade that he nearly failed altogether. He was really being driven along by his debts and the incredibly low rate of return on his investment – a fraction of one per cent – and it is doubtful whether he ever had any real alternative to what he did. The developer simply had to be prepared to plunge to the limit and hope to survive in the end only by his wits. As it was, Blake picked unreliable builders, lent heavily to another – even more adventurous – developer, and almost sank himself completely in a railway speculation in 1854–5: this drove him (all other efforts to pawn his personal estate having failed) into the hands of a firm of auctioneers to whom he had to give the option of selling his real property. Other mortgagees became threatening and he barely escaped being sold up altogether in 1859. The housing market revived the following year and Blake was helped out of his financial mess by a second firm of solicitors who took over some of his mortgages themselves, transferred others to another firm, and left him with enough cash to think of speculating all over again.

What now helped to ignite Blake's hopes was the revival of suburban railway promotion, especially as earlier schemes to take a southerly line to Hammersmith were, in 1861, supplanted by one that bisected Notting Hill. Blake, and three other large property-owners in the district, joined the provisional committee of what actually became the City and Hammersmith Railway (1864); other developers and builders were meanwhile taking shares in the Metropolitan Railway, which was opened to Paddington in the same year. Blake and his new solicitor both became directors of the Hammersmith Railway. They bought land ahead of the railway on borrowed money, Blake having to submit to some very tight conditions in order to guarantee the interest payments, and were happily selling and letting off land for building at a substantial profit almost at once: Blake's total investment (plus interest payments) in the Portobello estate, as it was known, between 1863 and 1870 was about £95,000, laid out on nearly 60 acres; and in return he got £56,000 from sales of land, £54,000 from sales of finished houses, and a little over £2,000 from rents. He still held some of the land, which was then worth three times what he had paid for it.

Operations like these could not be conducted by rule of thumb, and the developer had to be ready to assume any role that fell vacant. Blake was successful in the end because he responded in just this way and made the management of the estate his personal responsibility: he bought and leased land as the opportunity and need arose, made roads and sewers, hired builders, built himself, leased land to builders, granted them loans, made agreements with sub-developers who set up their own arrangements for building, bought back the freehold ground rents, offered mortgages to house-buyers. It was a versatile repertoire that, by the time of his death in 1872, had earned Blake a personal fortune of £35,000 and a real estate of £473,000. Whether his success was exceptional or not we do not know. Across the whole face of Victorian London it is not possible, unfortunately, to write the names of even a score of such men, nor to trace their business careers in any detail. Some of them are buried still in the deeds, bills of sale, building agreements, auction particulars and still more ephemeral documents which changed hands as deals went through or mortgages were foreclosed; not all these operations even took that tangible form which came in time to assume an archaeological meaning, and those that did are now being obliterated even faster than the first entries were made. If these men are ever to be known again it will only be by most diligent searching without delay.

2

When we turn to consider the builders themselves the names become more numerous, but authentic data about actual building operations are so scanty that it has come to be taken for granted that there are virtually none to be found. The structure of the house-building industry in London has long been regarded as a matter on which reliable statistics are just not available, even to show the number of the size of the building firms in existence.[8] Perhaps it is not surprising therefore that the only accepted version of the industry should have been one in which it shows a tendency towards large-scale enterprise, for this was a prominent feature of one type of development. It has been suggested indeed that the kind of firm first built up by Thomas Cubitt in his development of Belgravia, that of the master-builder employing large numbers of men on a permanent or semi-permanent basis, was becoming the typical form of enterprise.[9]

There is a certain amount of evidence for this view, fortified to some extent by the long and well-known ancestry which Cubitt's methods may be said to have had. They may be traced with no difficulty to that massively speculative builder of the seventeenth century, Nicholas Barbon, whose activities in Lincoln's Inn Fields, the Temple, Soho, the Strand and thereabouts, tended to create something of a standard method for suburban house-building by laying out an estate under single-handed control and then selling frontages by the foot to smaller speculators.[10] What is not clear from these operations is whether the various building craftsmen each stuck to their trades and were employed directly by an architect or surveyor of some kind, or whether the respective tradesmen – master-bricklayers, master-carpenters, master-masons – began to develop as general contractors who either employed other tradesmen themselves or sub-contracted such work as required. At any rate, when James Burton erected over 900 houses in the decade ending in 1803 on the Foundling Hospital and Bedford estates, which were being laid out between Bedford House and the New Road, he did so partly by following Barbon's method of bringing in smaller builders, to whom he appears not only to have sub-leased the plots but to have supplied some of the building materials and the capital as well. Both estates had overall development plans and made agreements with general contractors like Burton to take substantial blocks of land and develop them under their own architectural supervision.[11] The contractor was therefore now performing a well-recognised function. He was securing the uninterrupted progress of the works, keeping fairly tight control over the whole field of operations and making plenty of room for many smaller men.[12]

Thomas Cubitt's distinctive contribution to this tradition was to create the role of the general contractor in command of a regular labour force that included all the building trades and was held together from job to job. His career is well-known. Having formed the nucleus of this organisation around 1815 in the building of London Institution under contract – a bold stroke for a former ship's carpenter still in his twenties – he was not prepared to see it weakened by the ups and downs of this kind of contract work alone, and for this reason he began within another five years to edge his way into speculative building in the suburbs. His whole business career was now to be shaped by the great building boom of the early 1820s. By a series of rapid steps, during which he made repeated stabs at completing Burton's work on the less and less fashionable Bedford estate, he was ready by 1824 to lease 140 acres of the Marquess of Westminster's land on the more promising side of the town and to begin the almost single-handed creation of Belgravia and Pimlico. Presently, he was also committed to the development of an area of some 250 acres which was to become in effect the first garden suburb of London in the form of Clapham Park. He spent the years that followed virtually fulfilling these various undertakings, though he never completed them.

Cubitt's extraordinary ability of assimilating all the building trades into a single firm, and maintaining a weekly payroll of up to 2,000 employees (a strong cadre at least of which was kept in regular employment) was a truly remarkable feat. By everything he did it is clear that he was a leviathan among the builders of his generation. But it is equally clear, I think, that his imaginative genius for the organisation of his own enterprise did not start a revolution in the organisation of the building industry at large, let alone that part of it concerned with building houses. There certainly were some firms who began to combine all the building trades under single-handed control, as there were firms which were now conducting their operations on Cubitt's scale and would be ready, say, to take on 500 bricklayers of a Monday morning.[13] By mid-century or so there were, it was said, six master-builders at work in London each employing 1,500 men and that the leading hundred master-builders in the area employed 28,000 out of a total of 38,000 workers in the London building trade.[14]

Yet for the rest of the century there persisted much less highly organised methods: sub-contracting in particular remained a highly variable arrangement and even large building firms were inclined to contract out of quite routine jobs.[15] There is some doubt whether these large-scale activities were representative even of public contracting, much less of house-building. In Cubitt's heyday there were recognisable differences between the various branches of the building trade. Large-scale contracting for public buildings was in quite a different category from that of general building, and the speculative building of suburban houses was not only regarded as a thing apart but was conducted as such. A fairly typical general builder was Thomas Burton, who employed craftsmen in all branches of the trade on a daily basis, gave work on the average to 170 but never more than 235 men in the six or seven years before 1833, mainly on repair work and alterations in the City and West End; when he laid men off they went to work in the suburbs for speculative builders. These, it was widely felt, were less respectable men, whose eyes were fixed on quick profits rather than solid building and whose houses, in the opinion of the self-consciously respectable Burton just mentioned, 'rise up more like the creations of harlequin's wand in a pantomime than anything else'.[16]

Already, they were numerous: 78 different builders, for example, were engaged, between 1817 and 1850, in developing about 90 acres of land in Stepney belonging to the Mercers' Company, though 700 of the 1,100 houses built in the period – most of them having a value of no more than £250 – were put up by only three men. The largest of them, W. Dempsey, accounted for 570 of these, but the average commitment was for less than half-a-dozen, a great many of these being built by local builders.[17] It seemed so well established that 'great numbers of the small houses in the suburbs of all towns are built with the savings accumulated by carpenters, bricklayers, masons, plasterers, and others connected with Architecture' that J. C. Loudon published his monthly *Architectural Magazine* specifically for them in 1834.[18] It became so unremarkable to watch individual building tradesmen taking on general construction that one illustrated alphabet still current in the 1860s could declare that 'J was a Joiner and built up a house'.[19] Brick-work normally accounted for about 40 per cent of the work in building a dwelling house and the carpentry and joinery about 30 per cent,[20] so it was not a difficult matter for an individual bricklayer or carpenter to complete the job either by hiring the other trades, or by forming a partnership, or by setting up a kind of producers' co-operative such as the 'blood for blood' system of dividing the proceeds of a speculation according to the contribution made to it by the individual tradesman.[21] How long these traditions lasted is not clear but there does appear to have been some change in emphasis. Was what was happening, one wonders, simply a response to a rapidly expanding demand that was leading small jobbing builders who had once made a practice of having 'three or four houses upon the stocks, just to keep their men in constant employment', to reverse the order and do jobbing work to fill in time between speculations? The man whose words these are, a London surveyor speaking in the 1850s, thought that things had changed in the course of the previous forty years and that the builder must now 'have the houses ready to be sold when there is a demand for them. . . . he must not expect to get business by waiting till the order has been given for a house to be built'.[22] It is reasonable enough to think that the change in emphasis

161

occurred as the whole scale on which London was growing increased, and that the expanding demand for suburban houses led directly to a change in the structure of the industry which supplied them.

3

What evidence is there on this point? By the time the sixth census was taken in 1851 – the only one in the nineteenth century for which details of employers were published – the large contracting firm had already made a strong appearance. There were nine firms in London at that date describing themselves as 'builders' and employing 200 or more men apiece, and three of these actually employed over 350 men each; a mere 57 firms out of a total of 739 builders employed 50 or more.[23] Clearly enough, the most impressive feature of the industry as revealed in this way was not that the few were so large but that the many were so small. If it were possible to isolate the railway contractors known to have been included in these returns the large builder as such would have been even less conspicuous. As it is, 80 per cent of all firms employed fewer than 50 workers each. These figures put any tendency towards large-scale activity in its most favourable light because for three years beforehand the industry had been exceptionally prosperous – its physical output had trebled between 1848 and 1851[24] – and firms must have expanded to some extent as a result. Just the same, it would appear that the large firms of 'master-builders' or general contractors were outnumbered by the small by at least ten to one and that the master-builder, whom one writer has described as one of the 'typical industrial characters' of Victorian England,[25] does not seem to qualify even as a typical builder.

This is clear in other ways. One of the developments which has usually been regarded as indicating the advance of the really large firm was the formation of the Central Association of the Master Builders of London. It came into being in June 1872 as a building employers' defence against the demands of the unions for more pay and shorter hours: the masons, joined rather raggedly by the carpenters and joiners, had struck for a nine-hour day and ninepence per hour, and the whole of the London building trade was canvassed through the Builders' Benevolent Institution, a body which had grown out of the Builders' Society, founded in the 1830s.[26] A week later *The Builder* reported the London Master Builders' Association – as it quickly became known – as containing 352 members employing between them some 3,000 men, or an average of 94 each, and its secretary as declaring that there were 'fully 250 large building establishments in London'.[27] It seems very likely that all the big builders joined the association, especially as it had been one of the largest, Shaw and Jackson and Brass, then at work on the new Law Courts and employing 832 men, which had been selected for strike action.

It is hard to tell how comprehensive this body was. When it circularised the whole trade (as it did, for example, on the carpenters' and joiners' claim for 'grinding money' in 1875), it got in touch with about 500 firms, about twice as many as were then in the association.[28] However, it seems reasonable to assume that the largest firms were likely to be better represented than the smallest, and this would add to the significance of its actual membership structure. This is clear from the fees paid, which were pro rata to the number of employees in each member-firm, and ranged from the full rate of 10 guineas a year for firms employing over 800 to one guinea for those employing less than 50. When the Association was at full strength, in 1873, and contained 276 members, six firms employed more than 800, 41 more than 200, and 168 (61 per cent) less than 50.[29] It is not true, as Sir John Clapham is inclined to suggest, that none of these was a speculative builder[30] – some of the leading members' names, like Scrivenor and White, Gibbs and Flew, J. W. Hobbs, were household words in many of the newest suburbs – but just how many of these so-called master-builders did speculate on house-building cannot be known. The association's membership was certainly not a complete roll of all builders at work in London at the time: one trade directory for 1870 listed as many as 2,500 'builders' in London,[31] and the census of 1871 returned about three times the numbers in the building trades in London as a whole as were accounted for in the employment of members of the association in the following year.[32] Who made up the difference? Who were these thousands of builders who kept apart from the main professional body and have preserved their anonymity ever since? For it is surely among them that we have to look for the main body of the house-builders of Victorian London – not only, perhaps, for the small jobbing builders who broke off now and then from their repairs and alterations to put up a house or two, but also for both the large and the small speculative builders who kept in close pursuit of the suburban frontier and indeed, scarcely did anything else.

The most reliable and comprehensive information that is available to identify the house-builders of Victorian London is contained in the Monthly Returns of the fifty or sixty District Surveyors – the number increased as the built-up area spread – who were responsible to the Registrar of Metropolitan Buildings between 1845 and 1855, the Superintending Architect of the Metropolitan Board of Works between 1856 and 1888, and to his successor in the London County Council from 1889 onwards.[33] These still comprise a virtually untapped source of minute and authentic information about the making of Victorian London.[34] To discover the number of firms engaged in house-building and the number of houses they each built it is merely necessary to collate the details for the whole metropolitan area for selected years. On the reasonable assumption that the number of houses built normally bears some significant relationship to the overall size of the firm, it is then possible to visualise the whole structure of the housing industry. The years chosen for this essay coincide as nearly as possible with those in which the industry was known to be either at full stretch or at its slackest. These years of boom and slump were 1872 (in the trough of a building cycle), 1881 (crest), 1891 (trough), 1899 (crest), with an outside point of reference for 1845.

It must be admitted that there are some drawbacks to these figures. For example, they make no allowance whatever for different sizes of houses, and at the end of the period they are describing a rather unreal situation, circumscribed as it was by the limits to the LCC area which no longer contained the districts in which house-building was taking place on a large scale.[35] Yet they do have an inner consistency in that the general practice of the district surveyors did not change at all until after 1891, when they began to be appointed as full-time officials rather than as part-time architects or surveyors.[36] What a study of this evidence reveals very clearly is the persistence of the very small firm. Something like one-third of all house-builders in London in the last quarter of the nineteenth century built only one or two houses in the year. So far as can be told from the less satisfactory returns for 1845, practically half of all firms had been of this size then.

What is also evident is that throughout the period from the 1840s to the 1870s there was virtually no change in the overall structure of the London housing industry. The full figures are given in Appendix A but it can be noted here that about 80 per cent of firms built six houses a year or fewer, and hardly any built more than 50. What changed this was the great building boom which developed in the late 1870s and came to a head in 1880–1. The numbers of small firms rose, but those of medium-sized and large firms rose still more, and when the tide of prosperity turned it was the small firms that went under or out of house-building altogether. The proportion of medium-sized firms – those building more than six but less than 60 – remained extraordinarily constant at 37 per cent of the total right through the ups and downs of the 1880s and 1890s. When another considerable boom in house-building developed at the end of the 1890s it was the really large firm which moved in. A mere 17 firms – less than 3 per cent of the total – were in 1899 building well over 40 per cent of London's new houses. These were the builders of 60 or more houses in that year. The biggest of the day, Watts of Catford, was actually engaged in that single year in putting up over 400 houses in different parts of south-east London. Even at that date, however, there remained a considerable number of very small builders, for 60 per cent of the total were still building six houses or fewer in the year, and these accounted for about a fifth of all the new houses under construction. It is also clear from the monthly returns that at least 90 per cent of house-building was being conducted on speculation, in anticipation of the demand.[37] When one looks at a particular district as this tide rolled over it, the general impression built up from the more comprehensive data is confirmed: in Camberwell, for example, as the local building industry reached its peak between 1878 and 1880, as many as 200 firms, comprising 53 per cent of the total at work in the area, built six houses or fewer over this three year period; only 15 or less than 4 per cent of the total, built over 60 houses each. Here, too, the largest firms were responsible for a disproportionate share of the output, building something approaching a third of the total.

4

Who exactly were these builders? In what ways, if any, were their activities interrelated? How were they financed? The answers are not easy to find because the term speculative builder covered a range of functions and many degrees of financial independence. At one end of the scale there were men who were primarily financiers but who, for the sake of convenience or in order to keep control in a delicate situation, had men in their employment or on call who were capable of running up 'frontages' and creating the improved ground rents (the agricultural value of the land enhanced by housing development) which were the marketable products of building enterprise on the property market. Sometimes such a builder could manage his affairs so well that, by getting credit from the timber-merchant and brickmaker (a practice, incidentally, of declining importance from the 1850s), and by mortgaging his houses floor-by-floor or pair-by-pair or terrace-by-terrace to a building society, a money-lending solicitor or even to a bank, he needed virtually no fixed capital at all but could discharge all his obligations by finding a buyer for his houses in the nick of time and transferring the mortgage to his client. There were here some speculative builders who narrowly escaped being simple hirelings of the landlord or of the developer and who had come very quickly into a kind of financial servitude to more powerful men; there were also builders' merchants and building societies that had got involved in completing houses on which they had had to foreclose. Toward the other end of the scale there were developing family businesses, firms of jobbing builders built up through traditional apprenticeship and experience, or even individual builders, who, when new houses did not seem to hang on the market above a week or two, could be seen measuring the leap into full-scale speculative building, and taking it in a way that did not prevent them from returning to a jobbing business when the boom came to an end or when the tide of building, once again, passed out of their reach.

Getting into this business was not a difficult feat. There was by the 1850s a technical press of great versatility which was supplying what amounted to a complete kit of plans, designs and bills of quantities for almost any beginner in suburban estate development.[38] There may also have existed some more formal liaison between particular architects and builders for purveying working drawings for this purpose.[39] Apart from this, it seems to have been very easy for speculative builders to get finance. The general reasons for this are obvious enough from a glance at the unique circumstances in which the urban economy of London was expanding. This was more than a microcosm of the national economy, for London was not only the capital in the fullest sense of the term, but the chief port, commercial centre and industrial area in the whole country. Whether this meant that there was really free movement of capital between house-building in the suburbs and other kinds of enterprise is, perhaps, open to doubt. It has yet to be demonstrated empirically, for example, that capital going into house-building was actually diverted, say, from going abroad, or that capital sent abroad meant depriving suburban builders of it. It seems rather more credible that the money market operated in practice in more isolated departments and that, for example, developments overseas affected the flow of capital into house-building more indirectly. The supply of capital for house-building certainly ebbed and flowed, but there is no clear evidence that it was ever checked in such a way as to impede development at all seriously; there is, on the contrary, rather more evidence of over-building in periods of easy money than of under-building when money was tight.

If we do not draw too fine a distinction between builders and developers it might be said that 'speculative builder' was in effect a term that merely described the person who responded to these various pressures and opportunities, who bore virtually all the risks and took some, at least, of the profits of meeting an anticipated demand for houses. This was a function as easily met by men who in terms of previous occupation or professional commitment were totally unconnected with the building trade as by those who were. The Forsytes' fortune was laid, properly enough, by a mason from Dorset, but there were speculative builders who had been tailors, shopkeepers, domestic servants, publicans: a district surveyor was heard complaining in 1877 of one clergyman-cum-speculative builder whom he remembered only too well because he had been a builder of several hundred houses who had forgot to pay him his fees.[40]

How did speculative builders get their capital in practice? The most natural source of finance was the landlord himself, whose grant of a building lease involved in any case the transfer of a capital asset without immediate payment for it. It was widely believed that landlords were usually inclined to make cash advances, too, though there is very little direct evidence on this point. One instance of this is the Cotton estate at Bow Common where, in the 1860s, numerous builders were being given advances and supplied with bricks by the estate itself. These were meted out as the need arose, commonly reaching 50 per cent of the surveyor's valuation of the houses, sometimes substantially more, and were apparently regarded as a means of tiding the builder over the period between the start of his operations and his finding a buyer. Interest was generally at 5% for the first year but rose to 8% for longer periods: all advances seem to have been redeemed inside three years. The property ledger of this estate contains several entries that no advances were to be made to specific builders, and those that did look to the estate for finance accounted for only a fraction of the whole development.[41]

On the other hand, it is clear from the records of the de Beauvoir estate in Hackney that such advances could reach very substantial proportions.[42] This was a large estate of some 150 acres which had been the subject of an ambitious speculation by a local grazier and brick-maker in the early 1820s – the largest 'take' of land for speculative building known to James Burton – but which had been aborted by a protracted lawsuit brought by the heir to the landowner who had granted the disputed lease. The development of de Beauvoir Town started up again in the later 1830s under more effective control by the new landlord through his agent and solicitors. From this time the landlord produced bricks himself on the estate which he supplied on credit to builders, in addition to substantial cash advances which he was making to them. These may well have been financed in the beginning either out of his inheritance of over £750,000 or from his landed income of about £6,000 a year. But by the 1850s he was lending to at least 18 builders at a time annual sums ranging from less than £50 to more than £750 (usually in several instalments), and had put several of them into his debt for bricks and cash for sums of several thousand pounds. The total advances to builders for 1855, for example, were £6,900, which rose by annual jumps to over £39,000 in 1862, before tapering off completely by 1870. The aggregate of these sixteen years was over £176,000, all of it lent at 5%, and the whole of it repaid by 1878. However this whole process was financed at the start, it seems clear from the accounts which recorded these transactions that relatively small amounts were commonly raised within the building trade itself, either explicitly by loans between builders, or by a series of more or less loose partnerships between them.[43]

Capital raised outside the building trade came from quite a narrow range of institutions. Most London banks do not seem to have been at all ready to advance money on mortgage, at least to speculative builders, though there is no reason to doubt that they continued to make the kind of loans that they had traditionally made to the upper and professional classes on the security of their property, and that some of this will have found its way into builders' hands.[44] The London & Westminster and the London & County Banks were probably the only two joint stock banks in London to run the risk of getting a reputation for recklessness by lending direct to builders and property developers on the basis of a mortgage deed, though the general preference for transacting business on the basis of overdrafts and promissory notes almost certainly did lead to a certain amount of bank money being used to finance speculative building.[45]

Building societies were certainly of great importance, both directly and indirectly, particularly down to the 1870s. Their original role of creating a pool of capital from which the society's members drew in turn the sums necessary to build their houses, and which was replenished by their regular contributions until all had benefited, had fairly quickly been replaced by the perpetual balancing of the flow of capital between those willing to lend and those wishing to borrow. The change from the terminating to the permanent principle, which marked this differentiation in the membership of building societies, was occurring fast during the third quarter of the century. The main business of the building societies now became the advance of money to house purchasers on the security of mortgages. At the same time, many societies began to make substantial advances to builders for the purpose of financing building operations themselves. This occasionally meant taking over building speculations themselves, though building societies were disqualified in 1874 from holding on to such property.[46]

Two kinds of situations arose from these activities: one in which individual societies had their regional specialisms, the other in which particular estates literally swarmed with different societies. In Woolwich, it was said by the secretary to one small building society in the district in the early 1870s, there were five or six societies 'only too glad to advance money to any jerry-builder'.[47] On the Cotton estate in Limehouse a few years ealier there were around 45 building societies sharing 120 mortgage agreements between them.[48] Given the parochialism of this type of self-help, what the building societies may have helped to bring about, therefore, was a situation in which the capital resources of one locality were mobilised to finance the development of a neighbouring one, though far too little work has yet been done in this whole field to enable anyone to speak with real confidence on such points. In particular it is not known to what extent building societies went on lending direct to speculative builders during the 1880s and 1890s.[49] Jabez Balfour, the chairman of the largest and fastest growing building society in London in 1885, the Liberator, told the shareholders that no other society had done so little with the ordinary speculating builder in the suburbs of London. Yet it speculated, sometimes fraudulently, in ways that inflated the credit structure of the whole market in real property; and it was a small jobbing builder, J. W. Hobbs, who had started to speculate in the grand manner, first in houses and ultimately in palatial flats, that in 1892 helped to bring down one of the wobbliest giants in building society history.[50]

A substantial amount of money was also being provided for estate development on mortgage, and even by direct investment, by insurance companies. Some of this was simply in order to catch a good tide, some as an adjunct to straight fire insurance, and a little of it because investment in land itself tended to lead – as it did with many other corporate landowners – to direct participation in its development. It could thus happen that an insurance company found itself in the position of a developer, laying out an estate and making agreements with speculative builders, though this activity seems to have been rare. Investment by insurance companies appears to have been fairly discriminating, not to say fickle – even Thomas Cubitt was kept dangling for some £40,000 in and after 1835 – and it could be argued that it was occurring on such a scale that, by blowing hot and cold in times of easy and tight money, it probably helped significantly in accentuating the uncertainties of speculative building. Insurance companies were some of the biggest institutional financiers of urban development in the nineteenth century, and their readiness, especially in the 1860s and 1870s, to advance very substantial sums to the London vestries in order to finance various drainage and other sanitation schemes, and to support the great schemes of street improvement then being mounted, is well known. The comparative decline in returns on government stock during the nineteenth century made mortgages and other securities distinctly more attractive to insurance companies, which did not in any case need to keep their assets in any more liquid form, and as these investment opportunities widened so insurance companies spread their funds. Recent research is now beginning to show that several insurance companies were not only increasing their advances against the security of rural estates but were beginning to lend on a substantial scale to the larger speculative builders who were putting up superior houses: there is no evidence of any lending to small men or to large men who were building inferior houses. The Hand-in-Hand Insurance Company, for example, advanced £105,000 to six builders in Kensington and Paddington in 1868–78, over half of it in a single year (1877). In 1874 this company also lent £10,000 to a finance company, the Camberwell Association of Land Financiers, with more than 56 building plots as security.[51] What appears to have been the biggest portfolio of mortgage investments was that held by the London Assurance which had first turned, in the early 1830s, from its traditional preoccupation with marine insurance to lend to dock and railway companies, then to landowners opening up building estates, and finally (starting in 1839) to speculative builders, at least 80 of them in London. The highest peak in these advances was reached in 1865, with a total for the year of £113,000, and by 1870 this company had placed over half its assets – about £1½ million – in various kinds of mortgage loans, the majority of them still in country estates, however. From the 1880s lending to builders tended to evaporate somewhat as other investments, particularly debentures in various commercial undertakings, became easier and more profitable to hold.[52]

We come last to a source of building capital which has scarcely been noticed in the business annals of the period: the solicitor. He must be one of the most obscure characters, not only in the history of the Victorian period at large, but in a field of business activity in which he may well have been at one time the real fulcrum for the bulk of the capital movements. This certainly appears to be so for the housing industry of Victorian London and it may well have been so for other cities, too. Just when solicitors began to be important as a source of finance for speculative builders is not clear.[53] The only solicitors' records known to me to throw any light at all on this belonged to the firm of E. G. and J. W. Chester of south London. In the 1850s they had been concerned in their ordinary run of business with arranging house mortgages for their own clients with a number of London building societies – the Perseverance, the Amicable, the South London Tradesmen's; in the 1870s it is clear from their ledgers that they were advancing money on mortgage to builders direct. Between 1869 and 1882 this firm lent sums of £100 to £1,000 to builders in south and west London, along with loans to shopkeepers, publicans, pawnbrokers and other tradesmen. The firm's own investments seem to have gone into consols and industrial shares.[54] Not infrequently, solicitors were involved in speculations of their own; and, as we have seen, there were firms in west London who were engaged professionally in the 1860s with the promotion of suburban railways but who also tried to make money out of land deals along the route. There is little direct evidence of solicitors being used to any extent as channels for house-building investment before the second half of the century, and it seems quite possible that they did not become important until building society advances to builders began to flag for the first time following the recession of 1868–72.

5

It was certainly at this time that the one substantial speculative builder whose business records are known to have survived took to relying exclusively on this source of finance. Edward Yates was a self-made man who was financially as successful as Thomas Cubitt had been. When he came to London from the North in the early 1850s to start his career by digging foundations for army barracks at Aldershot, he is said to have had only pence in his pocket; when he died in 1907 after having built over 2,500 houses in south London and made some property deals elsewhere, he was a millionaire.[55]

How did he finance his business? His first loan was obtained from another builder who had sub-leased to him in 1867 part of an estate he was developing at Nine Elms, but this he had to supplement by mortgaging the twelve houses he was building to the London and Westminster Building Society.[56] At the end of 1868 he began to lay out £9,000, raised in small instalments from this and two other building societies, on building a whole street – Dragon Road – in Camberwell, and entered about the same time into a limited partnership with another builder, S. Sansom, which was to last seventeen years. Their first joint building operations were on the Ecclesiastical Commissioners' estates in Walworth, and these were financed by two further building societies along with an insurance company. Yates was now finding it possible to raise £500 or £600 a month on the average, but accepted no more loans until the summer of 1871, when the contraction of building in London was reaching its maximum. At this point, he opened an entirely new phase in his career by turning for the first time to a solicitor in Lincoln's Inn Fields to raise £500 at 5% on the security of the last four houses to be completed on Dragon Road. From this point, incidentally, his business expanded steadily and rapidly (despite another period of prolonged contraction in building as a whole throughout the 1880s), and the climax to his expansion came in 1888–90, when he was building around 150 houses a year, and the industry at large was at its slackest. By 1890 his total mortgages indebtedness stood at nearly £217,000, over 99 per cent of it in the form of mortgages that had been negotiated through solicitors. Within fifteen years he had completely redeemed them all and built up his fortune (see Appendix B).

Between 1867 and 1895 Yates raised altogether over £282,000 in about 270 instalments ranging from £200 to £20,000. Almost a third of this, £90,000, came from outside London, and though much of it had simply travelled up from the home counties there was a number of substantial sums raised farther afield, notably in the West Country, Yorkshire and the Midlands. About 16 per cent of the mortgages are not classifiable but it is possible to attribute the remainder without difficulty. Clergymen advanced £35,800, about 13 per cent of the total, and other professions (notably the Army) a further £11,450, about 4 per cent; women, especially widows and spinsters, produced over £58,000, or about 21 per cent of the total. The largest category of all, which accounted for about £85,000 or 30 per cent of the total, included executors and what seem from the number of names in each case to have been trustees. It should be added, however, that this proportion may well have been rather higher than this if, as seems quite possible, any of the solicitors named as mortgagees were in fact acting as trustees rather than as private lenders. The extent to which money held in trust was used to finance speculative building is, however, a little problematical. The law on this point seems clear but the practice somewhat variable. Trustees who did not have such powers under a deed of trust had been authorised in 1859, if not earlier, to invest in freehold mortgages but not in personal property, that is, leaseholds: according to a case settled on appeal in 1878 trustees had to have express authority in order to lend money on leasehold securities, and the Trustee Act of 1888 appears to have made statutory provision for this kind of investment for the first time, but only on leaseholds of 200 years or more which were subject to a peppercorn rent only.[57] The effect of the law may have been to reduce the supply of this kind of capital to speculative builders, as the Institute of Builders certainly seems to have thought.[58] Yates himself does not appear to have suffered by it, however. He also obtained about £39,000 (14 per cent of the total) from solicitors who were apparently acting on their own behalf. In a single case the landowner of a small estate which Yates was developing advanced £13,000.

The conclusion which is suggested by these data is that for the most part Yates was able to tap capital which was looking for a modest but safe and steady return rather than more definitely risk-bearing capital. The great majority of it was borrowed at 4½% and 5% (which was the normal rate) though a little was obtained at 4, 4¼, 4¾, 5½, and 6%. Yates's normal arrangement was to borrow for a minimum term of five years (though how often he was able to insist on this cannot be discovered), but on 6 per cent of the total borrowed – excluding the building societies' loans, which mostly had fixed terms of 14 years – was redeemed after five years or less, and the average length of the mortgage terms was 11.7 years for 4% mortgages or less, and 15.5 years for 5% mortgages or more. Mortgagees having a smaller rate of return were apparently more inclined to redeem their loans quickly in order to place their capital on better terms elsewhere, but except for a tiny fraction of rather more volatile capital the resources which Yates was able to call upon were content to earn a steady 5% or so until Yates himself was ready to pay back his borrowed capital.

Yates's business letters, of which between 5,000 and 6,000 have survived, do not always give a clear picture of the methods he used in raising this capital because much of his business was obviously done by word of mouth; his installation of a telephone in 1881 seems to have reduced the number of letters still more. Some of the statements made in the letters suggest that the financial scope of Yates's enterprise may have been rather broader than the property ledgers themselves imply. For example, in writing to would-be lenders Yates not infrequently referred to large loans – up to £30,000 – which had just been 'arranged for' but, as no entries justifying such statements can be traced in the property ledgers, it must be assumed that these loans were secured in other ways. Some other large transactions, too, especially dealings in land and licensed premises, appear only in tantalising snatches and leave the problem whether he made his fortune by speculative deals or speculative building.

The letters and the property ledgers do, however, make plain the nature of the connection between Yates as the speculative builder and the solicitors who acted as financial intermediaries for him. From 1870 he appears to have established a connection with a widening circle of solicitors, some at least of whom appear to have approached him first to inquire what securities he had to offer. It is striking that although he was occasionally driven to borrow on rather expensive terms – he once went so far as to propose paying 7½% to a building society in 1872 – he does not ever appear to have been held up for lack of capital. Practically every one of the houses he built was mortgaged within weeks of its completion and as often as not had become the subject of inquiries, on one side or the other, well before the lease was granted by the landlord. 'Referring to your enquiry about security for £2,000', Yates wrote to one solicitor in April 1872, 'I beg to say *that for the present* all that I have are arranged for – but it is possible I may have some a little time onwards.' In replying to another in October 1873 he said he had 'money advanced as required hitherto and do not contemplate needing more during the coming Winter, but may be glad of it in the Spring'. These are typical letters.

Frequently, solicitors who wrote to make firm offers of loans which had been the subject of verbal inquiries a fortnight or so before found that Yates had obtained the money elsewhere. On 2 December 1881, for example, Yates wrote to one solicitor referring to an inquiry he had made recently about security for £4,000 or £5,000, wanting to know whether this offer was still open and saying that if he had more money available Yates could use it as he now had securities for £7,000 or £8,000. On 16 December another letter followed thanking the solicitor for his reply but saying the amounts mentioned had, since writing, 'been arranged'. Sometimes, however, Yates evidently foresaw difficulties in raising capital just when he wanted it and suggested to inquirers that they should deposit the money they had available in the bank, and he promised to pay the difference between the bank rate and 5% until he was ready to take it on mortgage.

It is clear from his letters that one of Yates's business maxims was to make all his money work. The big fluctuations from year to year in his total mortgage indebtedness speak for his strictly empirical attitude to his capital needs; his obvious unwillingness to borrow money a fortnight before he had a use for it, and to borrow none at all if the proceeds of the sale of a piece of land or some other property brought him all that he required is evidence of the same kind. With more capital in hand than he could use himself, Yates occasionally became a financial intermediary and made loans of up to £1,000 to smaller builders in the locality. Though he kept all his resources employed, it is also clear that Yates's houses were neither mortgaged to the hilt nor let at high rents. From the little that can be discovered about the prime cost of the houses he built – usually around £350 for an eight-room house having an annual value of about £38 – Yates never aimed at getting much more than a 70 per cent loan; he frequently asked for no more than 50 per cent of the market value of the property.

6

Speculative builders, it is clear enough, came in all shapes and sizes and their operations were touched by many other kinds of business. This raises the familiar question: how much of a tool were they, as Charles Booth once suggested, in the hands of others? To what extent were they to blame for the palpable mistakes in layout and execution of Victorian London?

It is easy to pillory the speculative builder. The oral tradition that speculative building created 'cobweb houses' is a strong one. That 'He found a solitude and leaves a slum'[59] seems from a casual glance at the areas of urban blight that exist today an almost justifiable gibe. Here, surely, is the artful dodger of the suburbs, the builder of walls without footings, the bricklayer who knew how to mix mortar without cement, the carpenter who could lay floors over green joists, the plumber who knew just how to lay drains without traps or how to install cold water systems which had a positive, intimate and lethal acquaintance with the sewage arrangements. Even *The Builder*, perhaps the best champion of common sense and the public good in building (at least during George Godwin's tenure of the editorial chair, 1842–88), could not resist a sermon on the subject now and then. 'Among my people are found wicked men,' so ran one of these homilies on the basis of a text, appropriately enough, from *Jeremiah* (v: 26–27): 'They lay wait, as he that setteth snares; they set a trap, they catch men. As a cage is full of birds, so are their houses full of deceit: therefore they are become great and waxen rich.'

Actually, there is curiously little specific complain about bad speculative building in contemporary periodicals – say in *Household Words* or *All the Year Round* or even in *Punch*, except for a couple of memorable drawings by George du Maurier in 1871 – and as for a sustained criticism of it in a book or pamphlet I do not know of one.[60] Indeed, even the Blue Books contain virtually no hard evidence on this point, at least before the 1880s, and even then – for example in the voluminous data assembled by the Town Holdings Commission – references to the so-called scourge of the suburbs are scanty and subdued. The speculative builder kept surprisingly out of the news. The best blasts at him appeared in *The Builder*, and in what might almost be called the Christmas issue for 1889 some of the mysteries of the art of jerry-building were revealed by one of its practitioners: 'I think', he wrote, 'I may venture to style myself one of the wise men who build houses for fools to live in.'[61] If his elaborate deceptions were authentic, he amply justified the editorial comment of the *Law Times* a few years before that the frauds and peculations of the speculative builder had become the pest of suburban London. Yet such commentaries as there were on suburban builders were for the most part mocking rather than censorious, wistful rather than angry, at the brutal routing of soft fields full of buttercups and birdsong by the noisy, smelly paraphernalia of the builder and all the hard litter of suburban estates before they had been humanised. The very personification of the builder and his entourage – Mr Chips and Mr Hod, Mr Scampling, Mr Chisclem, Squire Graball, Messrs Rackem and Ruinem, solicitors – gave to this public spectacle an air almost of high melodrama, certainly not of tragedy.[62] Perhaps it is a matter for wonder that in the busless muddy wastes of half-finished estates people did not complain more. Perhaps it simply was that although everyone knew 'what serves to make a terrace, or constitute a villa in the neighbourhood of London' the people living in Tea-pot Terrace or Vanity Villa knew better than to spoil their dreams and their social aspirations by saying so.[63]

What proportion of the whole trade was made up of scamping or jerry-builders – a term apparently unknown before the 1870s – will never be discovered, but a really close inspection of what was being put up, even at this range of eighty or a hundred years suggests that it was a small one. No doubt these speculative suburbs were and remain the anguish of architects but they were not, by any means, the worst-built structures of Victorian London. Nor were most of them laid out regardless of all feeling for those that inhabited them. There was vastly more attention to detail in the houses of every class than a cursory glance at those that still stand would suggest; there were also more layers of romantic meaning to the siting and appearance of these family houses than their desolate condition now commonly reveals. There were builders, like Blake or Yates, who not only brought to their developments a shrewd business sense and the hopes, though never very rosy ones, of a fortune, but took from them some of the satisfaction of men of property, of petty potentates, of patrons of one of the more useful arts. One could almost mark off this class of builder from that below him by the names he chose for his terraces and streets; not for him mere family Christian names or military campaigns (unless worked into acrostics, perhaps), but the surnames of titled families, the heroes and landscapes of literature, new romantic words from his own imagination. Such men literally devoted their lives to their estates. There were others who seized every opportunity to make money fast. There was a residue who succeeded at neither.

The speculative builder was not the sole arbiter of the suburbia of Victorian London. He was indeed merely the most conspicuous contributor to a situation which had arisen in a society which was growing too fast for itself. His must be regarded simply as the last tittle of responsibility for the way in which his generation was making use of suburban land. The men who built Shepherds Bush or Balham were not only responding to demographic pressures but to an English tragi-comic romanticism that dwelt happily in *bijou* suburban houses, and to which most speculative builders seem to have responded with some versatility. They were operating, it is fair to say, under legal and financial conditions which precluded, or at any rate made improbable, any very radically different course of action from that which they followed. On the one side, the legal restrictions on their operations were grotesquely inadequate in a period in which the customary role of the State was largely limited to fields in which contractual obligations between its subjects did not apply. The piecing together since 1774 of the London building code, which became a national standard, was a very slow business. On the other side, it has to be remembered that, before 1851, indirect taxation on building materials was heavy enough to be reflected in the dimensions and specifications of the smallest houses, and that throughout the period builders could not escape the even more pervasive influence of changes in the price of borrowed money. The speculative builder had normally to rely far more heavily on his creditors than any other group of manufacturers or traders of his time. He was engaged, however unevenly, in a kind of joint enterprise of which we still know only a small part.

One of the ironies of this is that many of the houses of which I have been speaking go on still, serving and shaping the lives of hundreds of thousands of people who occupy them, but for whom they were not intended. The full story of the speculative builders and developers of Victorian London is therefore not yet over. Who occupied their houses then and who since, what use they made of them, and how the structure and development of a community was shaped by these, among other things, is only part of this story. This is the direction in which my current research on Camberwell is now taking me.

Appendix A: *House-builders in London, 1872–99*

Houses under construction	1872		1881		1891		1899	
	Firms	Houses	Firms	Houses	Firms	Houses	Firms	Houses
1–6	827 [75.1]	2,199 [37.2]	976 [62.8]	2,820 [23.0]	422 [61.9]	1,268 [24.0]	364 [59.3]	1,018 [14.3]
7–12	170 [15.4]	1,525 [25.8]	318 [20.4]	2,963 [24.1]	147 [21.6]	1,362 [25.8]	107 [17.4]	1,005 [14.1]
13–24	81 [7.4]	1,333 [22.4]	177 [11.4]	3,017 [24.6]	81 [11.8]	1,350 [25.5]	84 [13.7]	1,459 [20.4]
25–60	22 [2.0]	725 [12.2]	80 [5.1]	3,046 [24.8]	27 [4.0]	878 [16.6]	42 [6.9]	1,517 [21.3]
over 60	2 [0.1]	139 [2.4]	4 [0.3]	436 [3.5]	5 [0.7]	428 [8.1]	17 [2.7]	2,136 [29.9]
Totals	1,102	5,911	1,555	12,282	682	5,286	614	7,135

* Monthly Returns of the District Surveyors, *passim*. Percentages are in square brackets. See n. 33.

| Year | Edward Yates | | | New housing in south London (total fees of district surveyors) |
	New houses completed (leases granted)	Aggregate mortgage loan (at 31 Dec. in each year) £	Increase or decrease in mortgage debt £	£
1867	12			6,787
1868	44	2,100	2,100	7,677
1869	51	11,300	9,200	6,271
1870	43	16,670	7,470	5,027
1871	73	14,330	27,660	4,561
1872	39	56,480	12,150	4,289
1873	80	73,430	26,950	4,499
1874	45	89,921	16,491	5,604
1875	60	101,471	11,550	5,917
1876	69	116,471	15,000	7,983
1877	85	142,331	25,860	9,267
1878	50	157,541	15,210	9,621
1879	77	169,541	12,000	9,715
1880	89	194,075	24,534	12,570
1881	52	198,155	4,080	12,034
1882	86	209,755	11,600	10,281
1883	20	212,705	2,950	9,290
1884	113	219,255	6,550	9,588
1885	97	216,975	− 2,280	8,731
1886	98	202,235	− 14,740	8,524
1887	134	204,325	2,090	8,142
1888	149	217,469	13,144	7,944
1889	155	222,619	5,150	7,381
1890	98	223,919	1,300	7,009
1891	116	218,969	− 4,150	6,611
1892	125	219,239	270	7,788
1893	69	204,834	− 14,405	8,409
1894	98	191,414	− 13,420	8,096
1895	84	189,314	− 2,100	7,545
1896	92	111,230	− 78,084	9,852
1897	33	89,590	− 21,640	11,423
1898	25	54,450	− 35,140	11,535
1899	11	47,400	− 7,050	12,437
1900	42	31,800	− 15,600	11,765
1901	24	31,800	−	12,509
1902	60	13,300	− 18,500	11,394
1903	?	1,500	− 11,800	11,232
1904	?	1,500	−	11,029
1905	?	−	− 1,500	12,054

11

A Victorian speculative builder: Edward Yates

In Victorian England, the speculative builder was widely regarded as a kind of deadly spider, spinning houses in his cobweb to catch unsuspecting victims in, a jerry-builder, a scamping builder who mixed dust with his mortar, or who cut the footings, or quickly railed over the green timber, or got up to a thousand tricks to avoid building good and true. Despite the persistent lack of any substantial body of hard evidence on the matter, the legend took root, the familiar gibes were thrown, and the mud that stuck on the few also spattered many, especially at the lower end of the market, where operating margins were so slight that a few weeks of hot sun or of hard rain could wipe out any prospect of getting rid of a new house that had been scamped in some hidden way.

But the operations of Edward Yates, and the enduring condition of every one of his suburban houses that have descended into the third and, indeed, the fourth generation of him that built them, offer undeniably hard evidence that points to a different judgment on the speculative builders of the suburbs of Victorian London. In the course of this essay, I should like to set out his career as a builder and developer and, to some degree, as a landlord and man of property, in as much detail as his surviving business records permit us to do.[1] Just before I reached them down the Walworth Road some years ago, they had been largely consigned to the waste paper merchant, I'm sorry to say; but what remains are some five to six thousand business letters, and two huge property ledgers, setting forth all the relevant details of his property dealings. Alas, I have little information on the actual building operations; nor do I have much to tell about his private life and his other activities in the neighbourhood of his operations. Hence, I must largely confine myself to the financial aspects of his business career. These do in fact shed a good deal of light on the finance of speculative building in general and in the last quarter of the nineteenth century in particular. So, why don't we open up volume one of his property ledger, and simply keep his letter books at our elbows as we go along? They begin in January 1872.

179

The urban fabric

1

One of Yates's earliest building agreements, dated 19 March 1867, was with Henry Nixon, a builder well-known in south-west London, covering the building of twelve houses in Nine Elms on land evidently already leased by Nixon since Christmas 1866 on an 80-year lease. Yates was then a young man of about 25 and had come to London from Lincolnshire in his middle teens, as the saying goes, to seek his fortune. He had virtually nothing in his pocket nor any known skill, and his main employment, to begin with at least, was as a builder's labourer – digging foundations for army barracks on Aldershot plain and the like. By the time of this agreement he was living near Regent's Park and was prepared to describe himself as 'Builder' – something which it was tempting and easy to do in the upswing of the building cycle in the later 1860s. At that time, capital was in ready supply, and men at all levels in the building trades and outside them were naturally inclined to wonder whether the very varying methods of dividing the labour of building a house complete might not be adapted to their individual circumstances so as to permit them to take a piece of building land on a peppercorn, contrive some working relationship with building tradesmen from another trade, get credit on the supply of bricks, the timber, indeed the land, and get a house or two or more into carcass form at least so as to be able to raise more working capital on the security of the lease that would then be granted.

This *is* the house that Jack built, or rather the procedure followed, as an established custom of the trade. There were variations, such as differences in operational styles according to the scale of working and all kinds of almost idiosyncratic preferences. But in the circumstances in which Edward Yates found himself at the end of the 1860s, it was a perfectly straightforward matter to ask a building society for the initial capital and to discharge the loan by finding a buyer for the houses and investing the proceeds in the next take. Yates got nearly £750 here from the London & Westminster and cleared this off eleven years later just as another building boom got under way, having waited for the depression that arrived in 1872 to clear; some years later there was still some obscure correspondence with Henry Nixon about an I.O.U. of Yates's which he, as head lessee, still held, so it's clear that this page doesn't tell the whole tale.

On another page, we find an agreement concerning Dragon Road, now obliterated from the map, but once a shallow side-shoot along St George's Road, Camberwell. This was an important slip for Yates. He took the land on a 70-year lease in 1868–9 in order to build 46 small terraced houses, and to do so he raised about £7,000 in thirteen separate mortgage loans, all but one of them with building societies – the London & Westminster again, the Planet, and the Fourth City Mutual – at 5% and repayable in 14 years, in 1881–2, which was roughly when that happened. Yates reckoned he laid out an average £190 on each house and that they were each worth £26 a year.

The necessary sums yield the astonishing conclusion that his annual outgoings, if the full costs were to be cleared by the end of the building societies' terms, were not less than £1,150, and that if he let every house without a break at the full value he would fetch in no more than £1,200. This was cutting things fine, even for a beginner content to pick up barely ½% profit on his gross outlay so as to get into business.

Of course, he was lucky to survive during the recession that occurred before he had completed this little estate, and he had to scratch around fairly hard to find the last of the capital he required. He raised nothing here between the end of 1869 and the middle of 1871, and when he got hold of the last £500 that summer it was from a solicitor in Lincoln's Inn Fields. That was the most significant thing about Dragon Road. It opened a new phase in his business. By now, too, he had evidently decided to do three more related things: to go into a limited partnership with a well-established builder, S. Sansom of Kennington (which was to last for seventeen years), to make a more regular practice of buildings to let rather than for sale, and to concentrate his sphere of operations on Walworth and Camberwell. So, he opened a yard adjoining an office in one of his own houses down the Southwark Bridge Road, No. 2 York Street just off the Elephant.

At this point we can open Yates's property ledger at a page giving more of the contractual information I have been paraphrasing so far. It refers to the four houses in the north-east tip of his development, but is entirely typical of the entries that follow: another 70-year-term, expiring at Christmas 1939 and the following May, just when they were coming, it might be said, under their direct threat. These were much more substantial houses than those in Dragon Road. The owner of the land, a descendant of a cow-keeper hereabouts who still had a lot of land in south London (and who was the landowner for Dragon Road) was John Rolls who later became Lord Langattock.

On the facing page we see in effect some of the foundation stones of Yates's financial edifice. The first two houses he mortgaged to the full to the trustees of an estate managed by a solicitor in the City, in a form I confess I don't entirely understand since it appears to involve £1,000 of stock to be redeemed at a discount; and the second pair he mortgaged to some other trustees through another firm of solicitors altogether, this time in a straight mortage at 6%. He held on to both mortgages for what would appear to be a very long time, over 20 years, and this prompts one or two reflections before we try and fix in our minds the character and conditions of development of one estate in particular.

2

As I said, Yates built to let and was prepared to sell his properties only occasionally. Individual houses and shop premises were sold to their occupiers from time to time, but there was no large-scale transfer of his house property to other business interests. This had important financial implications. It meant that, with a regular income from rents, he wasn't so closely tied to the vicissitudes of the capital market as were most of his contemporaries in the trade, nor paradoxically enough to local eddies of confidence where a disproportionate increase in the number of empty houses in a particular neighbourhood might induce a certain nervousness. It was, of course, always fatally easy to overreach oneself and to misjudge the state of the housing market; but a point of less obvious significance is that in a business like this the impression of solidarity and general credit-worthiness which a broad base of property ownership gave was a distinct encouragement to mortgagees to place their loans with such a substantial man of property. For a man operating so much on other people's money, most of which could have been called in at only six months' notice, this was a vital consideration.

The other thing I'm prompted to say at this point is that letting rather than selling does seem to have contributed to the extraordinary evenness in the expansion of Yates's business over the thirty years when it was expanding, from 1867 to 1895. The peak was actually reached five years before, in 1890, when the flow of capital raised on mortgage reached a rate of £28,000 per annum and the production of houses around 150 a year. The highest level of mortgage indebtedness didn't occur, as I said, until 1895 though the rate of climb had by then markedly slackened off. The point reached by then was £282,000, an aggregate composed of around 270 separate loans varying in amount from £200 to £20,000.

I'll say something about the origins and composition of this fund later, but let us notice here the very striking fact that the profile of growth, as measured by mortgage indebtedness, was that quite simply of one long deep breath. It rose and it fell. It didn't flutter. Apart from one or two very minor hesitations the dominant trend of Yates's business was upward for the whole twenty-year period down to the end of the 1880s, the period when the London housing industry as a whole went through two slumps and a boom which had such a marked effect on its structure.[2] The final tally of houses built by Edward Yates was just over 2,500; his estate was valued after his death in 1907 at a little short of a million pounds.

3

Let us, against this background, now pursue him in his purpose and take the first of the radial roads available to him at the Elephant and Castle and go in the direction he first did down the Old Kent Road. Let's go to Surrey Square. In March 1872 Yates tendered for the ground that might have been used to complete the other sides of a square proper, if its projectors in the eighteenth century had been able to complete their plan. Here lived at the beginning of the 1870s a moderately respectable middling sort of person – a colour and varnish manufacturer, a Billingsgate fish salesman, a potato dealer, a publican, a couple of builders, a coach body and carriage manufacturer, two or three reverend gentlemen (2 MAs, 1 DD), and a scatter of maiden ladies of means – along with a decent enough church and a pub not too close at hand. The detailing is chaste and seemly, the tone discreet almost to a fault.

John Browne, Esq., of Chertsey House, Park Hill Rise, Croydon, owned the land to whom Edward Yates proposed that he should, within three years, put up on this uncompleted square 118 houses on a 90-year lease at a ground rent of £630 in a full year. The agreement was duly made, the carcasses raised, the leases granted, the mortgages obtained, and another terrace now faced across the square that had been thereby compressed into a street. This was all done in 1873. The capital to finance this operation had already been accumulated from the development around Princess Street and in one or two more scattered developments, including one much closer to hand that I'll mention later.

Yates now raised £7,300 in six instalments through a firm of solicitors in Bedford Row, Winter Williams & Co. The money itself had mixed origins: £2,800 of it came from a stockbroker; £1,400 from an architect and surveyor; £2,800 from a curious little consortium composed of one of the partners in the solicitors' office, a consulting marine engineer and an Oxfordshire cleric; £300 came from a nondescript merchant in the City. Yates apparently had had a little difficulty in fixing up this trio, for he had been touting the properties in question up St Swithin's Lane before he left the whole thing to Winter Williams & Co., and had originally been seeking rather more. The landowner had taken the precaution to appoint an architects with a practice in Kennington Road and to this Robert Parker Yates applied for various kinds of permission. He would be glad to have this, he wrote in February 1873, so as 'to substitute a moulded cornice and parapet with valley roof instead of span roof with dropping caves on the houses in Surrey Square, as I think a Molded Cornice with Parapet will give a boldness to the Elevation and very considerably improve the Elevation to the houses'.

These were solid and decent enough, letting for £36 p.a. (ground rent £6 6s 0d), and Yates was soon ready to launch himself on the larger operation of filling in the space behind. Into this he inserted Aldbridge Street. The connections with his own Surrey Square development couldn't have been closer, not only in terms of the street layout but in timing and finance. No doubt it helped that in the summer of 1873, when he began to open out his building operations independently of his associate Sansom of Kennington in a big way, that he had mortgage advances coming in from developments in Walworth on land belonging to the Newington Guardians and the Ecclesiastical Commissioners, as also from Kennington on land belonging to the Stockwell Orphanage. But what made the Aldbridge Street development go with such a swing was that he had the money raised on property just round the corner to operate on. And when he had carried the houses in Aldbridge Street to the roof, four or five of them at a time, he could set off to Bedford Row again to get the capital he needed for the next round.

Indeed, he now found himself in the position, rather suddenly, of having the money coming to him. Only the year before he had had to write to the Commercial Union Building Society and offer to pay 7½% on purely temporary advances, to no avail; now the tone of his letters becomes a little less wheedling, a little more lordly, as he explained to a newly established firm of estate agents in the City who had written to him, that he was *willing* to take within the next 12 months from £5,000 to £10,000 in sums varying from £500 to £1500 secured against his properties. Within a month he was writing to another potential mortgagee that he had had money 'advanced as required hitherto and does not contemplate needing more during the coming Winter, but may be glad of it in the Spring'. More than that, even, he was so flush as to lend out a bit of money himself to one or two other builders, who were working close at hand.

4

Aldbridge Street, which contained 71 houses, and Flinton Street adjoining, which contained 13, which Yates seems to have built in simple sequence up one side and down the other, were perhaps a surprisingly long time under construction. He completed the first of the houses in mid-summer 1873 and the last at the very beginning of 1876 – not less than 2½ years. These were on similar terms of tenure as those on Surrey Square except that the ground rent was a guinea per plot lower. What we see Yates doing at this stage in the development of his business is to widen his catchment area for capital beyond Bedford Row, not only from Gray's Inn to Lincoln's Inn, the Temple and Sergeant's Inn and other offices in the City but out into the provinces. Only one of the eleven firms of solicitors he was now dealing with on this one estate of 84 houses was actually outside London – a firm in Colchester – but well over half of all the money he raised on these houses (£22,000 or more all told) came up from the country.

Of the 29 separate mortgage transactions he entered upon no fewer than 17 involved the savings of people outside London – totalling just over £12,000 or 55 per cent of the money raised on these two streets. No one office yielded much above £4,000 and most of them produced less than £2,000, but what is so striking about the whole operation is the sense it gives of providing outlets for capital investment that accumulate on the suburban edges of London like a delta of a great river system which has been 'made fertile by the deposits collected in distant places and carried along irreversibly by superior force'. If we think of the London leasehold system that we see in operation here, not as the legal framework for placing houses on the ground, but as a kind of market for real property, we shall see that it was important above all as a means of transferring capital assets on credit. Cash left on trust in the country therefore made its way to the mouth of the river as readily as any that could be collected closer at hand, and followed the obvious course into the hands of the trusty ones in the inns of court. Who exactly have we got here, then?

We begin with that little consortium that turned up on Surrey Square including the rector from Wigginton in Oxfordshire, but go on to find money coming in from all parts of East Anglia, the southern counties, the West Country, and even a little from Wales. It ought, I suppose, not be so surprising, but a goodly number of these worthy mortgages were clergymen, one of them was the postmaster at Hull, and one a man of the greatest renown – none other than the Speaker of the House of Commons, Sir Thomas Erskine May. We see the second of his two investments here among the evenly numbered houses on Aldbridge Street – the four numbered 52–58. This was a mortgage in which he joined forces with a very reverend gentleman then living in a rectory in Crawley in Hampshire, Philip Jacob.

If we turn aside for a moment to consider this pattern of capital investment over Yates's entire career, we might note that almost a third of all the money raised came from outside London, about £90,000 out of the £282,000 I mentioned earlier. And, if we break the mortgages up into very roughly drawn categories, what we find is that nearly £36,000 came from clergymen (13 per cent of the total), about £11,000 from the professions, notably the Army (4 per cent), over £58,000 – just over a fifth – from women, especially widows and spinsters, and by far the largest amount, about £85,000 or 30 per cent of the whole, from executors and trustees – and, indeed, the figure may well have been higher than this if the various solicitors lending money against their own names turn out to have been acting as trustees rather than private lenders (14 per cent of the total, amounting to some £39,000, came from them).

5

After the Old Kent Road Yates turned back on the Walworth Road, where he established the yard that lasted until his building work was done (that on York Street was the one he shared with Sansom), just opposite the Southwark vestry hall and the estate he began to develop along now familiar lines along Larcom Street from the summer of 1875. Here are the proceeds of Aldbridge Street being put to work in turn, with Gray's Inn providing most of the capital once again. He also now began to operate on an altogether different wavelength, the signals of which I cannot pick up at all well.

Early in 1875 he entered with his partner Sansom on another kind of speculation altogether by building a pub – the White Lion Hotel at Brighton – and he was soon quoting terms for this to inquirers: £15,000 for the freehold, £10,000 of which could remain for a time on mortgage; if taken on a lease they would want a premium of £5,000 and £600 a year in rent; to another he was soon quoting a lease of £250 a year for 80 years with a premium of £10,000. It took in fact years to sell and Sansom & Yates appear to have become the licensees themselves in the meantime (they did nearly £3,000 of business in the year 1875–6 but I don't know whether that might be considered good or bad – they certainly were running at a loss five years later even though the business was then twice this), and they ended by selling it at the end of the 1880s, when the most they did get for it was £9,000.

That was something of a drain on resources even though the details are unclear; but there are other elements also at work which may have worked in quite the opposite direction. Yates did enter into a number of deals of which only the tips broke the surface of his letter books. He became a shareholder, for example, in the Home Counties Land & Investment Co. Ltd (not a lucky investment since it went into liquidation in 1896), and bought and sold freehold ground rents in various parts of London. But these extra-mural activities, which may have had an important bearing on the success of his building business, were often conducted by word of mouth, especially after the installation of a telephone in 1881. He also bought and sold land outside London, including some in north Essex in 1900, the Boarded Hall Barns estate near Bishop's Stortford, where he planned to retire.

His biggest operation of this kind was probably the purchase of over 12 acres of land at Blythe Road, Kensington in 1880 or 1881, which was worth something of the order of £70,000 or £75,000 and part of which was sold for the building of Olympia in three or four years after that. How much he made on that – some of it was in so-called National Agricultural Hall debentures – I don't know. It's impossible now to trace the transfer of his resources from one activity to another (though I suspect there were many of them), and this has to be borne in mind in considering how successful he was in his central concerns. The biggest of them was, in fact, yet to come. He was occupied for the rest of the 1870s in a whole series of sizeable estate developments. One of the smaller ones, at Domville Grove at the eastern end of Albany Road in Camberwell, had a certain practical elegance and even style for its neighbourhood and illustrates Yates's readiness to abandon set-piece routines.

This development was in 1875. The following year he began work on another Rolls property back up the Old Kent Road opposite the Bricklayers' Arms, on Danvin and Chatham Streets. Here is his archetypal estate so far as finance is concerned. It divides into the three estates of the realm: the church, the law and wealthy widows. Yates raised almost £23,000 here in 21 instalments, of which an astonishingly high proportion – 55 per cent of the money – came from clergymen, a third from the lawyers and the rest from the widows; the lawyers were really at the heart of it, though, because the partners in the practice in Lincoln's Inn each took part and their relatives (and no doubt their cousins, too) also came in.

6

This was the kind of operation that now began to gather momentum at very high speed within the angle of the Walworth and Old Kent Roads. It would be superfluous to go on illustrating it in any detail, and it isn't difficult to imagine how it all took place. Every one of Yates's estates at this point were within ten or fifteen minutes' walking distance of his office and yard in the Walworth Road, which was at the heart of an area which at the time was rapidly being populated by the lower-middle and working classes. Except for one small development that he appears to have had in mind on the north side of Clapham Common, and which he soon abandoned, Yates concentrated rather on the lower end of the market for houses in the suburbs, the kinds of houses that rising clerks or shopkeepers who were not disposed to live over the shop might attain to. Here, as he wrote to one solicitor in 1877, it was rare for any of his houses to be empty, nor did he ever lose a penny of rent. These were properties that let at £36 or £40 a year, or if they were designed to be let by the floor they would be rented at between five and six shillings or so per week for a suite of three rooms. If there was a change of tenancy, he used to explain, 'we increase the rents from £2 to £6 per year'.

Yates kept his own eye on things and tried to get his son to do the same. Indeed, here he tried a little too hard, making him queue for his wages with the men and trying to force him into his own mould. In this he failed and it is the third generation that has really got back into the business again. He was sharp on short time or short weight. To a timber merchant in Bedford who had supplied only 4,820 slates by rail instead of 5,040 as per invoice he suggested they should write to the railway about the missing 220; to Eastwoods in Belvedere Road he was always complaining about quantities – the barge *Alexandra* was short of 550 bricks in 40,000, he complained in September 1891, the *Promise* 150 in 28,000, but good old *Trotter* came up with an extra 150 on its 40,000 – and he duly reported that, too. He told a brickmaker at Sittingbourne to stop all supplies because the quality had fallen off. He pounced on one tenant for so losing sight of the meaning of the term dwelling as to instal sewing machines enough for a 'Manufactory' – this at No. 12 Aldbridge Street; and just across the street from his old office in York Street he came down on another of his tenants for turning his house into a brothel (1892).

He sought to protect his property from the contagion of non-residential use and strongly resisted all such proposals by local authorities as to build casual wards or Board Schools adjoining his properties, and campaigned against anything that might increase his rates, such as the proposal to introduce electric-lighting to the streets of Newington in 1882. Not

surprisingly perhaps he found himself taking small political offices – he was
for a time in the 1890s, for example, Treasurer of the London Freeholders
and Leaseholders Defence Association and Chairman of the Walworth
Conservative Association. Some of these were forlorn causes, and none
more so perhaps than the one he took up vehemently with the Southwark &
Vauxhall Water Company in 1895. Replying to their inquiries he told them
loftily that he had over 3,500 water closets in his property and considered the
two-gallon flush adequate for all practical purposes. He wanted to point out
to them the far-reaching implications in a city like London of 5 million
inhabitants of increasing the flush to three gallons. Would now that he had
been heeded!

I need perhaps say only a few words in conclusion about Yates's largest
single undertaking whose beginnings occurred at about the time he was
getting out of Chatham Street at the end of 1876 and the beginning of 1877.
This was the Waverley Park estate, as it came to be known, at Nunhead,
where he had bought four fields to the east and south of the new Nunhead
Cemetery in 1877 and which he had begun to use for brick-making, not only
to meet his own needs but to supply other builders and even the
Sittingbourne Brick Co. I need say comparatively little about this and the
huge developments that followed in the 1880s, because it's all already
accessible.[3]

The story, very briefly, is that he seized the opportunity that presented
itself in 1879 of adding a substantial chunk of land he took on lease from
Christ's Hospital, and from 1884 began on this land to erect some 120 houses
at an outlay of around £350/£450 each on payment of a ground rent of £225 a
year. At about the same time, in 1881 or 1882, he bought on its other side a
further tract of land and picked up a final crucial piece from a local resident –
four pieces of ground that formed an estate of about 50 acres. Here, in the
end, were to be found nearly a third of all his properties in 1905, and here too
was his largest single mortgage loan from the largest single cleric mortgagee
available – the Rector of Ashley near Market Harborough who was good for
£20,000.

Here all Yates's talents conveyed in the creation of the necessary
apparatus for a self-contained suburban community of impregnable respectability allied with the maximum economy and convenience. It may not
strike you so, for Ivydale Road is a wearisome length and its rather muscular,
uncommunicative villas do little to lighten the step or the heart. Remember,
though, that they were for their day the essence of modernity and
respectability – respectability in terms of a sufficiency of brass and coloured
glass at the front door and mahogany handrails and venetian blinds and
bright tessellated hallways within; modernity in terms of back-boilers and
gas-stoves, bathrooms and neatly fitted cupboards and separate washhouses;
economy in terms of rentals as low as £28 a year exclusive of rates. It was a

domain of domesticity all right and didn't, as things turned out, have much sense of community – though Frederick Willis managed to make it sound a good deal jollier in *101 Jubilee Road* (1948) and *Peace and Dripping Toast* (1950). And the pub which Yates carefully provided and the Anglican church, the mission hall and the Methodist chapel which he also helped forward, not to speak of the Board School in true E. R. Robson style, added something to the scale. The shops, which Yates scrupulously selected, did mitigate the pioneering atmosphere which was there at the start, just as it has always been among the busless muddy wastes of raw suburbia.

7

In the end it all comes good, so they say, or if it doesn't of its own accord the required effect is not beyond the ordinary handyman's skill. Suddenly, in the circumstances created by the wave of enthusiasm we have just been enduring for the wholesale refinestration of Victorian villas, we see something we had probably hardly noticed before – a sense of proportion a quiet delight in ordinary craftsmanship, a dignity that belonged in some degree to houses of a very ordinary kind. Other specimens of the speculative builders' labours may caution us from thinking that Yates was somehow typical of them all. No doubt it is already plain to you that he was not.

12

A guide to the streets of Victorian London

> Monstrous, marvellous, prodigious London, –
> Thou giant city, – mighty in thy size and power,
> Surpassing all that was, or is, or may be.
>
> From the title-page of [John Britton],
> *Picture of London* (26th edn, 1829)

'In the presence of London, it is just as it would be if you should meet a man fifty feet high . . . . You would be in a state of perpetual astonishment.' The words come from an obscure contributor to a family magazine, writing shortly before *Collins' Illustrated Atlas of London* was first published in 1854, but they express an attitude that was universal.[1] 'The extension of the metropolis of the British empire', declared the *Gentleman's Magazine*, 'is one of the marvels of the last century'[2] – a multiplication of numbers, and 'elasticity' and 'expansibility' that was 'almost oppressively palpable', that outdid all the capitals of Europe and was barely overtaken in the public mind by the gold-rushing growth of San Francisco.[3] 'London has not grown', complained one writer in *Household Words*,

in any natural, reasonable, understandable way . . . it has swollen with frightful, alarming, supernatural rapidity. It has taken you unawares; it has dropped upon you without warning; it has started up without notice; it has grown with stealthy rapidity, from a mouse into a mastodon.[4]

It had in fact multiplied only two and a half times in about two and a half generations, measured in London terms. In 1801 London was on the verge of becoming the world's first million-peopled city and its rate of growth since then had been exceeded by several northern industrial towns, but what so fascinated those watching was London's insatiable appetite for people. At the beginning of the nineteenth century the area later defined as the Metropolitan Police District – Greater London no less – already contained about 12 per cent of the population of England and Wales; by mid-century the figure was 15 per cent; at its close 20 per cent. On his second visit to London in 1847 Ralph Waldo Emerson had observed that 'the nation sits in the immense city they have builded, a London extended into every man's mind'.[5]

The convergence there of all the major institutions in the nation's life –
the Crown, parliament, government, law, commerce, industry, finance,
fashion – had long provided the ingredients for the national fixation of the
times: that London represented not so much the apex of provincial life as a
funnel for its wealth and its people.[6] Thomas de Quincey, who started life in
Manchester, had often felt its powerful suction, he said, since first visiting
London as a youth for a day in 1800 – a suction that was 'operating, night and
day, summer and winter, and hurrying for ever into one centre the infinite
means needed for her infinite purposes, and the endless tributes to the skill
or to the luxury of her endless population.'[7] Not surprisingly, Coleridge had
called London the 'Leviathan', Cobbett the 'Wen', Robert Mudie 'Babylon
the Great', Emerson 'the Rome of today', and to the widening circle of
writers who, in the 1830s and 1840s, were offering themselves as pathfinders
along its secret ways, it was a vast and mysterious continent demanding to be
explored.[8] 'Let us roll out the map of London', wrote one of them, 'and take a
glance at its terrible physiology. These fine streets that we trace are but the
frontier of a kingdom of which the upper classes know as little as of the
interior of Japan.'[9] Even a Londoner as knowledgeable as Sala had left great
tracts untouched. No one from Stowe to Dickens – no, not Pepys nor
Maitland – had done more, he thought, than scratch the surface of London.
'I never travelled in London', he wrote in 1857, 'though I am a cockney born.
. . I candidly confess that I never was in Bethnal Green in my life, that I have
a very indistinct notion of the latitude of Hackney, that I don't know where
Bluegate Fields are situated.' He must, he said, 'construe this metropolitan
Abracadabra . . . read this Rosetta inscription'.[10] What we can sense here is a
consciousness of the city as *terra incognita*, a man-made wilderness more
daunting than tropical forests, more inscrutable than the Sahara. London
was in truth a place with a regional geography of its own: it was a globe unto
itself: 'behold, within the Arctic circle the migratory Esquimaux of Camden
Town', declared John Fisher Murray; 'the Australasian territories of our
southern metropolitan hemisphere.'[11]

1

Here, indeed, was a place into which it was inconceivable that anyone,
visitor or native, dare go unaided: a map was indispensable; an atlas might be
better. When *Collins' Illustrated Atlas of London* offered itself for the second
time, in 1859, it was 'as a guide and friend to all who seek for information
through the labyrinths of the Metropolis'. Collins's was not in fact the first
street guide to London to describe itself as an atlas – a term hitherto kept for
collections of maps of some territorial substance.[12] The distinction of first
putting London on such a par belongs to James Wyld the younger, who had
assumed his father's style as Geographer to the Queen and H.R.H. Prince
Albert and produced five or six years before *An Atlas of London & its*

191

Environs, a portfolio of eight sheets measuring four feet square. This was something to be deliberated over, and never out of doors. *Collins' Illustrated Atlas*, on the other hand, was the first street guide specifically designed to go into the pocket and to be consulted under all street conditions, its plates being specially drawn for it, and every street that could be found being listed in it.

It had been a matter of common sense since the 1760s to fit fairly large-scale maps for the pocket simply by folding them sufficiently and carrying them in a slip-case, and this practice did not begin to change before about 1830.[13] Most maps of London produced in this period had fallen into two categories: small-scale maps of less than one inch to the mile encompassing a radius of around 15 miles of Charing Cross; large-scale maps upwards of four inches or so to the mile and covering the continuously built-up area to its limits. The second group was about twice as large as the first. About half of these larger-scale maps were either cut into sections or mounted for folding (almost all the smaller-scale maps were designed to be kept flat), and it was a natural step sooner or later to bind up maps prepared in this way into the form of a book. Cruchley's *Environs of London*, drawn to a scale of nearly five inches to the mile and first issued in a slip-case in 1825 or 1826, was presented in 1830, as its cartouche announced, 'bound in a novel form as a book'. There was an extra innovation because it included a paginated index to the streets and principal places of interest. Since fairly early in the eighteenth century the principal street-names were usually listed in the margins of so-called 'pocket maps' and 'city guides', and such maps were divided into squares for easy reference; sometimes important buildings were numbered and drawn into a decorative frieze, sometimes interspersed with awesome statistics. One idea was to provide a gazetteer in a booklet pasted inside the outer cover of a folding case. This was an advance on a much older idea used by Ogilby and Morgan as long before as 1677 in their *London Survey'd: or, an Explanation of the Large Map of London*, which was simply an index to the great survey of London they had completed following the Fire;[14] Rocque's plan of 1746 had also been augmented a year later by a substantial index of a similar kind;[15] Horwood's plan, too, was very effectively indexed; but perhaps the most developed form of index was that supplied as a *Companion* to Langley & Belch's *New Map of London* (1812), which ran to 172 pages. Although Cruchley's book-like plan of 1830 combined these possibilities in what now seems a most ingenious and convenient way, the idea failed to catch on: Deacon's small-scale map of the environs of London to a distance of 30 miles, published in 1831, was apparently its only imitator.

By the 1850s mapmaking had become all the same a notoriously derivative business. The six maps shown at the Great Exhibition in 1851 were versions of maps that had been available for anything up to sixty years, perhaps even more.[16] Advances were being made, for the trigonometrical survey of the country which had been started in 1784 had led to the publication of the one-inch Ordnance Survey for the four counties impinging on London in the years 1805–22, and its measurements must have passed fairly rapidly into the stock-in-trade of commercial mapmakers. More important for basic urban engineering was the completion, in 1851, of the central portion of the much larger-scale survey being conducted, on the double scale of five feet and 12 inches to the mile, at the instigation of the Metropolitan Commission of Sewers in 1847 – though the whole thing was not completed till 1871.[17]

In the meantime a vast but cruder stock of more easily adapted material was at hand to meet the growing demand of people visiting London who merely wanted to be able to find their way about. Richard Horwood's meticulous though imperfect survey, completed on a scale of 26 inches to the mile in 1792–9 covering the whole area between Islington and Kensington, Limehouse and Brompton, provided one such base. The conscientiously updated editions of John Cary's *New and Accurate Plan*, first issued in 1787, covering approximately the same extent but on a scale of 6½ inches to the mile, was another; and the scarcely less authentic and beautifully engraved maps of William Faden, Christopher and John Greenwood, George Cruchley and James Wyld (both father and son), and of one or two others besides, provided an abundant source for copyists, not to say one another, during the first half of the nineteenth century. The old plates were often handed down – as Horwood's were to Faden and then to Wyld – though this did not necessarily imply a failure to update the original version, and in this case thorough revision of a map of the City first issued in 1780 makes his edition of 1840 unusually valuable. However, sometimes the original plates were neither re-etched nor revised so carefully, even by the reputable mapmakers, and these occasionally became fuzzy or hopelessly outdistanced by the poliferating suburbs.[18]

2

Henry George Collins was one among many mapmakers and mapsellers who rose on the great tourist tide that engulfed London during and immediately following the exhibitions of 1851 and 1862. The market was a very large one. Over six million people were admitted to the Great Exhibition during the long season of 1851 (it was dismantled in 1852 and reopened at Sydenham in June 1854, ten days after *Collins' Atlas* appeared). The great aim of the publicists was to make London itself an exhibition of out-of-doors, a public show requiring the entrance fee merely of the price of a pocket map — something to be understood, used, enjoyed and finally disposed of. This was a time when old maps appeared unashamedly in disguise and new editions could masquerade under new names. James

Reynold's four-inch map of 1847, for example, already replete with a guide for viewing the 'sights and amusements of London' as a six days' wonder, merely needed redating 1851, the whereabouts of the Exhibition marked and tinted, and a new label affixed to the cover to become *The Exhibition Map of London*.

Novelty was inclined to breed novelty. The 'distance map' had a brief vogue following the publication of J. Friederichs' *The Circuiteer* about 1847, on which a continuous grid of half-mile circles was superimposed with the idea of making it easy to decide whether to walk or take a cab. John Tallis's highly original idea of providing 'a complete stranger's guide through London' by means of a series of detailed elevations to the main streets, coupled with street directories, views of the principal buildings and miniature street maps, had also reappeared in 1847.[19] *A Balloon View of London* covering eight square miles as seen from an altitude of a thousand feet above Hampstead Heath appeared in 1851. Skeleton maps that enabled the visitor to find without seeking, as in Virtue & Co.'s *The British Metropolis in 1851*, cut through the bewildering details in another way. The *Post Office Directory* map – the best cheap map of London according to Murray's[20] – came supplied in the 1855 edition with a patent index and a tape affixed to one edge for locating the place-names.

Collins' Illustrated Atlas was something of a novelty, too. Unlike almost all other maps of London ever known, each of its 36 sections was oriented on a different axis from the others, the sub-division of the ground being determined largely by the direction taken by the main thoroughfares between St Paul's and the suburbs but partly by the whimsical desire to stand the visitor, or the town, on their heads: the top of every map pointed in a different direction and every one overlapped the adjoining streets all round – St Paul's appeared on six of them. Turning the map sideways or upside-down to get one's bearings was supposedly unnecessary. There was some resemblance here to the maps in *Tallis's London Street Views*, which not only disregarded the compass completely but often inverted the street-names in an effort to square up with the views themselves. The *Atlas's* size permitted it, the introduction pointed out, to be used 'without notice or inconvenience of any kind'. Anyone unwilling to abandon the notion that the north is always uppermost must nevertheless have been driven to distraction.

This may help to explain why Collins himself did not last long as a mapseller. He disappeared within a decade. His first publication had been a small-scale map of London and its environs in 1851, and the following year he produced his *Pocket Ordnance Railway Atlas of Great Britain*. With some prescience he brought out in 1853 a map of Russia and Turkey and, when hostilities began in the Crimea the year after, put another half-a-dozen local charts and plans of the theatre of war on sale. He also produced two or three more railway maps. Very shortly after he had gone into partnership with his brother, Henry Edward Collins, and William Paprill in 1858 or 1859 the firm went bankrupt. His last publication seems to have been an *Indestructible Atlas of the Earth* (1858). The edition of the *Illustrated Atlas of London* that appeared in 1859 was published instead by Thomas Hodgson and that of 1862 by Darton & Hodge.[21]

It is clear from the plates themselves that they were not lithographic transfers from any existing map, though the claim that they are based on an independent survey must remain rather more open. The vignetted views bear a fugitive resemblance to some of the numerous engravings to be found in near-contemporary guide books – *Cruchley's Picture Book of London* (1846) offers two or three more positive likenesses – but it is hard to justify these suspicions. As for the street plan itself, it must be admitted that it would have been straightforward enough to take it straight off a number of existing maps. The inclination to block in back-streets and courts to a greater extent than most contemporary maps on the same scale did tends to diminish somewhat the claim that a survey was taken specially. The scale used was 3¾ inches to the mile, the same as that of Cruchley's famous *New Plan of London in Miniature* (1827) and Wyld's *Atlas of London & its Environs* (1848–9) – the first covering a rather smaller area and the second a much larger one than Collins's – and there had been a score of such maps published in the previous forty years, a number of them even distributed gratis with periodicals like the *Railway Bell and Illustrated London Advertiser* (1845) and the *United Kingdom Newspaper* (1832). Of Richard Jarman, the engraver of *Collins' Illustrated Atlas*, little is known beyond the fact that he also produced a map of Portsmouth and Southsea about 1865.

3

Despite the perverse arrangement of the plates, *Collins' Illustrated Atlas* had the great merit of imposing a rational order of some kind on London's apparently meaningless geography: it made the mass manageable. Though it covered not very much more than a third of London as delimited by the Registrar-General for census purposes, it included all but a fraction of the 40 or 50 square miles of its continuously built-up area and upwards of three-quarters of its total population of around 2½ millions. The line of the North London Railway, which traversed all the most northerly plates, roughly defined the built-up limits on that side, just as the line of the New Road had done up to forty years before and the Regent's Canal until the last twenty years. Beyond it, settlement was still fairly scattered, concentrated for the most part on villages not yet overtaken by the urban ooze. Down river, where Bromley and Bow and, more conspicuously, Poplar had opened salients across the lower Lea valley, and in a series of northerly uphill thrusts into Dalston, Islington, Kentish Town and Kilburn the growth points of the next ten or twenty years were already forming. Beyond the congested corner of the flood plain on the other bank the settlement was much looser and inderterminate: a great band of half-formed suburbs dotted across the higher ground between Blackheath, Denmark Hill, Brixton and Wandsworth.

Collins' Illustrated Atlas stopped a good way short of most of these newer places, but the direction in which it might be said to have stopped altogether too abruptly was in the west, especially towards Notting Hill and Kensington, which were beginning to grow fast. These limitations apart, it had kept up well with the developments closer to the centre: the Great Western Railway's new Paddington terminus on Praed Street, for example, which had not been opened till 1854, was duly shown; impending developments like the new cattle market in the Caledonian Road (opened in 1855) and Battersea Park (laid out and planted in 1856–7) were correctly indicated: the limits of the open ground were accurately shown. With one major exception, no change of any consequence on the previous decade had been overlooked.

The exception is the railway system. This also rather tells against *Collins' Illustrated Atlas* as an independent survey but it is something of a puzzle because the canals are all shown, as the railway termini are ('recent and novel creations', as one writer had lately put it, 'that as yet are in, but scarcely of London'[22]), and the lines themselves were added to the 1859 edition. The railways were neither inconspicuous on the ground nor insignificant in their operation, especially where they were carried on those long brick viaducts that marked the street plan so indelibly.

Yet it is important to remember how small a presence the railway had made within the central area as such by the 1850s. The lines built in the 1830s and 1840s had, with the exception of the Blackwall Railway, merely come to the edge of the built-up area and had not pierced it. From the mid-1840s till the end of the 1850s the railway was deliberately barred from central London: indeed, the bulk of its railway system, perforce a suburban one, did not come into being before the 1860s and 1870s. It was then that the railway became for a time a weapon of destruction, as lines that have been devised after the ground had been taken for houses and other buildings plunged remorselessly among them.[23] *Collins' Illustrated Atlas* belongs to the intervening lull, when the streets were virtually the only avenues of communication, when their superstructures were in form and substance largely an inheritance of the pre-Victorian past, and when London itself remained an inveterate, if diverting, obstacle to through travel between north and south.

The streets offered obstacles of their own. Despite the supposed abolition twenty-five years earlier, at the instigation of the Metropolitan Turnpike Commission, of the road tolls north of the river, there were within four miles of Charing Cross in the 1850s more gates and bars still standing than there had been in 1830, despite a well-packed lobby at Westminster to oppose them.[24] They were thickest on the ground in Notting Hill, Kentish Town, Holloway, Stamford Hill, Hackney, Peckham and Camberwell, and their virtual abolition did not come until 1865.[25] At the same time only London, Blackfriars and Westminster Bridges (the last newly built) were free of toll, and the other four – excepting Hungerford, which was a footbridge – were not completely cleared of theirs before 1879 (when the Chelsea, Albert and Battersea Bridges were also cleared, leaving only Wandsworth, Putney and Hammersmith to be made toll-free the following year). The *Illustrated London News* calculated in 1854 that, what with the toll and other inconveniences, 'five-sixths of the whole traffic of the largest city in the civilised world pours over one bridge'.[26]

London was not all it might have been, and there was a faint but increasingly nagging implication in remarks like this that the beautification of Paris, which was going ahead with such style and resolution, was a reproach on London. *Punch* was often carping about such things: 'Paris making such a movement in her buildings and her streets. How is it that all improvement here with opposition meets?'[27] The more London grew, grumbled the *Illustrated London News*, the more unwholesome it was becoming:

The new London of Belgravia and Tyburnia may stand comparison for beauty and splendour with any city in the world; but old London and Westminster, with their outlying boroughs of Southwark, Lambeth, the Tower Hamlets, and Finsbury, have positively nothing to recommend them but wealth, extent and populousness.

In Chancery Lane, the only direct connection between the parallel westward thoroughfares of Fleet Street and the Strand on one side and of Holborn and New Oxford Street on the other, the traffic was often brought to a standstill, it contemptuously declared, by a laundress's wheelbarrow.[28]

The truth of the matter is that the streets of London remained in 1854 roughly in the condition they had been twenty or thirty years before. A more sobering truth is that the road system of London as a whole scarcely changed, except at three or four crucial spots, over an ensuing period twice as long.

Taking New Oxford Street through the slums of St Giles separating Holborn and Tottenham Court Road in 1847 was one vital step, but the through-route it promised via Newgate, Cheapside, Cornhill, Aldgate and Whitechapel was frustrated by the steep and narrow crossing of the Fleet Valley, until Holborn Viaduct swept over it in 1869. The more southerly east–west route had a couple of serious bottlenecks in it, at Temple Bar and Ludgate Hill, but it was prevented from converging on the other route in Cheapside by the extension of Cannon Street straight to St Paul's, an improvement completed just in time for inclusion in *Collins' Illustrated*

Atlas. The City had never been seriously short of outlets to the north save at one point, beyond Holborn Circus, and the scheme to cut a new street to Clerkenwell Green, which had been initiated in 1832 as a means of extending Farringdon Street, was still incomplete when *Collins' Illustrated Atlas* appeared: it reached Bagnigge Wells Road (now King's Cross Road) in 1856 and was named Farringdon Road (having first been known as Victoria Street).

The only other major new streets to be imposed on central London in the sixty years after publication of the *Atlas* are the two constellations of Charing Cross Road–Shaftesbury Avenue (1867–7) and Theobalds Road–Clerkenwell Road–Rosebery Avenue (1878–1902), the Albert, Victoria and Chelsea Embankments (1868–74), Southwark Street (1862–4), and Kingsway (1905). Victoria Street, Westminster (1851), which, like its Clerkenwell namesake, was still being developed when *Collins' Illustrated Atlas* was published, Queen Victoria Street (1871), and Northumberland Avenue (1876) were all less important as traffic arteries.

4

What is not possible to discover from this street guide are the means of getting about, the way the city functioned, or the elements of its social geography.[29] What we have, apart from the maps, is a solemn enough roll-call of government buildings, almshouses, asylums, breweries, cemeteries, churches, hospitals, monuments, markets, prisons and the like, along with a brief flourish of theatres, pleasure gardens, museums, galleries, waxworks and peepshows of varying pretensions. It is not a complete list. Most obviously perhaps, it omits the recently established music halls and casinos, the widening range of hotels, clubs, shops and arcades, and necessarily offers few hints of that other London which became the subject of books like J. Ewing Ritchie's *The Night Side of London* (1857) or *London in the Sixties* (1908) by 'One of the Old Brigade'. The frivolities – and the miseries – of Victorian London constitute a whole library of their own.

On a more mundane level, *Collins' Illustrated Atlas* did not explain how to get about this bedevilling place. It offered no rules of thumb for reckoning cab fares – three shillings would take one almost anywhere – nor guidance on where to catch a bus or how much it would cost, but these mostly ran through the City or the West End and out to the suburbs so frequently and cheaply – sixpence or less all the way – while their service and direction were so mercurial that no comprehensive route map was ever offered to the general public before the more settled era of the London Passenger Transport Board's monopoly rule in the 1930s. *Collins' Illustrated Atlas* appeared, as it happened, at a moment of crisis for both the omnibus and coaching businesses: the latter because the railway had so lately driven the long-distance coaches off the roads and with them the business that had sustained the City's coaching inns; the former because, among other things, excessive numbers of buses brought onto the roads to cater for the tourist traffic of 1851 had led to fare-cutting at a time when operating costs were rising – the outbreak of the Crimean War in the spring of 1854 added to these by causing fodder to rise sharply in price. The formation the following year of an undertaking, soon to be known as the London General Omnibus Company, which would exercise a controlling hand over a large part of the omnibus business was the sequel to this. The tramway was a more distant development.

The mapmaker's is a lifeless art, and when applied to such a metropolis supremely so. He can supply no spot check of the human traffic passing through these streets – a mere 26,000 daily commuters, as it happened, in 1854[30] – that will restore their hubbub and incident; he can release none of the sensations of the prodigious daily act of provisioning the city – of close on two million livestock, for instance, being driven on the hoof into Smithfield in weekly instalments, of oxen that might have lined up ten abreast and stretched beyond Peterborough or of sheep all the way to Bristol, or supplied the thought that somewhere among those streets 20,000 cows were stalled up supplying milk.[31] The images he evokes, like those gathered at dawn from the crow's nest erected on the apex of the cross of St Paul's to conduct the Ordnance Survey in 1848, are of an 'empire of living mortality.... Could we unroof the houses and bare to the morning sun the vast congregated population beneath, what a motley, what a painful scene, would be developed.'[32]

That sensation of lurking truths about London was being evoked increasingly in the early 1850s. Henry Mayhew's encounters with the secret people of the streets, which were reported to readers of the *Morning Chronicle* in 1849–50 (and have never been repeated *in extenso* since), more than a decade of Dicken's explorations of the terrible interstices in London's familiar façade, the step-by-step accretion of social fact by fascinated statisticians, writings on every level from Max Schlesinger's *Saunterings in and about London* to Charles Manby Smith's *Curiosities of London Life: or, Phases, Physiological and Social, of the Great Metropolis* or John Garwood's *The Million-Peopled City; or, One-half of the people of London made known to the other half* – all of them published the year before *Collin's Illustrated Atlas* – and the curiouser and curiouser self-knowledge coming with the censuses (the final report of the 1851 census, the most searching yet, was not published until July 1854) – these were leading, in one direction, to new perceptions of social distance and to a new fashion for slumming and, in another, to more insistent demands that the amorphous lump be somehow shaped, that the polluting city be somehow cleansed.

What helped to clinch this question was the cholera, which in the course of the summer of 1854 carried off nearly 10,000 souls in London alone: less deadly at large than the visitation of 1849 had been, there were districts in London like St George's-in-the-East, Golden Square, the east side of Regent Street, parts of Deptford, where it took even more life.[33] That very spring a Royal Commission on the Corporation of the City of London – the second in Victoria's reign – had proposed the establishment of a board of management for London beyond the ancient square mile, which would do for it what the Corporation had disdained to do and the 78 assorted vestries and 300 or so other bodies that held disputed sway over it could never do – cleanse it, improve it, govern it.[34] And with the creation of the Metropolitan Board of Works for that purpose within the next 12 months came the need for more systemised knowledge about the mechanisms of the metropolis.

We see from this time therefore a new era of more searching and analytical mapping of London than *Collins' Illustrated Atlas* could provide. That was a job for a man who was only then seriously setting up as a mapmaker – Edward Stanford. He had acquired most of Collins's plates at the end of the 1850s, and his six-inch *Library Map of London*, published in 1862, was the first thoroughgoing survey of London for nearly forty years: it became the authentic basis for projecting the M.B.W.'s plans. The ultimate development of cartography of that order is the *Atlas of London and the London Region* prepared under the direction of Emrys Jones and D. J. Sinclair and published in 70 folio sheets in 1968. London is now so large and knowledge of it so liable to be fragmented that the chief need is to try to see the metropolitan city as a regional whole, and to map its social and economic elements within a context of town-planning.

5

Collins' Illustrated Atlas belongs to a different age and met a different need. The urban landscape had not up to that time been treated by mapmakers any differently from the rural landscape. The problem of handling its compacted form was still seen largely as one of scale. The idea of urban life as a new kind of social order, as a symbiosis of many species, that had to be represented in special ways, had scarcely yet occurred to cartographers. Why not show churches, schools and public buildings, suggested *The Builder* in 1856, on maps of their own: 'parts of another plan, differently shaded, might show the conditions of mortality, crime, or ignorance, or of property, or pauperism, and the latest census or enquiry'.[35] That suggestion was swiftly followed, and within the next two or three decades London got specialised maps galore.

Yet, apart from an incomplete Post Office list of streets dated 1857, with maps of the ten postal districts designated the year before, and a plethora of pocket-sized maps – including more than one for the waistcoat[36] – no other true pocket street atlas of London seems to have been published before the turn of the century.[37] What this suggests perhaps is that, for the great bulk of ordinary Londoners, continuous access to the larger mass, those outer corridors beyond the daily round, was not – as it must already have been for errand-boys, cab and delivery van drivers and policemen – an urgent social or economic necessity. What it certainly does mean is that *Collins' Illustrated Atlas of London* remains in a class of its own, the prototype of that now indispensable thing, a pocket atlas, not of the 7,000 streets of London in 1854 but of the 27,000 streets of London today.

Conclusion

Urban history in the United Kingdom: the 'Dyos phenomenon' and after

by DAVID CANNADINE

During the late 1960s and early 1970s, in Britain as in the United States, there was a marked proliferation of the sub-specialisms within the realms of historical scholarship – social history, oral history, women's history, family history, and so on. But of all Clio's new offsprings, none was so exuberantly expansive, nor so closely identified with one man (Jim Dyos) and one university (Leicester) as was urban history. Even social history, which was urban history's nearest rival among the burgeoning new fields of historical interest, was diffuse in its organisation and divided in its administration by comparison, with a wide proliferation of societies, series, conferences and journals. By contrast, urban history seemed a model of centralised organisation. As Bruce Stave rightly noted at the beginning of his interview with Jim Dyos, 'In terms of British urban history, all roads seem to lead to you and to the University of Leicester.'[1]

Indeed, the supreme paradox of urban history in the United Kingdom was that, as long as Dyos lived, it combined the maximum of organisational centralisation with the minimum of intellectual dogmatism – a position almost exactly the opposite of that which prevailed in the United States, where the New Urban History was being developed at the same time.[2] Zealous and indefatigable entrepreneurship was allied with a complete lack of scholarly imperialism or doctrinaire exclusiveness. It was this blending of a coherent and energetic organisation with a tolerant and encouraging intellectual milieu, which made the urban history explosion both the most spectacular and the most appealing of the historical booms in Britain during the late 1960s and 1970s.

In the last two or three years, however, urban history in England and the New Urban History in America have both experienced some loss of a sense of direction. In the United States, this has resulted from growing doubts about the quantitative methodology of the New Urban History. But with English urban history, true to its rather different character, the explanation lies elsewhere. For since Jim Dyos's death in 1978, there has been no one equipped, either as a personality or as a professor, to inherit or lead the historical sub-discipline which was his personal creation. And, thus weakened in its organisational zeal and coherence, there is a danger that a subject which has previously thrived on the complementary attribute of intellectual tolerance may become so diffuse and amorphous as to lose any real sense of identity.

But before investigating urban history's present position more fully, and speculating as to its future prospects and likely course of development, it is necessary to trace its evolution thus far. How, in the United Kingdom, did urban history evolve? What, if anything, does it stand for, intellectually and methodologically? And what, in particular, did Jim Dyos think urban historians ought to be doing?.

1

In his inaugural lecture as Professor of Urban History in the University of Leicester, Dyos self-effacingly thanked his colleagues for giving him 'the opportunity to indulge my historical curiosity in the way I chose', and coyly suggested that he had been 'lucky enough to catch one of the biggest breakers to have risen in modern history since the war'.[3] But he was doing himself less than justice. Like Rutherford who, on being told 'You're always at the crest of the wave', replied 'Well, after all, I made the wave, didn't I?', Dyos's contribution to the development of his subject was crucial.[4] For even if urban history did not, as two colleagues affectionately put it, 'spring from the head of Olympian Dyos as fully armed as Pallas Athene from the head of Zeus', he was in all ways its creator.[5] Unknown to themselves, some historians in the United Kingdom had written urban history before. But Dyos was the first man to tell them what they were doing, why they should do more of it, and how they might do it better.

He was born in London in 1921, and remained at heart a Londoner all his life.[6] He left school at the age of fifteen, saw war service in the Royal Artillery, and only then made his way into university at the London School of Economics as a result of the army scholarship scheme. He stayed on to research, and in 1952 completed his doctoral dissertation on 'The suburban development of Greater London, south of the Thames, 1836–1914', under the guidance of H. L. Beales. A year later, he was appointed to an assistant lectureship in economic history (with special reference to transport) at the University College of Leicester. Two areas in which it specialised and was soon to excel were in local and transport history, the one thanks to the presence of Hoskins and Finberg,[7] the other because of the zeal of Simmons,[8] and both had their influence on Dyos, and on the urban history he was to write. Throughout the late 1950s and early 1960s, the university (as it had now become) acquired a growing reputation for its history departments, largely because of its vigorous sponsorship of these subjects. At the same time, its press supported these developments by launching, under Finberg's editorship, the series of *Occasional Papers in Local History*, by establishing, with Simmons's guidance, the *Journal of Transport History*, and by publishing a variety of miscellaneous books of (in retrospect) pre-Dyos urban history.[9]

Dyos's early work was heavily indebted to this tradition, while at the same time already beginning to go beyond it in a direction of its own. His first articles concerned the impact of railways on London, and his abiding interest in transport history was evidenced in other, later publications, culminating in a co-authored history of British transport.[10] But, as even this early work suggested, his real interest lay in trying to understand how London worked *in its totality* as a city: the history of urban transport, which for him was as much concerned with the social consequences of railways as with their construction, was but a means to a greater end. Other work followed, on suburban development and on the transformation of London's West End by the Prince Regent, giving promise of what might be to come.[11] Then, in 1961, there appeared *Victorian Suburb: A Study of the Growth of Camberwell*, published by Leicester University Press, and originally intended for their series *Occasional Papers in Local History*.[12] In that work he laid bare as no one had before the way in which a suburb was created, and with rare style and perception evoked the 'feel' of suburban life, with reference to a particular time and place.

Within a year, Dyos sensed a quickening interest in the history of urban life and city growth, and began to produce twice-yearly the *Urban History Newsletter*, which provided a small but growing body of adherents with news and a sense of corporate identity.[13] Further publications followed, some of a specialised kind, pushing further his work on the making of London's fabric, others more general in scope, feeling their way towards a more self-conscious articulation of urban history as a subject in its own right.[14] In 1963, he formed the Urban History Group as a loyal offshoot of the Economic History Society, and in 1966 organised the first major British conference on urban history at Leicester, the proceedings of which were published two years later and, in the words of one reviewer, 'put British urban history on the map'. The bandwagon had begun to roll. Only forty people had attended that first conference; but by the mid-1970s, there were usually one hundred and fifty or more. For his services in identifying, creating and promoting the subject, Dyos was awarded a personal chair at Leicester in 1971. His choice of title – Professor of Urban History – aptly reflected the fact that both he and his subject had arrived.

In retrospect, it is clear, the 1970s were a halcyon decade for urban history, which expanded with zest, buoyancy and success which made all of Clio's other recent offsprings seem but ugly ducklings by comparison. 'The present mood of urban history', Dyos proclaimed with characteristic gusto in 1970, 'is . . . experimental and exploratory. The field is wide open and world wide.'[15] 'There is no denying it', he stated four years later, 'urban history is booming.'[16] And so, indeed, it was. 'Happily'. he wrote with pardonable pride in one of the last issues of the *Newsletter*, 'no-one expects me to keep them thoroughly informed in these columns of the thousand and one things happening nowadays within the orbit of urban history.'[17] And in the concluding pages of his most massive publishing venture, devoted to exploring the Victorian city in all its multifarious aspects, he could write with complete sincerity of 'not having brought our subject to a finish, but of having barely opened it up'.[18] Yet, however much the subject expanded, Dyos remained creatively eager to enlarge its horizons and opportunities still further. As David Reeder so appropriately puts it 'for those who set him going, there were occasional but memorable ascents to the top of some historical Darien peak, from which to survey the landscape of seemingly limitless possibilities'.[19]

'Limitless' was, indeed, the operative word. In 1970, Dyos began his first series, *Studies in Urban History*, of which five volumes appeared in rapid succession, and at the same time began to steer other works into print through Leicester University Press. By 1974, the *Urban History Newsletter* had burst its bounds, and was transmogrified into the more durable and substantial *Urban History Yearbook*, again published by Leicester University Press, and edited by Dyos. In the following year, the *London Journal* appeared, a periodical which Dyos had done much to promote, and it was learned that he was at work on a book entitled *London, 1870–1914: The World Metropolis*. Two years before he had published his most ambitious work, *The Victorian City: Images and Realities*, which he co-edited with Michael Wolff – a *tour de force* of editorial inspiration and skill, which won immediate and widespread acclaim. By 1978, *Victorian Suburb* was in paperback and in its fourth impression; two new series – *Themes in Urban History* and *Explorations in Urban Analysis* – were on the stocks; and he was actively planning a super-conference, scheduled for 1979, intended to chart the progress which urban history had made in the preceding decade.

The 'Dyos phenomenon' was, in terms of the historical profession, without precedent in England or parallel in America. As Sydney Checkland observed when reviewing the collected volumes of *Studies in Urban History*:

He is not only the parent and editor of the present series: he is in the rare, if not unique, position of acting as midwife to an emergent branch of history in Britain, a complex phenomenon of entrepreneurship and guru-ship worthy of the attention of the sociologist of scholarship.[20]

Every year at the Urban History Conference, the faithful gathered in increasing numbers, and Dyos held court – dominant but never assertive, avuncular without being patronising, advising and encouraging with zest and gusto. He sought out contacts in America, Australia, Scandinavia, Holland and India. He extended the scope of the subject backwards to the early modern period, and outwards to other cultures and other continents. From the most junior graduate students to the most senior patriarchs in the historical profession, the lure of urban history seemed irresistible. And yet, however much the subject grew and blossomed in these heady days, it remained, in organisational terms, Leicester-located and Dyos-dominated.

2

Such was urban history in the United Kingdom when Dyos died, too young, in 1978: but what, if anything, did it stand for intellectually? In fact, it stood for very little. For, having identified, established and promoted a subject with a distinctive label and a large following, Dyos stubbornly refused to be dogmatic as to what, exactly, urban history was. As Checkland explained, Dyos was 'a centre of focus and endeavour'; but he did not 'preside over a school of urban history', nor was that his wish. In the words of two other colleagues:

Unlike other pioneers, he laid no claim to the territory he had marked out, but generously supported every kind of initiative . . ., irrespective of their congruence with his own research preoccupations. Organisationally fertile and inventive, he was personally reticent, and did nothing to attempt to impose his stamp on the projects he helped to encourage.[21]

In the light of his extraordinary entrepreneurial energy, this well-attested lack of intellectual imperialism was all the more remarkable. He resolutely refused to separate the meetings to the Urban History Group from those of the Economic History Society. He would not found a separate journal devoted to urban history – as happened in the United States. Even the *Yearbook*, far from being a surrogate vehicle for propaganda, was merely a market place for the exchange of information and ideas. As he noted in an editorial:

We content ourselves . . . with gauging the many-sided approach to the urban past, taking stock of what is being done, adding where we can to the effectiveness of such teaching and research as are moving in this direction, becoming more indeed the necessary adjunct of them both, but stopping short of presenting the findings of research as such.[22]

In his inaugural lecture, he went to even greater lengths to describe and defend this tolerant approach. 'Urban history', he explained,

it must by now be clear, is a field of knowledge, not a single discipline in the accepted sense but a field in which many disciplines converge, or at any rate are drawn upon. It is a focus for a variety of forms of knowledge, not a form of knowledge in itself.[23]

So, to those of his colleagues who occasionally 'express embarrassment on account of the considerable variety of approaches that are being made in their subject', he replied:

I do not think they need do so. On the contrary, the lack of agreement as to whether to pursue the ecological approach . . ., or the more generally environmental approach . . ., or the approach through the comparative study of institutions..., or the approaches through locational and small area analysis..., or even the approach through first and last things...: the lack of agreement, I say, as to which of these and other approaches to follow gets neither rebuke nor dogmatic guidance from me. I find their catholicity positively healthy.[24]

What mattered – *all* that mattered – was not so much the particular methodology brought to bear, but rather the *commitment* to the city *as a whole*. For urban historians, Dyos once explained, 'the crucial thing' was that they 'must go on addressing the total phenomenon of the city as directly as they can'.[25] 'What distinguishes the urban historian', he wrote on another occasion, 'from the innumerable scholars who may be said merely to be passing through their territory', was the 'totality of their commitment to it.'[26] It was this commitment to the subject, to the city *as a whole* and *as a field of study* which was of first importance; the methodology, the ideology of approach, was very much of secondary significance.

All this was spelt out plainly in his inaugural lecture, where he made his most systematic plea for urban history's autonomy as a field of study, while eschewing any claims to its coherence as a methodology:

What is, I think, already clear is that the authentic measure of urban history is the degree to which it is concerned directly and generically with cities themselves, and not with the historical events and tendencies that have been purely incidental to them: and that, whether concerned with cities as more or less isolated or systematic or universal phenomena, it is the study of the ... ways in which their components fitted together or impinged on other things, that distinguishes urban historians from those who may be said to be merely passing through their territory.

Their subject differs from local history to the extent that it is concerned with a more pervasive historical process, and from municipal history in being occupied with vastly more than certain types of local government; it differs, on the other hand, from social history in its quite specific commitment to explaining the development of the urban milieu and its uses, and from sociology in its dominant concern in explaining the urban past; it differs, too, from its first cousins in this country, economic history and geography, in being more interested than they can afford to be, in their different ways, in the humanistic and functional elements composing the urban scene; and it differs, incidentally, from a variety of other historical specialisms, such as agricultural, industrial, business, transport, military or town-planning history, in not being concerned with specific forms of activity.[27]

So, whereas other historians were primarily committed to a particular methodology, and only incidentally and occasionally addressed themselves to the city, urban historians primarily addressed themselves to the city, and were only incidentally and occasionally committed to a particular methodology.

This elaborate attempt to define the subject as intellectually interdisciplinary, methodologically eclectic and spatially autonomous was not met with approval in all quarters.[28] Some criticised urban history for being merely 'a fashionable bandwagon' which had 'falsely claimed credit, in the name of spurious interdisciplinarism, for work which would have proceeded in any case in disciplines such as geography and economic history'. Thus it was argued that work in urban history which concentrated on a particular town was in practice but local history under a more fashionable name; and that historians who were investigating the general effects of urban growth on economic development were really writing economic history. The most telling criticism was that, since almost everyone in an industrial and post-industrial world lived in cities, *urban* history was merely a synonym for a *social* history. As Sidney Pollard explained, 'apart from some specific aspects of rural life like agriculture, modern British social history *is* urban history'.[29] And Stephan Thernstrom, notwithstanding his role as transatlantic patriarch of the 'New Urban History', agreed:

The decisive features of urban life in modern times are not spatially distributed in a way that justifies urban history, or for that matter urban sociology, as a special field.... For the student of modern society, it is indeed nearly co-terminus with social history.[30]

A further problem was that, as Dyos himself admitted, urban history was 'vulnerable to the charge of becoming a portmanteau subject'.[31] For if, in the words of Eric Hobsbawm, it included 'everything about cities', then it might degenerate into becoming merely 'a large container, with ill-defined, heterogenous and sometimes indiscriminate contents'.[32] Other critics, too, implied that urban history was 'a kind of historical variety store', an 'academic "come-all-ye" ', into which all subjects remotely connected with cities, but intellectually quite unrelated, were being put.[33] And the problem was further complicated because, having defined urban history as including all things concerned with cities, it was extraordinarily difficult to decide what was or was not urban, in any satisfactory operational sense.[34] To say that urban history was a field of knowledge was one thing; to locate that field and delimit its boundaries was quite another.

For some reviewers, *The Victorian City: Images and Realities*, showed up these shortcomings only too plainly. Its editors hoped that the logic of the book's structure and of the links between the contributions, would become apparent as the reader made his way through its pages. But in practice, as E. P. Thompson noted, no such structure or links emerged. Was there such a thing as *the* Victorian city? Or the *Victorian* city? Or even the Victorian *city*? Although the two volumes contained an impressive array of essays, their only unity derived from their common but unrelated preoccupation with what was at best an ideal type, and at worst an undefinable abstraction. As some said of urban history itself, the contributions did not add up to anything coherent: the whole was not greater than the sum of its parts.[35]

But while some critics thought urban history was too broad and populated by too many heterogeneous and unrelated disiplines, others took the opposite view and argued that in some senses its scope was too narrow. For by focussing attention so singlemindedly on the city, there was a real danger of ignoring themes, issues and development which were spatially outside the city, but still of prime importance in understanding it. As Dyos himself admitted, there was a strong case for seeing the city as the 'dependent variable, the outcome of larger forces commonly studied more explicitly by demographers or economic historians'.[36] Asa Briggs agreed, stressing the need for historians of the modern world to weigh a variety of different variables, 'of which urbanisation is only one', and went on to urge urban historians to be 'historians of something else as well as the city'.[37] And Derek Fraser has recently posed the question most starkly: 'Does urban history get in the way of analysis by posing as a discrete focus of historical explanation that which was merely a part of the wider whole?'[38]

Ever since William Diamond's reply to Arthur Schlesinger Sr, there have always been some historians who have answered this question in the affirmative.[39] For it is, in practice, exceedingly difficult to see what, exactly, *is* uniquely urban. Class consciousness, for example, is an urban phenomenon: but since it is also manifest in the countryside, it is not at all clear what is the urban contribution to this form of social relationship. In the same way, it is hard to see how the evolution of any large or small city, be it administrative centre, industrial metropolis or market town, can be fully understood without seeing it in a regional (or even national and international) context. Eric Lampard summed up the problem well:

> To be sure, topics such as public health, housing, city politics, municipal finance or 'the ghetto' might appear to be the intrinsic stuff of urban history regardless of *how* they are handled by the urban historian. Yet they all have obvious counterparts in the histories of non-urban (rural?) settlements, and can also be studied in the context of reform movements, state or congressional politics, public finance, racial relations or even national history. To treat such matters as though they were exclusively 'urban' . . . is myopic and often misleading.[40]

A glance at the register of research published annually in the *Urban History Yearbook* only serves to confirm the force of some of these criticisms. As Dyos himself admitted, the main characteristic of urban history which stood out when looking at the work in progress was 'its empiricism, its eclecticism, its lack of theoretical rigour, its failure to pursue more systematically the urban variable in historical causation'. More particularly, he admitted that some four-fifths of the research was being directed at what might, on the face of it, be represented as 'more or less incidental to the central concerns of urban history'.[41] In short, few people – in their research interests at least – shared Dyos's *total* commitment to the city. Most were merely 'passing through': they were not urban historians in the sense that Dyos had sought to define them. On the contrary, they were social, local, economic, administrative historians who had chosen research topics which were *incidentally* urban. When put between the covers of the *Yearbook*, it did, indeed seem that all these endeavours added up to something called urban history. But in practice, most of the work seemed more appropriately categorised under one or other of the more traditional historical sub-disciplines.

Nevertheless, what *could* be said in favour of urban history was that it had made popular and respectable a whole variety of important subjects which might not otherwise have been taken so seriously as objects of scholarly endeavour. Sydney Checkland once listed them, and the catalogue is impressive:

Housing, building, land use, land tenure, transportation, administration, finance, politics, health, sanitation, food supplies, population, family, social class, elites, power structure, sub-cultures, crime, conflict, protest, philanthropy, welfare, architecture, spatial planning, the demands of terrain, the aesthetics of the city, locational advantage, the industrial mix, the commercial facilities of the central business district.[42]

Perhaps this list did not really add up to anything coherent which could with intellectual conviction be labelled urban history. But it did mean that, for the first time, many aspects of city life were being taken seriously as objects of historical study.

3

Although as a propagandist Dyos limited his activities to urging historians to address the city directly, he did have a careful idea himself as to the type of urban history which, ideally, ought to be written. To begin with, he was anxious to chart a course between the Scylla of old-fashioned city biographies, and the Charybdis of galactic surveys of the urbanisation process. When reviewing Sir Francis Hill's *Victorian Lincoln*, which he rightly recognised as a classic of its genre, he labelled it a 'splendid failure' because, although its sense of place and 'feel' for the town was unrivalled, it lacked any perception of the broader process of urbanisation of which Lincoln's development was a part. For all its merits, it remained an 'individually-posed, idiosyncratic study of a town that has no particular analytical purpose or significance'.[43] But at the same time, he was equally sceptical of those who aspired to write galactic accounts of the urbanisation process, with little reference to time or place. 'At best', he argued,

that way leads to what historians are bound to regard as rather inchoate studies . . . At worst, it leads rapidly to the city in history, to unhistorical and even apocalyptic visions which, like Mumford's, convey all the images and excitement of a fireworks display that fizzles out in chilling caricature of reality itself.[44]

For Dyos, the essence of urban history was to eschew the vices but combine the virtues of these two approaches, by linking process in general to a sense of place in particular, and by rooting an appreciation of the broad themes of urban growth in the context of a specific example. 'The test of whether urban history is succeeding', he observed, is the degree to which the analytical themes and structures are recognisable on the ground; not in terms of a series of local mysteries penetrable in their own terms ... but in as many dimensions as will allow their particularity and their universality to come out.[45]

'What we have to explain', he once wrote in a similar vein,

are the origins and the outcome of an historical process that can be conceived on two levels: the relatively abstract level of discerning in largely aggregative terms how and why urbanisation came about in a series of different societies; [and] the more concrete but closely related level of making out where and to what effect this gathering of people into towns actually took place.[46]

In his study of suburban Camberwell, Dyos showed that he could practice what he preached. Fully aware of the urbanisation process in general and of the growth of London as a whole, the book was on one level remarkable for its perception of the urbanisation process *tout court*. Yet is also succeeded in describing a *particular* nineteenth-century suburb with such vividness and immediacy that one closes the book with a real feeling of what it must have been like to walk through late-nineteenth-century Camberwell.

Equally important to Dyos was the need to link the way in which the urban fabric was made with the kind of life that was actually lived in it, and to see how the two interacted. By definition, this was something which only those historians who addressed the city as a whole and with total commitment would be willing and able to do. The historian of housing or of architecture might be interested in the buildings; the social or family historian might be concerned with the life that was lived within them. But only the urban historian would be equally interested in both 'the generations of buildings and generations of men' – anxious to discover how the urban fabric influenced the urban family, and *vice versa*. 'We have watched and learned', he wrote in an appreciative review of one distinguished account of the making of part of suburban London,

how these castles were placed upon the ground. Let us hope that someone will now go on and tell us what *happened* – or failed to happen – when the building came to an end and a hundred thousand drawbridges went up.[47]

Indeed, his own early railway articles had investigated how their impact on the town fabric had influenced the lives of the people who lived close by, and in his projected second volume on Camberwell, he proposed to complement his study of the making of the suburb with an account of the life the suburbanites actually lived.

A third way in which Dyos hoped urban history would develop was in the establishment of some comparative methodology. 'By this', he argued,

we mean not only comparisons of different places at the same time and of the same place over time, but also comparisons between different elements, institutions and phenomena abstracted from different types of society.[48]

But in order to accomplish this, it was first necessary to agree on terms. 'If we want to develop more sustained comparisons', he noted, 'it is vital that we identify the basic variables unequivocally, and define the standard terms quite precisely.' This, he argued, would provide the 'typological framework into which to fit particular cases'. But at the same time, so as to establish 'a general scaffolding for historical research', he also urged the need for a 'thorough statistical survey' of the 'basic features' of nineteenth-century towns, so as to produce some relatively simple, but systematic data, largely derived from the census material. 'These exercises', he warned, 'are conceptually and technically difficult, and run the danger of encouraging the study of purely numerical orders of magnitude which, when widely applied, could become an end in itself.'

Here, indeed, Dyos touched upon his greatest anxiety about the writing of urban history, namely his fear that a growing preoccupation with quantification might take urban historians away from their primary obligation, which was to evoke the urban past in human and comprehensible terms.[49] Indeed, one reason why the second volume on Camberwell was never written was his increasing conviction that the anaylsis of the census data, far from making it easier to evoke life as lived in the urban past, actually made it more difficult to do so in a historically convincing and humane manner. Significantly, he acclaimed E. P. Hennock's study of town councillors because the data had been his servant and not his master: his great triumph was 'to have broken through the thicket of statistics which must inevitably guard the entrance to any real understanding of the machinery of modern society, and to discover the human material behind it'.[50] And he applauded Richard Cobb's *Paris and Its Provinces* because of its 'capacity for imaginative insight and historical feeling that stands in such stark contrast to the more theoretical and systematic analysis that is now *de rigeur*'.[51]

Of necessity, this brought Dyos into conflict with the New Urban History in the United States, with its passion for quantitative computerised studies of census data. Indeed, in his inaugural lecture, he registered his doubts and criticisms in uncharacteristically strident terms:

as I sample the first fruits of this new growth I do grow somewhat apprehensive of its outcome for the study of urban history at large.... Historians are always being asked to jump through new hoops. That is their occupational hazard. But what concerns me about these particular hoops is their diameter. They are so narrow.[52]

In part, he was worried that the concern with quantification, allied with the sociological interests of many of the New Urban Historians, meant that their work would be only incidentally concerned with the city and with its past history. To him, it seemed 'somewhat indifferent to the human content of the city', with 'no place for the individual's experience of it', and offered 'little scope for the elucidation of its culture'. The obsession with counting had, he felt, taken the historians away from their prime concern – the urban fabric and its people, and the links between process in general and place in particular. Significantly, it was not Stephan Thernstrom but Sam Bass Warner, Jr, whom Dyos most admired of American urban historians, whose publications received the most fulsome treatment in the *Yearbook* and whose evocative and non-quantitative work of the urban past approximated most closely to Dyos's own.[53]

But there was a further reason for Dyos's doubts about the all-pervasive fashion of quantification. For he believed passionately that the purpose of urban history was not only to evoke the urban *past* for its own sake, but also to provide a perspective on the urban *present*. Just as the Victorian city was 'a foretaste of the way we live now', so Victorian city-dwellers were 'the prototype of modern urban man'. 'The characteristic setting for modern man', he once wrote, 'is the city, and his urban history [is] a necessary dimension in understanding his predicament and potential.'[54] At one level, the whole point of urban history was that it might help in 'dispelling widely-held fears of the urban present and the urban future'. The very fact that he saw a profound and important link between 'the way we lived then', 'the way we live now' and 'the way we might live' meant it was more than ever necessary for urban historians to write stylishly and humanely of the urban past so as to be comprehensible to a wide audience in the urban present.[55] Indeed, it was largely because he believed this that he helped to found the *London Journal*, which was to bridge the gaps, not only across the disciplines, but between past, present and future, by forming a 'primarily *historical* focus for the comprehension of London's *contemporary* culture, its social issues, fabric, and economic and political life'. And in the same way, he acclaimed Sam Bass Warner's most ambitious book, *The Urban Wilderness*, because 'the interconnection between the urban past and present could not conceivably be better demonstrated'.[56]

Of course, doing urban history in this way was no more immune from criticism than were his more abstract attempts to define urban history in methodological terms. The capacity to synthesise process and place was all very well: but was it really realistic, as one colleague had the temerity to ask, to imagine an endless proliferation of case-studies like Camberwell? The commitment to relating the making of the urban fabric to the nature of the urban life lived there sounded sensible in the abstract: but the conviction that there is any necessary connection of this kind remains unproven. The problems of quantification are undeniable: yet it probably offers the only way in to some more rigorous form of comparative framework still conspicuously lacking in British urban history. And the belief that understanding the urban past would help to throw light on the urban present was more easily asserted than proved.

4

Such, briefly, was urban history in the United Kingdom as it evolved in the late 1960s and 1970s until Dyos's death in 1978 – a story in marked contrast to the simultaneous development of the New Urban History in America. Self-evidently, Dyos's role in creating, defining and promoting the subject was crucial, as was his own lack of scholarly dogmatism and the example of his own writings and exhortations. But, of course, most of the work actually produced, although indebted to Dyos in one way or another, came from pens other than his. What, insofar as others were writing urban history in Britain, was it like? How far did it benefit from the entrepreneurial flair of Dyos, from the tolerant and encouraging intellectual milieu he had created and from the particular example of his writings? It is only possible to give the briefest answers to these questions here, and to mention a limited number of publications. For the fullest account of research in urban history, the *Yearbook* remains the indispensable guide. But here are a few general impressions.

It is arguable that the two books which have influenced British urban history most by their example appeared before Dyos had given the subject any real sense of self-awareness. Both were by Asa Briggs: the first was his volume of the *History of Birmingham*, the second his more wide-ranging survey of *Victorian Cities*.[57] Today, perhaps, the novelty and audacity of these books seems limited. But when published, they were both quite extraordinarily innovative. In part, this was because Briggs was the first important British historian to take the city seriously as a legitimate field of historical study, to address it directly for its own sake. Moreover, in order to do this, he was obliged to break down conventional barriers between economic, political and social history, in his attempt to relate the economic and social sub-structure of the city to the pattern of local politics and government. Equally significant was the way in which, in *Victorian Cities*, he introduced a comparative dimension, by building the book around the contrast between the Manchester of Cobden and Bright and the Birmingham of Joseph Chamberlain. Some indication of the novelty of this book may be gleaned from the fact that, in a relatively recent text book on nineteenth-century English history, its bibliography is divided into 'general', 'economic and social', 'political and constitutional', 'foreign and imperial' and 'art, culture and religion'; but *Victorian Cities* is placed in a separate section labelled 'other books not fitting well into this classification'.[58]

In retrospect, these two books were the fountainhead of urban history in the United Kingdom and, significantly, it was Briggs whom Dyos asked to write the foreword to *The Study of Urban History*. Indeed, in many ways, urban history in Britain may be seen as the offspring begotten from the union of Briggs's writing and Dyos's entrepreneurship. But even so, much writing of urban history even in the 1970s has continued in a pre-Briggs, pre-Dyos mould, as a clutch of old-fashioned town biographies have continued to appear – all with a strong antiquarian commitment to one place, but lacking any awareness of the larger process of urbanisation, ignoring many of the themes and subjects which urban historians now treat as serious and important, and devoid of that conceptual breadth which urban history has increasingly and rightly come to demand.[59] Such works still appear – a rich quarry of material for the urban historian, and an eloquent reminder of how far the subject has travelled since this was the only urban history available.

Other studies of cities, however, have sought to extend and deepen the approach pioneered by Briggs, by looking not only at social and economic sub-structure as well as at local government and politics, but also at the making of the urban fabric. The most ambitious attempt to do this is Daunton's book on Cardiff, which starts with the economic base of the town, then looks at the way in which it was made physically, and finally investigates the nature of local municipal and political life.[60] More impressionistically, Checkland has written a brief, beguiling and evocative pen-portrait of industrial Glasgow, while Sutcliffe and Smith, in the most recent volume of the *History of Birmingham*, go to the other extreme, with their careful, precise, densely evidenced analysis, shorn of the heroic element or personal viewpoint.[61] Somewhere between these two can be located Yeo's study of Reading, which investigates the links between the mode of production and the nature of social relationships in a town dominated by one large capitalist.[62]

However much their particular approaches and methodologies differ, all these books are characterised by their attempts – consciously or unconsciously – to emulate Briggs's work and heed Dyos's exhortations by addressing the city directly and in its totality. On another tack, some other studies of individual cities confine themselves to single themes of a type which would not have received serious attention in pre-Briggs and pre-Dyos days. Thus Sutcliffe, in his study of nineteenth- and twentieth-century Paris, looks at the way in which the urban fabric was made, and at the constraints which this has imposed on subsequent town planning schemes.[63] Meller's book on late-nineteenth-century Bristol uncovers the links between the philanthropic activities of the town's nonconformist elite and the changing patterns of working-class leisure in a period of major social and economic change.[64] And Bater's pioneering work on nineteenth-century St Petersburg investigates the shattering impact of sudden, large-scale industrial development on a town originally founded as a political and administrative centre.[65]

These single-city studies bear eloquent witness to the Dyos revolution in urban history, showing an awareness of both the urbanisation process in general, and of the need to study it with reference to a particular time and place. Equally significant has been the development of comparative studies, not so much in emulation of Briggs's total evocation, but rather by taking one specific urban theme, and investigating it with reference to several similar towns. The pioneer work here was Kellett's brilliant study of *The Impact of Railways on Victorian Cities*, with special reference to London, Birmingham, Manchester, Glasgow and Liverpool.[66] In a similar vein, there is Fraser's investigation of urban politics in the major provincial cities of Victorian England, Hennock's work on the personnel and role of local government in Leeds and Birmingham, Cannadine's book on the influence of the old, landed elite on the new urban world of the nineteenth century, and Chalklin's study of the making of the urban fabric in seven Georgian towns.[67]

In his introduction to Chalklin's book, Dyos again asserted that one of the most important topics which only urban historians would be willing to tackle was the way in which the urban fabric was made, and there have been a variety of books on this subject. Suburban development has been looked at in a symposium on middle-class housing, which investigates several large nineteenth-century towns, but leaves the reader to make most of the comparisons for himself.[68] A companion volume investigates the housing of the working class, and there have been several other books devoted to this topic.[69] Whether the time is yet ripe for a grand synthesis on urban housing is unclear: Burnett's book is a brave attempt in that direction.[70] But the outstanding work here is Thompson's study of Hampstead, which brilliantly relates the forces making for urban growth in the metropolis as a whole with the actual physical creation of its most renowned suburb.[71]

London, as always, remains *sui generis*: an irresistibly fascinating city, which defies conceptualisation, categorisation or comparison. The most explicit attempt to confront the 'world metropolis' directly is to be found in Secker & Warburg's *History of London*, of which three volumes have so far appeared: each, in its own way, bears witness to the changed priorities of urban historians during the last decade and a half.[72] Another book which takes a broad theme is Olsen's beautifully produced account of the building of Victorian London, a marvellously perceptive evocation of place, but so intuitive and impressionistic that the substance of the urbanisation process seems somehow lost sight of.[73] More restricted in their scope, but thorough in their research, are Young's study of some aspects of the politics of London's government, and Wohl's investigation of slum-dwelling and reform in the metropolis.[74] Two other books which add immeasurably to our knowledge of social relations are Stedman Jones's investigation of metropolitan problems and tensions of the 1870s and 1880s, and Crossick's more specific study of the mid-nineteenth-century artisan elite of Kentish London.[75]

Conclusion

Both of these books are primarily concerned with social relationships which are incidentally urban, rather than with urban relationships which are incidentally social. Indeed, as the criticisms of urban history implied, many books appeared in the 1960s and 1970s which were self-consciously works of social history, but which were eagerly annexed for review in the *Urban History Yearbook* because they were incidentally urban as well. In this category came Foster's neo-Marxist book on Oldham, Gray on the labour aristocracy of late-Victorian Edinburgh, Macleod on religion and class in late-nineteenth-century London, and Tholfsen on the mid-Victorian working classes.[76] None of these books addressed the city directly, in the manner that Dyos urged: rather, their prime aim was to contribute to debates within the realm of social history via a single, urban case study. And in a similar way, the investigations of Armstrong of York and Anderson of Preston, although crammed with important findings on social structure and family life, were not much interested in the urban fabric and leave little abiding impression of what it was like actually to live in the town.[77]

5

In one way or another, most of these works are direct or indirect products of the 'Dyos phenomenon'. Some arose out of theses examined by him, which were transmogrified into books at his suggestion; some appeared in series initiated and edited by him; some sought to emulate the example of his own writings; some tried to practise what he urged others to do, but never had time to do himself. So, whether English urban history can be satisfactorily defined intellectually or not, there has certainly been an impressive body of published work which to a lesser or greater degree merits that name. Moreover, the variety of methodological approaches, and the diversity of ideological standpoints displayed by the writers bear eloquent witness to that very catholicity which Dyos so happily welcomed. Yet, at the same time, almost all of these studies may be seen as products of the dominant empirical tradition of English historical scholarship – sceptical of the values of large-scale, collaborative ventures, uneager to embrace wholeheartedly conceptual frameworks drawn from economics or sociology, and unwilling to make more than minor and occasional concessions to quantification.

All this serves to illustrate how English urban history, so much indebted to economic, local and transport history, has developed along a trajectory fundamentally different from that of the New Urban History in the United States, with its leanings towards sociology and statistics. Assuredly, these two new sub-disciplines developed at almost the same time: *Poverty and Progress* and *Victorian Suburb* appeared within three years of each other, and the seminal conferences at Yale and Leicester were only two years apart.[78] But the contrasted interests of those early path-breaking books only serves to underline the different approaches to the subject on both sides of the Atlantic. If Anderson's study of Preston had set the fashion here, or if Warner's *Streetcar Suburbs* had spawned numerous imitators in America, then the Anglo-American developments would have proceeded in more comfortable alliance. But as it was, the parting of the ways had already taken place by the time Dyos registered his protest against the development of the subject in America, and the gap only widened in the years which followed.

Ironically, urban history as it developed in England had more in common with that earlier tradition of American city histories which runs from Arthur Schlesinger, Sr to Richard Wade, than it did with the New Urban History of Thernstrom *et al.*[79] So while, in America, the New Urban History was reacting against this older tradition, in Britain, urban history came nearer to emulating it. Like this earlier phase of American scholarship, the urban history which developed in England under Dyos in the 1960s and 1970s was primarily a *subject* and a *field of study*, while the New Urban History was more self-consciously a *methodology* and a *way of doing things*. In Britain, it was the commitment to the city which mattered; the methodology was incidental. In America, it was the commitment to the methodology which mattered; it was the city which was incidental.

Yet both disciplines, although they have evolved along such different lines, are today less sure of themselves than they were five years ago. In America, the problem for the New Urban History is that, as the whole cult of quantification and census analysis comes increasingly under attack, the very existence of a subject almost exclusively identified with this criticised methodology seems threatened. The endless replication of studies of social mobility in American towns seems increasingly hard to justify, and it is highly unlikely that there will be a second Philadelphia project.[80] In Britain, conversely, because urban history thrived on intellectual tolerance and eclecticism, it has not suffered from being identified with a single approach, and can absorb and abandon new methodologies as they come and go. To that extent, the subject has benefited from the way Dyos chose to mould it, and may well survive more successfully than will the New Urban History across the Atlantic.

In terms of its zest, confidence and organisation, however, there can be no doubt that British urban history suffered a severe blow as a result of Dyos's untimely death. Leicester University has refused to appoint another Professor of Urban History, so that the whole urban history organisation, perhaps over-centralised under Dyos, now lacks a central inspirational figure. Under these circumstances, the subject's lack of intellectual coherence, which was so appealing when allied with real administrative centralisation, is now in danger of becoming a weakness, as more and more historians are beginning to ask themselves what, if anything, urban history is. As the essays collected in this book must effectively demonstrate, Dyos had an answer to that, albeit more convincing in the realm of practice than of definition. But there is no one today in the Urban History Group who radiates his influence, his confidence or his vision.

There are a variety of other reasons why the future of the subject may not appear as bright as the past, and why the expansive impulse of the 1970s cannot be sustained indefinitely. Most of the research being undertaken in urban history (as in all branches of the subject), is by graduate students reading for higher degrees. Some of it, therefore, will never be finished; a great deal of it will go unpublished; and the majority of those who complete their dissertations will never become practising urban historians employed in British universities. Moreover, as the numbers starting research in urban (and all other) history lessen dramatically, there must be a significant diminution in the total amount of work being done. Indeed, if the size of the register of research in the *Yearbook* is any guide, then urban history has already begun to contract.

In the higher reaches of the profession, too, there are difficulties. Many of the most outstanding works of urban history were written by academics whose commitment to the city as a field of historical study was not total, but only partial, for the duration of one research project which was only incidentally urban. They moved into urban history – perhaps attracted by the allure of Dyos himself and by the exciting things he seemed to be doing or promising – and then moved out again when they had completed their specific project. This could be said, for instance, of the work of Thompson, Hennock and Crossick, all of whom are now working on projects less directly urban than those in which they were involved a decade ago. So, it seems likely that in future the number of senior historians who will embrace urban history will also be reduced. And with fewer grandees as exemplars, there will inevitably be fewer graduate students to follow, so that the whole trend away from urban history may become self-reinforcing.

But it would be misleading to paint too pessimistic a picture. The Urban History Group has recently been established on a more formal basis, and attendance at its conferences – if no longer as large as in the mid-1970s – is still impressively high. The commercial future of the *Urban History Yearbook* also seems assured for the time being, and its indispensability as a research tool is widely recognised, even by those who do not believe that there is such a thing as urban history. The super-conference which Dyos had planned duly took place in August 1980, and may spark off a second generation of urban historians, who will have all the advantages of a decade's consolidated work to build on.[81] Likewise, the series which Dyos set up, *Studies in Urban History*, *Themes in Urban History* and *Explorations in Urban Analysis*, are still in being, and may enjoy a period of fertile expansiveness as some of the projects conceived in the mid and late 1970s finally appear in print.

Indeed, it is important to remember how many of the subjects listed by

Dyos in his agenda for future research in 1966 have still only received the most limited attention. The speculative and financial aspects of the housing industry; the functioning and amenities of towns; patterns of holiday-making; the urban underworld; the links if any between social, political and religious divisions; the identification of middle-class elites; the politics of small towns and suburbs: all these areas need more extensive investigation. And, at the most general level of all, his lament in 1973 – 'even now, the number of absolutely first-class studies of individual towns is painfully small, and scarcely a major city in this country has yet been given definitive treatment' – remains, a decade later, still valid.[82] Extraordinary though it is, there is no equivalent for Liverpool, Leeds, Manchester or Glasgow (to name only the towns of first rank) of Briggs's history of Birmingham. There is much to do and, thanks to Dyos, much which it is recognised needs to be done.

Moreover, in a variety of ways, the achievements of urban history in the 1970s already stand permanent and significant. For even if few historians have been bred who share Dyos's total commitment to the city, he certainly succeeded making the city a serious, respectable and recognised area of historical inquiry, in a way that had not been generally true before. Most of the people whose projects are listed in the *Yearbook's* register of research are, perhaps, only passing through; but twenty years ago, they would not even have been doing that. And, since almost any research into the recent British past must be concerned in part with towns and cities, history about urban life (if not urban history as defined by Dyos), will continue to be written. In future, there will be few who will share Dyos's commitment to addressing the totality of the city directly, who will see it as that unique conjuncture of the particular and the general, the cynosure where process and place interact. But much of the research which will be undertaken in the next decade, although less self-consciously urban history, will remain profoundly influenced by the topics opened up, the questions posed, the methodologies developed, and the findings published, by urban historians of the 1970s.

6

So, while for urban history in England, the 1980s in prospect do not look quite as buoyant as do the 1970s in retrospect, its future can certainly be viewed with more optimism than that of the New Urban History in America. In organisation, in research interests and in published output, the nature of modern British history has been irrevocably altered and fundamentally enriched as a result of the 'Dyos phenomenon', and that fruitful impulse is by no means yet spent. In Britain, at least, urban history is here to stay.

Appendix
A bibliography of
the published writings of H. J. Dyos

This listing attempts to cover all books and articles as well as review articles, but leaves out individual book reviews. Arrangement is chronological and, within each year, items are listed alphabetically by title. Articles reprinted in this volume are marked with an asterisk (*). Unless otherwise stated, the place of publication is the United Kingdom.

* 'Workmen's fares in south London, 1860–1914', *Journal of Transport History*, I (1953), 3–19
  'The growth of a pre-Victorian suburb: south London, 1580–1836', *Town Planning Review*, XXV (1954), 59–78
* 'Railways and housing in Victorian London. 1. Attila in London', *Journal of Transport History*, II (1955), 11–21
* 'Railways and housing in Victorian London. 2. Rustic townsmen', *Journal of Transport History*, II (1955), 90–100
  'Counting the cost of railways', *Amateur Historian*, III (1957), 191–7
  'The literature of transport history', *Library Association Record*, LIX (1957), 388–92
* 'Some social costs of railway building in London', *Journal of Transport History*, III (1957), 23–30
* 'Urban transformation: a note on the objects of street improvement in Regency and early Victorian London', *International Review of Social History*, II (1957), 259–65
  'A survey of specialist historical journals. 2. *The Journal of Transport History*, volumes I–III', *Amateur Historian*, IV (1959), 116–19
  'Economic forces leading to urban concentration – a contribution to a discussion on papers given at the International Centre for Regional Planning and Development', British Group (November, 1959), *Report*, 2, 2–3
  'The annals of suburbia', *Amateur Historian*, IV (1960), 275–81
  'Transport history in university theses', *Journal of Transport History*, IV (1960), 161–73
  Victorian Suburb: a study of the growth of Camberwell (1961; 2nd imp. 1966; 3rd imp. 1974; 4th imp. 1977)
  'A bibliography of urban history, 1962–64', *Urban History Newsletter*, III (1964), 3–17; and 'Current bibliographies', *Urban History Newsletter*, V (1965), 21–43; VII (1966), 16–33; IX (1967), 32–43; XI (1968), 40–66; (1969), 35–63; XV (1971), 25–50; XVII (1972), 37–49
  'British university theses on the urban history of Great Britain, 1911–65', *Urban History Newsletter*, V (1965), 9–21

Appendix

'Transport history in university theses, 1959–63', *Journal of Transport History*, VII (1965), 54–6

'The growth of cities in the nineteenth century', *Victorian Studies*, IX (1966), 225–37

'The making and unmaking of slums', in *The Victorian Poor: fourth conference report of the Victorian Society*, ed. P. Thompson (1967), 26–33

'The study of urban history: a conference report', *Victorian Studies*, X (1967), 289–92

'Agenda for urban historians', in *The Study of Urban History*, ed. H. J. Dyos (1968), 1–46

'The possibilities of computerising census data', by H. J. Dyos and A. B. H. Baker in *The Study of Urban History*, ed. H. J. Dyos (1968), 87–112

'The slum observed', *New Society*, 279 (1968), 151–4

'The slum attacked', *New Society*, 280 (1968), 192–5

* 'The slums of Victorian London', *Victorian Studies*, XI (1968), 5–40

* 'The speculative builders and developers of Victorian London', *Victorian Studies*, XI (1968), suppl., 641–90

'Stadtgeschichte in Grossbritannien', *Archiv für Kommunalswissenschaften*, VII (1968), 199–201

The Study of Urban History: the proceedings of an international round table conference of the Urban History Group at Gilbert Murray Hall, University of Leicester, 23rd–26th September, 1966 (1968; reprinted 1971; paperback 1976)

British Transport: an economic survey from the seventeenth century to the twentieth, by H. J. Dyos and D. H. Aldcroft (1969; 2nd imp. 1971; paperback 1974)

* 'Some historical reflections on the quality of urban life', in *The Quality of Urban Life*, ed. H. J. Schmandt and W. Bloomberg (Beverly Hills, 1969), 31–60

Editorial foreword to *The Autumn of Central Paris: the decline of town planning, 1870–1970*, by A. R. Sutcliffe (1970), v–viii (Studies in Urban History, I)

Digest of the Urban History Newsletter, nos. 1–13 (1963–9), ed. H. J. Dyos (1971)

* 'Greater and greater London: notes on metropolis and provinces in the nineteenth and twentieth centuries', in *Britain and the Netherlands*, ed. J. S. Bromley and E. H. Kossman (The Hague, 1971), vol. IV: *Metropolis, Dominion and Province*, 89–112

'Urban history', in *Research and Economic History*, ed. B. E. Supple (1971), 47–54

'List of theses completed in urban history, 1965–1969', *Urban History Newsletter*, XVIII (1972), 9–13

Editorial foreword to *Fit and Proper Persons: ideal and reality in nineteenth-century urban government*, by E. P. Hennock (1973), vi–viii (Studies in Urban History, 2)

'Images of urban life in the nineteenth century', *Devon Historian*, VII (1973), 3–4

* Introduction to *Collins' Illustrated Atlas of London* (1973), 7–26

'Lament for East London: an obituary, *East London Papers*, 1958–73', *East London Papers*, XV (1973), 61–8

'Monuments of modernity. I. The Victorian city', *New Society*, XXV (1973), 447–50

'The records of the recent urban past: the threat and the opportunity', *Archives*, XI (1973), 19–26

'Slums and suburbs', by H. J. Dyos and D. A. Reeder, in *The Victorian City: Images and Realities*, ed. H. J. Dyos and M. Wolff (1973), 1, 359–86

'Urban history in Britain: the last decade, 1 and 2', *British Book News* (August and September 1973), 492–8, 564–8

Urban History Newsletter, nos. XIX and XX (1973); XXI (1974); XXII (1976)

* *Urbanity and Suburbanity: an inaugural lecture delivered in the University of Leicester, 1st May 1973* (1973)

The Victorian City: Images and Realities, ed. H. J. Dyos and M. Wolff (2 vols., 1973; part reissued in paperback, 1976 and 1978)

* 'The way we live now', by H. J. Dyos and M. Wolff, in *The Victorian City: Images and Realities*, ed. H. J. Dyos and M. Wolff (1973), 2, 893–907

Bibliography of the published writings of H. J. Dyos

Editorial, *Urban History Yearbook* (1974), 3–10; (1975), 3–5; (1976), 3–6; (1977), 3–5; (1978), 3–6

Editorial foreword to *The Provincial Towns of Georgian England: a study of the building process, 1740–1820*, by C. W. Chalklin (1974), v–viii (Studies in Urban History, 3)

'A castle for everyman', *London Journal*, I (1975), 118–34

'The English approach to the urban past and the task of the urban historian', in *Convegne Internazionale di Storia urbanistica 'Gli studi di storia urbanistica: confronto di metodologie e risultati* (Lucca, 1975), 17–44, 247–74

Foreword to *Printed Maps of Victorian London, 1851–1900*, by Ralph Hyde (1975), xi–xii

'Speechesse delineations pace Camden', *Bulletin of Society of University Cartographers*, IX (1975), 10–12

'Dear, damned, distracting town: a survey of recent writings on London', *British Book News* (November 1976), 798–815

Editorial foreword to *St Petersburg: industrialisation and change*, by J. Bater (1976), v–viii (Studies in Urban History, 4)

'The hunting ground beyond Covent Garden', *London Journal*, II (1976), 97–100

'Jack Simmons: an appreciation', *Journal of Transport History*, new ser., III (1976), 133–44

'The Victorian city in perspective', by H. J. Dyos and M. Wolff, in *The Urbanization of European Society in the Nineteenth Century*, ed. A. Lees and L. Lees (Lexington, 1976), 107–13

Editorial foreword to *The Eternal Slum*, by A. Wohl (1977), v–viii (Studies in Urban History, 5)

'The language of the walls', *London Journal*, III (1977), 85–101

'A conversation with H. J. Dyos: urban history in Great Britain', by Bruce M. Stave, *Journal of Urban History*, V (1979), 469–99

Notes

The following abbreviations have been used throughout the notes:

EcHR	*Economic History Review*
HC	House of Commons
HL	House of Lords
HLM	*House of Lords Minutes of Evidence*
JEcH	*Journal of Economic History*
JRSS	*Journal of the Royal Statistical Society*
JSSL	*Journal of the Statistical Society of London*
LCC	London County Council
MSESS	*Manchester School of Economic and Social Studies*
PP	*Parliamentary Papers*
RC	*Royal Commission*
SC	*Select Committee*
SJPE	*Scottish Journal of Political Economy*
TNAPSS	*Transactions of the National Association for the Promotion of Social Science*
TPR	*Town Planning Review*
VS	*Victorian Studies*

Unless otherwise stated, the place of publication of all books is England.

2. *Urbanity and suburbanity*

1. D. C. Coleman, *What has happened to Economic History?* (1972), I.
2. T. B. Macaulay, *The History of England* (1862 edn), II, 12–13.
3. C. F. G. Masterman, *The Heart of the Empire* (1902), 15–17; *idem, Alarms and Discussions* (1939 edn), 138.
4. H. G. Wells, *Anticipations of the Reaction of Mechanical and Scientific Progress upon Human Life and Thought* (1901), 64.
5. F. W. Maitland, *Township and Borough* (1898), 13.
6. R. Williams, *The Country and the City* (1973), 154.
7. G. Eliot, *The Mill on the Floss* (1863), IV, ch. 3.
8. C. F. G. Masterman, *From the Abyss* (1902), 12.
9. Maitland, *Township and Borough*, 24.
10. B. Disraeli, *Coningsby* (1844), bk IV, ch. 1; H. James, 'London' (1888), reprinted in *English Hours* (1905), 31.
11. W. Cowper, *The Task* (1785), bk 1.
12. H. James, 'The suburbs of London', *Galaxy*, XXIV (1887), 778.
13. N. Taylor, *The Village in the City* (1973), 95.

14. R. Fogelson, *The Fragmented Metropolis: Los Angeles, 1850–1930* (Cambridge, Mass., 1967), 3.
15. A. J. P. Taylor, 'The world's cities (I): Manchester', *Encounter*, VIII (1957).
16. E. Hobsbawm, 'From social history to the history of society', *Daedalus*, C (1971), 34.
17. *Hansard*, third series (1831), 1193–4; A. Strauss, *Images of the American City* (New York, 1961), 9.
18. S. Thernstrom, 'Reflections on the new urban history', *Daedalus* C (1971), 361–2.
19. N. Birnbaum, 'Afterword', in S. Thernstrom and R. Sennett (eds.), *Nineteenth-Century Cities: essays in the New Urban History* (1969), 430.

3. Greater and greater London

1. John Fisher Murray, *The World of London* (2 vols., 1844), I, 7.
2. Walter Bagehot, *Literary Studies* (1878), II, 301.
3. Richard Jefferies, *Nature near London* (1883), iii.
4. The phrase is Chesterton's, quoted by my colleague, Alan Everitt, in an unpublished paper entitled 'Victorian literature and local history', which he kindly allowed me to read.
5. Oliveira Martins, *The England of Today*, trans. C. J. Willdey (1896), 9.
6. T. C. Barker, 'London and the great leap forward', *The Listener*, 29 June 1967, 845–7.
7. Henry James, *English Hours* (1905), 30.
8. See Donald Read, *The English Provinces, c. 1760–1960: a study in influence* (1964), 1–3, and S. W. Dawson, ' "Provincial" – a modern critical term', *Essays in Criticism*, V (1955), 275–80.
9. Quoted by G. M. Young among his essays, *Daylight and Champaign* (1937), 20.
10. Pierce Egan, *Life in London* (1821), and Anon., *Real Life in London* (2 vols., 1822).
11. Murray, *The World of London*, I, 20–1.
12. See Jean-Paul Hulin, 'Exetisme et littérature sociale au début de l'ère victorienne', *Études Anglaises*, XVI (1963), 23–37.
13. Murray, *The World of London*, I, 13.
14. For a brief, general treatment of these matters, see Sir Gwilym Gibbon and Reginald W. Bell, *History of the London County Council, 1889–1939* (1939), pt 1.
15. Quoted by Read, *The English Provinces*, 117, who deals very thoroughly with the provincial emphasis in the popular movements of this period, and whose work I have drawn upon here.
16. Paul Thompson, *Socialists, Liberals and Labour: the struggle for London, 1885–1914* (1967), 39.
17. H. M. Pelling, *Social Geography of British Elections, 1885–1910* (1967), 56–9.
18. A. Briggs, *Victorian Cities* (1963), 336.
19. Royston Lambert, 'Central and local relations in mid-Victorian England: the Local Government Act Office, 1858–71', *VS*, VI (1962), 121–50. See also [F. O. Ward], 'Sanitary consolidation, centralisation, local self-government', *Quarterly Review*, CLXXVI (1851), 435–92.
20. The data underlying the statements made here have been gathered from the *Census Reports, London Statistics* for 1936–8, and *Annual Abstract of Statistics* for 1967.
21. Report of the RC on the Distribution of the Industrial Population (Cmd. 6153) (1940), 15; Ministry of Housing and Local Government, *The South East Study, 1961–81* (1964), *passim*.
22. Such an attempt is E. A. Wrigley, 'A simple model of London's importance in changing English society and economy, 1650–1760', *Past and Present*, XXXVII (1967), 44–70.
23. *Macmillan's Magazine*, X (1864), 310.

24. See below, Ch. 10.
25. E. G. Ravenstein, 'The laws of migration', *Journal of the Royal Statistical Society*, XLVIII (1885), 167–227.
26. A. K. Cairncross, *Home and Foreign Investment, 1870–1913* (1953).
27. See below, Ch. 9.
28. See J. A. Banks, 'Population change and the Victorian city', *VS*, XI (1966–7), and John Friedman, 'Cities in social transformation', *Comparative Studies in Society and History*, IV (1961–2), 86–103.
29. Jefferies, *Nature near London*, 26–7.
30. M. Arnold, *Culture and Anarchy*, ed. J. Dover Wilson (1960), 59.
31. T. S. Eliot, *Notes towards the Definition of Culture* (1948), 58.
32. George Wilson M'Cree, *The Moral Condition of London* (1869), 7, 13, 16.
33. *The Spring of Shillelah*, ed. Dinny Blake (1852), 55, quoted in L. H. Lees, 'Social change and social stability among the London Irish, 1830–1870' (Ph. D. thesis, Harvard University, 1969), 11.
34. In his review of Pelling's *Social Geography* for the *Bulletin of the Society for the Study of Labour History*, XVIII (1969), 54.
35. I must thank Mr R. J. Morris of the University of Edinburgh for the information concerning Leeds.
36. Arts Council of Great Britain, *Annual Report for 1967*. Cf. Paul Banks, *Metropolis, or the Destiny of Cities* (1930).
37. J. Roland Phillips, 'Local taxation in England and Wales', in *Local Government and Taxation in the United Kingdom*, ed. J. W. Probyn (1882), 465–506.
38. George C. Brodrick, 'Local government in England', *ibid.*, 81.
39. Another Frenchman, recalling his impressions of 1932, had this to say: 'There were, I found, more years than miles between London and any town that I discovered' (Pierre Maillaud [pseud. P. Bourdan], *The English Way* (1945), 13).
40. On this, see T. F. Tout, 'The beginnings of a modern capital: London and Westminster in the fourteenth century', in his *Collected Papers* (3 vols., 1934), III, 249–75.
41. See, for example, Graham Turner, *The North Country* (1967), and D. Elliston Allen, *British Tastes: an enquiry into the likes and dislikes of the regional consumer* (1968).
42. Murray, *The World of London*, I, 208.

5. The objects of street improvement in Regency and early Victorian London

1. D. H. Pinkney, 'Napoleon III's transformation of Paris: the origins and development of an idea', *Journal of Modern History*, XXVII (1955), 125–34.
2. His first four reports were reprinted in *PP*, 1812 (274), XII.
3. *PP*, 1812 (357), XII, *First Report, HM Commissioners of Woods, Forests and Land Revenues*, 9–12.
4. *Ibid.*, 1816 (147) XV, *Second Report, HM Commissioners of Woods, Forests and Land Revenues*, 122–3.
5. *Ibid.*, 1844 (15), XV, *First Report, RC on Metropolis Improvements*, 5.
6. J. Summerson, *Architecture in Britain, 1530–1830* (1953), 299.
7. *PP*, 1812 (357), *First Report, HM Commissioner of Woods*, 89.
8. J. Elmes, *Metropolitan Improvements; or London in the nineteenth century* (1828), 1–2.
9. *PP*, 1836, XX, *Report, SC (HC) on Metropolis Improvements*, QQ 8, 20.
10. *Ibid.*, QQ 21, 285.
11. *Ibid.*, Q 375.
12. *PP*, 1837–8, XVI, *Second Report, SC (HC) on Metropolis Improvements*, iii.
13. *Ibid.*, vii.

14. *Ibid.*, viii.
15. This was the formative stage in the financial development of public works of this kind: the largest single source of income was the London Bridge Approaches Fund, formed mainly from the proceeds of a duty on all coal brought into London; this was supplemented by local rates, private subscriptions and loans raised on the security of the coal duties and of the land revenues of the Crown. Details of metropolitan improvements financed by the coal duties before 1838 may be found in *PP*, 1837–8 (475), XV, *Report, SC (HC) on the Coal Trade (Port of London) Bill*, Appendix 5; further details are available in *PP*, 1851 (1356), XXIX, *Seventh Report, RC on Metropolis Improvements, Appendix*.
16. *PP*, 1840 (410), XII, *First Report, SC (HC) on Metropolis Improvements*, v.
17. *PP*, 1845 (348), XVII, *Second Report, RC on Metropolis Improvements*, QQ 31, 40. Pennethorne continued to have an eye for this type of street improvement: some of his suggestions in the Covent Garden Improvement, for example, were aimed primarily at slum clearance: *PP, Seventh Report, RC on Metropolis Improvements*, 5.
18. *Ibid.*, iv.
19. Metropolitan railways, it is worth adding, were also regarded in this role: see below, Ch. 7.
20. B. Chapman, 'Baron Haussmann and the planning of Paris', *TPR*, XXIV (1953–4), 191; S. E. Rasmussen, *London: the unique city* (2nd edn, 1948), 134–5. Cf. below, Chs. 7–8.
21. See D. H. Pinkney, 'Money and politics in the rebuilding of Paris', *JECH*, XVII (1957), 45–61; Chapman, 'Baron Haussmann', 189–90.
22. (Unsigned), 'The financial question of the works in Paris', *The Builder*, XXI (1863), 874; (Editorial), 'A quarter of a century of London street improvements', *ibid.*, XXIV (1866), 877.
23. *The Times*, 25 February 1861.
24. See W. Ashworth, *The Genesis of Modern British Town Planning* (1954), 65 ff.
25. (Unsigned), 'The question between London and Paris street improvements', *The Builder*, XIX (1861), 870; (Editorial), 'A quarter of a century of London street improvements', *ibid.*, XXIV, 898–9; report of a meeting of the Royal Institute of British Architects, 18 December 1871, *The Builder*, XXX (1872), 22–4.
26. W. Tite, 'On the Paris street improvements, and their cost', *Journal of the Statistical Society*, XXVII (1864), 385.

6. Workmen's fares in south London, 1860–1914

1. *Hansard*, 4th series, LXXXIII (1900), 517.
2. This paper is based in part on H. J. Dyos, 'The suburban development of Greater London, south of the Thames, 1836–1914' (Ph.D. thesis, University of London, 1952).
3. General Booth, *In Darkest England and the Way Out* (1890), 210.
4. C. Gatliff, 'On improved dwellings and their beneficial effect on health and morals', *JRSS*, XXXVIII (1875), 34–5.
5. *Ibid.*, 45. See also A. Newsholme, 'Vital statistics of the Peabody Buildings and other artisans' and labourers' block dwellings', *JRSS*, LIV (1891), 70–99.
6. V. Zoond, 'Housing legislation in England, 1851–67' (M.A. thesis, University of London, 1932), and *PP*, 1884–5, XXX (C. 4402), *RC on the Housing of the Working Classes*.
7. *LCC Report on the Housing of the Working Classes, 1855–1912* (1913); P. J. Edwards, *History of London Street Improvements, 1855–97* (1898); *PP*, 1902, V, *Joint SC on Housing of the Working Classes*, Appendix H.

8. *The Builder,* III (1845), 61.
9. *London* (1841–4), I, 254.
10. *Hansard,* 3rd series, CLXI (1861).
11. In particular, W. Denton, *Observations on the Displacement of the Poor by Metropolitan Railways* (1861); J. Hole, *The Housing of the Working Classes* (1866); *PP,* 1881, VII, and 1882, VII, *SC on Artisans' and Labourers' Dwellings Improvement*; *PP,* 1884–5, XXX, *RC on the Housing of the Working Classes*; *PP,* 1906, XLI, *RC on London Traffic.*
12. *The Tramway and Railway World,* XI (1902), 165, report on a meeting of the Society of Arts, February 1902.
13. C. Booth, *Improved Means of Locomotion as a First Step Towards the Cure of the Housing Difficulties of London* (1901), 13.
14. W. Glazier, 'A workman's reflections', *The Nineteenth Century,* LXXXII (1883), 954.
15. A witness to a parliamentary inquiry in the 1850s, for example, pointed out the illogicality of the working classes occupying central, highly-rated districts, when twenty minutes' travelling would have taken them into the suburbs, at a rate, he proposed, of a farthing a mile. (*PP,* 1854–5, X (415), *SC on Metropolitan Communications,* Q 1356.)
16. Browning Hall Conference, *Synopsis of Report of Sub-Committee on Locomotion* (1902), 6–7.
17. See C. E. Lee, *Passenger Class Distinctions* (1946).
18. See S. A. Pope, *The Cheap Trains Act, 1883* (1906).
19. J. M. McCabe, *Life and Letters of George Jacob Holyoake* (1908), II, 152.
20. The legal decision was reached in the Court of Exchequer in July 1874, in an action against the North London Railway Company, when the ruling stated that the Board of Trade could not dispense with this necessity. (Lee, *Passenger Class Distinctions,* 43.)
21. *Interim Report: SC on Artisans' and Labourers' Dwellings Improvement,* QQ 921–6, 2397–403, 2434–41, 2455–63, 2864–5, 5275.
22. *Ibid.,* QQ 3857–61; *Final Report,* QQ 704–7; *PP,* 1902, V, *Joint SC on Housing of the Working Classes,* QQ 413, 499–502, 726–31, 752–3; C. Booth, *Improved Means of Locomotion,* 12, 15; H. P. Boulnois, *Housing of the Labouring Classes* (1896), preface.
23. *Final Report, SC on Artisans' and Labourers' Dwellings Improvement,* QQ 1188, 2458–9.
24. M. S. Pember Reeves, *Round About a Pound a Week* (1913), 39.
25. D. Pasquet, *Londres et les ouvriers de Londres* (Paris, 1913), 125.
26. *Hansard,* 3rd series, CLXI (1861), 1073.
27. Reeves, *Round About a Pound a Week,* 22.
28. For example, Godwin in *The Builder,* I (1843), 271; and *RC on Housing of the Working Classes, 1884–5,* 18
29. *Final Report, SC on Artisans' and Labourers' Dwellings Improvement,* Q 1328.
30. *Ibid.,* Q 2198.
31. *Ibid.,* QQ 2993–5.
32. Lee, *Passenger Class Distinctions,* 23, 32, gives details of a fourth class at various dates from 1841 in several parts of the country.
33. *Ibid.,* 51. The Metropolitan District Railway Act, 1864 (27 and 28 Vict., C. CCCXXII), Sect. 90 required workmen's trains north of the river only.
34. *The Illustrated London News,* 22 April 1865, quoted Lee, *Passenger Class Distinctions,* 53.
35. 23 and 24 Vict., C. CLXXVII.
36. H. Roberts, *The Dwellings of the Labouring Classes* (1867), 72.
37. 27 and 28 Vict., C. CXCV, Sect. 134.

38. 28 Vict., C. LI, Sect. 144.
39. The section from New Cross to Wapping was opened in 1869, and to Shoreditch in 1876.
40. Lee, *Passenger Class Distinctions*, 54.
41. *Ibid.*, 55.
42. *PP*, 1894, LXXV (C. 7541).
43. *RC on the Housing of the Working Classes, 1884–5*, QQ 10, 113.
44. *Ibid.*, Q 9962.
45. Pope, *The Cheap Trains Act, 1883*, 15; Ludwig Sinzheimer, *Der Londoner Grafschaftsrat* (1900), 375.
46. *PP*, 1882, VII, *SC on Artisans' and Labourers' Dwellings Improvement*, Rep., X.
47. The Metropolitan Association for Procuring Cheap and Regular Railway Accommodation for the Working Classes, which was established in 1868, was an earlier organisation devoted to a similar end. It held public meetings and petitioned parliament, but had little publicity in the railway press. (Lee, *Passenger Class Distinctions*, 53–4.)
48. He was chairman for 24 years.
49. An incomplete series, 1878–99, is deposited in the Gladstone Library at the National Liberal Club, London, and Nos. 1–13 (1878–83) are available in the British Library of Political and Economic Science (HE 2231 (42)). Pamphlets are deposited at the British Museum (Cat. No. 08228 i 46).
50. G. J. Holyoake, *Byegones Worth Remembering* (1905), I, 42–3. See also G. J. Holyoake, *History of the Travelling Tax* (1901), and C. D. Collet, *Reasons for the Repeal of the Railway Passenger Duty* (1877). There was one interesting parallel between the propaganda methods of the Travelling Tax Abolition Committee and the 'Newspaper-stamp Abolition Committee' (later, 'Association for Promoting the Repeal of the Taxes on Knowledge') formed by C. D. Collet, Francis Place, Richard Cobden and others, to which Holyoake was soon recruited, twenty-seven years before. An effective device was used to discredit the administration of the 'taxes on knowledge' and to expose their anomalies. The Abolition Committee first forced the Commissioner of Stamps to prosecute the proprietors of a small provincial newspaper whose omission to stamp their issues had been gratuitously overlooked, and then had the question asked in Parliament why *Punch*, the *Athaneum* or *The Builder* escaped prosecution. In the cheap fares campaign, this device was resurrected. Holyoake then blandly urged the taxing of the tramways, which he tried to show were just as liable to pay the passenger duty, in order to precipitate a public agitation on the whole question. (See McCabe, *Life and Letters of Holyoake*, I, 261–3, II, 153–4.)
51. *LCC Report of the Public Health and Housing Committee on Workmen's Trains for Districts South of the Thames* (1892), *passim*; *PP*, 1890, LXV, includes a paper giving full details of services at that date.
52. Sinzheimer, *Der Londoner Grafschaftsrak*, 392–3.
53. *LCC Report of the Public Health and Housing Committee on Workmen's Trains* (1892), 40.
54. *Ibid.* (1893).
55. J. Hole, *National Railways* (1893), 162.
56. According to Sinzheimer (*Der Londoner Grasschaftsrat*, 382), one train on this line did not arrive till 8.40 a.m.
57. *Hansard*, 4th series, LXXXII, 349.
58. *LCC Report on the Inadequacy of Workmen's Train Services on the South London Railways* (1897).

59. *London Reform Union Pamphlet* no. 79 (1899); Sinzheimer, *Der Londoner Grafschaftsrat*, 393.

60. *LCC Report on the Inadequacy of Workmen's Train Services on the South London Railways* (1897), 16.

61. *Ibid.*, 2.

62. The author of the campaign behind this bill was J. Blundell Maple, MP of Maple and Co. Ltd. His letters to the press on the subject, the text of the bill and a report of the debate are included in his pamphlet, *Cheap Trains for the London Workers* (1891).

63. *Annual Report, Battersea Vestry* (1897), 78.

64. See correspondence in *PP*, 1895, LXXVI (C. 7657).

65. *PP*, 1903, VIII, *SC on Workmen's Trains*, *passim*; Sinzheimer, *Der Londoner Grafschaftsrat*, 379–80, enumerates the special needs of certain groups of workers.

66. *London Reform Union Pamphlet* no. 79: *The London Reform Union and Workmen's Trains* (1899), *passim*. Workmen's fares not unnaturally became a political question in the struggle between the Moderates and Progressives for control of the Council. See, for example, *London Reform Union Leaflet* no. 50: *Workmen's Trains*, of which the final paragraph reads: 'A few Railway Directors and the Railway Shareholders don't like cheap fares. A few Railway Companies are still obstinately holding out against the Council. The slum landlords in the middle of London want to keep the workmen in the slums. A determined attempt is therefore being made to defeat the Progressives, so as to stop all pressure in favour of more Workmen's Trains.'

67. *RC on London Traffic*, Q 5141.

68. *43rd Annual Report, Wandsworth Board of Works* (1899), 19.

69. *PP*, 1904, VII, *SC on Workmen's Trains*, Q 692 (evidence of Chairman of LCC Housing Committee). According to Pasquet (*Londres et les ouvriers de Londres*, 161), the failure of the Board of Trade to take a firm hand in the provision of workmen's trains in some areas north of the Thames resulted in extremely scanty provision being made. The Midland Railway and Great Western Railway provided the fewest trains, the latter having no workmen's services in 1890, one train in 1894, three in 1902 and 16 in 1909.

70. *SC on Workmen's Trains*, 1904, QQ 713, 722–3, 760–9.

71. *Ibid.*, QQ 869–72, 858, 870. This may be compared with the admission at a shareholders' meeting by the Chairman of the Great Eastern Railway that the extremely low fare of 2d for the 21 miles from Enfield to Liverpool Street and back was remunerative: *The Times*, 28 January 1891.

72. *SC on Workmen's Trains*, 1904, QQ 74–80.

73. *PP*, 1905, VIII, *SC on Workmen's Trains*, Rep. VII.

74. *Report of the Public Health and Housing Committee on Metropolitan Workmen's Trains* (1896), *passim*; *SC on Workmen's Trains*, 1904, Q 22.

75. *Hansard*, 4th series, LXXXII, 355.

76. *PP*, 1884–5, XXX, *RC on Housing of the Working Classes*, 49.

77. *PP*, 1908, CVII, *Board of Trade Report on the Cost of Living of the Working Classes*, Rep. XXXI, 21.

78. *RC on London Traffic*, Q 5064.

79. *LCC Workmen's Trains Inquiry* (1898), I, 11–14.

80. *RC on London Traffic*, Q 5064.

81. *Ibid.*, QQ 5124–5.

82. *Ibid.*, Q 4982.

83. *Ibid.*, Q 5011.

84. *Ibid.*, Q 5180.

85. *LCC Report on Third Class Season Tickets*, 1902, xxiv.

86. A complete analysis of these variations is contained in two tables, and a comparison is made with much lower Continental workmen's fares, in Sinzheimer, *Der Londoner Grafschaftsrat*, 383–7. See also *PP*, 1903, LXIII, for a return showing numbers of workmen's trains, distance run and the fare charged.

87. An illustration of the connection between housing development and workmen's fares is provided by the spectacular rise in workmen's tickets issued on the tramway to Tooting, where a large LCC housing estate was developed. Numbers of workmen's tickets rose from 581,626 in 1902–3, to 3,342,277 in 1906–7, and to 8,812,041 in 1913–14. (*Seventh Annual Report of the London Traffic Branch, 1914; PP*, 1914–16, XXVI (Cd 7757), 79.)

88. *LCC Report on Housing Development and Workmen's Fares* (1912).

89. *Ibid.*, Appendix 5.

90. Between 1889 and 1906. See *London Statistics*, XVII, 330.

91. *LCC Report on Locomotion Service* (1895), 32 ff. Also *Quarterly Returns, Workmen's Trains and Trams, LCC*, 1906–14, and *RC on London Traffic*, Appendix 77, *passim*.

92. A. F. Weber, *The Growth of Cities in the Nineteenth Century* (1899), 463, Table clxv.

93. R. Price-Williams, 'The population of London, 1801–81', *JRSS* XLVIII (1885), 376.

94. See Minutes of Evidence to *SC on Artisans' and Labourers' Dwellings Improvement* (1881), *passim*.

95. See, too, Alexander Patterson, *Across the Bridges* (1911); J. Hollingshead, *Ragged London in 1861* (1861); J. Greenwood, *The Seven Curses of London* (c. 1870); Anon, *The Bitter Cry of Outcast London* (1883); 'The charities of London', *Quarterly Review*, XCVII.

7. Railways and housing in Victorian London

1. This is a subject which has seldom attracted much attention. See W. M. Ackworth, *Railways of England* (1889), 147–8; G. A. Sekon, *Locomotion in Victorian London* (1938), 172; R. W. Kinder, *The London, Chatham & Dover Railway* (1952), 11; H. Ellis, *The Midland Railway* (1953), 35.

2. The 'Metropolitan Railway District' was bounded by Edgware Road, Marylebone Road, Euston Road, City Road, Finsbury Square, Bishopsgate, London Bridge, Borough High Street, Lambeth Road, Vauxhall Road, Vauxhall Bridge, Park Lane: *PP*, 1846, XVII, 21.

3. The City authorities persistently opposed all railways which affected their interests. It was probably due to their support for its scheme that the Metropolitan Railway obtained its original act in 1854: see *HLM*, XXXV, 19 July 1864, 31–2. Thus, although numerous schemes were proposed from time to time, no surface railway ever penetrated the Metropolitan Railway District: the Metropolitan Railway, the first section of which was opened between Paddington and Farringdon Road in 1863, followed the perimeter of this area below street level.

4. 'Grand railway from England to China', *Punch* III (1842), 205.

5. *An Appeal to the Public on the Subject of Railways* (1837).

6. *London Shadows* (1854), 71.

7. *Another Blow for Life* (1864), 30.

8. *Fortnightly Review*, IV (1866), 362–3.

9. *The Working Man*, II (1866), 110–11; see, too, *Hansard*, 3rd series, CLXXXI (1866), 1025.

10. *The Working Man*, I (1866), 30.

11. T. B. Smithies, *TNAPSS* (1871), 529.

12. Originally, the 'Commercial Railway Company' (changed 2–3 Vict., C. XCV).

13. Corporation of London, *Common Council Minutes*, 1 March 1836. I owe this reference to Prof. J. Simmons.
14. The *RC on London Termini* (1846) had specially emphasised the need for all London communications improvements to be 'part of one well-considered scheme' (Rep., 8). According to the Board of Trade, little attention seems to have been paid to this recommendation: *The Times*, 24 March 1863; *PP*, 1863, LXII, 2. This was particularly urgent by the 1860s, when 'the railway map of England (was) excuse enough even for a Whig Minister's interference with the random projects with which the metropolis (is) menaced': *Illustrated London News*, XLIX (1863), 219.
15. *Hansard*, 3rd series, CXXV (1853), 402; CLXI (1861), 64.
16. Emanuel, *TNAPSS* (1864), 731.
17. *The Builder*, XXV (1867), 37.
18. *Hansard*, 3rd series, CXXVI (1853), 1292; *Lords Journals*, LXXXV (1853), 244, Standing Order 191.
19. For Present Standing Order 47, see *Standing Orders of the House of Lords relative to Private Bills* (1951), 30–1; *Standing Orders of House of Commons* (1953), 138–9.
20. E.g., Housing Act, 1936, Sect. 6 and Sched. XI.
21. W. Denton, *Observations on the Displacement of the Poor by Metropolitan Railways, and by other Public Improvements* (1861), *passim*, and his evidence to *PP*, 1884–4, XXX, *RC on Housing of the Working Classes*, QQ 10563 ff.; *Hansard*, 3rd series, CLXI (1861), 1083, 1704, 1707.
22. Analytically, these may be considered as the negative elements involved in the computation of social net product, as elaborated by A. C. Pigou, *The Economics of Welfare* (4th edn, 1932), 134.
23. Denton, *Observations*, 23; E. Lankester, MOH St James's, *Seventeenth Annual Report of Westminster Board of Works* (1872), 36.
24. T. Hammond, *A Few Cursory Remarks on Railways* (1835), 9; cf. *Morning Herald*, 26 and 28 September 1834.
25. *PP*, 1846, XVII, 7, 9; cf. H. Clarke, *London Street Improvements, 1855–89* (1892), 4.
26. Lord Shaftesbury: *Hansard*, 3rd series, CXXV (1853), 401.
27. The LC&D and SE (Kennington, Clapham and Brixton) Railways Bill, 1866, though abortive, provided the following typical observation on the accompanying demolition statement (3,743 persons would have been involved): 'It is not apprehended that any inconvenience will arise, inasmuch as the Railways will offer facilities for Residences in suburban parts of the Metropolis not at present overcrowded with houses and population.'
28. McCullagh Torrens: *Hansard*, 3rd series, CLXXXI (1866), 821.
29. See part of the text of one petition, presented by the Corporation of the City of London against the London & Blackwall Railways Bill in 1836; J. Simmons, 'Railway history in English local records', *Journal of Transport History*, I (1953–4), 163.
30. *The Builder*, XXV (1867), 33.
31. *The Times*, 7 January 1867. The Association included several MPs and clergymen.
32. *The Working Man*, II (1866), 110–11.
33. *All the Year Round*, XV (1866), 466 ff.
34. W. Ashworth, *The Genesis of Modern British Town Planning* (1954), 106, gives some examples of these changes in land values following improvements.
35. E. Clarke, *The Hovel and the Home* (c. 1863), 6.
36. G. Godwin: *The Builder*, III (1845), 61; XII (1854), 25; XIX (1861), 169; *London Shadows* (1854), 28, 33; *TNAPSS* (1862), 595; (1864), 516; H. Roberts, *The Dwellings of the Labouring Classes* (1850), 3 (4th edn, 1867), preface, 47; *Annual*

Report, British Association (1860), Transactions of Sections, 198; J. Hole, *The Homes of the Working Classes* (1866), 5; W. Druce, *The Builder*, IX (1851), 449.

37. C. Pearson, *PP*, XVII, Q 2351; Lord Shaftesbury, *Hansard*, 3rd series, CXXV (1853), 403; CLXXXIII (1866), 569. Bishop of London, *Hansard*, 3rd series, CXXV (1853), 408; CLXI (1861), 1054–5. *Eighth Annual Report, St Giles' District Board of Works* (1864), 16; *Sixteenth Annual Report, St Giles' District Board of Works* (1872), 3; *Ninth Annual Report, Westminster District Board of Works* (1865), 16; *Eleventh Annual Report, St Martin's Parish* (1867); *Eleventh Annual Report, Strand District Board of Works* (1867), 5. Dr G. Ross (MOH Bloomsbury), *PP*, 1874, X, Report, *SC on Metropolitan Buildings and Management Bill*, QQ 3966, 3968. H. Potter (vice-chairman, Board of Guardians, Farringdon Street), *HLM*, 1860, XVII, 80–1.

38. Rev. C. Girdlestone, *Letters on the Unhealthy Condition of the Lower Class of Dwellings* (1845), 61. W. Denton (Curate, St Bartholomew's, Cripplegate), *Observations on the Displacement of the Poor*, 10–11. (N.B., the Rector and Churchwardens repudiated Denton's interpretation: *Hansard*, 3rd series, CLXI (1861), 1705; *HLM*, 1864, XXVI, 26.)

39. *Friend of the People*, I (1860), 155–6, 560; II (1861), 121–2. *The Working Man*, I (1866), 13.

40. *Quarterly Review*, CVII (1860), 270; *Illustrated London News*, XLII (1863), 83; L. Faucher, *Études sur l'Angleterre* (2nd edn, 1856), 37; H. D. Davies, *The Way Out* (1861), 4; T. Worthington, *TNAPSS* (1864), 732; Dodd, *Fortnightly Review*, IX (1866), 362–3; P. Greg, *Macmillan's Magazine*, VI (1862), 65; H. W. Rumsey, *Journal of Social Science*, VII (1866), 354; T. Beggs, *ibid.*, IV (1866), 70, and *Social Science Review*, VI (1866), 204; *Report, Committee on Dwellings for the Labouring Class* (C. B. P. Bosanquet, E. Chadwick, Prof. Fawcett, G. Godwin, C. Wren Hoskyns, E. Lankester, J. S. Mill, Lord Shaftesbury, Sir J. Kay-Shuttleworth, Alderman Waterlow), *Journal of the Society of Arts*, XII (1864–5), 430; Anon., *Work About the Five Dials* (1878), 47.

41. The Author of 'The Autobiography of a Beggar Boy' (J. D. Burn), *Commercial Enterprise and Social Progress* (1858), 12.

42. *The Workman's Friend*, I (1862), 2–3.

43. E.g., *The Times*, 25 February 1861; Ashworth, *Genesis of Modern British Town Planning*, 74.

44. B. Chapman, 'Baron Haussmann and the planning of Paris', *TPR*, XXIV (1953), 191; S. E. Rasmussen, *London: The Unique City* (2nd edn, 1948), 134–5.

45. *Punch*, XL (1861), 98; XLIV (1863), 128, 146 (the reference is to the LC&D Ely's viaduct over Ludgate Hill).

46. T. Hole, *TNAPSS* (1871), 524.

47. H. W. Rumsey, *Journal of Social Science*, VII (1866), 353.

48. *Hansard*, 3rd series, CXXV (1853), 400.

49. M. Gore, *On the Dwellings of the Poor* (2nd edn, 1851), 15; also, G. B. Tremenheere, *Dwellings of the Labouring Classes in the Metropolis* (1856), 23.

50. *Hansard*, 3rd series, CXXV (1853), 406.

51. *HL, SC, Proceedings*, 1853, V, 108–11.

52. *Hansard*, 3rd series, CXXV (1853), 417.

53. R. J. Simpson, *TNAPSS* (1874), 614–15.

54. *Commons Journals*, CXXIX (1874), 351.

55. For terminology, see *PP*, 1882, VII, 216–18.

56. *PP*, 1884–5, XXX, QQ 8838–9, 8386–8, 9984, 9987, 10412; Q 10676 (Denton); Q 9940 (Surveyor to Metropolitan Board of Works); QQ 10777–8 (Clerk of Public Bills).

57. C. Booth, *Life and Labour of the People in London* (1903), 3rd series, I, 214.

58. *PP*, 1902, V. *Report, Joint SC on Housing of the Working Classes*, 147.

59. E.g., Booth, *Life and Labour*, 3rd series, IV, 166.
60. *Ibid.*, 3rd series, II, 166; III, 132.
61. *HLM*, XXVI, 1 July 1864, 3–32.
62. *HLM*, I, 11 March 1861, 183 ff.
63. Details of season tickets and suburban bus services may be found in H. J. Dyos, 'The suburban development of Greater London, south of the Thames, 1836–1914' (Ph.D. thesis, University of London, 1952), 214–40, 275–80, 320–1.
64. See H. J. Dyos, 'The growth of a pre-Victorian suburb: south London, 1580–1836', *TPR*, XXV (1954), 59–78.
65. *Railway Register*, II (1845), 495–9; III (1846), 34; see, too, Anon., *Railways; their Uses and Management* (1842), 28–9.
66. *Monthly Paper* (1847), 4.
67. *PP*, 1846, XVII, QQ 2320 ff.: I am most grateful to Prof. O. H. K. Spate, Australian National University, Canberra, for making several helpful references on this topic, and for permitting me to use the substance of an unpublished note of his own.
68. See A Shareholder, *Railroads: Statements and Reflections thereon* (1836), 7 n. Similar proposals, and action on them, later became almost conventional: G. W. Jones, *The Million on the Rail* (1874), 19, proposed third-class fares of a penny for 5–10 miles; and by 1912 twopenny return workmen's fares were widely available for comparable distances in London.
69. Davies, *The Way Out*, 22.
70. *PP*, 1854–5, X, QQ 1355–62.
71. *HLM*, I, 12 March 1861, 121 ff.
72. *The Builder*, XVI (1858), 801, 836.
73. *Ibid.*, XIX (1859), 138.
74. T. Hare, *Thoughts on the Dwellings of the People* (1862), 19–20, and *TNAPSS* (1862), 807–8, and their elaboration in *Macmillan's Magazine*, VII (1863), 441–7; also W. Hardwicke, *TNAPSS* (1862), 226–30.
75. E.g., Slaney: *Hansard*, 3rd series, CLXI (1861), 1809–12.
76. E.g. (1864), 586 (Sir G. Stickland); 739 (H. W. Rumsey).
77. W. B. Adams, *Roads and Rails* (1862), 226–30.
78. Clarke, *The Hovel and the Home*, 32.
79. Also advocated by H. Roberts, *TNAPSS* (1858), 613–14, and (T. Wright), *The Great Unwashed* (1868), 44–5; see also Ashworth, *Genesis of Modern British Town Planning*, Ch. 5.
80. G. Godwin, *Another Blow for Life* (1864), 31.
81. *The Builder*, XXII (1864), 161.
82. *Cottager & Artisan*, VII (1867), 92: Clarke, *The Hovel and the Home*, 10.
83. Davies, *The Way Out*, 25–39.
84. J. Hole, *The Homes of the Working Classes* (1866), 63–4.
85. *The Working Man*, I (1866), 139; see, too, T. Beggs, *Journal of Social Science*, VI (1866), 205.
86. *The Working Man*, II (1866), 136. See, too, *The Builder*, XX (1862), 86, in which the idea that suburban cottages might be built, and railway companies offer cheap fares (2d per day for bulk travel of 1,000 passengers) is warmly welcomed, with the practical suggestion that such property should be spoken in advance.
87. C. D. Collet, *Reasons for the Repeal of the Railway Passenger Duty* (1877), 27.
88. J. Parslee, *Workman's Magazine*, I (1873), 288.
89. Davies, *The Way Out*, 13. The nomenclature of the worst City slums is recorded in H. Letherby, *Report on the Sanitary Condition of the City of London for the Year 1855–6*, 13–14.
90. See H. Roberts, *The Dwellings of the Labouring Classes* (4th edn, 1867), 48.

91. 24–5 Vict., C. CXCVI, Sect. 45.
92. 24–5 Vict., C. CCXXXIII, Sect. 24.
93. *PP*, 1905, VIII, Rep. vii.
94. A series of letters and reports in *The Times* provides the main arguments in favour of widespread workmen's services, and gives the government attitude: 28 January 1870, 6 April 1870, 23 June 1870, 24 February 1874, 18 March 1874, 11 September 1874. See also above, Ch. 6.
95. T. Beggs, *Journal of Social Science*, IV (1866), 87–8.
96. When first introduced it was lost through ministerial changes, but became law in 1868 (31–2 Vict., C. 130): *The Times*, 7 January 1867.
97. *Railway Register*, II (1845), 496.
98. 8–9 Vict., C. 18.
99. See *Railway Register*, II (1845), 203–6; H. Riddell, *Railway Parliamentary Practice* (1846).
100. Sections 63 and 68 respectively.
101. *Ricket v. Metropolitan Railway Company* (1867), LR 2 HL 175.
102. *Ibid.* (1865), 34; *LJQB*, 261.
103. For the full text and annotations to the 1845 Act, see A. W. Nicholls, *Compensation for the Compulsory Acquisition of Land* (1952), 31–121. A contemporary examination of the legal position may be found in T. D. Ingram, *A Treatise on the Law & Compensation for Interests in Lands, etc., payable by Railway and other Public Companies* (1862).
104. *The Builder*, XXIII (1865), 914. The lack of any legal claim was also noted in Denton, *Observations on the Displacement of the Poor*, 25; *The Working Man*, II (1866), 98.
105. *Thirteenth Annual Report, Westminster District Board of Works* (1869), 7.
106. *The Times*, 23 March 1861.
107. *RC on Housing of the Working Classes*, Q 10771 (Clerk of Public Bills, Lords), Q 10678 (Denton).
108. *Hansard*, 3rd series, CLXI (1861), 67.
109. *HLM*, I, 12 March 1861, 74, 181, 220.
110. Dodd, *Fortnightly Review*, IX (1866), 362.
111. *PP*, 1882, VII, Q 234; 1884–5, XXX, QQ 10400–8, 10676.
112. *HLM*, I, 13 March 1861, 77; 11 March 1861, 181.
113. H. Letherby, *Report on Sanitary Condition of the City of London*, 1856–7, 8.
114. Sir George Clark, *The Idea of the Industrial Revolution* (1953), 30–1.
115. *The Times*, 12 and 23 March 1861.
116. G. B. Longstaff, *Studies in Statistics, Social, Political and Medical* (1891), 180.
117. H. L. Beales, 'The making of social policy', *Hobhouse Memorial Lectures, 1941–50* (1951), 12; see, too, J. B. Brebner, 'Laissez faire and state intervention in nineteenth-century Britain', *JEcH*, VIII (1948), suppl., 59–73.

8. Some social costs of railway-building in Victorian London

1. See above, Ch. 7.
2. It should be added that thousands of people had already been evicted for street improvements and dock extensions as well as railways, and these evictions increased at the time railway demolitions were increasing after 1853. Earlier clearances included: London Docks (1800–5), 1,300 houses; Regent Street (1814–23), 750 houses; St Katherine's Dock (1827–8), 1,250 houses; between 1853 and 1901 at least 28,500 people were evicted for street improvements and dock extensions.
3. See *PP*, 1884–5, XXX, *RC on Housing of the Working Classes*, QQ 10056–7 (evidence of H. G. Calcraft, Assistant Secretary to Board of Trade).

4. Lord Derby: *Hansard*, 3rd series, CLXI (1861), 1698–9.
5. Lord Redesdale: *Hansard*, 3rd series, CLXXVII (1865), 553.
6. I am grateful to my former colleague, Mr J. A. Banks, for pointing this out to me in Karl Renner, *The Institutions of Private Law and their Social Functions*, ed. O. Kahn-Freund (1949), 64.
7. See Great Eastern Railway Bill, 1887, Sub-section (13), and compare with Schedule XI to Section 6 of the Housing Act, 1936, and other references, in H. A. Hill and D. P. Kerrigan, *The Complete Law of Housing* (4th edn, 1947), 348–50.
8. *HLM*, I, 11 March 1861, 159, 255–7, 264; 13 March 1861, 2.
9. See, too, *PP*, 1874, LIX, *Copy of Correspondence between Home Office and Solicitors to the Midland Railway Company in reference to a proposal of the Railway Company to pull down nearly 700 houses at Somers Town occupied by the Labouring Classes*, 159–62.
10. O. C. Williams, *The Historical Development of Private Bill Procedure and Standing Orders in the House of Commons* (1948), I, 169; II, 65, where the subsequent history of Standing Order 49 is traced in detail.
11. See above, Ch. 7.
12. In the 1851 census, a block of flats or model dwellings counted as a single house, as did a conventional dwelling, whether sub-divided into separate tenements or not.
13. Sir Francis Fox, *Sixty-three Years of Engineering* (1924), 48; I am grateful to Prof. J. Simmons for pointing this out to me.

9. The slums of Victorian London

1. George Orwell, *The Road to Wigan Pier* (1937).
2. George Augustus Sala, *Gaslight and Daylight, with Some London Scenes they Shine Upon* (1860), ch. 1, 'The Key of the Street'.
3. W. J. Loftie, *A History of London* (2 vols., 1884).
4. Two notable exceptions are G. L. Gomme, *London in the Reign of Victoria* (1898), and Sir Walter Besant, *London in the Nineteenth Century* (1909).
5. H. J. Dyos, 'The growth of cities in the nineteenth century: a review of some recent writing', *VS*, IX (1966), 225–37.
6. See Francois Bedarida, 'L'histoire sociale de Londres au XIXe siècle', *Annales*, XV (1960), 949–62.
7. E. R. Dewsnup, *The Housing Problem in England: Its Statistics, Legislation and Policy* (1907); see, too, J. S. Nettlefold, *Practical Housing* (1909).
8. W. Ashworth, *The Genesis of Modern British Town Planning* (1954). Leonardo Benevolo, *The Origins of Modern Town Planning*, trans. Judith Landry (1967), is of no particular value.
9. J. N. Tarn, 'Housing in urban areas, 1840–1914' (Ph.D. thesis, Cambridge University, 1961); A. S. Wohl, 'The housing of the artisans and labourers in nineteenth-century London, 1815–1911' (Ph.D. thesis, Brown University, 1965); W. Vere Hole, 'The housing of the working classes in Britain 1850–1914: a study of the development of standards and methods of provision' (Ph.D. thesis, London University, 1965). See, too: Vera Zoond, 'Housing legislation in England, 1851–1867, with special reference to London' (M.A. thesis, London University, 1931); J. H. Cheetham, *Working-Class Housing in England*, Royal Institute of British Architects (1945).
10. One monograph of value is Desire Pasquet, *Londres et les ouvriers de Londres* (Paris, 1914), which takes careful stock of slum formation. There is also a valuable analysis of the origins of slums in The Land Enquiry Committee, *The Land*, vol. II, *Urban* (1914), especially in pts I and III. G. H. Duckworth, one of Charles Booth's

collaborators, wrote a useful article on the subject, 'The making, prevention and unmaking of a slum', *Journal of the Royal Institute of British Architects,* XXXIII (1926), 327–37. There is a valuable discussion and other points of reference arising from a study of the Bedford estate in D. J. Olsen, *Town Planning in London: the Eighteenth and Nineteenth Centuries* (1964). Harry Barnes, *The Slum: Its Story and Solution* (1931), is a polemic aimed at invigorating slum clearance in the early 1930s, but it does contain some rather disorganised historical data; his *Housing: the Facts and the Future* (1923), is still more generalised. Of more value for historical purposes is B. S. Rowntree, *The Slum Problem* (1928). It should be noted that the *Report of the Committee on Housing in Greater London* (The Milner-Holland Report), HMSO, Cmd 2605 (1965), is not only the first major investigation of the subject since the *RC on the Housing of the Working Classes, 1884–85,* but contains what is in many respects as valid an analysis of the situation that existed at the end of the Victorian period as that existing in the 1960s. Valuable bibliographies covering periodicals, books and pamphlets directly related to the subject are contained in K. C. Brooks, *A Bibliography of Municipal Administration and City Conditions* (1897); Sidney Webb, *The House Famine* (1900); M. J. Elsas, *Housing Before the War and After* (1942); W. F. Stolper, 'British monetary policy and the housing boom', *Quarterly Journal of Economics,* LVI (1942), 165–6; J. B. Cullingworth, *Housing Needs and Planning Policy* (1960); Ruth Glass, 'Urban sociology in Great Britain: a trend report', *Current Sociology,* IV (1955), 5–76.

11. See (Charles Hindley), *'The Catnach Press': A Collection of the Books and Woodcuts of James Catnach* (1869), and *The Life and Times of James Catnach* (1878).
12. See also Jon Bee, *A Dictionary of the Turf, the Ring, the Chase, the Pit, of Bon-Ton, and the Varieties of Life* (1823), 161.
13. Pierce Egan, *Life in London* (1821), 274, 288, 343, 345–6.
14. To Daniel Maclise, 20 November 1840. I am grateful to my colleague, Philip Collins, for this reference, as I am for his help with Dickens's periodicals.
15. Henry Mayhew, *The Great World of London* (1856), 46; J. S. Farmer and W. E. Henley, *Slang and its Analogues* (1890–1904), *s.v.* 'slum'.
16. *The Times,* 17 January 1845: 'My reason for troubling you with this letter is to inform you that, in the thick of the once renowned "slums" of St Giles's, there has existed one of the finest springs in the metropolis.'
17. See Cardinal Wiseman, *An Appeal to the Reason and Good Feeling of the English People on the Subject of the Catholic Hierarchy* (1850), 30 – the passage referring to the 'labyrinths of lanes and courts, and alleys and slums, nests of ignorance, vice, depravity and crime' around Westminster Abbey was widely quoted in the national press. See also F. Cross, 'A word to the wise: dwelling houses', *The Builder,* VII (1849), 411; 'As the homes, so the people', *Ragged School Union Magazine,* XIV (1862), 145. Interest in the etymological origins of the term was aroused long before it had ceased to be slang: see *Notes & Queries,* III (1851), 224, 284; VI (1852), 111; XLVIII (1873), 328–9, 413.
18. See Stanley Alderson, *Britain in the Sixties: Housing* (1962), especially ch. 2.
19. Statutory overcrowding did not become punishable in the courts until the passage of the Housing Act in 1935.
20. As suggested, perhaps, by Marcel Cohen's study *Pour une sociologie du language* (Paris, 1956).
21. A slum has recently been defined as 'a building, group of buildings, or area characterised by overcrowding, deterioration, unsanitary conditions or absence of facilities or amenities which, because of these conditions or any of them, endangers the health, safety or morals of its inhabitants or the community': United Nations, *Urban Land Policies* (New York, 1952), 173, quoted by Nels Andersen, *The Urban*

Community: A World Perspective (New York, 1959), before going on (191–3) to enumerate its salient characteristics.

22. See Robert A. Woods *et al.*, *The Poor in Great Cities; Their Problems and What is Being Done to Solve Them* (1896).

23. For a general view of the relationship between the heritage of nineteenth-century slums and the process of urbanisation considered globally, see Andersen, *The Urban Community*, especially ch. 8, and Charles Abrams, *Man's Struggle for Shelter in an Urbanizing World* (Cambridge, Mass., 1964); Marshall B. Clinard, *Slums and Community Development* (1966), is the most thorough historical survey yet to appear on the slum and specifically deals with British slums of the nineteenth century. See, too, Lewis Mumford, *The City in History* (1961).

24. Leo F. Schnore and Henry Fagin (eds.), *Urban Affairs and Annual Reviews*, vol. I, *Urban Research and Policy Planning* (Beverly Hills, 1967). For a more specific example, see Jane Jacobs, *The Death and Life of Great American Cities* (New York, 1961), especially ch. 15. An unusually suggestive view of the relation between the products of the past and the problems of the present is offered by C. J. Stokes, 'A theory of slums', *Land Economics*, XXXVIII (1962), 187–97.

25. Charles Booth, *Life and Labour of the People in London*: 1st series, *Poverty* (4 vols.); 2nd series, *Industry* (5 vols.); 3rd series, *Religious Influences* (7 vols.); *Notes on Social Influences and Conclusion* (1 vol.) (1902–3).

26. H. W. Llewellyn-Smith (ed.), *The New Survey of London Life and Labour* (9 vols., 1930–5).

27. For example, Howard Marshall and Avice Trevelyan, *Slum* (1933); C. R. A. Martin, *Slums and Slummers: A Sociological Treatise on the Housing Problem* (1935).

28. Quoted by Mumford, *The City in History*, 433.

29. See Henry Jephson, *The Sanitary Evolution of London* (1907); S. E. Finer, *The Life and Times of Edwin Chadwick* (1952); R. A. Lewis, *Edwin Chadwick and the Public Health Movement* (1952); David Roberts, *Victorian Origins of the British Welfare State* (New Haven, 1960); Royston Lambert, *Sir John Simon, 1816–1904, and English Social Administration* (1963); M. W. Flinn (ed.), *Report on the Sanitary Condition of the Labouring Population of Great Britain, 1842, by Edwin Chadwick* (1965).

30. It was subtitled, *Being Sketches and Illustrations, of Bethnal Green. A Type of the Condition of the Metropolis and other Large Towns* (1848); see R. J. Roberts, 'Sanitary Ramblings: being Sketches and Illustrations of Bethnal Green, by H. Gavin', *East London Papers*, VIII (1965), 110–18. See, too, his *The Habitations of the Industrial Classes: Their Influence on the Physical and Moral Conditions of those Classes* (1851).

31. William Felkin, 'Moral statistics of a district near Gray's Inn Court, London, in 1836', *JSSL*, I (1839), 541–2; Rev. George Weight, 'Statistics of the Parish of St George-the-Martyr, Southwark', *JSSL*, III (1840), 50–71; 'Report of a committee of the Statistical Society of London on the State of the Working Classes in the Parishes of St Margaret and St John, Westminster', *JSSL*, III (1840), 14–24; R. W. Rawson, 'Results of some inquiries into the condition and education of the poorer classes in the Parish of St Marylebone in 1838', *JSSL*, VI (1843), 44–8; C. R. Weld, 'On the condition of the working classes in the inner ward of St George's Parish, Hanover Square', *JSSL*, VI (1843), 17–27; 'Report of a committee of the Statistical Society of London to investigate the state of the inhabitants and their dwellings in Church Lane, St Giles', *JSSL*, XI (1848), 1–18; 'Report to the Council of the Statistical Society of London from a committee appointed to make an investigation into the state of the poorer classes in St George's-in-the-East', *JSSL*, XI (1848), 193–249. See, too, Charles Cochrane, *How to Improve the Homes of the People!* (1849); (R. H.

Cheney?), 'The charities and the poor of London', *Quarterly Review*, CXCIV (1855), 407–50, and Thomas James, 'Labourers' homes', *Quarterly Review*, CVII (1860), 267–97 (attributions for the last two articles are from *The Wellesley Index to Victorian Periodicals*, ed. by Walter E. Houghton).

32. Henry Mayhew, *London Labour and the London Poor: A Cyclopaedia of the Conditions and Earnings of Those That Will Work, Those that Cannot Work, and Those that Will Not Work* (4 vols., 1861–2). It is interesting to compare his work with that of Charles Manby Smith, *Curiosities of London Life: or, Phases, Physiological and Social of the Great Metropolis* (1853), in which more street-folk are paraded, along with the kind of low-life reporting that soon became more widespread. His *The Little World of London; or, Pictures in Little of London Life* (1857), contains more general clippings, including one on the slum 'Crocodile Court'. Mayhew's own *London Characters* (1870, 1874, 1881), is a light-hearted, even comic, view of the passing show.

33. See also Douglas Jerrold, *St Giles and St James* (1851); Augustus Mayhew, *Kitty Lamere; or, A Dark Page in London Life* (1855), and *Paved with Gold* (1857, 1884). Apart from fictional writing, there are numerous references available. Note, for example: John Garwood, *The Million-Peopled City: or, One-half of the People of London made known to the Other Half* (1853); Catherine Sinclair, *London Homes* (1853); Viscount Ingestre (ed.), *Meliora; or, Better Times to Come: First Series* (1852), containing, along with clergymen's essays on topics like 'The beer-shop evil', 'Popular investments', 'Rich and poor', Henry Mayhew's 'Home is home, be it never so homely' – a revolting description of that 'Venice of drains', Jacob's Island in Bermondsey, and a rare glimpse of Mayhew's own incredulity; *Second Series* (1854) is equally valuable – the article by the Hon. and Rev. Sidney Godolphin Osborne entitled 'Immortal sewerage', though pertaining to Glasgow, is valuable as a description of slum life and of a type of middle-class attitude towards it. One of the periodicals that most clearly revealed this polarisation of social attitudes was the *Ragged School Union Magazine*: see particularly 'The poor' and 'The low haunts of London', III (1851), 14, 200–5. The *Illustrated London News* dwelt on these themes occasionally at this time, as in the verses entitled 'A scene from London life' (13 December 1851). For a foreigner's comment on 'cette antithèse sociale . . . cette société monstreuse', see Edmond Texier, *Lettres sur l'Angleterre* (Paris, 1851), 10–15. Compare this tradition with Walter Greenwood's *How the Other Man Lives* (1939).

34. Examples of this genre are: Max Schlesinger (trans. Otto Wenckstern), *Saunterings in and about London* (1853); J. E. Ritchie, *The Night Side of London* (1857, 1858, 1861), *Here and There in London* (1859), *About London* (1860). See also 'The perils of the city', *Ragged School Union Magazine*, XI (1859), 61–4; 'Our workfield', *ibid.*, XIV (1862), 51, and the works of Charles Manby Smith cited in n. 32.

35. John Knox, *The Masses Without! A Pamphlet for the Times, on the Sanitary, Social, Moral and Healthier Condition of the Masses, who inhabit the Alleys, Courts, Wynds, Garrets, Cellars, Lodging-houses, Dens, and Hovels of Great Britain* (1857), 4, 30.

36. *The Servant Girl in London* (1840), 1.

37. R. Vaughan, *The Age of Great Cities: or, Modern Society Viewed in its Relation to Intelligence, Morals and Religion* (1843).

38. For the work of the community reformers like J. Minter Morgan, James Silk-Buckingham, Henry Solly, Ebeneezer Howard and others, see Ashworth, *Genesis of Modern British Town Planning*.

39. James Hogg, *London as It Is; being a Series of Observations on the Health, Habits and Amusements of the People* (1837).

40. Richard Seeley, *The Perils of the Nation: An Appeal to the Legislature, the Clergy, and the Higher and Middle Classes* (1843).

41. James Grant, *Lights and Shadows of London Life* (2 vols., 1842), I, 163–5; this work was regarded by the author as a companion to his earlier writings – *The Great Metropolis* (2 vols., 1836–7), and *Travels in Town* (1839). His *Sketches in London* (1838, 1840, 1850, 1861), despite some excellent lithographs by Halbot K. Browne, is less useful here; compare this with his *Pictures of Life: The Dwellings of the Poor* (1855).

42. Thomas Beames, *The Rookeries of London: Past, Present, and Prospective* (1851).

43. Henry Morley, 'Wild court tamed', *Household Words*, XII (1855), 85–7.

44. George Godwin, *London Shadows* (1854), *Town Swamps and Social Bridges* (1859), and *Another Blow for Life* (1864); John Hollingshead, *Ragged London in 1861* (1861) – a valuable review of this work in conjunction with Mayhew appeared in *Meliora*, IV (1862), 297–312. The same writer's *Under Bow Bells: A City Book for All Readers* (1860), reprinted pieces from *Household Words* and kept clear of the slums.

45. See Henry Morley, *Gossip* (1857), and *Early Papers and Some Memories* (1891); W. H. Wills, *Old Leaves: Gathered from Household Words* (1860); (James Payn), *Lights and Shadows of London Life* (1867). The most prolific and revealing writer on the slums and the curiosities of the back-streets in this whole group was James Greenwood, the self-styled 'amateur casual', who for a time edited the *Pall Mall Gazette*. All the following are what he once described as 'public faithful photographs, open pictures of daily life in London', and are in some respects a unique record: *A Night in a Workhouse* (1866); *The Seven Curses of London* (1869); *The Wilds of London* (1874); *Unsentimental Journeys; or, Byways of the Modern Babylon* (1867); *Undercurrents of London Life* (1880); *Low-Life Deeps; an Account of the Strange Fish to be Found There* (1876, 1881); *In Strange Company; being the Experiences of a Roving Correspondent* (1883). Some shorter, and semi-fictional writings of his having definite value are: *Odd People in Odd Places; or, the Great Residuum* (1883); *Dining with Duke Humphrey; or, Curiosities of Life* (c. 1875); *Tag, Rag & Co.: Sketches of the People* (1883); *Almost Lost: A Tale of Old Pye Street* (1883); *The Little Ragamuffins; or, Outcast London* (1884); *Jerry Jacksmith of Lower London* (1890). He also wrote a number of somewhat melodramatic stories on similar themes, such as *Jack Stedfast; or, Wreck and Rescue* (c. 1875); *By Hook or By Crook* (c. 1875); *On the Tramp* (1883). For other material of this kind, though not exclusively concerned with the slums, see: G. A. Sala, *Twice Round the Clock; or, The Hours of the Day and Night in London* (1859), which was admiringly dedicated to Augustus Mayhew for his 'Photographs of fact', and tellingly illustrated by William McConnell; his *London Up to Date* (1894), was a much less successful attempt on the same theme; *Gaslight and Daylight, with some London Scenes they Shine Upon* (1860), is more useful; J. E. Ritchie, *Days and Nights in London; or, Studies in Black and Gray* (1880). Among the articles from Dickens's periodicals which provide valuable material and have not been printed elsewhere, are the following: *Household Words*: (G. A. Sala), 'Down Whitechapel, far away', VII (1853), 569–73; 'Bright chanticleer' (Seven Dials), XI (1855), 204–9; (Henry Morley), 'Death's doors', IX (1854), 398–402; 'Piping days' (Somers Town), X (1854), 196–9; 'Turpin's corner' (A Southwark slum), XVII (1858); 'Life and death in St Giles', XVII (1858), 525–8: *All the Year Round*: 'Every man's poison' (South London), XIV (1865), 372–6; 'Home, sweet home' (Westminster), XV (1866), 303–6.

46. *Punch* had surprisingly little comment to offer, either verbal or visual, on life in the slums until the appearance of *The Bitter Cry of Outcast London* in 1883, but see 'The nemesis of neglect', 29 September 1880. The *Illustrated London News* had little more

that was specifically representative of the slums themselves: see 'The dwellings of the poor in London', 13 March 1875; also 19 November 1887, 10 and 31 January 1891.

47. An East End Incumbent (G. H. MacGill), *The London Poor and the Inequality of the Rates Raised for their Relief* (1858).

48. (Mrs) L(ydia) N. R(anyard), *The Missing Link; or, Bible-women in the Homes of the London Poor* (1859). See the valuable commentary on this by R. H. Cheney, 'The Missing Link and the London poor', *Quarterly Review*, CVIII (1860), 1–34. See, too, L., A. V., ed. Mrs Mary Bayly, *The Ministry of Woman and the London Poor* (1870), which describes such activities in the East End. The soup tradition is an old one; a Leicester Square Soup Kitchen was established in 1847: Anon., *A Plan for Preventing Destitution and Mendicancy in the British Metropolis* (1850).

49. C. B. P. Bosanquet, *London: Some Account of Its Growth, Charitable Agencies and Wants* (1868). For some indication of the scope of formal charitable endowments, see Sampson Low, Jr, *The Charities of London* (1850); see, too, H. Bosanquet, *Social Work in London, 1869 to 1912: A History of the Charity Organisation Society* (1914); C. L. Mowat, 'Charity and casework in late Victorian London: the work of the Charity Organisation Society', *Social Service Review*, XXXI (1957), 258–9; and David Owen, *English Philanthropy, 1660–1960* (1965), especially chs. 5 and 8.

50. Mrs (Mary) Bayly, *Ragged Homes and How to Mend Them* (1860), and *Mended Homes, and What Repaired Them* (1861); G. W. M'Cree, *Day & Night in St Giles'* (1862), *Twenty Years in St Giles'* (1869) and *The Moral Condition of London* (1869); Robert Gregory, *Sermons on the Poorer Classes of London* (1869); 'The riverside visitor' (Thomas Wright), *The Great Army: Sketches of Life and Character in a Thames-side District* (2 vols., 1875); Rev. D. Rice Jones, *From Cellar to Garrett* (1875); Anon., *Work About the Five Dials* (1878); A Parish Deaconess, *Sketches from Life, or Work Among the Poor of London* (1879).

51. Douglas Jerrold, *St Giles and St James* (1851), 16. In this connection, see 'The natural history of society', *Westminster Review*, XXXVI (1841), 358–80, and 'The geology of society', *Punch*, I (1841), 157.

52. See also *Our New Masters* (1873), in which he maintained that a great gulf was fixed between the 'idle' and 'industrious' poor, and that 'by far the largest proportion of the suffering incidental to poverty is to be found on the industrious side of it' (360–1). His novels – e.g., *Johnny Robinson: the Story of the Childhood and Schooldays of an 'Intelligent Artisan'* (2 vols., 1858) and *The Bane of Life* (3 vols., 1870) – are far less useful.

53. Henry Morley, 'The quiet poor', *Household Words*, IX (1854), 201–6.

54. 'The low haunts of London', *Ragged School Union Magazine*, III (1851), 200.

55. K. J. Fielding, 'Sir Francis Burdett and Oliver Twist', *Review of English Studies*, II (1951), 157.

56. J. G. Lockhart, *Cosmo Gordon Lang* (1949), 96. He was a curate in Leeds, 1890–3, and later Bishop of Stepney, 1901–8; the comment refers to Leeds – 'I never saw anything worse, or indeed as bad, in East London,' he wrote.

57. Walter Besant, 'A riverside parish', in Robert A. Woods, *The Poor in Great Cities*, 273.

58. (John Pearce), *Mr George R. Sims* (1882), provides a brief biography.

59. G. R. Sims, *How the Poor Live* (1883), and *How the Poor Live and Horrible London* (1889) comprised the two sets of essays bound together; his *The Social Kaleidoscope, 1st and 2nd series* (1881), *Ballads of Babylon* (1880), and other numerous writings contain little of interest in this respect, but *Living London: Its Work and Its Play, Its Sights and Its Scenes* (3 vols., 1901–3 and 1904–6), is an illustrated record of

considerable value. There is a little about this aspect of his writing career in his autobiography, *My Life* (1917), 135–8.

60. (W. C. Mearns), *The Bitter Cry of Outcast London: An Inquiry Into the Condition of the Abject Poor* (1883). It has also been attributed to W. C. Preston. It went through several editions; one, dated 1913, and apparently published on behalf of Frederick N. Charrington, the temperance reformer, was superscribed 'Tower Hamlets Mission', and the reference to Collier's Rents and the mission work of the Congregational Union was replaced by a more general homily. Rev. Brooke Lambert, 'The outcast poor', *Contemporary Review*, XLIV (1883), 916–23; Rev. Andrew Mearns, 'The outcast poor', *ibid.*, XLIV (1883), 924–33.

61. *Punch*, 10 November 1883. The highlights of the campaign were: 'The Devil's walk', 17 November 1883; 'A sigh from the slums', 'Seeing's believing', 'The house that capital built' and 'Unjust rates', 1 December 1883; 'Strangers', 29 December 1883; 'The slum-dwellers' Saturday night', 26 January 1884.

62. Hugh MacCallam, *The Distribution of the Poor in London* (1883); Rev. Christopher Carruthers, *The Root of the Matter; or, the only Cure for the Bitter Cry of Outcast London, and other Similar Evils of the Present Day* (1884); Rev. J. Edmond Long, *The Hopeful Cry of Outcast London* (1884); G. W. M'Cree, *Sweet Herbs for the Bitter Cry; or, Remedies for Horrible and Outcast London* (1884); Henry Clarke, *Dwellings for the Poor* (1884); Rev. David Rice Jones, *In the Slums* (1884); Countess of Tankerville, *A Bright Spot in Outcast London* (1884) and *From the Depths* (1885); Forster Crozier, *Methodism and 'The Bitter Cry of Outcast London'* (1885); Anon. (W. D. Preston?), *'Light and Shade': Pictures of London Life* (1885); Andrew Mearns, *London and Its Teeming Toilers: Who They Are, and Where They Live* (1885); Alfred Jones, *The Homes of the Poor in Westminster* (1885); F. E. Smiley, *The Evangelisation of a Great City; or, The Churches' Answer to the Bitter Cry of Outcast London* (Philadelphia, 1890); General Booth, *In Darkest England and the Way Out* (1890); Rev. A. Osborne Jay, *Life in Darkest London: A Hint to General Booth* (1891) and *A Story of Shoreditch* (1896); 'The riverside visitor' (Thomas Wright), *The Pinch of Poverty: Sufferings and Heroism of the London Poor* (1892); Arthur Sherwell, *Life in West London: A Study and a Contrast* (1897); George Haw, *No Room to Live: The Plaint of Overcrowded London* (1900).

63. Some of the evidence relevant to his point is in C. J. Stewart, *The Housing Question in London, 1855–1900* (1900), and LCC, *Housing of the Working Classes in London* (1913), and the works by E. R. Dewsnup and J. S. Nettlefold (see n. 10); see J. F. Sykes, 'The results of the state, municipal and organized private action on the housing of the working classes in London . . .', *JRSS*, LXIV (1901); see, too, *SC on Artisans' and Labourers' Dwellings Improvements Acts and Metropolitan Streets Improvements Acts, 1872 and 1877, First and Second Reports and Minutes of Evidence, PP*, 1881 (358), VII, 395 ff., and 1882 (235), VII, 249 ff.; *RC on the Housing of the Working Classes, First Report and Minutes of Evidence, PP*, 1884–5 (C. 4402, C. 4402-I, C. 4402-II), XXX; *Buildings erected within the Metropolis and City of London in pursuance of the Artisans' and Labourers' Dwellings Improvement Acts, PP*, 1886, LVII 297–8. An important source of information on the connections between systems of land tenure and the development of slums is the *SC on Town Holdings*, 1886–92, which covered the whole country: *PP*, 1886 (213), XII; 1887 (260), XIII; 1888 (313), XXII; 1889 (251), XV; 1890 (341), XVIII; 1892 (214), XVIII.

64. To ship the poor abroad was an old cry: for some characteristic ways of putting it in an urban context, see: James Greenwood, *The Seven Curses of London* (1870), ch. 24; Edward White, *Land Reform and Emigration, the Two Remedies for Overcrowding* (1884); Arnold White, *The Problems of a Great City* (1886); Lord Brabazon, *Social*

Arrows (2nd edn, 1887), 252–70; General Booth, *In Darkest England*. For one type of home colonisation as a solution to the slums and general overcrowding, see Henry Solly, *Home Colonisation: Rehousing the Industrial Classes: or Village Communities v. Town Rookeries* (1884).

65. For two very different kinds of negative answer, see E. S. Robertson, *The State and the Slums* (1884), which was published by the Liberty and Property Defence League, and William Morris, *News from Nowhere* (1891).

66. A complete bibliography would be very extensive, but the following represent the most important reactions: Sir Richard Cross, 'Homes for the poor in London', *Nineteenth Century*, XII (1882), 231–41; 'Homes of the poor', *ibid.*, XV (1884), 150–66; 'Housing the poor', *ibid.*, XVII (1885), 926–47; George Howell, 'Dwellings of the poor', *ibid.*, XIII (1883), 992–1007; Octavia Hill, Lord Shaftesbury, H. O. Arnold-Foster and William Glazier, 'Common sense and the dwellings of the poor', *ibid.*, XIV (1883), 925–63; Lord Salisbury, 'Labourers' and artisans' dwellings', *National Review*, II (1883), 301–16; Alfred Marshall, M. G. Mulhall, Elijah Hoole, 'The housing of the London poor: (1) Where to house them; (2) Ways and means; (3) The cost of tenements', *Contemporary Review*, XLV (1884), 224–40; Edwin Chadwick, 'London centralised', *ibid.*, XLV (1884), 794–810; John Rae, 'State socialism', *ibid.*, LIV (1888), 224–45, and 'The betterment tax in America', *ibid.*, LVII (1890), 644–60; Joseph Chamberlain, 'Labourers' and artisans' dwellings', *Fortnightly Review*, XXXIV (1883), 761–76; D. F. Schloss, 'Healthy homes for the working classes', *ibid.*, XLIII (1888), 526–37. See also F. H. Millington, *The Housing of the Poor* (1895); C. F. G. Masterman, *The Heart of the Empire* (1901), and his chapter on the English city in L. R. F. Oldershaw (ed.), *England: a Nation* (1904), 44–94.

67. For a useful brief guide and commentary, which has been of some value in writing this paper (especially in its analysis of anti-urbanism), see Ruth Glass, 'Urban sociology in Great Britain' (n. 10). For a more general assessment of Booth and his work, see T. S. Simey and M. B. Simey, *Charles Booth, Social Scientist* (1960).

68. The Booth Collection at the British Library of Political and Economic Science contains 57 volumes of loose papers and 392 notebooks, and appears to be little used.

69. For example, three-deckers like Joseph Hatton, *Cruel London* (1878), or B. L. Farjeon, *Toilers of Babylon* (1888).

70. Not without some argument: H. D. Traill, editor of *Literature*, considered Morrison's portrayal of the Jago as 'a monstrous libel' on the ground that in a 'very slum selected by an enterprising realist as material for "copy", one of our great Free Churches has been for many years providing the means of grace and kindling the hope of glory': unattributed newspaper cutting, Booth Collection, vol. B 392, 41. Note also Morrison's *The Hole in the Wall* (1902).

71. See Joseph Leftwich, 'Israel Zangwill and the East End', and Eric Domville, 'Gloomy city, or the depths of Hell': the presentation of the East End in fiction between 1880–1914', *East London Papers*, VIII (1965), 29–39 and 98–109.

72. 'Ragged London'. *Meliora*, IV (1862), 300.

73. (Thomas Wright), *The Pinch of Poverty* (1892), 187.

74. There is no comprehensive published account of the history of building regulations during this period. C. C. Knowles, 'A history of the London Buildings Acts, the District Surveyors, and their Association' (author's MS, 1947) is the only account available in the Members' Library, Greater London Council, County Hall.

75. For an interesting comment on this, see: J. M. Mackintosh, *Trends of Opinion about the Public Health*, 1901–51 (1953), 1–2.

76. C. F. G. Masterman, *The Condition of England* (1909), 72.

77. Except where indicated otherwise, all references to population figures that follow have been taken from the censuses.

78. See, for example, *Household Words*, I (1850), 297.
79. The information on Sultan Street belongs to a much larger piece of research I am doing on the social structure of Camberwell in the nineteenth century as a complementary study to my *Victorian Suburb: a study of the growth of Camberwell* (1961), and I am grateful to acknowledge the financial help given to me in this connection by a Leverhulme Research Award. Some of the methods and materials involved are described in a paper written jointly with Mrs Bannon Baker, my research assistant on the project, entitled, 'The possibilities of computerising census data', in H. J. Dyos (ed.), *The Study of Urban History* (1968).
80. It does also make the more straightforward point, perhaps, that the families concerned may simply have become relatively immobile once the children had been born, because the proportion of Camberwell children at large who were born outside London was roughly twice as great.
81. Dyos, *Victorian Suburb*, 1, 9–13.
82. The agricultural value of land 'improved' by building development, i.e., the rent paid to the ground landlord under the leasehold system of land tenure.
83. *PP*, 1887 (C. 5228), XV, *Condition of the Working Classes: Tabulation of the Statements made by Men living in Certain Selected Districts of London in March, 1887*. The areas it covered were the registration sub-districts of St George's-in-the-East, Battersea, Hackney and Deptford. Despite the warning given that the details of the returns were 'of very small statistical value', there is a very general pattern discernible in them.
84. See E. J. Hobsbawm, 'The nineteenth-century London labour market', in *London: Aspects of Change* (1964), Report no. 3, edited by the Centre for Urban Studies by Ruth Glass and others, 3–28.
85. B. F. C. Costelloe, 'The housing problem', *Transactions of Manchester Statistical Society* (1898–9), 48, quoted in Ashworth, *Genesis of Modern British Town Planning*, 20.
86. See John Nelson Tarn, 'The Peabody Donation Fund: the role of a housing society in the nineteenth century', *VS*, X (1966), 7–38.
87. See above, Chs. 6 and 7, and H. J. Dyos, 'Counting the cost of railways', *Amateur Historian*, IV (1957), 191–7.
88. Rev. G. W. M'Cree, *Day & Night in St Giles'* (1862), 6.
89. (C. G. Stonestreet), *Domestic Union, or London as it Should Be* (1800).
90. See above, Ch. 5. For other contemporary attitudes, see 'A quarter of a century of London street improvement', *The Builder*, XXIV (1866), 877–8, 988–9, and 'Victoria Street', *The Builder*, IX (1851), 516; also Thomas Miller, *Picturesque Sketches of London, Past and Present* (1852), ch. 15: St. Giles's.
91. See Sir John Summerson, *John Nash* (1935); James Elmes, *Metropolitan Improvements; or, London in the Nineteenth Century* (1827).
92. See the references above in Ch. 7, n. 87.
93. Ebeneezer Clarke, Jr. *The Hovel and the Home; or, Improved Dwellings for the Labouring Classes, and how to obtain them* (1863), 31.
94. William Acton, *Prostitution . . . in London and Other Large Cities* (1857), 180.
95. Quoted from the Demolition Statement submitted with its Bill by the Metropolitan Board of Works under the provisions of a HL Standing Order adopted in 1853: HL Record Office.
96. See Tarn, 'The Peabody Donation Fund', and his references.
97. These are mostly embodied in LCC (Local Government and Taxation Committee), *London Statistics* (since 1890), though there are numerous separate memoranda compiled by special committees.
98. See, for example, Robert Williams's analysis of London's one-room dwellers in his

The Face of the Poor (1897), 10–11, which he drew from his own elaborate classification of London tenements into 32 categories, ranging from 1,864 persons in Class I who had 2,840 cubic feet apiece, to the 84 persons he could identify in Class XXXII, who were living, moving and breathing in 80 cubic feet of space, 12 or more to the room. He reckoned to have identified about 326,000 people then living in London two or more to a room.

99. Robert Williams, *More Light and Air for Londoners* (1894), 6.
100. There is very little evidence on landed proprietors in towns, for example, in F. M. L. Thompson, *English Landed Society in the Nineteenth Century* (1963). London was excluded from the HL, *Owners of Land: England and Wales, Return for 1872–3, PP,* 1874 (Cmd 1097) (The 'New Domesday'), summarised by John Bateman in *The Great Landowners of Great Britain and Ireland* (1883). But see Frank Banfield, *The Great Landlords of London* (1888), and 'Noblesse Oblige' (Howard Evans), *Our Old Nobility* (2 vols., 1879). For the arithmetic of radicalism in this regard, see Fabian Tract No. 5, *Facts for Socialists* (London, 1887).
101. Henry Lazarus, *Landlordism; an Illustration of the Rise and Spread of Slumland* (1892).
102. See n. 10.

10. The speculative builders and developers of Victorian London

1. E. W. Cooney, 'Capital exports and investment in building in Britain and the USA', *Economica*, XVI (1949), 347–54; A. K. Cairncross, *Home and Foreign Investment, 1870–1913* (1953); Brinley Thomas, *Migration and Economic Growth* (1954); B. Weber, 'A new index of residential construction, 1830–1950', *SJPE*, I (1954), 104–32; Hamish Richards and J. Parry Lewis, 'House building in the south Wales coalfield, 1851–1913', *MSESS*, XXIV (1956), 289–301; A. K. Cairncross and B. Weber, 'Fluctuations in building in Great Britain, 1785–1849', *EcHR*, IX (1956), 283–97; J. Parry Lewis, 'Building cycles: a regional model and its national setting', *Economic Journal*, LXX (1960), 519–35, and 'Indices of house-building in the Manchester conurbation, South Wales and Great Britain, 1851–1913', *SJPE*, VIII (1961), 148–56; E. W. Cooney, 'Long waves in building in the British economy of the nineteenth century', *SJPE*, XIII (1960), 257–69; A. R. Hall, 'Long waves in building in the British economy of the nineteenth century: a comment', *SJPE*, XIV (1961), 330–3; H. J. Habakkuk, 'Fluctuations in house-building in Britain and the United States in the nineteenth century', *JEcH*, XXII (1962), 198–230; S. B. Saul, 'House building in England, 1890–1914', *EcHR*, XV (1962), 119–37; A. G. Kenwood, 'Residential building activity in north-eastern England, 1853–1913', *MSESS*, XXXI (1963), 115–28; J. Parry Lewis, *Building Cycles and Britain's Growth* (1965).
2. G. T. Jones, *Increasing Returns*, ed. Colin Clark (1933), Pt II; H. W. Singer, 'An index of urban land rents and house rents in England and Wales, 1845–1913', *Econometrica*, IX (1941), 221–30; K. Maiwald, 'An index of building costs in the United Kingdom, 1845–1938', *EcHR*, VII (1954–5), 187–203; B. Weber, 'A new index of house rents for Great Britain, 1874–1913', *SJPE*, VII (1960), 232–7.
3. R. W. Postgate, *The Builders' History* (1923), is concerned essentially with trades unionism; Norman Davey, *Building in Britain* (1964), and Marian Bowley, *The British Building Industry* (1966), do not treat the nineteenth century in any detail; H. M. Colvin, *A Biographical Dictionary of English Architects, 1660–1840* (1954), mentions some organisational changes among building firms. Sir Stephen Tallents' *Man and Boy* (1943), deals briefly with his great grandfather, Thomas Cubitt; some information on James Burton is given in Sir John Summerson, *Georgian London*

(1945); both Burton and Cubitt figure importantly, among others, in D. J. Olsen, *Town Planning in London in the Eighteenth and Nineteenth Centuries* (1964). K. A. Middlemass, *The Master Builders* (1963), is about a number of public works contractors. Among unpublished works that touch on the building process in London are R. C. W. Cox, 'Some aspects of the urban development of Croydon, 1870–1940' (M.A. thesis, Leicester University, 1966); D. A. Reeder, 'The use of short-term building and repairing leases by the crown and corporate landowners on English urban estates in the nineteenth century, with special reference to London' (M.A. thesis, University of Leicester, 1961); and his Ph.D. thesis mentioned above; Brenda Swann, 'A study of some London estates in the eighteenth century' (Ph.D. thesis, London University, 1964).

4. See E. L. Tarbuck, *Handbook of House Property* (1875); Alfred Emden, *The Law Relating to Building Leases and Building Contracts, the Improvement of Land by, and the Construction of, Buildings* (1882); Fowler Maitland, *Building Estates: A Rudimentary Treatise on the Development, Sale, Purchase, and General Management of Building Land* (1883); C. H. Sargant, *Ground Rents and Building Leases* (1886), and *Urban Rating* (1890); and Tom Bright, *The Development of Building Estates* (1910). For the general background, see F. M. L. Thompson, *English Landed Society in the Nineteenth Century* (1963), though there is little here on estate development as such.

5. As, for example, on St George's Fields on Southwark, where the Hedger family seized their opportunity between 1773 and 1810 in a massive building speculation beyond the control of the landlord, the commissioners of the Bridge House Estates. See *The Survey of London*, XXV: *St George's Fields*, ed. Ida Darlington (1955), 52–6. An interesting brief review of estate management in fifteen towns before the Victorian period is C. W. Chalklin, 'Urban housing estates in the eighteenth century', *Urban Studies*, V (1968), 67–85.

6. For more sanguine control of rapidly appreciating land, see H. J. Dyos, *Victorian Suburb: a study of the growth of Camberwell* (1961), 91–6.

7. I owe all the information I have on Blake to Dr Reeder.

8. Marian Bowley, 'Housing statistics', in *Sources and Nature of the Statistics of the United Kingdom*, ed. M. G. Kendall (1952), 317; G. T. Jones, *Increasing Returns* 87–8.

9. E. W. Cooney, 'The origins of the Victorian master builders', *EcHR*, VIII (1955), 167–76.

10. For some general information about Barbon, see N. G. Brett-James, 'A speculative London builder of the seventeenth century, Dr Nicholas Barbon', *Transactions of the London and Middlesex Archaeological Society*, VI (1933), 110–45; and Summerson, *Georgian London*, 28–35.

11. On Burton, Cubitt and their contemporaries, see particularly the works of Summerson, Olsen and Cooney already cited. A full-length study of Cubitt based, I am told, on a wide selection of new material, is being written by Miss Hermione Hobhouse, to whom I am grateful for some general information. There are useful obituaries of Cubitt in *The Builder*, XIII (1855), 629–30; *Gentleman's Magazine*, XIV (1856), 202–5, 382; and *Minutes of the Proceedings of the Institution of Civil Engineers*, XVI (1857), 158–62.

12. On the general tendency in the building trade toward the practice of contracting in gross, see M. H. Port, 'The Office of Works and building contracts in early nineteenth-century England', *EcHR*, XX (1967), 94–110. See also J. Nisbet, 'Quantity surveying in London during the nineteenth century', *Journal of the Royal Institution of Chartered Surveyors*, XXXI (1951–2), 522–8.

13. For example, Smith and Taylor, who were the contractors for both the Foreign Office and the India Office: *PP*, 1867 (3873), XXXII, *Report of the RC on Trade Unions, Minutes of Evidence*, Q 2854 (George Francis Trollope).

14. J. R. T. Hughes, 'Problems of industrial change', in *1859: Entering an Age of Crisis*, ed. P. Appleman, William A. Madden, and Michael Wolff (Bloomington, 1959), 53, using data from G. Shaw Lefevre, *Trade Societies and Strikes* (1860), and the *Economist*, 6 August 1859.

15. *PP*, 1867 (3873), XXXII, *Report, RC on Trades Unions*, QQ 2767–2854 (George Smith of Smith & Taylor); *PP*, 1892 (C. 6795–VI), XXXVI, *Report, RC on Labour*, 1892, Pt II, QQ 17382–5 (George Dew); Q 18460 (William Knox).

16. *PP*, 1833 (690), VI, *Minutes of Evidence, Report of the SC on Manufactures, Commerce, and Shipping*, Q 1690.

17. Jean M. Imray, 'The Mercers' Company and east London, 1750–1850: an exercise in urban development', *East London Papers*, IX (1966), 3–25.

18. See also James Noble, *The Professional Practice of Architects, and that of Measuring Surveyors, and Reference to Builders* (1836).

19. (Charles Hindley), *'The Catnach Press': A Collection of Books and Woodcuts of James Catnach* (1869).

20. Masonry, plumbing, painting, and plastering contributed around 7% each, and tiling 2% (G. T. Jones, *Increasing Returns*, 93).

21. *PP*, 1833 (690), VI, *Report of SC, Manufactures, Commerce and Shipping*, Q 1700 (Thomas Barton).

22. *PP*, 1857 (220), X, *Report, SC on Bank Acts*, QQ 5411–15 (Edward Capps).

23. *Census of England and Wales, 1851* (1851): 85 builders, or 11.5% of the total, were entered as having no employees or no numbers stated.

24. As calculated from the District Surveyors' fees.

25. Cooney, 'Master builders', 167.

26. This was a purely welfare organisation, whose records have totally disappeared. It does not appear to have had any formal connection with the London Master Builders' Society which was formed in 1834 to combat trade unionism in the industry: its initial membership had been 15, but by 1867, when its secretary alleged that it contained all substantial builders in London, this had grown to 76. See *PP*, 1867, XXXII, *Report, RC on Trade Unions*, QQ 2580 ff. (Thomas Piper); see, too, Q 340 (G. Potter); QQ 386 ff. (G. F. Trollope). There had also come into existence some working builders' associations like the North-London and the Pimlico Working Builders' Associations, though very little seems to be known about them. See (J. M. Ludlow and C. Sully), The *Society for Promoting Working-Men's Associations* (1850).

27. *The Builder*, XXX (1872), 990.

28. London Master Builders' Association, Minute Book, 15 March 1875. I am grateful to the London Master Builders' Association for permission to use their records, which would make an excellent starting-point for the general study, which we lack, of industrial organisation and industrial relations in the building trade. There is no full-length study of the Association, though a brief history, entitled *Seventy-five Years On: 1872–1947*, was published in 1947, and there is a short history of the Association contained in the *London Master Builders' Association Handbook* for 1903, 10–19. There is also a certain amount of information in *Minutes of Evidence and Appendices*, *PP*, 1892 (C. 6795), XXXVI, *Report, RC on Labour*.

29. London Master Builders' Association, Minute Book, 10 February 1874.

30. J. H. Clapham, *An Economic History of Modern Britain*, vol. II, *Free Trade and Railways, 1850–1886* (1952), 146.

31. *The Post Office Directory of the Building Trades; comprising every trade and*

profession in any way connected with the Architectural and Building Trades throughout England, Scotland and Wales (1870), 30–54.

32. 1872 was a slacker year for building in London than 1871, and the physical output of the housing industry had probably fallen by about a third since 1869.

33. There are altogether nearly 1,000 large folio volumes covering the period 1845–1914, of which approximately one hundred belonging to the years 1853–70 are unfortunately missing; there are also the Quarterly Returns made to the Justices under the London Building Act of 1774, a somewhat patchy series extant for the years 1831–44, and the individual certificates which the district surveyors completed on examining a new house or other building – affidavits, in effect – for the whole area south of the Thames right back to 1774. All these are housed in the Record Room at County Hall, London. Seven volumes of similar papers covering 1764–1846, though more ravaged by mice, are kept at the old Middlesex County Hall, Westminster. Some of these records, and the administrative machinery of which they are the product, are described by Ida Darlington, 'The Registrar of metropolitan buildings and his records', *Journal of the Society of Archivists*, I (1955), 17–19. On the district surveyors, see Bernard Dickee, 'An enquiry into the origin of the office and title of "District Surveyor" ', *Journal of the Royal Institute of British Architects*, XII (1905), 256–8; and C. C. Knowles, 'A history of the London Building Acts, the District Surveyors, and their Association' (1947), which is an unpublished MS held by the Members' Library, Greater London Council. See also Appendix A.

34. They are divided into three parts, the first of which records the builder, owner, situation, height and number of storeys of all houses noticed as under construction or alteration; the second part mainly records action taken and fees due; the third part records fees received, abated or lost. The entries all appear to have been made with care and were serially numbered; this makes it possible to trace the completion of any building.

35. This is also a serious limitation on using the fees charged by the district surveyors as an index of building activity at this time (see E. W. Cooney, 'Capital exports', 347–54).

36. There are some grounds for thinking that the office of district surveyor was normally sought, not so much for the fee income it brought, but for the opportunities it gave for enlarging professional practices. There were complaints from time to time that district surveyors were not doing their jobs at all efficiently, but they never suggested that the district surveyors were backward in taking account of new building, which provided the largest and most easily earned fees.

37. It is possible to ascertain this by a comparison of the columns listing builders and owners in the returns.

38. The lithograph was coming in so helpfully, as for example, in *The Builders' Practical Director; or, Buildings of All Classes making every Freeholder to be his Own Builder, with Plans, Elevations and Sections for the Erection of Cottages, Villas, Farm Buildings . . . with detailed Estimates, Quantities, Prices, etc.* (2 vols., c. 1855). *Weale's Rudimentary Series*, among others, supplied a want in works like Edward Dobson, *Rudiments of the Art of Building* (1849), which had thirteen editions in forty years. S. H. Brooks, *Designs for Cottage and Villa Architecture* (1839), was written 'for a builder who has no leisure to travel and copy widely . . . Our object throughout has been to prepare such a series of drawings as should convey a few hints to the architect, direct the builder, and instruct those intended to build' (iv, 145). This author's major work went further in this direction: *The Erection of Dwellinghouses: or, The Builder's Comprehensive Director, explained by a Perspective View, Plans, Elevations, and Sections of a Pair of Semi-detached Villas . . . to which is added the Specification, Quantities, and Estimate . . . calculated to render Assistance to the*

Young Artizan in every Department of the Building Art (1860). See, too, C. Wilkes, *A Handy Book of Villa Architecture* (1897).

39. My colleague in the Victorian Studies Centre, Miss Priscilla Metcalf, tells me that James Thomas Knowles, both father and son, had some connections of this kind. The elder (1806–84) had moved up from the family business of plumbers and glaziers in Reigate around 1830 to become a London contractor before styling himself architect around 1838: he appears to have supplied some drawings to speculative builders, at least during the 1840s. The younger Knowles (1831–1908) – who is interesting on other accounts, as editor of *Contemporary Review*, 1870–7, founder-editor of *Nineteenth Century*, friend of Gladstone, Tennyson and other notabilities – undertook some extensive estate development at Clapham, Sydenham and Hove, in which these relations with builders seem to have been continued.

40. *The Builder*, XXXV (1877), 42.

41. Greater London Council Record Office, E/COT/1652.

42. *Ibid.*, E/BVR/191, 194. I am grateful to Mr R. F. Kelsall of the Historic Buildings Division of the Architect's Department at County Hall for drawing these papers to my attention, and for his preliminary researches into the earlier history of the estate, especially among the Chancery proceedings: Public Record Office, C. 13/2184/22. Their full contents merit a separate study.

43. See, for example, *PP* 1833 (690), VI, *Report, SC on Manufacturers, Commerce, and Shipping, Minutes of Evidence*, Q 1691 (T. Burton, builder); *PP*, 1887 (260), XIII, *Report, SC on Town Holdings, Minutes of Evidence*, Q 2963 (E. Towson, estate dealer); C. M. Smith, *Curiosities of London Life* (1853), 367–8; Charles Booth, *Life and Labour in London* (1900–3). 2nd ser., I, 51; E. G. Howarth and Mona Wilson, *West Ham* (1907), 10.

44. Bankers' loans to building societies on the security of promissory notes was one way of putting bank credit at the disposal of speculative builders about which very little seems to be known. From 1854, for instance, the Temperance Permanent Building Society of London was borrowing for periods of up to six months at 5 and 6% from the Commercial Bank in order to make advances to its members, including speculative builders; on one occasion, the Society mortgaged its own premises to the bank for an advance. These loans were, to begin with, for a few hundred pounds at a time, but by 1858 sums of £1,000 and £2,000 were being raised frequently, occasionally at weekly intervals. See Temperance Permanent Building Society, Directors' Minute Books, 27 June, 11 July, 21 November, 5 December 1854; 5 and 12 October 1858 ff.

45. T. E. Gregory, *The Westminster Bank through a Century* (1936), I, 371–2. Bank advances are known to have been important in a number of provincial towns and there seems to have been a general presumption that London banks also made loans on the security of leases. See a letter entitled 'One sort of speculative builder', *The Builder*, XXXVIII (1880), 424–5.

46. Building Societies Act, 1874, Sect. 37. Before this date, there is some evidence that building societies were prepared to develop building estates themselves: the Temperance Permanent Building Society, for example, undertook the full role of the developer on its Forest Gate estate almost from the date of the foundation of the society in 1853, and was regularly inspecting other sites in various parts of London over the next few years (Directors' Minute Books, *passim*). The Secretary to this Society said later that this kind of enterprise was not pursued more, simply 'because more money could be made out of advancing upon houses'; the Forest Gate estate had been a modest development of ten acres divided into 227 plots, of which a few had still not been taken up in 1871. See *PP*, 1871 (C. 452), *RC on Friendly and Benefit Building Societies*, Q 6137 (H. J. Phillips).

47. *PP* 1887 (260), XIII, *Report, SC on Town Holdings*, Q 10537 (John Green, a part-time agent to a small building society).

48. Greater London Council Record Office, E/COT/260. Another five building societies on this estate were head lessees of houses.

49. The Temperance Permanent Building Society, which had considered as early as 1872 whether it should continue making advances to builders on unfinished houses and had decided to leave the matter to the discretion of its Secretary, resolved in 1879 (following the report of a Special Committee on Advances) to discontinue advances on 'mills or manufacturing premises, unfinished houses and in unfinished neighbourhoods where surrounding property is unlet, except for owner-occupation or where a margin of 50 per cent is offered' (Directors' Minute Books, 4 February 1879).

50. The best general accounts of the history of the building society movement in the nineteenth century are: Sir Harold Bellman, *Bricks and Mortals* (1949); J. Seymour Price, *Building Societies, their Origin and History* (1958); E. J. Cleary, *The Building Society Movement* (1965).

51. Hand-in-Hand Securities Book, MS 10687, Guildhall Library.

52. Reeder, 'Capital investment', 162–73. There is nothing useful in this respect in Bernard Drew, *The London Assurance* (1949), but on the investment policies of other leading insurance companies in relation to the finance of house-building, see P. M. G. Dickson, *The Sun Insurance Office, 1710–1960* (1960), ch. 12; M. E. Ogborn, *Equitable Assurances* (1962), especially chs. 12–14; and A. W. Tarn and C. E. Byles, *A Record of the Guardian Assurance Company Limited, 1821–1921* (privately printed, 1921), ch. 9.

53. The role of the solicitor as a financial intermediary in the seventeenth and eighteenth century is well known, primarily through the work of Robert Robson, *The Attorney in Eighteenth-Century England* (1959). So far as the nineteenth century is concerned, the only specific reference worth making appears to be J. D. Bailey, 'Australian borrowing in Scotland in the nineteenth century', *EcHR*, XII (1959), 268–79, which analyses the role of the Scottish solicitor in this respect.

54. Greater London Council Record Office, B/CHE/42.

55. *The Times*, 15 August 1907.

56. The data that follow have been abstracted from the property ledgers and ledger books of the Trustees of the Estate of the late Edward Yates, 194 Walworth Road, London, to whom I am much indebted, especially to Mr R. F. Osborne, Manager of the Estate, for his thoughtful help. It is only to be regretted that these valuable records have already been so depleted by salvage drives.

57. *In re Chennell* (1878) 8 Ch. D. 492. The 1859 legislation authorising trustees to lend funds on freehold property was contained in the Law of Property and Trustee Relief Amendment Act, Sect. 32 (22 and 23 Vict. C. 35); the Act of 1888 giving the first explicit authority for lending on lease-hold property was the Trustee Act (51 and 52 Vict., C. 59, S. 9). There is some guidance on these points in *Lewin on Trusts*, ed. W. J. Mowbray (16th edn, 1964), 322, 369–70.

58. *The Builder*, L (1886), 63.

59. *Ibid.*, XLVIII (1885), 896. See also *PP*, 1887 (260), XIII, *Report, SC on Town Holdings*, QQ 1382–411 (Robert Vigers, a leading surveyor in the City of London).

60. The anonymous author of *In Contracting with Builders, Beware!* (1851), for example, was letting fly at competitive tendering and the large contractor, not at the speculative builder; but for two brief and comparatively rare indictments of the jerry-builder, see G. Laurence Gomme, *London in the Reign of Victoria (1837–1897)* (1898), 24–5; and George Haw, *No Room to Live: The Plaint of Overcrowded London* (1900), 90–3.

61. *The Builder*, LVII (1889), 460. The most critical commentaries on speculative building in this journal are: XI (1853), 709; XV (1857), 220–1, 232–4; XVI (1858), 176–8; XXIX (1871), 833; XXXIV (1876), 1156; LXI (1881), 680; LVI (1889), 403–4.
62. See *ibid.*, XXXVIII (1880), 424–5.
63. *Post Magazine*, XII, no. 16 (19 April 1851) – a reference I owe to Prof. Barry Supple.

11. A Victorian speculative builder: Edward Yates

1. For the sources on which this essay is based, see Ch. 10, n. 56.
2. For the general background of the building world of Victorian London, see above, Ch. 10.
3. H. J. Dyos, *Victorian Suburb: a study of the growth of Camberwell* (1961), 130–7.

12. A guide to the streets of Victorian London

1. 'The greatness of London', *Working Man's Friend*, new ser., I (1852), 59.
2. 'The map of London a hundred years ago', *Gentleman's Magazine*, new ser., XLII (1854), 17.
3. (George Dodd), 'Growth of the map of London', *Edinburgh Review*, CIV (1856), 52.
4. (G. A. Sala), 'The great invasion', *Household Words*, V (1852), 70.
5. Ralph Waldo Emerson, *English Traits*, ed. Howard Mumford Jones (Cambridge, Mass., 1966), 59.
6. See above, Ch. 3.
7. 'The nation of London', being ch. 7 of his *Autobiographic Sketches, 1790–1803* (1862), 179. I owe this reference to my colleague, Philip Collins.
8. See, for example, John Hogg, *London As It Is* (1837); Paul Pry (pseud. Thomas Hill), *Oddities of London Life* (2 vols., 1838); (James Grant), *Travels in Town* (2 vols., 1839), and *Lights and Shadows of London Life* (2 vols., 1842).
9. Andrew Wynter, 'Country houses for the working classes', *People's Journal*, II (1846), 134.
10. G. A. S(ala), 'Fishers of men: or recruiting for Her Majesty's Forces in London', *Illustrated Times*, V (1857), 379.
11. J. F. Murray, *The World of London* (1844), I, 20–1.
12. See J. B. Harley, *Maps for the Local Historian* (1972), 7, 15.
13. See Ida Darlington and James Howgego, *Printed Maps of London, circa 1553–1850* (1964), an invaluable source of information from which much of my information about earlier maps has been derived.
14. The whole work, edited by Charles Welch, was published in facsimile by the London & Middlesex Archaeological Society in 1895.
15. A facsimile edition of this plan was published for the London Topographical Society in 1913–19, and a new reproduction, including the index, has recently been issued by Harry Margary and Phillimore & Company.
16. Ralph Hyde, 'Printed maps of London: 1851–1900' (F.L.A. thesis, 1971), 2. I am most grateful to the author, not only for giving me access to his sterling work, but for commenting most helpfully on the draft of this essay.
17. See R. A. Skelton, 'The Ordnance Survey, 1791–1825', *British Museum Quarterly*, XXI (1957–9), 59–61, and Ida Darlington, 'Edwin Chadwick and the first large-scale Ordnance Survey of London', *Transactions of the London & Middlesex Archaeological Society*, XXII (1969), 58–63; J. B. Harley and C. W. Phillips, *The Historian's Guide to Ordnance Survey Maps* (1964).
18. See Philippa Glanville's luxurious anthology, *London in Maps* (1972), especially 39.
19. *Tallis's London Street Views* had originally been issued in 88 parts in 1838–40, and

these were reprinted by Nattali & Maurice in association with the London Topographical Society in 1969, along with the 1847 edition and a most useful introduction and biographical note by Peter Jackson.

20. Peter Cunningham, *Hand-Book of London* (enlarged edn, 1850), xxxiii.

21. (a) *London at a Glance: An Illustrated Atlas of London* appeared in September 1859 little different from the 1854 edition except for the addition of a list of about 250 hotels, the new postal districts, and the railways; the original publisher's and engraver's names were cut out. (b) *London at a Glance: A Guide for Visitors to the International Exhibition*, appeared in 1862 identical in all respects to the 1859 edition except for the addition of more railways and a separate postal district map: it was, however, worse printed on inferior paper and filled out by advertisements.

22. (Cyrus Redding), 'London from the crow's nest', *Fraser's Magazine*, XXXIX (1849), 63.

23. On this episode, see above, Ch. 7.

24. See J. E. Bradfield, *Notes on Toll Reform and the Turnpike and Ticket System* (1856).

25. 'The toll-bar nuisance', *Illustrated London News*, XXX (1857), 535–6; for a map of London tollgates, see 554–5.

26. 'The wants of London', *Illustrated London News*, XXV (1854), 294.

27. 'Our mean metropolis', *Punch*, XXVII (1854), 158. See above, Ch. 5, and Anthony Sutcliffe, *The Autumn of Central Paris* (1970), ch. 2.

28. *Illustrated London News*, XXV (1854), 293; for more complaints about the inadequacies of the streets, see *ibid.*, XXIV (1854), 18, 24.

29. For a side-light on the social significance of street names, see (E. Fairfax Taylor), 'London topography and street nomenclature', *Edinburgh Review*, CXXXI (1870), 155–93.

30. Based on an estimate formed by evidence supplied to the *SC on Metropolitan Communications*, 1854–5: T. C. Barker and Michael Robbins, *A History of London Transport*, vol. I, *The Nineteenth Century* (1963), ch. 2.

31. (Andrew Wynter), 'The London commissariat', *Quarterly Review*, XCV (1854), 284, 292, 305.

32. Cyrus Redding, 'London from the crow's nest', 60.

33. *Annual Register*, Chronicle for 1854, 159–60; *Illustrated London News*, XXV (1854), 230.

34. On the state of the public administration of London at this time, see Sir Benjamin Hall's introductory speech on the Metropolis Local Management Bill in March 1855: *Hansard*, 3rd series, CXXXVII (1855), 699–722; it was reprinted at some length in G. Laurence Gomme, *London in the Reign of Victoria (1837–1897)* (1898), 42–56.

35. Quoted by Hyde, 'Printed maps of London: 1851–1900', 44.

36. J. Skinner, *Waistcoat Pocket Map of London* (c. 1876); *Lett's Waistcoat Pocket Map of London* (c. 1884), which was in fact an updated version of B. R. Davies's map of 1843, originally published for the Society for the Diffusion of Useful Knowledge, and now given a new format; there was another edition in 1887.

37. Bacon's *Up to Date Pocket Atlas and Guide to London* (1894) seems to have been the first that did not need a poacher's pocket to hold it; another was Philip's *A.B.C. Pocket Atlas Guide to London* (1902). Those described as 'portable' or 'handy' were generally about six inches by nine.

Conclusion: Urban history in the United Kingdom: the 'Dyos phenomenon' and after

1. Bruce M. Stave, 'A conversation with H. J. Dyos: urban history in Great Britain', *Journal of Urban History*, V (1979), 469.

2. For the development of urban history in the United States, both new and old, see: M.

Frisch, 'American urban history as an example of recent historiography', *History and Theory*, XVIII (1979), 350–77; Z. L. Miller and C. Griffen, 'Urban history in North America', *Urban History Yearbook* (1977), 6–23.

3. See above, 19.
4. C. P. Snow, *Variety of Men* (1969), 12.
5. M. W. Flinn and T. C. Smout (eds.), *Essays in Social History (1974)*, x.
6. Most of this section is based on D. Reeder, 'H. J. Dyos: an appreciation', *Urban History Yearbook* (1979), 4–10; *The Times*, 25 August 1978; A. R. Sutcliffe, 'The condition of urban history in England', *Local Historian*, XI (1975), 278–84.
7. See in particular: W. G. Hoskins, *Local History in England* (1959); H. P. R. Finberg, *The Local Historian and His Theme* (1952).
8. See H. J. Dyos, 'Jack Simmons: an appreciation', *Journal of Transport History*, new ser. III (1976), 133–44.
9. E.g., B. R. Smith, *A History of Malvern* (1964); G. Hart, *A History of Cheltenham* (1965); A. Rogers (ed.), *The Making of Stamford* (1965).
10. See above, Chs. 6–8; H. J. Dyos and D. H. Aldcroft, *British Transport: an economic survey from the seventeenth century to the twentieth* (1966).
11. See above, Ch. 5; H. J. Dyos, 'The growth of a pre-Victorian suburb: south London, 1580–1836', *TPR*, XXV (1954), 59–78; *idem*, 'The annals of suburbia', *Amateur Historian*, IV (1960), 275–81.
12. H. J. Dyos, *Victorian Suburb: a study of the growth of Camberwell* (1961).
13. H. J. Dyos (ed.), *Urban History Newsletter*, nos. I–XXII (1963–76).
14. See above, Chs. 3, 4, 9, 11: H. J. Dyos, 'The growth of cities in the nineteenth century', *VS*, IX (1966), 225–37; *idem*, 'A castle for everyman', *London Journal*, I (1975), 118–34.
15. H. J. Dyos, Foreword to A. Sutcliffe, *The Autumn of Central Paris: The Defeat of Town Planning, 1850–1970* (1970), vi.
16. *Urban History Yearbook* (1974), 4.
17. *Urban History Newsletter*, XXII (1976), 1.
18. H. J. Dyos and Michael Wolff, 'The way we live now', in H. J. Dyos and Michael Wolff (eds.), *The Victorian City: images and realities* (2 vols., 1973), II, 907.
19. Reeder, 'H. J. Dyos: an appreciation', 8.
20. S. G. Checkland, 'Urban history in the British idiom', *Urban History Review*, VII (1978), 58.
21. G. Stedman Jones and R. Samuel, obituary notice of H. J. Dyos, *History Workshop Journal*, VII (1979), 247.
22. *Urban History Yearbook* (1976), 3.
23. See above, 31.
24. See above, 35.
25. H. J. Dyos to D. N. Cannadine, 24 January 1977.
26. *Urban History Newsletter*, XX (1973), 3.
27. See above, 36.
28. The best summary of the critics' case is in Sutcliffe, 'The condition of urban history in England', 279.
29. S. Pollard, 'Two visions of the city', *Times Higher Education Supplement*, 7 September 1973.
30. S. Thernstrom, 'Reflections on the "New Urban History"', *Daedalus*, C (1971), 34.
31. Eric Hobsbawm, 'From social history to the history of society', *Daedalus*, C (1971), 34.
32. *Urban History Yearbook* (1977), 4.
33. S. Glynn, 'Approaches to urban history: the case for caution', *Australian Economic*

History Review, x (1970), 219; R. Lubove, 'The urbanisation process: an approach to historical research', *American Institute of Planners Journal*, XXXIII (1967), 33.

34. See above, 32.
35. E. P. Thompson, 'Responses to reality', *New Society*, 4 October 1973.
36. *Urban History Yearbook* (1977), 4.
37. Asa Briggs, 'History goes to town', *Times Literary Supplement*, 27 December 1974.
38. Derek Fraser, 'Politics and the Victorian city', *Urban History Yearbook* (1979), 37.
39. W. Diamond, 'On the dangers of an urban interpretation of history', in E. F. Goldman (ed.), *Historiography and Urbanisation* (Baltimore, 1941), 67–108.
40. E. Lampard, 'The dimensions of urban history: a footnote to the "urban crisis" ', *Pacific Historical Review*, XXXIX (1970), 264. For a fuller criticism along these lines, see two essays by P. Abrams, 'Introduction' and 'Towns and economic growth: some theories and problems', both in P. Abrams and E. A. Wrigley (eds.), *Towns in Society: Essays in Economic History and Historical Sociology* (1978), 1–7, 9–33.
41. *Urban History Yearbook* (1976), 158–9.
42. S. G. Checkland, 'Towards a definition of urban history', in H. J. Dyos (ed.), *The Study of Urban History* (1968), 351–2.
43. *Urban History Yearbook* (1975), 3.
44. H. J. Dyos, 'Agenda for urban historians', in Dyos, *The Study of Urban History*, 9.
45. *Urban History Yearbook* (1976), 6.
46. *Urban History Yearbook* (1977), 3.
47. Dyos, 'A castle for everyman', 134.
48. *Urban History Yearbook* (1974), 7.
49. Reeder, 'H. J. Dyos: an appreciation', 6.
50. H. J. Dyos, Foreword to E. P. Hennock, *Fit and Proper Persons: ideal and reality in nineteenth-century government* (1973), viii.
51. *Urban History Yearbook* (1976), 6.
52. See above, 34.
53. *Urban History Yearbook* (1975), 3, 45–6; Dyos, *Victorian Suburb* (3rd imp.), 14.
54. H. J. Dyos, Foreword to J. H. Bater, *St Petersburg: Industrialisation and Change* (1976), v.
55. See above, 18.
56. *Urban History Yearbook* (1975), 45; *ibid.*, (1976), 4–5.
57. Asa Briggs, *The History of Birmingham*, vol. II, *Borough and City, 1867–1939* (1952); *idem, Victorian Cities* (1963). Other works of similar scope written at this time include: W. H. Chaloner, *The Social and Economic Development of Crewe, 1780–1923* (1950); T. C. Barker and J. R. Harris, *A Merseyside Town in the Industrial Revolution: St Helens, 1750–1900* (1954); J. D. Marshall, *Furness and the Industrial Revolution* (1958); J. Prest, *The Industrial Revolution in Coventry* (1960).
58. Derek Beales, *From Castlereagh to Gladstone, 1815–1885* (1971), 187–93.
59. The best of these books are as follows: R. Newton, *Victorian Exeter, 1837–1914* (1968); A. T. Patterson, *Southampton, 1700–1914* (3 vols., 1969–75); J. Simmons, *Leicester Past and Present* (2 vols., 1969–75); Sir Francis Hill, *Victorian Lincoln* (1974); A. F. J. Brown, *Colchester, 1815–1914* (1980); P. J. Waller, *Democracy and Sectarianism: A Political and Social History of Liverpool, 1868–1939* (1981).
60. M. J. Daunton, *Coal Metropolis: Cardiff, 1870–1914* (1977).
61. S. G. Checkland, *The Upas Tree: Glasgow, 1875–1975* (1976); A. Sutcliffe and Roger Smith, *The History of Birmingham*, vol. III, *Birmingham, 1939–1970* (1974).
62. S. Yeo, *Religion and Voluntary Societies in Crisis* (1976).
63. Sutcliffe, *The Autumn of Central Paris*.
64. H. E. Meller, *Leisure and the Changing City, 1870–1914* (1976).

65. Bater, *St Petersburg.*
66. J. R. Kellett, *The Impact of Railways on Victorian Cities* (1969).
67. D. Fraser, *Urban Politics in Victorian England* (1976); idem, *Power and Authority in the Victorian City* (1979); Hennock, *Fit and Proper Persons;* D. Cannadine, *Lords and Landlords: the aristocracy and the towns, 1774–1967* (1980); C. W. Chalklin, *The Provincial Towns of Georgian England: a study of the building process, 1740–1829* (1974).
68. M. A. Simpson and T. H. Lloyd (eds.), *Middle-Class Housing in Britain* (1977).
69. S. D. Chapman (ed.), *The History of Working-Class Housing: a symposium* (1971); J. N. Tarn, *Five Per Cent Philanthropy: an account of housing in urban areas between 1840 and 1914* (1973); E. Gauldie, *Cruel Habitations: a history of working-class housing, 1780–1914* (1974); A. Sutcliffe (ed.), *Multi-Storey Living: the British working-class experience* (1974).
70. J. Burnett, *A Social History of Housing, 1815–1970* (1978).
71. F. M. L. Thompson, *Hampstead: building a borough, 1650–1970* (1978).
72. C. N. L. Brooke and G. Keir, *London, 800–1261: the shaping of a city* (1975); G. Rudé, *Hanoverian London, 1714–1808* (1971); F. H. W. Sheppard, *London, 1808–1870: the Infernal Wen* (1971).
73. D. J. Olsen, *The Growth of Victorian London* (1976).
74. K. Young, *Local Politics and the Rise of Party: the London Municipal Society and the Conservative intervention in local elections, 1894–1963* (1975); A. S. Wohl, *The Eternal Slum: housing and social policy in Victorian London* (1977).
75. G. Stedman Jones, *Outcast London: a study in the relations between classes in Victorian society* (1971); G. Crossick, *An Artisan Elite in Victorian Society: Kentish London, 1840–1880* (1978).
76. J. Foster, *Class Struggle and the Industrial Revolution: early industrial conflict in three English towns* (1977); R. Q. Gray, *The Labour Aristocracy in Victorian Edinburgh* (1977); H. McLeod, *Class and Religion in the Late Victorian City* (1974); T. R. Tholfsen, *Working-Class Radicalism in Mid-Victorian England* (1977); P. Joyce, *Work, Society and Politics: the culture of the factory in late Victorian England* (1980).
77. W. A. Armstrong, *Stability and Change in an English Country Town: a social study of York, 1801–1851* (1974); M. Anderson, *Family Structure in Nineteenth-Century Lancashire* (1971).
78. S. Thernstrom, *Poverty and Progress: social mobility in a nineteenth-century city* (Cambridge, Mass., 1964); S. Thernstrom and R. Sennett (eds.), *Nineteenth-Century Cities: essays in the New Urban History* (New Haven, Conn., 1969). For an analysis of their influence in the United States, see: Frisch, 'American urban history', 356–60.
79. For the most outstanding exemplars of this earlier tradition, see: Arthur M. Schlesinger, Snr, 'The city in American history', *Mississippi Valley Historical Review,* XXVII (1940), 43–66; C. M. Green, *Washington* (2 vols., Princeton, N.J., 1962–3); O. Handlin and J. Burchard (eds.), *The Historian and the City* (Cambridge, Mass., 1963); Richard Wade, *The Urban Frontier: the rise of the Western cities, 1790–1850* (Cambridge, Mass., 1963); idem, *Slavery in the Cities: the South, 1820–1860* (New York, 1964).
80. For a summary of recent criticisms, and full references, see: Frisch, 'American urban history', 363–71.
81. See the proceedings, published in D. Fraser and A. R. Sutcliffe (eds.), *The Pursuit of Urban History* (2 vols., 1982).
82. See above, 35.